Padwick's
BIBLIOGRAPHY OF CRICKET
Volume II

compiled by

Stephen Eley and Peter Griffiths

LIBRARY ASSOCIATION PUBLISHING
FOR
THE CRICKET SOCIETY

© The Cricket Society 1991

Published by
Library Association Publishing Ltd
7 Ridgmount Street
London WC1E 7AE

First published 1991

British Library Cataloguing in Publication Data

Padwick's bibliography of cricket: 2
  I. Eley, Stephen   II. Griffiths, Peter
  796.358016

  ISBN 0-85365-528-6

Typeset by Peter Griffiths.
Printed and made in Great Britain by Bookcraft (Bath) Ltd.

PREFACE

In his preface to the second edition of *A Bibliography of cricket*[1], Tim Padwick expressed the hope that it would be regularly updated by supplements. In compiling this bibliography we have begun to fulfil that expectation. It contains not only publications of the 1980-89 period but also 816 items published before 1980 which were not recorded in the earlier work. It provides details of those serial publications (annuals and periodicals) which continued publication into the 1980s, records new editions of single works but does not otherwise amend existing entries in '*Padwick I*'. Such amendments await inclusion in a future consolidated edition.

This publication was produced on a personal computer. The raw data for each entry is held as a record in a database file and formatted data was output by several programs for eventual input to a desk-top publishing program. The final camera-ready copy was produced using Ventura Publisher[2].

The entries in this book, apart from serials, stand as separate works. We decided at an early stage not to interpolate the numbers in this volume into the existing '*Padwick I*' sequence. Instead we have assigned to the entries numbers from 0001 onwards. We hope that, to distinguish books which bear the same number in different volumes, the designation '*Padwick I*' will be used for the 1977 and 1984 editions, and '*Padwick II*' for this volume.

We have followed, with minor adjustments, Tim Padwick's classification scheme. Such changes as we have made reflect the changing nature of cricket publications. As well as the flood of limited overs tournament material, tour brochures published by schools, clubs and youth organisations have proliferated. Academic writing on cricket is on the increase, most notably in the fields of sport history and performance measurement. We have been more proscriptive in selecting match programmes for inclusion. Items have been classified, wherever possible, under one specific heading, thus avoiding large numbers of duplicate entries. We hope that any omissions and incomplete entries can be rectified in future editions in the same way that we have repaired some omissions in '*Padwick I*'.

In some respects the 1980s has been an easy decade to register bibliographically. A wider range of publications than ever before are reviewed or recorded; national bibliographical control is tighter. But the impact of new technology on home publishing coupled with the growth in the market for specialised publications such as statistical works, have ensured that the task has not been simple. Without the assistance of many within the cricket fraternity it would have been impossible.

First, we are indebted to **John Arlott** for writing the foreword to this volume as he did for the earlier ones. **Nigel Haygarth**, Chairman of the Cricket Society, was involved in the project throughout and his encouragement and support, particularly at times of difficulty, were crucial to its realisation. **Tim Padwick** himself was available at all times to offer help and guidance; it is fitting that the *Bibliography of cricket* be continued under his name.

Many enthusiasts - collectors, researchers, librarians and booksellers - have given us invaluable help. In particular, **Tony Woodhouse** and **Bob Jones** have given generously of their time in making their collections available to us over a number of visits and in patiently meeting all the demands we made upon them. We also enjoyed the hospitality of **Geoffrey Copinger**, whose collection is a model in its scale and organisation, **Tony Laughton**, who has much that was not recorded in '*Padwick I*', **Malcolm Lorimer, William Powell, Tony Debenham, Tony Dey, Michael Pearce, George Langdale, Brian Heald** and **Brian Croudy**. Among booksellers, **John McKenzie** and **Roger Page**, gave us access not only to their stock but also to rarities in their own collections. **John Gaustad** of Sportspages and **Martin Wood** also let us peruse their stock at leisure.

In public collections, much of the research was undertaken at the M.C.C. Library at Lord's. We are greatly indebted to **Stephen Green** and his colleagues for their help over the duration of the project. The libraries of Lancashire C.C.C. and Nottinghamshire C.C.C. were also visited and thanks are due to **Peter Wynne-Thomas** (Trent Bridge) and **Malcolm Lorimer** and **Don Ambrose** (Old Trafford) for their assistance and co-operation. **Howard Milton**, Librarian of the

---

1   The first edition (1977) and the second edition (1984) are referred to throughout this volume as '*Padwick I*'
2   Ventura Publisher ® is a trademark of Ventura Software Inc., a Xerox Company.

Cricket Society, was always on hand - drawing our attention to new stock in the Library, checking and adding to the Kent material, and assisting with some of the cataloguing. In Australia, visits were made, at the start of the work, to the New South Wales Cricket Association Library in Sydney where **Cliff Winning** extended a cordial welcome, and, at the very end of our researches, to the Melbourne Cricket Club Library which has recently acquired the collection of Pat Mullins. We gratefully acknowledge the help and the professional expertise of the Librarian, **Catherine Geary**, the Museum Curator, **Jena Pullman**, and her assistant, **Kristen Thornton**. We also exploited the reference, bibliographical and archival resources of Enfield Libraries, Westminster City Libraries and Cambridge City Library.

Chris Harte was ubiquitous, providing information on a regular basis, checking sections of the Bibliography where his eye for detail spotted many an error or ambiguity, and, not least, notifying us of potential helpers in Australia and worldwide. Another who provided details of contacts was **Peter Hargreaves** whose knowledge of cricket in Europe is unrivalled. In Sydney, **Stephen Gibbs** systematically worked his way through the stock at the New South Wales Cricket Association Library, keeping us informed of items he came across not recorded in '*Padwick I*'; he also undertook much bibliographical research on our behalf. **Richard Cox**, whose monumental *Sport in Britain: a bibliography of historical publications 1800-1988* was published by Manchester University Press in March 1991, kindly supplied us with proofs of his book, and the details of a number of those U..K. club histories which have not been seen by us are taken with grateful acknowledgement from his work.

Many correspondents in the U.K. and abroad checked their own and, in some cases, other private and public collections to help us fill gaps. We would particularly like to thank **Robin Abbott** (South Africa), **Sandeep Nakai** (India), **Jimmy Richards** (West Indies), **Stan Cowman** and **David Archer** (New Zealand), **Andrew Hignell** (Wales), **Bob Harragan** (Wales and the West Country), **Ric Finlay** (Tasmania), **Christopher Saunders** (Fiction), **D.L.Ingelse** (Netherlands), **Derrick Townshend** (Zimbabwe), **Tony Bradbury** (Law Reports), **Norman Epps** (Sussex), and **Neil Leitch** (Scotland).

We owe a debt to many others who provided information and assistance, principally, **David Rayvern Allen, Robert Brooke, Derek Barnard, Richard Cashman, Philip Daniel, Derek Deadman, John Eastwood, Duggie and Lennie Ettlinger, John Featherstone, T.J.Finlayson, David Frith, Norman Gannaway, Ricky Gunn, Roger Hancock, John Hurst, John King, Sue Lambert, Roger Burford Mason, Terry Needham, H.A.Osborne, Frank Peach, Tony Percival, Gordon Phillips, Clive Porter, John Prickett, Percy Samara-Wickrama, Rolf Schwiete, Philip Scowcroft, Steven Smallwood, Philip Snow, Mike Spurrier, Mike Winder, Ken Woolfe** and all those league, club and association historians and secretaries who sent us copies of their own publications.

Finally, a word of thanks to **Jamie Cameron** and his colleagues at Library Association Publishing who smoothed our path and carried us through to publication, and to our wives, **Teng Lin** and **Jenny** for their forbearance during the time we spent on the project.

Stephen Eley   May 1991
Peter Griffiths

FOREWORD

By JOHN ARLOTT

Any attempt to compile a bibliography of cricket was bound to be daunting. Few, however, including Mr. Padwick, can have guessed quite how vast was their task. His has been a most refreshing mixture of professionalism and amateur enthusiasm. The outcome, of course, is the biggest bibliography of any sport or game in existence, for the elementary reason that it covers more titles than any other sport. The main contents of this edition are items published between 1980 and 1989 - even so, some 15 per cent consists of items which lie outside the given dates, that is to say items published earlier but overlooked in the previous volume.

The layout and main classifications are as before, with new headings such as 'Indoor Cricket', and 'Youth Cricket'. The most striking single accession has been of publications from Australia, but not only have there been additions within the main known body of the game, but the growth of the International Cricket Conference has drawn in records of completely fresh countries, who, in their turn, have spawned other references. As was pointed out previously, much of value for the researcher is to be found in the inclusion of volumes whose titles would not indicate offhand that they contain cricket material.

It is to be hoped that, eventually, some major body - like, for instance, the great library of Melbourne / Victorian Cricket Association - will make the uniquely complete collection of the subject. The ordinary human collector long ago recognized that such a goal was beyond his powers. Meanwhile, the present volumes indicate the magnitude of the task and fill the ordinary amateur with dreams of the greatness of completion.

This continuation of Tim Padwick's major undertaking has been commissioned by Library Association Publishing, undertaken as a Cricket Society project and in detail by Stephen Eley, a professional Librarian and Bibliography Officer of the Society, and Peter Griffiths, a computer consultant, who is also a student of cricket. Mr. Griffiths has been able to produce camera-ready copy with his own desk-top publishing system, which has made the whole operation more economical.

It is a happy coincidence that the Chairman of the Cricket Society, whose name heads the notepaper, should be Haygarth - a historic name in the study of the game. But while all the credits can be allocated, no mention can be made of the countless collectors and students whose amateur detective work helped to create such a remarkable healthy and thorough whole. Cricket may well be proud of this accession to its riches.

CONTENTS

GENERAL WORKS

CONTENTS

CRICKET IN SOUTH AFRICA AND ZIMBABWE

CRICKET IN THE WEST INDIES

CRICKET IN NEW ZEALAND

CRICKET IN INDIA

CRICKET IN PAKISTAN

CRICKET IN SRI LANKA

CRICKET IN THE REST OF THE WORLD

INTERNATIONAL CRICKET

INTERNATIONAL CRICKET - ENGLAND

INTERNATIONAL CRICKET - AUSTRALIA

INTERNATIONAL CRICKET - SOUTH AFRICA and ZIMBABWE

INTERNATIONAL CRICKET - WEST INDIES

INTERNATIONAL CRICKET - NEW ZEALAND

CONTENTS

INTERNATIONAL CRICKET - INDIA

INTERNATIONAL CRICKET - PAKISTAN

INTERNATIONAL CRICKET - SRI LANKA

INTERNATIONAL TEAMS

CRICKET IN LITERATURE

PICTORIAL RECORDS

SPORTS AND GAMES

REMINISCENCES AND BIOGRAPHY

MISCELLANEOUS

APPENDIX

INDEX

EXPLANATORY NOTES

1. Scope.

The intention in this volume is to list all books, periodicals, brochures and yearbooks on cricket published during the decade 1980 to 1989. In addition, books that contain passages on cricket are included. Some unpublished manuscript material is also included where it is of special interest or is accessible in a public collection.

Specifically excluded are individual periodical articles, large print and braille editions, audio-visual material, instruction books for table cricket, cricket games of all sorts (board, computer, etc.) and (except where of special interest) match programmes, scorecards, fixture lists, diaries and equipment catalogues.

† against an entry indicates that the item was published in full or in part prior to 1980 and was not recorded in 'Padwick I'.

2. Authority.

■ against an entry indicates that the item has been seen by the compilers.

□ against an entry indicates that some, but not all, editions of a work, or issues of a serial, have been seen by the compilers.

Where neither ■ nor □ is shown against an entry, the item has not been seen by the compilers.

3. Arrangement.

Entries are arranged under subject content (except for 'Cricket in Literature' where they are under literary form). Some items appear under more than one subject heading. Within each subject heading, entries are arranged alphabetically by author or title (except where noted). Under each author, entries are arranged alphabetically by title.

4. Entries.

The entries consist of author, editor or compiler; title; sub-title; publisher's series (where applicable); illustrator; place of publication (London is omitted unless publication occurred simultaneously somewhere else); name of publisher (or printer if publisher not known); date of publication; pagination (except where more than one volume as in a yearbook); illustrations; maps; match scores; statistics; glossary; bibliography; index.

The entry is followed as appropriate by notes.

Page size is not given, neither is a description of the binding except in a few special cases.

5. Dates.

The date of the work is given as stated on the title page or elsewhere in the publication. If it is inferred, the date is enclosed in '[ ]'. If there is doubt about the inferred date, it is followed by a '?'.

In a serial publication, inclusive dates of publication are given. Those issues seen or notified are shown between oblique strokes. The following examples show the method:

a. 1981/1983,1987/ to date
   the run is from 1981 to 1989 with the issues 1983 and 1987 having been seen.

b. 1970/1980...1987/ to date?
   the run is from 1970 probably to 1989 although this has not been verified. Various issues between 1980 and 1987 have been seen.

c. ?/1983/ to date?
   the start of the run is unknown, 1983 issue has been seen, and it probably continues to 1989.

6. Index.

The index is a single sequence by author and title. It refers to entry numbers.

7. Abbreviations.

adverts.	advertisements
bibliog.	bibliography
bs.	broadsheet
c.	circa
ch.	chapter
col.	coloured
diagr.	diagram
ed.	edition
facsim.	facsimile

figs.	figures
frontis.	frontispiece
illus.	illustrations
incl.	including
ms.	manuscript
n.d.	no date given or inferred
no.	number
n.p.	no publisher given or inferred
p. or pp.	page or pages
pbk.	paperback
pseud.	pseudonym
pub.	published
rev.	revised
scores	full match scores
stats.	statistics and records of individual or team performances
vol.	volume
v.p.	various pagination
v.y.	various years

8. *References.*

Allen C	A catalogue of cricket catalogues, booklists, bibliographical sources and indexes etcetera; compiled by David Rayvern Allen. (See 'Padwick I' 0-1)
Allen EBC	Early books on cricket; by David Rayvern Allen. (See item 0001)
Mullins	A catalogue of the cricket and sporting collection of P. J. Mullins. (See item 0022)
Padwick I	A bibliography of cricket (second ed.); compiled by E.W. Padwick. (See item 0023)

GENERAL WORKS

BIBLIOGRAPHIES, BOOKLISTS AND CATALOGUES

0001 Allen, David Rayvern
■ Early books on cricket. Europa Publications, 1987. 128p. facsims. index.

0002 Samuel Britcher: the hidden scorer. [The Author, 1982]. 16p. illus.
limited ed. of 100 numbered and signed copies.

0003 † Ashley-Cooper, Frederick Samuel
■ Catalogue of cricket library formed by Mr F.S. Ashley-Cooper; acquired by Sir Julien Cahn, December, 1931. [i], 93 leaves. *typescript.*
arrangement of books by title.

0004 † Berkelouw, *fine and rare booksellers*
☐ An interesting collection of books on sport with a separate section [on] cricket. (Catalogue no. 179). Sydney, Berkelouw, c.1972. 33p.
——*also Catalogue no. 337, 'Cricket' c.1985. illus.*

0005 † Bibliography of Fiji, Tonga and Rotuma. Canberra, Australian National University, 1969.
contains a bibliography of Fijian cricket by Philip A. Snow.

0006 † Blyth, Henry Arthur
■ Catalogue of the sporting library of Henry Arthur Blyth Esq. ... will be sold by auction ... on Thursday, March 14, 1901. Christie, Manson & Woods, [1901]. 37p.
10 cricket lots, nos. 92-101.

0007 Brockbank, William
The Brockbank cricket collection: catalogue. Manchester, John Rylands University Library, 1987.
photographic reproduction of handwritten cards used by Dr William Brockbank to record his collection of over 1100 volumes.

0008 The game of cricket: an exhibition of books based on the Brockbank Cricket Collection [at the] John Rylands University Library of Manchester, ... August 11 - December 19 1986. [Compiled by John P. Tuck]. Manchester, the Library, 1986. [i], 64p. illus. facsims.

0009 The C.C. Morris Cricket Library Association
☐ Newsletter. Haverford, the Association. *biannual.*
continues 'Padwick I' 30-1 to date.

0010 Clinton, Peter Edward
■ Cricket libraries. Littleborough (Lancs.), the Compiler. *irregular.* illus.
24 issues pub. from 1982 to date.

0011 † Cole, Roland *and* **Cole, Betty,** *booksellers*
[Cricketana]
catalogues issued from 1960s until 1973 when stock sold to J.W.McKenzie.

0012 Cox, Richard William
Sport: a guide to historical sources in the UK. Sports Council, 1983 61p.

0013 The Cricket Society
■ Library catalogue, 1982; [compiled by Howard R. Milton]. The Society, 1982. iv, 87p.
——*new ed. 1988, compiled by Howard R. Milton, as print-out from computer database; subsequent copies issued, fully updated, on demand.*
later eds. of 'Padwick I' 11.

0014 † Davies, Tony *and* **Dey, Anthony,** *booksellers*
Cricket classics.
catalogues of books for sale; 10 issued between April 1971 and Spring 1975.

0015 Dyer, Ian Claude, *bookseller*
☐ Cricket books. Birmingham, the Compiler. *irregular.*
19 issues pub. from 1981 to date.

0016 Gibbs, Stephen W.
■ The development of a bibliography of cricket. [i], 16p.
paper presented at the 7th A.S.S.H. Conference, Sydney, July 1989.

0017 Gibbs, Stephen W., *compiler*
■ A cricket index. [Sydney], the Compiler, 1988. [446]p. in v.p. spiral binding.
on cover: 'The Gibbs cricket index'.
copy of ms. available at Melbourne Cricket Club Library.

0018 † Goldman, Joseph Wolfe
Catalogue of cricket books. 162 leaves. *typescript.*
typed to March 1937.
see also 'Padwick I' 20 and 21.

0019 † 'Collection of cricket books, prints, pictures and
■ engravings in possession of J.W.Goldman as at 1st March 1935'. [62]p. *typescript.*
title inscribed by Goldman on inside front cover.

0020 † Hudson, Ernest F., *bookseller*
[List of book for sale]. Birmingham.
Hudson founded his shop in 1906; lists particularly issued in the 1930s; stock sold to Epworth's in the 1950s after Hudson's death.

0021 McKenzie, John William, *bookseller*
■ [Catalogue]. Ewell (Surrey). *irregular.* illus. facsims.
nos. 39, 42, 43, 46, 48-73 inclusive; no. 46, devoted to 'Wisden Cricketers' Almanack', contains 'A history of Wisden' by L.E.S. Gutteridge.
additionally:
——*'A catalogue of new books for Christmas', [1986], 20p.*
——*'A special catalogue', [1989], 20p. illus. facsims.*
continues 'Padwick I' 28.

0022 Mullins, Patrick J.
■ A catalogue of the cricket and sporting collection of P. J. Mullins. Coorparoo (Qld.), the Compiler, December 1987. v.p. *typescript.*
handwritten on title page: 'subject to physical checking'; many ms. annotations and additions; collection now housed at Melbourne Cricket Club Library.
updated ed. of 'Padwick I' 30-3.

0023 † **Padwick, Eric William,** *compiler*
■ A bibliography of cricket. The Library Association for The Cricket Society, 1977. xxi, 649p. index.
comprehensive bibliography of cricket to the end of 1973.
——*2nd ed. rev. and enlarged to the end of 1979,* The Library Association in association with J.W. McKenzie (Bookseller) on behalf of The Cricket Society, 1984. xxxiv, 877p. illus. index.

0024 † **Page, Roger,** *bookseller*
□ Catalogue. Yallambie (Vic.), the Compiler. *bimonthly. typescript.*
pub. monthly Oct. 69 - Dec. 72; bimonthly to date.

0025 **Prance, Claude Annett**
■ E.V. Lucas and his books. West Cornwall (Connecticut), Locust Hill Press, 1988. xxxvi, 243p.
bibliography of the writings of E.V.Lucas with introductory biographical note.

0026 † **Southern Booksellers & Publishing Co.**
■ [Cricket] catalogues. St Leonards on Sea, the Compiler. *irregular. typescript.*
proprietor: C.W.Steggell.
1977? to date.

0027 † **Weston, George Neville**
■ The cricketers' manual by 'Bat' (Charles Box): a short bibliography; further details of the several editions and their variations. 12p. *typescript.*
supplementary information on 'Padwick I' 44 updated to 13 December 1941.

0028 † **Wood, Martin John Boniface,** *bookseller*
■ [Cricket book catalogues]. Sevenoaks, the Compiler. *annual.*
40 catalogues pub. from 1970 to date.
prior to 1980 pub. more frequently at irregular intervals.

CRICKETANA

(See also under Prints and Illustrations)

0029 **Bouwmann, Richard**
■ Glorious innings: treasures from the Melbourne Cricket Club collection. Hawthorn (Vic.), Hutchinson Australia, 1987. xi, 131p. illus. (some col.) bibliog. index.

0030 **Burlington Gallery**
■ [Catalogue].
'Second innings: an exhibition to celebrate the Bicentenary M. C. C. 1787-1987'. [1987], 31p. illus.
'Following on: an exhibition of cricket's history'. [1989], 35p. illus.
'Double century: two hundred years of cricket prints'. [1986], 24p. illus.

0031 † **Catalogue** of an exhibition on the history of Worcestershire C. C. C. [Worcester, Worcester City Library], 1975.

0032 † **Catalogue** of the rural game of cricket, a loan exhibition by the Museum of Rural Life. Reading, Reading University, 1975.
scenes, personalities, craft industry.
mentioned in 'Allen C'.

0033 **Centenary** 1880-1980 cricket stamp album. Worthing, Stamp Publicity, [1980]. 36p. illus.
lists all known cricket stamps.

0034 **Christie's,** *auctioneers*
■ [Catalogue]. *irregular.*
including
'M. C. C. Bicentenary auction'. 13 April 1987, 109p. illus.
'Cricket and sport ...'. 9 Oct. 1987, 78p. illus.

0035 **Colin** Johnson Appreciation Fund sale by auction of
■ cricketana and sporting items, Thursday 21st August 1986 ... Headingley Cricket Ground. [8]p. incl. covers.
auction of books, clothing, equipment and pictorial material.

0036 **Deadman, Derek**
■ Cricket cigarette and trade cards: an extended listing. Murray Cards (International), 1985. xiv, 254p. illus.

0037 Cricket cigarette and trade cards: an initial listing. Part 1:
■ tobacco issues. Leicester, [the Author], 1983. [iv], 79p.

0038 Cricket cigarette and trade cards: an initial listing. Part 2:
■ trade issues. Leicester, [the Author], 1983. [iii], 135p.

0039 † **Gloucester City Library**
Catalogue of the Grace centenary. 1948.
Graciana exhibition; 91 cricket items.

0040 **Green, Stephen Edgar Alexander**
■ Cricketing bygones. Princes Risborough (Bucks.), Shire Publications, 1982. 32p. illus. facsims. bibliog.

0041 **Jennings, Grenville**
■ Cricket on old picture postcards. Nottingham, Reflections of a Bygone Age, 1985. 64p. ports. illus. (some col.).

0042 **John** Abrahams testimonial year: cricket & sporting
■ memorabilia auction ... Wednesday 31st August 1988 ... Old Trafford Cricket Ground, Manchester. [10]p incl. covers. illus. *typescript*
an auction of bats, books, ties, autographs, ephemera etc.

0043 **Lewis, Vic**
■ Cricket ties: an international guide for cricket lovers. Ebury Press, 1984. 112p. col. illus. bibliog. index.

0044 **Nottinghamshire** cricket cards. West Bridgford
■ (Notts.), Sport-in-Print, [1989].
pub. in four albums: 'Batsmen', 'Bowlers', 'All-rounders', 'In the field'; each album contains 16p. with spaces provided for cards to match accompanying text.

0045 **Phillips, Son** *and* **Neale,** *auctioneers*
■ [Catalogue]. Phillips, Son & Neale. *biannual.* illus.
including 'An important collection of cricket books, pictures and ephemera'. 20 and 21 Nov. 1985, [The Winder collection].
'The Pilkington Collection of sporting items'. 27 and 28 Sep. 1989.

0046 **Rice, Timothy Miles Bindon**
■ Treasures of Lord's. (The MCC Cricket Library). Willow Books, 1989. 160p. illus. (some col.) bibliog. index.

0047 **Stanley, Louis T.**
■ The sporting collector. Pelham Books, 1984. 170p. illus. index.
includes four chapters on cricket and many other references.

0048 † **Sussex County Cricket Club**
■ Bazaar, Clarence Rooms, Hotel Metropole, December 4th, 5th & 6th: catalogue of articles for sale and exhibition only ... Brighton, John Beal & Son, [1894]. 10p.

0049 Catalogue of cricketana; sale, Saturday 17 May 1980, the
■ County Gournd, Hove ... Hove, the Club, 1980. 14p.

0050 **Tomkins, Richard**, *editor*
■ Classic cricket cards: 154 collector's cigarette cards
authentically reproduced in original colours perforated
for easy detaching; from the collection of M. A. Murray;
with an introduction by John Arlott. Constable, 1980.
20p. incl. covers, ports. (some col.) index.

0051 More classic cricket cards: 160 collector's cigarette cards
■ reproduced in original colours; with an introduction by
Brian Johnston. Constable, 1981. 20p. incl. covers,
ports. (some col.) index.

0052 **Walker, Walton, Hanson**, *auctioneers*
■ Trent Bridge '84': sale by auction of cricketana and
sporting items, Thursday, 9th, August, 1984 ... in the
Pavilion, Trent Bridge Cricket Ground ... Nottingham,
Walker, Walton, Hanson, 1984. [ii], 17p.

0053 **Walton Fine Arts Limited**
■ Catalogue & price list. Chertsey, 1987.
unnumbered catalogue; 134 entries.

ENCYCLOPAEDIAS

0054 **Arnold, Peter**
■ The illustrated encyclopedia of world cricket. Marshall
Cavendish for W. H. Smith & Son, 1986. 320p. illus.
(some col.) stats. index.
*parts of this book adapted from earlier Marshall
Cavendish publications, viz: 'Padwick I' 73-2, 4347-1.*

0055 **Barclay's** world of cricket: the game from A to Z;
■ general editor E. W. Swanton, associate editor John
Woodcock, assistant editors George Plumptre and A. S.
R. Winlaw, statistician G. A. Copinger. Collins in
association with Barclays Bank, 1980. x, 662p. col.
frontis., illus. stats. index.
——*new and rev. ed.* Willow Books in association with
Barclays Bank, 1986.
later eds. of 'Padwick I' 47.

0056 **Wynne-Thomas, Peter** *and* **Arnold, Peter**
■ The Hamlyn encyclopedia of cricket; colour photography
by Patrick Eagar. Twickenham, Hamlyn, 1987. 176p.
illus. (some col.) bibliog.

DICTIONARIES AND CRICKET TERMS

0057 **Burgschmidt, Ernst**, *compiler*
■ Linguistischen landeskunde und sprachpraxis.
Braunschweig, 1980. 145p. diagrs. bibliog.
*pp. 95-131 deal with the language and description of
bowling techniques.*
in German.

0058 **Considine, Tim**
The language of sport: a handy dictionary of sporting
terms. North Ryde (N.S.W.), Angus & Robertson,
1986. iii, 333p. illus.
cricket pp. 105-133.
——*first pub.* New York, Facts on File, 1982.

0059 **Dunstan, Keith**
■ A cricket dictionary; illustrated by Jeff Hook. Newton
Abbot, David & Charles, 1984. iv, 84p. illus.
humorous definitions.
——*first pub.* Melbourne, Sun Books, 1983.

0060 **Emery, Llewellyn** *and* **Horton, Walt**
Cricket: the off side. Hamilton (Bermuda), Emerton
Productions, 1987. 56p. illus.

0061 **Rundell, Michael**
■ The dictionary of cricket. George Allen & Unwin, 1985.
viii, 272p. illus. diagrs. bibliog.

0062 **Western Australian Cricket Umpires Association**,
compiler
Cricket dictionary. Perth, the Association, 1984. 44p.

GENERAL BOOKS AND HISTORY

0063 **Allen, David Rayvern**
■ The Guinness book of cricket extras; drawings by David
Arthur. Enfield, Guinness Publishing, 1988. 128p.
illus. bibliog.

0064 **Andrew, Keith Vincent**
■ The handbook of cricket. Pelham Books, 1989. x, 230p.
illus. (some col.) diagrs. glossary, index.

0065 **Association of Cricket Statisticians**, *compiler*
■ First class cricket matches. Haughton Mill (Notts), the
Association. scores, index.

1855-1859 with title 'Cricket matches', [1989]		
1860-1863 with title 'Cricket matches', [1984]		
1867-1869, [1980]	1883, [1981]	1891, [1984]
1870-1872, [1980]	1884, [1982]	1892, [1985]
1873-1874, [1980]	1885, [1982]	1893, [1985]
1875-1876, [1980]	1886, [1983]	1894, [1985]
1877-1878, [1981]	1887, [1983]	1895, [1986]
1879-1880, [1981]	1888, [1983]	1896, [1988]
1881, [1981]	1889, [1983]	1897, [1988]
1882, [1981]	1890, [1983]	

addenda to 1897, [1989] 4p.
continues 'Padwick I' 900-1.

0066 **Bailey, Trevor Edward**
■ The greatest since my time: the best cricketers of the last
twenty years and the major changes in the game. Hodder
and Stoughton, 1989. 272p. illus.
major changes in the game pp. 223-272.

0067 **Birley, Derek**
■ The willow wand: some cricket myths explored. Simon &
Schuster, 1989. [ix], 211p.
*reprinted ed. of 'Padwick I' 61-1 with a new afterword by
the author.*

0068 **Brayshaw, Ian John**
■ ABC of cricket: the history, the laws, a glossary of terms.
Sydney, ABC Enterprises for the Australian
Broadcasting Corporation, 1985. 96p. diagrs.

0069 † **Brooks, C. C. P.**
Cricket as a vocation: a study of the development and
contemporary structure of the occupation. University of
Leicester, 1974.
unpub. thesis.

0070 **Brown, Ashley**
■ The pictorial history of cricket. Bison Books, 1988.
208p. illus. (some col.) index.
——*another ed.* 1989, *updated to include 1989 Ashes
series.*

0071 **Brown, Craig** *and* **Brown, David**, *compilers*
The book of sports lists. Arthur Barker, 1983. xiii, 226p.
some cricket.

0072 **Cowdrey, Christopher Stuart** *with* **Lemmon, David
Hector**
■ Cricket. (What's your sport? series). Partridge Press,
1989. 96p. illus.
'all aspects for those who have a passion for the game'.

0073 **Cricket.** St Peter's (N.S.W.), Gregory's Publications, 1983. 129p. incl. adverts. index. glossary.
cover title: 'Gregory's cricket: history of the game, equipment, field positions, skills, laws of cricket, glossary'.

0074 **Cricket.** (Hamlet Sports Special series). Hamlyn, 1980. 95p. illus. (some col.)

0075 **Formhals, Hugh**
The jolliest game under the sun: a beginner's guide to cricket. Albuquerque (New Mexico), Western Mountain Press, 1983. xv, 104p. diagrs. bibliog.

0076 **Frith, David Edward John**
The golden age of cricket 1890-1914. Ware, Omega Books, 1983. 192p. illus. (some col.) index.
reissued ed. of 'Padwick I' 67-4.

0077 **Giller, Norman,** *editor*
The book of cricket lists; photographs by Patrick Eagar. Sidgwick & Jackson, 1984. 216p. illus.
——*pbk. ed.* Futura, 1985.
——*reissued.* Treasure, 1987.

0078 **Graveney, Thomas William** *and* **Giller, Norman,** *editor*
Tom Graveney's top ten cricket book. Harrap, 1982. 192p. stats.

0079 **Green, Benny**
A history of cricket. Barrie & Jenkins, 1988. 288p. illus. (some col.) bibliog. index.

0080 **Green, Benny,** *editor*
Wisden cricketers' diary 1986. John Wisden & Co., 1985. [120]p. illus. maps. stats.
each week's diary pages contain historical information; additional facts and figures at front and back.
only ed. pub.

0081 **Harrison, M.,** *editor*
The summer games: baseball and cricket. Sleaford (Lincs), the Author, [1989]. [32]p. incl. covers, illus.
typescript.

0082 **Harriss, Ian**
Cricket and rational economic man. Canberra, Australian Society for Sports History, 1985. 18p.
how cricketers have developed 'cost-benefit' techniques.
paper originally given at A.S.S.H. conference in Adelaide 1985.

0083 **Hayter, Reginald James**
The new observer's book of cricket. (The New Observer's series, no. 6). Warne, 1983. 192p. illus.
3rd. rev. ed. of 'Padwick I' 76-2.

0084 **Howat, Gerald Malcolm David**
Cricket's second golden age. Hodder & Stoughton, 1989. 300p. illus. bibliog. index.
cover sub-title: 'the Hammond - Bradman years', [1919 - 1949].

0085 **Johnston, Brian Alexander**
Brian Johnston's guide to cricket. W. H. Allen, 1986. 239p. illus. diagrs. scores. stats. glossary. index.
rev. and updated ed. of 'Padwick I' 73.

0086 **Lodge, Derek Harry Alan**
Figures on the green. George Allen & Unwin, 1982. xii, 188p. stats. index.

0087 **Mangan, James Anthony**
The games ethic and imperialism: aspects of the diffusion of an ideal. Viking, 1986. 239p. illus. bibliog. index.
several cricket references.

0088 **Marks, Victor James**
The Wisden illustrated history of cricket; records compiled by Bill Frindall. Queen Anne Press, 1988. 256p. illus. (some col.) scores. stats. index. bibliog.

0089 **Martin-Jenkins, Christopher Dennis Alexander**
Cricket - a way of life: *The Cricketer* illustrated history of cricket; photographs by Adrian Murrell. Century, 1984. 224p. illus. (some col.) scores. index.

0090 Twenty years on: cricket's years of change 1963 to 1983. Willow Books, 1984. 159p. illus. index.

0091 **Morrison, Ian**
Cricket. (Play the game series). Ward Lock, 1989. 80p. illus. diagrs. index.

0092 **Naik, Vasant K.**
Jengalik cricketeka itihas. Salsette (Goa), Bandodkar, 1981. 424p.
in Marathi: 'A history of world cricket'.

0093 **Nandy, Ashis**
The tao of cricket: on games of destiny and the destiny of games. New Delhi, Penguin Books, 1989. 150p. index.
the cultural psychology of cricket.

0094 **Patherya, Mudar**
Cricket. (Wills Book of Excellence series). Edited by M. A. K. Pataudi, designed by Sunil Sil. Hyderabad (India), Orient Longman, 1987. 208p. illus. (some col.) stats. index.

0095 **Patherya, Mudar** *and* **O'Brien, Barry**
The Penguin book of cricket lists. Harmondsworth, Penguin, 1988. 239p.
'a fascinating compendium of cricket trivia'.
——*first pub. by* Penguin Books (India), 1987.

0096 **Radhakrishnan, K.**
Cricket scene from 'silly positions'. Madras, Panu Publications, 1985. xxvi, 168p. illus.

0097 **Rhys, Chris,** *compiler*
The Cricketer book of cricket days. Oxford, Lennard Publishing, 1989. 150p. illus.

0098 **Rhys, Chris,** *compiler and editor*
The Courage book of great sporting teams. Stanley Paul, 1985. 128p. illus. stats.
cricket pp. 23-26, 37-39, 44-48, 52-55, 86-88, 127-128.

0099 **Rippon, Anton**
Cricket around the world. Ashbourne, Moorland Publishing, 1982. 192p. illus.

0100 **Salberg, Derek**
Much ado about cricket. Studley, K. A. F. Brewin Books, 1987. [viii], 140p. illus.

0101 † **Scott, James W.**
A cricketing miscellany: being a collection of odds and ends. Sydney, [the Author], 1942. 281p.
ms. in New South Wales Cricket Association Library.

0102 † Unorthodox cricket. Sydney, [the Author], 1933. 296p.
ms. in New South Wales Cricket Association Library.

0103 **Scott, John**
Caught in court: a selection of cases with cricket connections. Andre Deutsch, 1989. xii, 276p. illus. bibliog. index.

0104 Surrey County Cricket Club
Cricket: the English ball game. Management Public Relations Ltd in conjunction with Walter Judd Ltd, [1980]. [16]p. incl. covers, illus.
to celebrate the centenary of the first Test match in England, 1880.

0105 Synge, Allen
Cricket: the men and the matches that changed the game. Century Benham for Marks and Spencer, 1988. 192p. illus. (some col.) index, scores.

0106 Wagholikar, G. A.
Careers in cricket and other sports. Delhi, Creative Career Publishers, 1989. [viii], 90p.

0107 Walker, Maxwell Henry Norman with Piesse, Ken
Hooked on cricket: an addict's A-Z guide. South Melbourne, Macmillan of Australia, 1989. xiii, 122p. illus.

0108 Walmsley, Christopher
Cricket through the year: a day-by-day account of cricketing events 1586-1984. Lewes, Book Guild, 1987. 581p. index.

0109 [Watson, Thomas Mead]
Le jeu de cricket. [Lord's Taverners, 1986?] [4]p. folded sheet.
introduction to the game for French speakers.

0110 Willis, Robert George Dylan ('Bob') and Murphy, Patrick
Starting with Grace: a pictorial celebration of cricket 1864-1986. Stanley Paul, 1986. 188p. illus. (some col.) stats. index.

0111 Wooldridge, Ian Edmund
Great sporting headlines. Collins, 1984. [128]p. illus.
includes 25 cricket stories.

0112 Wynne-Thomas, Peter and Arnold, Peter
Cricket in conflict. Feltham, Newnes, 1984. 176p. illus. bibliog. index.

GENERAL BOOKS FOR CHILDREN

0113 Barclay, Patrick
The Puffin book of cricket; illustrated by Raju Patel. Harmondsworth, Puffin, 1986. 156p. illus. diagrs. index.

0114 Blackall, Bernie
Cricket. South Melbourne, Macmillan Australia, 1989. 30p. col. illus.

0115 Bradshaw, Tony
Cricket; illustrations by Chris Reed; photographs by Tim Clark. Loughborough, Ladybird Books, 1982. 52p. + end covers, col. illus. diagrs. index.

0116 Cricket activity book. Gladesville (N.S.W.), Golden Press, 1983. 32p. incl. covers, col. illus. diagrs. stats.

0117 Freeman, Gill
Cricketer. (People series). Franklin Watts, 1986. 32p. illus. (some col.) index.
based on Warwickshire C.C.C. and Andy Lloyd.

0118 [Keane, Gary and Randall, Neville]
'Cricket, lovely cricket'. Wickford (Essex), W. Bourne & Co., 1985. [32]p. illus.
'specially produced to celebrate Ian Botham's successes in 1981 and incorporating "Focus on fact" strip cartoon from "The Daily Mail"'.

0119 Knight, Barry Rolfe
Stumpy and Bails all about cricket; illustrated by Bill Mitchell. Sydney, Lansdowne Press, 1982. 30p. illus.

0120 Palmer, Robert
It's a great game cricket: fun facts and figures. Cammeray (N.S.W.), Horwitz Grahame Books, 1985. 63p. illus.

0121 Perchard, Peter
Cricket. (World of Sport series). Hove, Wayland, 1988. 64p. illus. (mostly col.) diagrs. glossary, index.

MEMORABLE MATCHES

0122 Colabawalla, J. K.
Cricket's unforgettable cliff-hangers. Bombay etc., Jaico, 1982. xv, 160p. illus. scores.

0123 Murphy, Patrick
Fifty incredible cricket matches. Stanley Paul, 1987. x, 293p. illus. scores, bibliog.

RECORDS AND STATISTICS

0124 Bhalla, Surjit Singh
Between the wickets: the who and why of the best in cricket. New Delhi, Living Media, 1987. x, 196p. illus. stats. index.
statistical analysis of cricket's great players.

0125 Brooke, Robert William
The Cricketer book of cricket milestones. Century Benham for Marks and Spencer, 1987. 191p. illus. (some col.) stats.

0126 Brooke, Robert William and Matthews, Peter
Guinness cricket firsts. Enfield, Guinness Publishing, 1988. 160p. illus. index.

0127 † Cricket records. Sydney, William Brooks & Co., [1911]. 32p. incl. adverts. illus. stats.

0128 [Ford, Alfred Lawson]
Curiosities of cricket by an Old Cricketer. [Ewell, Epsom], J. W. McKenzie, 1989. [x], 39p.
facsim. ed., of 'Padwick I' 108 with a new introduction by Irving Rosenwater.

0129 Frindall, William Howard ('Bill')
The Guinness book of cricket facts and feats. Enfield, Guinness Superlatives, 1983. 256p. illus. (some col.) stats. glossary, index.
——*2nd. ed. with title 'Guinness cricket facts & feats', 1987.*

0130 Frindall, William Howard ('Bill'), compiler & editor
The Wisden book of cricket records. Queen Anne Press, 1981. 618p. stats.
——*2nd. rev. ed. 1986.*

0131 Melford, Michael Austin and Frindall, William Howard ('Bill')
Cricket (*Daily Telegraph* pocket sports facts). Telegraph Publications, 1984. 128p. illus. stats.

0132 † Roberts, Edward Lamplough, compiler
Cricket facts and feats. [1938]. 37p. stats.
additional ed. of 'Padwick I' 125.
——*rptd. 1946.*

0133 Sharma, Ram Dutt
Cricket ke aankre. Narnaul, Indian Sports Lovers Club, 1980. 80p. incl. adverts. stats.
in Hindi: 'Figures of cricket'.

0134 **Trueman, Frederick Sewards** *and* **Mosey, Don**
■ Cricket statistics year by year 1946-1987; statistics compiled by Wendy Wimbush. Stanley Paul, 1988. 206p. illus. stats.

0135 **Wat, Charlie,** *compiler*
□ Subscribers' bulletin. Prahran (Vic.), Cricket Stats Publications. *monthly?* stats.
six? issues in 1988-89.
continued in 1989-90 season.

0136 **Wynne-Thomas, Peter**
■ The Hamlyn A-Z of cricket records. Hamlyn, 1983. 192p. illus. (some col.) stats. index.
——*pub. in Australia with title 'The Rigby A-Z of cricket records'.*
——*rev. ed.* 1985.

QUIZ BOOKS

0137 **Coley, Chris** *assisted by* **Nocton, Bob**
The cricket quiz book. East Ardsley (Yorks.), EP Publishing, 1983. 64p. illus.

0138 **Crampsey, Robert Anthony**
■ The Somerset cricket quiz book. Edinburgh, Mainstream Publishing, 1988. 160p. illus.

0139 The Surrey cricket quiz book. Edinburgh, Mainstream
■ Publishing, 1988. 156p. illus.

0140 **Dawson, Marc Brian,** *compiler*
■ ABC cricket quiz. Sydney, ABC Enterprises for the Australian Broadcasting Corporation, 1986. 126p. illus.

0141 Cricket in question. Cammeray (N.S.W.), Horwitz Grahame, 1989. iv, 135p. illus.

0142 Howzat? Australian cricket quiz. Sydney, Australian
■ Broadcasting Corporation, 1984. 128p. illus.

0143 **Giller, Norman,** *compiler*
Greavsie's sports quiz challenge. Hamlyn, 1987. 192p. illus.
some cricket.

0144 **Hatton, Leslie Walter**
■ The Worcestershire cricket quiz book. Edinburgh, Mainstream Publishing, 1989. 144p. illus.

0145 **Hickey, Peter** *and* **Williamson, Malcolm**
■ Trivia Test match. BBC Books, 1988. 106p.
general knowledge questions in cricket scoring format based on BBC radio series.

0146 **Hughes, Emlyn**
■ A question of cricket: an Arthur Barker quiz book. Arthur Barker, 1988. 110p. illus.

0147 **Lewthwaite, Hazel**
A question of sport: questions and answers from the BBC TV quiz game; illustrated by Alan Burton. BBC, 1985. 128p. illus.
some cricket.
——*rev. eds. compiled by Mike Adley and Mick Dempsey* 1988 and 1989.

0148 **Lodge, Derek Harry Alan**
■ A question of cricket. Unwin Paperbacks, 1983. 128p. illus.

0149 **Lorimer, Malcolm George** *and* **Warburton, Bob**
■ The Lancashire cricket quiz book. Edinburgh, Mainstream Publishing, 1989. 142p. illus.

0150 **Martin-Jenkins, Christopher Dennis Alexander**
■ Stumped? a cricket quiz. Orbis, 1984. 159p. illus.

0151 **Monster** quiz poster cricket book: packed with facts and
■ statistics on international one day limited-over cricket. North Sydney, Underline, 1984. 31p. col. illus. stats.

0152 **Puri, Narottam**
1000 cricket quiz. Calcutta etc., Rupa, 1989. 145p.

0153 One-day cricket quiz. Calcutta etc., Rupa, 1987. 85p.
illus.

0154 Power quiz book of cricket. New Delhi, Konark
■ Publishers, 1987. xi, 132p. illus.

0155 **Rhys, Chris**
Brain of sport: questions and answers from the Radio 2 quiz game. BBC, 1980. 80p. illus.

0156 **Sarin, Ashok Kumar**
Cricket quiz. New Delhi, Current Scientific Literature, 1986. 119p. index.

0157 **Scholefield, Peter,** *compiler*
■ Cricket trivia declared; illustrated by Greg Wilson. Axiom Publishing, [1989]. 65p. glossary.
includes terms and field positions.

0158 **Shahid Mahmood**
■ Cricket quiz book. Karachi, Liliana International Publishers, 1989. 100p. incl. covers and adverts.

0159 **Szumski, A. J.**
■ 'Light meters stopped play' cricket quiz. Sheffield, T/A Damson Publishing, 1988. [i], 55p. *typescript.*

0160 **Tarrant, Graham**
■ The Lord's Taverners cricket quiz book. Newton Abbot, David & Charles, 1984. 92p. illus.
——*Australian ed. pub. as 'Cricket quiz book',* Macmillan Australia, 1984.

0161 The new Lord's Taverners cricket quiz book. Newton
■ Abbot, David & Charles, 1989. 90p. illus.

0162 **Thomson, Ian** *and* **Davies, Mansel**
■ Cricket quiz book. Sphere, 1988. [192]p.

0163 **Trivial** challenge cricketer quiz. Little Berkhamsted
■ (Herts.), PWA Services, [1988]. [80]p.
'the pull-out game in a magazine'.
vol. 1 no. 1 pub. in Spring 1988; the only issue?

0164 **Woodhouse, Anthony**
■ The Yorkshire cricket quiz book. Edinburgh, Mainstream Publishing, 1989. 140p. illus.

THE CONDUCT OF THE GAME

LAWS
(Arranged in order of date of publication)

0165 † The **sky-lark**: containing a new, elegant, and much more
■ numerous collection of well chosen English songs, than
any other book hitherto published ... to which are added
... rules and laws to be observed at the game of cricket ,
as settled at the most respectable meetings. Printed for
T. Evans, 1772. [272]p.
*contains 2 pages on 'Rules to be observed by the players at
cricket'.*

0166 † The **laws** of cricket. Robert Dark, 1850. bs. on cloth.
■ *'by authority of the Mary-le-bone Club'.*

0167 † **Victorian Cricket Association**
The laws of cricket as revised by the Marylebone Club
1884, 1889, 1894, 1899, 1900, 1902 and 1906. (With
decisions and interpretations authorized by the
Marylebone Club.) Melbourne, the Association, 1906.
28p.
cover sub-title: 'instructions to umpires'.

0168 † **Marylebone Cricket Club**
Laws of cricket with decisions & interpretations
authorized by the M.C.C. Rules of county cricket,
instructions to umpires, county qualifications, minor
county rules, Advisory Cricket Committee and Board of
Control rules. The Club, 1923. 27p.
13th ed. of 'Padwick I' 205.

0169 † The **laws** of cricket 1925 (Cricket Press Rules of Sport &
Games series). Cricket Press, 1925. 16p.

0170 † **New South Wales Cricket Association**
Laws of cricket with decisions & interpretations and
instructions to umpires authorised by the Marylebone
Cricket Club; rules and conditions governing Test
matches. Sydney, the Association, 1925. 26p.

0171 † **Sporting** teasers asked and answered. *Topical Times*,
■ n.d. 40p. incl. covers, illus.
*cricket laws queries asked and answered by George
Duckworth, pp. 17-24.*

0172 † **Victorian Cricket Umpires' Council**
■ Laws of cricket with decisions, interpretations and knotty
points, together with hints to umpires. Melbourne, the
Council, 1932. 28p.

0173 † **Cricket-regeln.** Berlin, Ausgabe, 1952. 32p. diagrs.
in German.
later ed. of 'Padwick I' 208?

0174 † **McMenamin, Jim**
'Ask the umpire!': 173 questions and explained answers
on the laws of cricket. Sydney, Excelsior Publishing,
[1963]. 56p. incl. adverts. index.

0175 **Marylebone Cricket Club**
■ The laws of cricket: 1980 code. The Club, 1980. 56p.
index.

0176 The laws of cricket. (Know the Game series). Wakefield,
■ EP Publishing, 1980. 48p. illus. diagrs. index.
*reprint of 'Padwick I' 222, 9th ed., with the addition of the
1980 code of the laws of cricket.*

0177 **Dansk Cricket Forbund**
■ Love for cricket. The Forbund, 1980. 72p. index.
in Danish.

0178 The **laws** of cricket (1980 code). South African Cricket
Umpires Association on behalf of the South African
Cricket Union, [1980]. 100p.
in English and Afrikaans.

0179 **Marsden, J. Trevor**
■ A league players guide to the new laws of cricket; edited
& verified by Frank Richardson. The Author?, 1980.
12p.
abridged from the laws of cricket (1980 code).

0180 **Permainan** krekit (sic). (Siri sukan, no. 10) Kuala
■ Lumpur, Fargoes, 1980. 63p. illus. diagrs.
in Malay: 'The game of cricket'.

0181 **Smyth, W. J.**
A guide to the laws of cricket, 1980 code. Melbourne,
Victorian Cricket Association, 1980. 23p.

0182 **Boxall, Thomas**
■ Rules & instructions for playing at the game of cricket ...
Ewell, J. W. McKenzie, 1981. [x], 92, [v]p. illus.
*reprint of 'Padwick I' 164 (2nd ed. 2nd issue) with
foreword and appendices by Diana Rait Kerr.*
limited ed. of 150 numbered copies.

0183 **Marylebone Cricket Club**
■ The laws of cricket. 9th ed. A. & C. Black, 1984. 48p.
illus. some col.
'incorporating 1980 code of the Laws of Cricket'.

0184 **Vermaak, C.M.**
■ Die Suid-Afrikaanse krieketreëls: soos vasgestel deur die
S.A. Krieketunie met verklareude komentaar. Cape
Town, Perskor, 1984. 94p. diagrs.
in Afrikaans.

0185 **Brodribb, [Arthur] Gerald Norcott**
■ Next man in: a survey of cricket laws and customs.
Pelham Books, 1985. x, 261p. illus. diagrs. stats. index.
rev. ed. of 'Padwick I' 223.

0186 **Roy, Samar**
■ Cricketer umpire. Calcutta, 1985. 270p. illus. diagrs.
index.
the laws of cricket and their interpretation.
in Bengali.

0187 **Hales, Geoff**
■ Cricket rules OK: the laws of cricket; illustrations by
Brian Flaherty. A & C Black, 1986. [72]p. illus. index.

0188 **Asad Sherzad**
■ Adabe cricket; cartoons by Javed Iqbal. Lahore, Aleel
Publishers, 1987. 36p. illus.
in Urdu: 'Etiquettes of cricket'.

0189 **Sanglikar, V. N.**
Cricket rules & regulations. 1988?
in Marathi.

UMPIRING

0190 **Naik, Vasant K.**
Cricket kayade. Bombay, Bombay Cricket Association, 1989.
in Marathi: 'Laws of cricket'; standard text book for umpires' examination.

0191 **Association of Cricket Umpires**
☐ How's that?: the official organ of the Association of Cricket Umpires. Hatfield, the Association, *bi-monthly.*
continues 'Padwick I' 244 to date?

0192 **Berkshire Association of Cricket Umpires and Scorers**
☐ Play: the news letter of the Berkshire Association of Cricket Umpires. The Association. *irregular.*
?/series 2, no. 1, Oct. 1983 - no. 4, Oct. 1985/ to date?

0193 **Bird, Harold Dennis ('Dickie')**
■ That's out! Arthur Barker, 1985. 160p. illus.
——*pbk ed.* 1989.

0194 **Bristol and District Cricket Association *and* Bristol and District Cricket Umpires' Association**
Official handbook. Bristol, the Association. *annual.* stats.
sponsored successively by Halls, Bowdens and Sun Life. continues 'Padwick I' 254? to date.

0195 **Bristol and District Cricket Umpires' Association**
The appeal: the news-sheet of the ... Association; edited by H. C. Cook. Bristol, the Association. *seven issues per year.*
continues 'Padwick I' 254-1 to date?

0196 **Constant, David John *with the assistance of* Murphy, Patrick**
■ Cricket: umpiring (Sporting Skills series). Pelham Books, 1981. 120p. illus. diagrs.

0197 **Federation of Australian Cricket Umpires**
☐ Over: the official journal of the Federation ... The Federation. *3 issues per season.* illus.
format changed, Oct 1985.
continues 'Padwick I' 257-2 to date?

0198 **Jamaica Cricket Umpires Association**
Jamaica Cricket Umpires Association commemorates the hosting of the 12th biennial convention of the West Indies Cricket Umpires Association ... May 1985. Kingston, the Association, 1984. 26p. incl. adverts. illus.

0199 **Jew, Keith**
History of South Australian Cricket Umpires Association. Adelaide, the Association, [1980]. [24]p.
——*another ed.* 1981.
includes list of umpires officiating at Adelaide Oval since 1892.

0200 **Kidson, Hayward C.**
■ Over and time. Cape Town, Howard Timmins, [1983]. [xvi], 449p. illus. scores.
sub-title on cover: 'An umpire's autobiography'.

0201 **McLean, Teresa**
■ The men in white coats: cricket umpires past and present. Stanley Paul, 1987. xiv, 176p. illus. index.

0202 **New South Wales Cricket Umpires' Association**
Training officers manual. Sydney, Management Development Publishers for the Association, 1989. 249p. diagrs.

0203 Umpires manual and handbook Sydney, Management Development Publishers for the Association, 1989. v, 47p. index.

0204 † **New Zealand Cricket Umpires' Association**
■ The umpires' companion. The Association, 1978. 16p.

0205 † **Roach, J. E.**
Cricket teasers for junior umpires. King William's Town (Border), 1956. 18p. illus.

0206 **Smith, Thomas Edward**
■ Cricket umpiring and scoring. Dent, 1980. 192p. diagrs. index.
completely rev. ed. of 'Padwick I' 277.
contains 1980 M.C.C. official laws of cricket with interpretations and definitions for umpires, scorers, players and spectators.
——*2nd ed.* 1989. *includes new laws and extension of definitions.*

0207 **South Australian Cricket Umpires Association**
Newsletter.
edited by M.G.Gandy.
1980? - 1984

0208 **Whiting, Herbert Haig**
New Zealand Cricket Umpires' Association: a brief history. Hastings (N.Z.), [the Association], 1986. 28p. illus.

SCORING

0209 The **official** cricket scorer's book. Pymble (N.S.W.),
■ Playbill in co-operation with the Australian Cricket Board, 1981. 56p. illus. scores.
mostly empty scoresheets.
includes 'Scoring - and how to do it' by Irving Rosenwater and a completed ball by ball sample scoresheet.

0210 **Smith, Thomas Edward**
■ Cricket umpiring and scoring. Dent, 1980. 192p. diagrs. index.
completely rev. ed. of 'Padwick I' 277.
contains 1980 M.C.C. official laws of cricket with interpretations and definitions for umpires, scorers, players and spectators.
——*2nd ed.* 1989. *incorporates changes in the official method of scoring.*

CARE OF GROUNDS

0211 **Burdett, Les**
Pitch preparation and turf maintenance. Adelaide, South Australian Cricket Association, 1983. 28p. diagrs.

0212 Turf cricket pitches: construction, preparation and
■ maintenance. [Adelaide, South Australian Cricket Association, 1989]. 28p. illus. diagrs.

0213 **Challenger, Ian**
Cricket and cricket wickets: a discussion of the two. Lincoln College (N.Z.), 1986. 55 leaves, illus.
dissertation submitted in partial completion of the Diploma in Parks & Recreation Management.

0214 **Cricket** wicket preparation and maintenance: a practical guide for groundsmen. [Wellington], N. Z. Local Government Training Board, [1981]. 25p. illus.
based on a seminar held in Dunedin, 1980.

0215 † **Division of Recreation, Tasmania**
Preparation and maintenance of turf cricket wickets: seminar July 19-21, 1976. Hobart, the Division, 1976. 45p.

0216 Dury, Peter *and* **Dury, Peter L. K.**
■   To play like grass: an investigation into the use of particular and synthetic materials in the provision of sports facility base; drawings by Neil Parkes. Nottingham, Nottinghamshire County Council, 1985. 77p. illus. diagrs. glossary, bibliog.

0217 Dury, Peter L. K.
■   To play like natural turf. (Cricket pitch jottings); drawings by Neil Parkes. Nottingham, Nottinghamshire County Council, 1985. 72p. illus. diagrs.

0218 Dury, Peter L. K. *compiler, and* **Slater, Colin,** *editor*
■   Cricket pitch research. (Cricket pitch jottings). Nottingham, Nottinghamshire County Council, 1985. 108p. illus. diagrs.

0219 Enoch, Maldwyn David
    Concrete bases for non-turf cricket pitches. Slough, Cement and Concrete Association, 1980. [ii], 14p. illus. (one col.) map.

0220 Fairbrother, Jim *and* **Moore, Reginald**
■   Testing the wicket: from Trent Bridge to Lord's. Pelham Books, 1984. 144p. illus. index.

0221 Liffman, Karl, *compiler*
    Sports grounds and turf wickets: a practical guide. Collingwood (Vic.), TAFE Publications Unit, 1986. 102p. illus. diagr.

0222 Lock, Herbert Christmas
■   Cricket - take care of your square; revised by P. L. K. Dury. 1987. 33p. illus. diagrs.
    rev. ed. of 'Padwick I' 306.

0223 Mansfield, Peter
    Maintenance of the club ground. Ashurst (Kent), *The Cricketer,* 1983.

0224 † Nottinghamshire County Council. *Education*
■   The construction of non-turf cricket pitches including 'The Nottinghamshire pitch'. Nottingham, the Council, [1979]. 18p. incl. inside covers, illus. diagrs.

0225 Nottinghamshire cricket pitch. Nottingham, the
■   Council, n.d. [10]p. incl. inside back cover, illus. (one col.)

0226 Nottinghamshire County Council. *Education Playing*
■   *Fields Service*
    Cricket pitch research supplement. Nottingham, the Service, [1980]. 18p. illus. diagrs.
    supplement to 'Padwick I' 310-2.

0227 Royal Australian Institute of Parks and Recreation
    Proceedings of the National Seminar on turf management; Canberra, 3-5 May 1983. Dickson (A.C.T.), the Institute, [1983].
    includes 'Cricket wicket construction' by Peter S. Semos, 23pp; 'Cricket pitch preparation' by Les Burdett, 5pp; 'Australian cricket pitch soils and profiles' by Don S. McIntyre, 13pp.; 'A report on cricket wickets' by Bob Simpson, 8pp.

0228 Turf cricket wicket seminar; University of New South Wales, September 14, 1988. [Dickson (A.C.T.)], the Institute, [1988]. 42 leaves, illus.

0229 Turf wicket seminar; 10 September 1986. [St. Albans (Vic.), the Institute, 1986]. [21]p. illus. (some col.)

0230 † Watt, W. B., *compiler*
    Turf wickets: their overhaul, preparation and repair. Sydney, New South Wales Cricket Association, 1949. 8p. diagr.
    earlier ed. of 'Padwick I' 314-2.

EQUIPMENT

0231 Ackland, Timothy Robert
    Physical and impact characteristics of aluminium and wooden cricket bats. University of Western Australia, 1981. vii, 105 leaves.
    unpub. thesis.

0232 British Standards Institution
■   British Standard protective equipment for cricketers. Part 1: specification for batting gloves, leg guards and boxes. (BS 6183: Part 1). The Institution, 1981. [12]p. incl. covers, diagrs.
    part 2 not yet published.

0233 British Standard specification for leather-covered cricket
■   balls. (BS 5993). The Institution, 1987. [16]p. incl. covers, diagrs.
    revised ed. of BS 5993, 1980.

0234 † The '**Cambridge**' bowler. F. H. Ayres, [1909]. [8]p.
■   illus.
    bowling machine invented by Dr Venn and Mr J.A. Venn

0235 † Clark, William
■   Improvement in cricket bats. (Patent no. 9,398). HMSO, 1893. 2p. diagr.

0236 † Hartleys Ltd.
■   Cricket catalogue 1951-52. Melbourne, Spectator Publishing Co. 16p. illus.
    other years pub?

0237 † Illustrated catalogue of cricket goods. Bristol, J. R.
■   Painter, [1896]. 12p. illus.

0238 † James Martin & Co.
■   [Catalogue]. Sydney, printed by J. A. Campbell, c.1902. 16p.
    on cover: 'To the cricketers of Australasia - you get the enjoyment, we provide the means'.

0239 Junior cricket safety. Melbourne, Victorian Dept. of Youth, Sport and Recreation, 1981. folded sheet, col. illus.
    helmets and protective clothing.

0240 † The **M.S.D.** cricket catalogue. Melbourne, Melbourne
■   Sports Report, n.d. 12p. incl. covers, illus.

0241 Martin, D. R.
    Cricket bat manual: a guide to the selection, purchase, care and maintenance of a cricket bat. [Charmhaven (N.S.W.)], the Author, 1983. 22p.

0242 † Ruston, William *et al*
    Cricket bat handle. (Patent no. 14,566). HMSO, 1898. 2p. diagr.

0243 † Sandham, Andrew *et al*
    Ess Ess Bee: catalogue of cricket equipment. 1920. 32p. illus.

THE TECHNIQUE OF THE GAME

GENERAL INSTRUCTIONAL

(See also Coaching)

0244 **Abrahams, John** *and* **Watkinson, Michael**
■ Basic cricket skills. Canberra, Canberra Times, [1984]. 23p. illus. diagrs.

0245 **Andrew, Keith Vincent**
■ The skills of cricket. Marlborough (Wilts.), Crowood Press, 1984. viii, 136p. illus. (some col.) diagrs. index.
——*rev. pbk. ed.* 1989.

0246 **Andrew, Keith Vincent** *et al*
Cricket. Wakefield, EP Publishing, 1981. 116p. illus. diagrs.
pbk. ed. of 'Padwick I' 554-1.

0247 **Bailey, Trevor Edward**
■ Cricketers in the making. Queen Anne Press, 1982. 119p. illus.
includes chapter on softball cricket.
updated ed. of 'Padwick I' 557.

0248 **Barlow, Edgar John ('Eddie')**
Cricket: a guide for young players. Cape Town, Mobil Oil Southern Africa, [1980]. 62p. col. illus. diagrs.
pub. simultaneously in Afrikaans.

0249 † **'A batsman'**, *pseud.*
■ The cricketers' pocket companion: or, field-sportsman's guide. Printed for J. Bysh, 1818. 63p. illus. index.
on cover: 'printed by and for Hodgson & Co.'
earlier ed. of 'Padwick I' 372?

0250 **Botham, Ian Terence**
■ Ian Botham on cricket; photographs by Geoff Goode. Cassell, 1980. 88p. illus. glossary.

0251 **Botham, Ian Terence** *with* **Bannister, John David**
■ **('Jack')**
Cricket my way. Willow Books, 1989. 208p. illus. diagrs. index.

0252 **Boxall, Thomas**
■ Rules & instructions for playing at the game of cricket ... Ewell, J. W. McKenzie, 1981. [x], 92, [v]p. illus.
reprint of 'Padwick I' 373 (2nd ed. 2nd issue) with foreword and appendices by Diana Rait Kerr.
limited ed. of 150 numbered copies.

0253 † **Boxhammer, F.**
Leitfaden des Torballspiels (Cricket). Crefeld, Gustav Hohns, 1912. 15p.
in German: 'Introduction to wicket-ball-play (cricket)'.

0254 **Boycott, Geoffrey**
■ Master class; drawings by George Stokes. Arthur Barker, 1982. [148]p. chiefly illus. stats.

0255 **Bradman, Sir Donald George**
■ The art of cricket. Lane Cove (N.S.W.), Hodder & Stoughton Australia, 1984. 255p. illus. diagrs.
rev. and updated ed. of 'Padwick I' 564.

0256 † **Bradman, Sir Donald George** *et al*
'The News' cricket hints. Sydney, Sun Newspapers, 1934. 40p. illus. stats.
variant ed. of 'Padwick I' 503-1.

0257 **Carr, John Donald**
■ Guide to cricket skills. Holder (A.C.T.), Weston Creek Cricket Club, [1987]. [12]p. diagrs.

0258 **Carstens, Thys** *and* **Barnard, Sollie**
Korrekte krieket. Bellville (W.P.), Gedruk deur Renee Press, 1984. 74p. illus. diagrs.
in Afrikaans.

0259 † **Christian, Arthur**
Hints to cricketers. Perth, Paramount Press, [1934]. 48p. incl. adverts. illus.
articles previously published in 'The West Australian'.

0260 **Club** cricket for you. (TSB Bank Play the game series).
■ [TSB for the National Cricket Association, 1989?] [14]p. incl. inside covers.
maxims and advice for club cricketers.

0261 † The **cricketers'** handbook: containing the origin of the
■ game, remarks on recent alterations, directions for bowling, striking, and placing the players, and the laws as altered by the Marylebone Cricket Club; with a view of Lord's Cricket Ground. London, Robert Tyas; Edinburgh, J. Menzies, 1838. [viii], 37p. frontis.
2nd ed. of 'Padwick I' 377.

0262 † The **cricketer's** pocket book, 1868-9. 2nd. ed. E. J. Page, [1868].

0263 **Davies, Jan**
■ Basic cricket. New Plymouth (N.Z.), the Author, 1983. 38p. diagrs.
pub. for New Zealand Women's Cricket Council.

0264 **Dexter, Edward Ralph**
■ You can play cricket; illustrated by Mike Miller. Severn House, 1982. 128p. illus. diagrs.
——*pbk. ed.* Carousel Books, 1982.

0265 **Farmer, Bob**
■ Cricket (Play the Game series). Hamlyn, 1984. 61p. illus. index.
cover title: 'Cricket: a step by step guide to skills and tactics'.
reprint of 'Padwick I' 575-1.
——*reprinted. ed.* Treasure Press, 1989 *with title 'How to Play Cricket'.*

0266 **Freeman, Gill**
■ Cricket (Sportmasters series). Cambridge, Cambridge University Press, 1984. 48p. illus. diagrs.
for children.

0267 **Gore, Chris** *and* **Woods, Kym**
It's just not cricket: an open-ended guide for teachers and learners. n.p. 1982. x, 87, xxiip. illus.

0268 **Gover, Alfred Richard**
■ Alf Gover's cricket manual: a pictorial guide to batting, bowling, wicket-keeping and fielding; illustrated by Geoff Jones. Guildford, Lutterworth Press, 1980. 160p. illus.

0269 **Gower, David Ivon** *with* **Hodgson, Derek**
■ A right ambition. Collins, 1986. 127p. illus.

0270 **Hadlee,** *Sir* **Richard John**
■ Hadlee on cricket: the essentials of the game.
Wellington, Reed; Sydney, Lansdowne Press, 1982.
viii, 145p. illus. diagrs.
——*UK ed.* Angus & Robertson, 1983.

0271 **Hutchinson, Garrie**
■ How to play cricket; illustrated by Tony Ward.
Melbourne, McPhee Gribble Publishers, 1982. 64p.
illus. diagrs. glossary.
——*new ed.* 1988.

0272 **Imran Khan Niazi**
■ Imran Khan's cricket skills; edited by Peter Ball; specially
commissioned photographs by Action Plus. Hamlyn,
1989. 127p. illus. (some col.) diagrs, glossary, index.

0273 **Johnston, Brian Alexander**
■ Brian Johnston's guide to cricket. W. H. Allen, 1986.
239p. illus. diagrs. scores, stats. glossary, index.
rev. and updated ed. of 'Padwick I' 590.

0274 **Lenham, Leslie John** *and* **Dellor, Ralph**
■ Copybook cricket: the guide to more sucess and
enjoyment. Robson Books, 1989. 188p. illus. diagrs.

0275 **[Lillywhite, Frederick William],** *editor*
■ Lillywhite's illustrated hand-book of cricket. [Ewell], J.
W. McKenzie, 1988. [viii], 22p. illus.
*facsimile reprint of 'Padwick I' 386 with a new
introduction by John Arlott.*

0276 The **Lord's** Taverners' cricket clinic: tactics, technique,
■ training (a Graham Tarrant book). Newton Abbot,
David & Charles, 1986. 128p. illus. diagrs.

0277 **Main, Jim,** *editor*
■ Greg Chappell's cricket clinic; photographs by Roger
Gould. South Yarra (Vic.), Lloyd O'Neil for Currey
O'Neil, 1983. [iv], 60p. col. illus. diagrs.

0278 How to play cricket Australian style. South Yarra (Vic.),
■ Currey O'Neil, 1981. 135p. illus. diagrs.
3rd ed. of 'Padwick I' 592-1.

0279 **Mallett, Ashley Alexander**
■ 100 cricket tips. Adelaide, Rigby, 1982. 109p. illus.

0280 **Marks, Thomas Geraint**
Criced (Dewch i chwarae). Y Loffa, 1985. 108p. illus.
diagrs. glossary.
in Welsh.

0281 **Marks, Victor James**
■ The Test & County Cricket Board guide to better
cricket. Octopus Books, 1987. 175p. illus. (mostly col.)
diagrs. index.
sponsored by National Westminster Bank.

0282 † **Meuleman, Kenneth Douglas**
Basic cricket for West Australian schools. n.p. 1960?
16p. incl. adverts.

0283 **Middlebrook, Ralph,** *principal contributor*
■ Take up cricket. Huddersfield, Springfield Books, 1989.
56p. illus. diagrs.

0284 **Mushtaq Ali, Syed**
How to play cricket. New Delhi, Vikas, 1981. [vi], 145p.

0285 **Philpott, Peter Ian**
■ Cricket fundamentals. Batsford, 1982. 111p. illus.
U.K. ed. of 'Padwick I' 603-1.
——*rev. ed.* Frenchs Forest (N.S.W.), Reed, 1983.
——*pbk. ed.* Reed, 1988.

0286 **Pollard, Jack,** *editor*
■ Cricket: the Australian way. Sydney, Jack Pollard
Publishing, 1980. [vi], 154p. illus. diagrs.
rev. ed. of 'Padwick I' 604.

0287 **Puri, Narottam** *and* **Gothi, Dilbar**
Cricket guide. Calcutta, etc., Rupa, 1989. [iv], 116p.

0288 **Randall, Derek William** *with* **Bowles, Terry**
■ The young players guide to cricket. Newton Abbot,
David & Charles, 1980. 112p. illus. index.

0289 **Rice, Peter**
■ How to play cricket. Enfield, Guinness Books, 1988.
127p. illus. diagrs.

0290 **Richards, [Isaac] Vivian Alexander** *with* **Foot, David**
■ Learn cricket with Viv Richards: a young players guide.
Stanley Paul, 1985. 96p. illus.

0291 **Richards, [Isaac] Vivian Alexander** *with* **Murphy,**
■ **Patrick**
Viv Richards' cricket masterclass. Queen Anne Press,
1988. 160p. illus. (some col.) diagrs.

0292 **Skills** and tactics: the Australian Test team cricket book.
■ Dee Why West (N.S.W.), Lansdowne Press, 1982. 127p.
col. illus. diagrs. index.

0293 **Smith, Michael John Knight**
Better cricket for boys. Kaye and Ward, 1980. [vi], 87p.
illus.
2nd rev. ed. of 'Padwick I' 614.

0294 **Sobers,** *Sir* **Garfield St Aubrun** *with* **Smith, Patrick**
■ Gary Sobers' way of cricket; illustrated by John Spooner.
Hawthorn (Vic.), Five Mile Press, 1985. x, 78p. illus.
diagrs.

0295 **Steel, Allan Gibson** *and* **Lyttelton,** *Hon* **Robert Henry**
■ Cricket: with contributions by A. Lang, W. G. Grace, R.
A. H. Mitchell and F. Gale. (The Badminton Library of
Sports and Pastimes). Southampton, Ashford Press
Publishing, 1987. xv, 429p. illus. diagrs. index.
*facsimile reprint of 'Padwick I' 473 with a new
introduction by His Grace, the 11th Duke of Beaufort.*

0296 **Stretch, Richard Aldworth**
Validity and reliability of an objective test of cricket
skills. Grahamstown, Rhodes University, 1984. x, 150p.
stats.
unpublished thesis.

0297 **Tyson, Frank Holmes** *and* **Harris, John**
■ Cricket skills. Lane Cove (N.S.W.), Doubleday, 1983.
viii, 151p. illus. diagrs.
——*rev. ed.* 1985.

0298 † **Walters, Kevin Douglas ('Doug')**
Doug Walters' cricket book: complete guide to
techniques of batting, bowling, fielding, wicket-keeping,
captaincy. Sydney, for the National Fitness Council,
1969. 48p.
blank pages designed for cut-outs from newspaper.

0299 **Webster, Rudi Valentine**
■ Winning ways: in search of your best performance; with
tips from Ian and Greg Chappell, Dennis Lillee, Greg
Norman, Sir Garfield Sobers and others. Sydney,
Fontana, 1984. 234p. diagrs. bibliog.

0300 **Wettimuny, Sunil Ramsay de Silva**
■ Cricket: the noble art. Colombo, Lake House, 1985. [x], 186p. illus. (some col.)

0301 **Whimpress, Bernard**
■ Understanding cricket; illustrations by Bob Dikkenberg. Adelaide, Rigby, 1985. [vii], 115p. illus. diagrs.

0302 **Worcestershire Cricket Coaches Association**
■ Introduction to cricket for juniors. [Worcester], the Association, 1984. 28p. illus. diagr.

SPORTSMANSHIP

0303 **Booth, Brian Charles** *and* **White, Paul**
■ Cricket and christianity: to help you live with a straighter bat and to maintain a better line and length; illustrated by Graham Wade. Homebush West (N.S.W.), Anzea Publishers, 1985. 103p. illus.

0304 **Vagrants Cricket Club**
Cricket: a code of good sportsmanship and good temper. East London, the Club, n.d. 28p.

FITNESS

0305 **Australian Cricket Board**
The place of fitness in cricket. Jolimont (Vic.), the Board, 1987.
listed in Mullins.

0306 † **Fry, Charles Burgess**
Training and diet for cricket, football, and athletics ... with diary for 1904. Bedford Publishing Press, [1904]. 95p. frontis.
see also 'Padwick I' 635.

0307 **Jamison, Bob**
■ Fitness and fielding activities for cricket training. [McKinnon (Vic.)], the Author, 1987. v, 107p. illus.

0308 **National Cricket Association**
■ Physical fitness for cricket. [The Association, 1980]. 20p. diagrs.

COACHING

0309 **Abberley, [Robert] Neal**
■ The basic principles of cricket. Birmingham, Warwickshire County Cricket Supporters' Association, [1988]. 32p. diagrs.

0310 **Andrew, Keith Vincent**
■ Coaching cricket. Marlborough (Wilts.), Crowood Press, 1986. 134p. illus. diagrs. bibliog. index.

0311 **Association of Cricket Coaches**
□ Cricket coach: the journal of the Association of Cricket Coaches. The Association. *annual.* illus. diagrs.
continues 'Padwick I' 645-1 to date?.

0312 **Australian Council for Health, Physical Education and Recreation**
Cricket: Aussie sports coaching program. Parkside (S.A.), the Council, 1987. v.p. illus.

0313 **Bairan, Erkin I.** *et al*
Production functions in cricket: Australian and New Zealand experience. Dunedin, University of Otago Department of Economics, 1989. 18p.
attempt to measure performance and success of teams according to performers' input.

0314 Production functions in cricket: one and three day games in New Zealand. Dunedin, University of Otago Department of Economics, 1989. 17p.

0315 **Cricket Coaches Association of N.S.W.**
Aims of the Association. Dee Why (N.S.W.), the Association, [1981]. 14p.

0316 Blueprint: journal of the Cricket Coaches Association of New South Wales. The Association. *biannual.* diagrs.
vol. 1, no. 1, Aug. 1982 - vol. 6, no. 1, June 1987; prior to 1984 entitled 'Cricket Coaches Association of N.S.W. newsletter';
edited by Laurie Lawrence and Howard Reay.

0317 Cricket: a guide book for teachers, coaches and players.
■ Wellington, New Zealand Department of Education, 1984. 52p. illus.
rev. ed. of 'Padwick I' 673.

0318 **Dawkins, P.** *and* **Cope, John H. C.**
■ Nottinghamshire 'Test cricket' award scheme: a teaching guide to the NCA Proficiency Award Scheme. Nottingham, Nottingham C. C. C., 1986. [i], 59 leaves. illus. diagrs.
first pub. 1982.

0319 **Diamond, Philip** *et al*
Physport. Cricket/vigoro & ball handling. Townsville (Qld.), Townsville and District Education Centre, 1986. 33p. illus.

0320 † **The Faulkner School of Cricket Ltd.**
Prospectus. The School, [1928]. 10p. illus.
later ed. of 'Padwick I' 654, excluding statistics of Faulkner's career.

0321 **Ford, Graham**
Cricket: teaching material for physical education teachers. Ballarat (Vic.), Ballarat Community Education Centre Co-operative Society, 1987. 131p. illus.

0322 † **Garnsey, George Leonard**
■ Handbook for the cricket coach. Department of Education, N.S.W. for the New South Wales Cricket Association, 1947. 64p. illus.
edited by M. Matheson.

0323 **Gloucestershire Schools Cricket Association**
■ Cricket for the eighties: a booklet of hints and information for Gloucestershire teachers. Cheltenham, the Association, [1983]. 37p. diagrs. bibliog.

0324 **Hope, Mark**
Coaching young cricketers. Cammeray (N.S.W.), Martin Educational, 1987. 52p. illus. diagr.

0325 **Horton, Martin John**
Cricket: a guide book for teachers, coaches and players. Wellington, N. Z. Dept. of Education, 1984. 54p. illus.
rev. and enlarged ed. of 'Padwick I' 657-1.

0326 **Irvine, Greg** *and* **Samara-Wickrama, Percy**
■ A guide to cricket skills and drills for use by coaches of junior cricketers. Weston (A.C.T.), the Authors, [1986]. 32p. illus. diagrs.

0327 † **Kingsmead Mynahs Club**
Cricket coaching manual. [Durban], the Club, 1974. 20p. illus. diagrs.

0328 **Kourie, Alan John,** *editor*
Super C cricket coaching manual. [Johannesburg], Central News Agency, 1987. 32p. illus. diagrs.
short articles by South Africa's top players.

0329 **Marylebone Cricket Club**
■ M.C.C. cricket coaching book. 5th edition. Kingswood Press, 1987. x, 175p. illus. diagrs.
rev. ed. of 'Padwick I' 666.

0330 National Cricket Association
■ N.C.A. coaches courses handouts. [The Association, 1987]. 17p. diagrs.

0331 The national coaching scheme. The Association, [1984].
■ 32p. illus.

0332 † New South Wales Cricket Association
Coaching bulletin. Sydney, the Association, *irregular*. diagrs.
no. 1, 14 May 1976 to no. 8, June 1979.

0333 † New Zealand cricket coaching bulletin; edited by Martin
□ Horton. Auckland, [the Editor]. *irregular?* illus. diagrs. *typescript.*
undated issues nos. 13-20 seen.

0334 The Notts Association of Cricket Coaches
□ The 'Coil': newsletter of the Notts Association of Cricket Coaches. The Association. *quarterly.* illus. diagrs. in various issues.
vol. 1 no. 1 1983 to date.

0335 Oakman, Alan Stanley Myles
■ Games for cricket training. Pelham Books, 1980. 127p.

0336 Payne, W. *et al*
A critical review of current research information relative to exercise physiology and cricket performance. Belconnen (A.C.T.), National Sports Research Program, 1986. 44p.

0337 † Queensland Cricket Association
Cricket syllabus. [Brisbane], Department of Public Instruction for the Physical Education Branch and the Association, 1948? 48p. illus. diagrs.
instruction book for Queensland teachers.

0338 Radford, Brian
■ From the Nursery End: cricket's 18 top coaches reveal how players are made. Arthur Barker, 1985. viii, 216p. index.

0339 Rice, Clive Edward Butler
■ Coaching tips; illustration by Ivor van Rensburg. Parow (South Africa), printed by National Commercial Printers, 1985. 100p. illus. *strip cartoon format.*
sponsored by Benson & Hedges.

0340 Sands, R., *editor*
The world of sociology. Melbourne, Rusden CAE, 1982. *includes 'A comparison of orientations towards cricket of the individual members of a cricket team with regard to their goals, priorities and expectations ...' by J. F. Harris, pp. 199-241.*

0341 South African Cricket Union
Bakers Biscuits mini cricket teachers handbook. [Johannesburg, the Union, 1988]. [32]p. illus.

0342 † Spence, Peter R.
■ Cricket action: an approach to teaching and coaching the game of cricket. Sydney, New South Wales Cricket Association, 1975. [vii], 63p. diagrs.

0343 The cricket decathlon: a realistic approach to cricket for beginners (under 10 years). Sydney, Rothmans National Sport Foundation, n.d. 16p. illus.

0344 † Spence, Peter R., *compiler*
Cricket: a game to be enjoyed. Sydney, [New South Wales Cricket Association] for A.C.H.P.E.R. (NSW Branch) with ... N.S.W. Department of Education, 1976. 43p. illus. diagrs.

0345 Spence, Peter R. *and* **Shepherd, Max,** *compilers*
Senior player development handbook. Jolimont (Vic.), Australian Cricket Board National Coaching Committee, 1987. 13p.

0346 Tyson, Frank Holmes
■ The cricket coaching manual. Melbourne, Thomas Nelson in association with the Victorian Cricket Association, 1985. viii, 207p. illus. diagrs. index.
——*UK ed.* Pelham, 1986.
some parts of this work originally appeared in 'Padwick I' 681-1.

0347 Victorian Cricket Association
■ Cricket for everyone. [Jolimont (Vic.), the Association, n.d.] [8]p. incl. covers.
V.C.A. coaching scheme.

0348 Wyman, Grant A.
Cricket coaching. Adelaide, [South Australian Cricket Association], 1987. 23p. illus. (some col.)
sponsored by 5DN Radio Station.

BATTING AND BATSMEN

0349 Abernethy, B.
A cinematographic investigation of decision-making in highly skilled and lesser skilled cricketers. University of Queensland, 1981. v.p.
reaction time of batsmen.
unpub. thesis.

0350 Arlott, [Leslie Thomas] John
■ John Arlott's 100 greatest batsmen. Queen Anne Press, 1986. 280p. illus. (some col.) stats.
——*rev. ed.* 1989 *with figures for current players updated to end of 1988 English season.*

0351 Barker, Ralph
■ Innings of a lifetime. Collins, 1982. 256p. illus. scores, index.
great innings by Colin Cowdrey, Peter Burge, Graeme Pollock, Bob Barber, Gary Sobers and David Holford, Asif Iqbal, Glenn Turner, Doug Walters, Dennis Amiss, Derek Randall.

0352 Barras, N.
Looking while batting in cricket: what a coach can tell a batsman. Belconnen (A.C.T.), National Sports Research Program, 1989. 10p.

0353 Vision and batting in cricket. Belconnen (A.C.T.), National Sports Research Program, 1989. 67p.

0354 Basic Group of Companies
■ Hit for six: commemorating the first year of Basic Six 6-Hit Awards. Wisden Cricket Magazines, [1987]. 16p. incl. covers. illus.

0355 Bearshaw, Brian
■ The big hitters. Queen Anne Press, 1986. 200p. illus. bibliog. index.

0356 Biomechanics VIII-B: proceedings of the Eighth International Congress on biomechanics. Nagoya (Japan), 1983.
includes 'Discovering biomechanical principles of batting in cricket' by K. Davis, pp. 915-922.

0357 Boycott, Geoffrey
■ Geoff Boycott on batting. Stanley Paul, 1980. [xii], 99p. illus.

0358 **Crowley, Brian Mathew**
■ A history of Australian batting, 1850-1986. South Melbourne, Macmillan, 1986. xii, 211p. illus. stats. bibliog. index.

0359 **Dexter, Edward Ralph**
■ From Bradman to Boycott: the master batsmen. Queen Anne Press, 1981. 159p. illus.

0360 **Frindall, William Howard ('Bill')** *et al*
■ The century makers. Richard Publications, 1984? 64p. illus. (some col.)
'personal profiles of eleven of England's leading century makers past and present'.

0361 † **Fry, Charles Burgess**
How to bat and how not to bat. Adelaide, South Australian Cricket Association, [1913]. 16p.

0362 **Gooch, Graham Alan** *with the assistance of* **Murphy, Patrick**
■ Batting (Sporting Skills series). Pelham Books, 1980. 152p. illus.

0363 **Lee, Alan**
■ The Wisden book of cricket heroes: batsmen. Stanley Paul, 1989. 96p. illus. line drawings. stats.
for children.

0364 **Murphy, Patrick**
■ The centurions: profiles of the 20 batsmen who have scored a hundred 100s - from Grace to Zaheer. Dent, 1983. viii, 277p. illus. bibliog. stats. index.
——*pbk. ed.* Dent, 1986 *includes extra chapter on Dennis Amiss.*

0365 **Synge, Allen** *and* **Anns, Derek**
■ Master strokes; cricket's timeless batting lessons. Kingswood Press, 1987. xi, 120p. illus. bibliog.

BOWLING AND BOWLERS

0366 **Australian Cricket Board**
Prevention of lower back injuries in fast bowlers. Jolimont (Vic.), the Board, 1987.
listed in Mullins.

0367 **Bailey, Trevor Edward** *and* **Trueman, Frederick Sewards**
■ From Larwood to Lillee. Queen Anne Press, 1983. 207p. illus. index.
——*pbk. ed.* 1984.

0368 The spinners' web. Willow Books, 1988. 224p. illus.
■ stats. index.

0369 **Crowley, Brian Mathew**
■ A history of Australian bowling and wicket-keeping, 1850-1986. South Melbourne, Macmillan, 1986. xii, 212p. illus. stats. bibliog. index.

0370 † **Davis, K. H.**
A cinematographic analysis of fast bowling in cricket. University of Western Australia, 1974. vii, 95p. *unpub. thesis.*

0371 **Edmonds, Philippe-Henri** *with* **Berry, Scyld**
■ Phil Edmonds' 100 greatest bowlers. Queen Anne Press, 1989. 256p. illus. (some col.) stats.

0372 **Elliott, Bruce** *et al, editors*
■ Send the stumps flying: the science of fast bowling. Nedlands (W.A.), University of Western Australia Press, 1989. x, 96p. illus. index.

0373 **Embury, John Ernest** *with* **Gibson, Pat**
■ Spinning in a fast world. Robson Books, 1989. 160p. illus. index.

0374 **Foster, D. H.** *and* **John, D.**
The inter-relationship between fast bowling techniques, physical characteristics and physiological capacities of junior fast bowlers to injuries in cricket. Belconnen (A.C.T.), National Sports Research Program, 1987. 53p. *final report.*
——*interim report with title 'A study of junior fast bowlers: findings and recommendations' pub. in* 1987.

0375 **Frith, David Edward John**
■ The fast men: a 200-year cavalcade of speed bowlers. George Allen & Unwin, 1982. 177p. illus. bibliog. index.
rev. and updated ed. of 'Padwick I' 751-1.
——*pbk. ed.* Corgi, 1984.

0376 The slow men. George Allen & Unwin, 1984. 198p.
■ illus. index.
——*pbk. ed.* Corgi, 1985.

0377 † **Grimmett, Clarence Victor**
■ Tricking the batsman. Adelaide, R. M. Osborne, 1932. 138p. illus.
earlier Australian ed. of 'Padwick I' 729.

0378 **Hill, Alan**
■ A chain of spin wizards. Keighley, Kennedy Brothers, 1983. x, 147p. illus. scores, index.
Yorkshire slow left arm bowlers from Peate to Wilson.

0379 **John, David**
A prospective study of back injuries to young fast bowlers in cricket. [University of Western Australia], 1989. 133 leaves, illus.

0380 **Lee, Alan**
■ The Wisden book of cricket heroes: bowlers. Stanley Paul, 1989. 96p. illus. line drawings. stats.
for children.

0381 **Murphy, Patrick**
■ The spinner's turn. J. M. Dent & Sons, 1982. ix, 208p. illus. stats. index.

0382 **Shaikh, Anwar**
■ The making of a fast bowler. Pune, Rukhsana Shaikh, [1987]. xvi, 72p. illus.

0383 **Willis, Robert George Dylan ('Bob')**
■ Fast bowling with Bob Willis. Willow Books, 1984. 112p. illus. diagrs.

ALL-ROUNDERS

0384 **Lemmon, David Hector**
■ The great all-rounders. Marlborough (Wilts.), Crowood Press, 1987. 180p. illus.

FIELDING

0385 **Jamison, Bob**
■ Fitness and fielding activities for cricket training. [McKinnon (Vic.)], the Author, 1987. v, 107p. illus.

0386 † **Weekes, Everton de Courcy**
'To the youth of the West Indies': aspects of fielding. Bridgetown, the Author, n.d. 16p. illus.

WICKET-KEEPING AND WICKET-KEEPERS

0387 **Crowley, Brian Mathew**
■ A history of Australian bowling and wicket-keeping, 1850-1986. South Melbourne, Macmillan, 1986. xii, 212p. illus. stats. bibliog. index.

0388 **Evans, [Thomas] Godfrey**
■ Gordon's Gin wicket-keepers of the world. Sevenoaks, New English Library, 1984. [ix], 136p. illus.

0389 **Lemmon, David Hector**
■ The great wicket-keepers. Stanley Paul, 1984. 176p. illus. stats. index.

0390 **Sundaresan, P. N.**
■ Navle to Kirmani: story of Indian stumpers. Madras, Free India Publications, 1985. viii, 86p. incl. adverts. illus.

CAPTAINCY AND CAPTAINS

0391 **Brearley, John Michael ('Mike')**
■ The art of captaincy. Hodder and Stoughton, 1985. 288p. illus. (some col.) bibliog. index.
——*pbk. ed.* Coronet, 1987.

0392 **Gibson, Alan**
■ The cricket captains of England: a survey. Pavilion Books, 1989. xi, 242p. illus. index.
reprinted ed. of 'Padwick I' 767-1 with additional chapter 'Ten more years' written in 1988.

0393 **Illingworth, Raymond** *with the assistance of* **Calvin, Mike**
■ Captaincy (Sporting Skills series). Pelham Books, 1980. 118p. illus.

0394 **Lemmon, David Hector**
■ The crisis of captaincy: servant and master in English cricket. Bromley, Christopher Helm, 1988. vii, 150p. illus. index.

0395 **Robinson, Raymond John**
■ On top down under: Australia's cricket captains. North Ryde (N.S.W.), Cassell Australia, 1981. 285p. illus. bibliog. index.
pbk. ed. of 'Padwick I' 767-3, updated to include Greg Chappell, Graham Yallop and Kim Hughes.

0396 **Rose, Edward McQueen**
■ How to win at cricket: or the skipper's guide; cartoons by Albert Rusling. Hodder & Stoughton, 1988. 267p. illus. diagrs. bibliog. index.

INDOOR CRICKET

0397 **Cosier, Gary John** *and* **Smithers, Patrick**
■ Indoor cricket: the history, the rules and how to play the game. Hawthorn (Vic.), File Mile Press, 1986. 79p. illus.

0398 **Harris, John**
■ Indoor cricket: the game, the skills, the rules. Sydney, Doubleday, 1986. 107p. col. illus. diagrs.

0399 **Hough, Greg** *and* **Cobb, John**
New Zealand indoor cricket: skills and tactics: the sport of the eighties. Auckland, Cobb-Horwood, [1986]. 63p. col. illus.

0400 **Indoor** cricket. (Know the Game series). A & C Black in
■ collaboration with the National Cricket Association, 1989. 32p. illus. diagrs.

0401 **Official 'ICA' rules.** Perth, Indoor Cricket Arenas (Australia), 1982. 16p. illus.
——*another ed.* 1985.

0402 **Starling, Avril** *and* **Lear, Megan**
■ Indoor cricket. Poole, Blandford Press, 1986. 96p. illus. diagrs. index.

0403 **Supertest** indoor cricket: official rules handbook. 2nd.
■ ed. Sydney, Supertest Sports Centre, 1984. 8p.

0404 **Underhill, G.**
'Howzat': a handbook on indoor cricket. Perth (W.A.), Northern Districts Indoor Cricket Centre, 1983. 30p. illus. facsim.

ADAPTED CRICKET

0405 † **Cricks:** the new & fascinating ball game: ... a modification of cricket for playing indoors or on lawns. Newtown (N.S.W.), 1930? [30]p.
score-book and laws governing all interstate and competition matches throughout Australia.

0406 **Evans, John Robert**
The analysis, evaluation and implementation of game modifications in junior cricket. n.p. 1982. viii, 236 leaves. illus.

0407 **O'Driscoll, Ken**
So your club wants to play Kanga cricket this summer? Perth, Western Australia Cricket Association, 1984? v.p. illus. facsims.

0408 **Spence, Peter R.**
Kanga cricket: teacher's handbook. Jolimont (Vic.), Australian Cricket Board, 1984. v.p. illus.

0409 **Stumpy and Bails** cricket games; illustrations by Bill
■ Mitchell. Dee Why West (N.S.W.), Lansdowne Press, 1981. 32p. incl. covers. col. illus.
produced in co-operation with the Australian Cricket Board.
for children.

0410 **Victorian Cricket Association,** *compiler*
Modified cricket games and activities for schools. Perth (W.A.), the Association in conjunction with Dept. for Youth, Sport and Recreation, Western Australia, n.d. 30p. illus.

WATCHING CRICKET

0411 **Arlott, [Leslie Thomas] John**
■ How to watch cricket. Willow Books, 1983. ix, 111p. illus. diagrs. bibliog.
rev. ed. of 'Padwick I' 771.
——*pbk. ed.* Fontana, 1984.

0412 **Johnston, Brian Alexander**
■ Chatterboxes: my friends the commentators. Methuen, 1983. 214p.
'voices of cricket' pp. 119-149.
——*pbk. ed.* Star, 1984.

CRICKET IN ENGLAND AND WALES

ADMINISTRATION

0413 **Concentrating** resources on cricket in the Eastern region. Sports Council (Eastern region) in co-operation with the County Cricket Association. 28p. illus.
cover title.

0414 † **The Cricket Council**
■ Review of the arrangements of the Cricket Council. Cooper Brothers & Co. [for the Council], 1973. [iii], 46 leaves + [22]p. of appendices.

0415 **National Cricket Association**
■ County championship: sponsored by Notts Sport. The Association, [1989]. [12]p. incl. covers.
rules and fixtures for the NCA County Championship.

0416 Handbook. The Association. *annual.* illus. scores.
□ *continues 'Padwick I' 791-1* to date.

0417 † Indoor cricket facilites. The Association, 1971. 13p.
■ *schedule of facilities in the U.K.*

0418 **Test and County Cricket Board**
■ Report of the T.C.C.B. enquiry into the standards of play of English cricket in Test and first class county cricket. The Board, 1985. [30]p. *typescript.*
'The Palmer report'.

0419 TCCB newsletter. The Board. col. illus.
■ *first issue, Spring 1989.*

HISTORY

0420 **Andrews, Gordon B.**
■ The Datasport 1940-45 cricket annual. [Shipston-on-Stour (Warwicks.), the Author, 1986].
2 vols.
part 1: complete war period playing record. [ii], 74p. [i.e. 102p.] illus. scores.
part 2: diary, records and averages. [ii], 64p. [i.e. 88p.] illus. stats.

0421 † **Armitage, John**
■ Man at play: nine centuries of pleasure making. Frederick Warne, 1977. 192p. illus. index.
many cricket references.

0422 **Association of Cricket Statisticians,** *compiler*
■ A guide to first class cricket matches played in the British Isles. Haughton Mill (Notts), the Association, 1982. 40p. scores.
2nd. ed. of 'Padwick I' 797-1.

0423 A guide to important cricket matches played in the
■ British Isles 1709-1863. Haughton Mill (Notts), the Association, 1981. 40p.
——*2nd. ed. [1707-1863],* 1985.

0424 A statistical survey. Haughton Mill (Notts), the
■ Association. illus. stats.
for 1864, pub. 1985.
for 1865, pub. 1985.
for 1866, pub. 1987.

0425 **Borsay, Peter**
The English urban renaissance: culture and society in the provincial town 1660-1770. Oxford, Oxford University Press, 1989. xxii, 416p. illus.
discusses development of high status leisure, paying particular attention to the transformation of cricket and horse-racing.

0426 **Brasch, Rudolph**
How did sports begin?: a look at the origins of men at play. Sydney, Fontana, 1986. 437p. illus. index.
cricket pp. 83-88.
rev. ed. of 'Padwick I' 828.

0427 **Cashman, Richard I.** *and* **McKernan, Michael,** *editors*
■ Sport: money, morality and the media. Kensington, New South Wales University Press, [1982]. illus. bibliog. index.
includes 'Playing for pay: the earnings of professional sportsmen in England 1870-1914' by Wray Vamplew, pp. 104-130.

0428 † **Cheyne, George**
An essay of health and long life. Printed for George Strahan ... and J. Leake, 1725. 6th. ed.
another ed. of 'Padwick I' 863-2.

0429 **Craven, Nico**
■ Summer and sunshine; illustrations by Frank Fisher. [Seascale, the Author], 1985. 86p. illus. scores.
personal impressions of 1982 and 1983 seasons.

0430 **Down, Michael G.**
■ Is it cricket? power, money & politics in cricket since 1945. Queen Anne Press, 1985. 160p. figs. bibliog. index.
changes in English first class cricket between 1946 and 1963.

0431 **Epps, William**
■ The grand matches of cricket played in England from 1771 to 1791. [Ewell], J. W. McKenzie, 1989. [ix], 104p. frontis. scores.
facsimile reprint of 'Padwick I' 877 with a new introduction by David Rayvern Allen.

0432 **Goulstone, John**
The midsummer games: elements of cult and custom in traditional English sport. [The Author], 1982. [70]p. bibliog.
several cricket references.

0433 **Holt, Richard**
■ Sport and the British: a modern history. [Oxford Studies in Social History]. Oxford, Clarendon Press, 1989. xiii, 396p. bibliog. index.
many cricket references.

0434 Jones, Stephen Glyn
Sport, politics and the working class: organised labour and sport in inter-war Britain. [International Studies in the History of Sport]. Manchester, Manchester University Press, 1988. xi, 228p. bibliog. index.
some cricket.

0435 Kingwell, Patrick, *compiler*
A *Clarion* cricket mixture. The Author, [1983]. [12]p. illus. facsims.
facsimile reprints from 'The Clarion' 1892-1905.

0436 Lemmon, David Hector
Cricket mercenaries: overseas players in English cricket. Pavilion Books, 1987. 167p. illus. index.

0437 McCarthy, Tony
War games: the story of sport in World War Two. Queen Anne Press, 1989. 192p. illus. bibliog. index.
many cricket references.

0438 Mangan, James Anthony, *editor*
Pleasure, profit, proselytism: British culture and sport at home and abroad 1700-1914. Frank Cass, 1988. xiii, 284p. illus. index.
includes 'Cricket and colonialism: colonial hegemony and indigenous subversion?' by Richard I. Cashman, pp. 258-272.

0439 Martin-Jenkins, Christopher Dennis Alexander
Sketches of a season; illustrations by Jack Russell. Oxford, Lennard Publishing, 1989. 151p. illus.
diary, January-September 1989.

0440 Martin-Jenkins, Christopher Dennis Alexander, *editor*
Seasons past: *The Cricketer* diaries of John Arlott, Alan Gibson, Tony Lewis, Mike Brearley, Peter Roebuck. Stanley Paul, 1986. 224p. illus. (some col.) scores, stats. index.
seasons 1967-85.

0441 Mason, Tony
Sport in Britain. Faber, 1988. xii, 128p. bibliog. index.
cricket throughout.

0442 Mason, Tony, *editor*
Sport in Britain: a social history. Cambridge, Cambridge University Press, 1989. vii, 363p. illus. index.
'Cricket' by Jack Williams, pp. 116-145.

0443 Midwinter, Eric Clare
The lost seasons: cricket in wartime, 1939-45. Methuen, 1987. [vi], 218p. index.

0444 Moorhouse, Geoffrey
The best loved game. Pavilion Books, 1987. 188p. scores.
reprinted ed. of 'Padwick I' 974-3 with a new introduction by Matthew Engel.

0445 Morrah, Patrick
Alfred Mynn and the cricketers of his time. Constable, 1986. 224p. illus. stats. bibliog. index.
reprinted ed. of 'Padwick I' 882 with a new introduction by the author.

0446 † Principal matches played in 1881. [iv], 136p. scores.
scores of first class and other matches played in 1878!

0447 † A proper reply to a late infamous and scurrilous libel intitled a congratulatory letter to a certain Right Honourable person upon his late disappointment. Printed for J. Robinson, 1743. [ii], 28p.
references to 'sitting a quiet spectator of a cricket-match on the Green' pp. 16-17.

0448 [Pycroft, James]
Cricketana. Clacton-on-Sea, Tyre Industry Publications, 1987. iv, 106p. illus.
new ed. of 'Padwick I' 909.

0449 Sissons, Ric
The players: a social history of the professional cricketer. Sydney, Pluto Press; London, Kingswood Press, 1988. xiv, 336p. illus. bibliog. index.

0450 Sloane, Peter J.
Sport in the market? The economic causes and consequences of the 'Packer Revolution'. (Hobart Paper no. 85). Institute of Economic Affairs, 1980. 74p. bibliog.
the economic viability and marketing of team sports in the U.K. with special reference to cricket and football.

0451 Steel, Allan Gibson and Lyttelton, *Hon* **Robert Henry**
Cricket: with contributions by A. Lang, W. G. Grace, R. A. H. Mitchell and F. Gale. (The Badminton Library of Sports and Pastimes). Southampton, Ashford Press Publishing, 1987. xv, 429p. illus. diagrs. index.
facsimile reprint of 'Padwick I' 913 with a new introduction by His Grace, the 11th Duke of Beaufort.

0452 Swanton, Ernest William and Plumptre, George, *editor*
Back page cricket: a century of newspaper coverage. Queen Anne Press, 1987. 208p. illus. facsims, scores, index.

0453 Vamplew, Wray
Play up and play the game: professional sport in Britain 1875-1914. Cambridge, Cambridge University Press, 1988. xix, 394p. tables, bibliog. index.
many cricket references, especially pp. 90-99, 115-124.

0454 † [Warner, *Sir* **Pelham Francis,** *editor]*
British sports and sportsmen past and present; compiled and edited by 'The Sportsman'. British Sports and Sportsmen, [1908-1936?]. 16 vols. illus.
vol. 5 'Cricket and football', 1917. xiii, 579p.
limited royal ed. of 250 numbered copies of 'Padwick I' 822.

0455 West, G. Derek
The elevens of England. Darf, 1988. viii, 190p. illus. scores, stats. bibliog. index.
history of the All England Eleven and other contemporary itinerant elevens.

0456 † Woods, S.
A history of cricket: first period, from the earliest times to the end of 1748. c. 1878. 50p.
original ms. in 2 vols. of unpub. work formerly in the collection of G. Neville Weston. 'Mr Woods ... used to write on cricket in the London 'Evening News' and some times for C. W. Alcock'.

CRICKET GROUNDS

0457 Heald, Timothy Villiers
The character of cricket; illustrated by Paul Cox. Pavilion Books, 1986. 207p. illus.
——*pbk. ed.* Faber, 1987.

0458 Plumptre, George
Homes of cricket: the first-class grounds of England and Wales. Queen Anne Press, 1988. 224p. illus. (some col.) index.

0459 Powell, William Ahmed *with* **Powell, Peter William George** *and* **Bannister, Alexander James**
The Wisden guide to cricket grounds. Stanley Paul, 1989. 416p. illus. diagrs. stats.
directory of U.K. first class grounds.

0460 Sampson, Aylwin
■ Grounds of appeal: the homes of first-class cricket; written and illustrated by Aylwin Sampson. Robert Hale, 1981. xiv, 206p. illus. map, bibliog. index.

0461 The Tiger Club
■ Dawn-to-dusk competition: county cricket clubs. The Club, 1983. 84p. col. illus. maps.
report of overflight of all county headquarters' grounds on 11 Jun 83.

Hastings: Central Cricket Ground

0462 Brodribb, [Arthur] Gerald Norcott
□ Cricket at Hastings: the story of a ground. Speldhurst (Kent), Spellmount, 1989. 128p. illus. frontis. map, scores, stats. bibliog.
——de luxe limited ed. of 100 numbered copies signed by the author and Jim Parks, 1989.

Leeds: Headingley

0463 Dalby, Ken
■ The Headingley story vol. 3: white is the rose: a record of county cricket at Headingley 1891-1980. Leeds, the Author, [1981]. [iv], 146p. illus. scores, stats.
vols. 1 and 2 cover rugby.

London: Lord's

0464 Bradley, H. Gilbert
■ Dorset Square in the parish of St. Marylebone: a short history. Dorset Square Trust, 1984. [ii], 16p.
Lord's cricket ground, pp. 1-2.

0465 Green, Benny, *editor*
■ The Lord's companion. Pavilion Books, 1987. 460p. scores, index.

0466 Hodgkinson, Harry
■ Lord's Dukes & Dorset Square. The Author?, 1987. 18p.

0467 Margetson, Stella
■ St John's Wood: an abode of love and the arts. Home and Law Publishing for the St John's Wood Society, 1988. [ii], 30p. illus.

0468 Marylebone Cricket Club
■ Lord's, headquarters of cricket and of M.C.C. The Club, 1987. 24p. illus. (some col.) plan.
lists dates in the history of Lord's.

0469 Moorhouse, Geoffrey
■ Lord's. Hodder and Stoughton, 1983. 256p. illus. (some col.) stats. index.

0470 Rait Kerr, Diana Mary *and* Peebles, Ian Alexander Ross
■ Lord's 1946-1970. Pavilion Books, 1987. 349p. illus. stats. index.
reprinted ed. of 'Padwick I' 1016 with a new introduction by Jeffrey Archer.

0471 Slatter, William H.
■ Recollections of Lord's and the Marylebone Cricket Club. [Ewell], J. W. McKenzie, 1989. [vi], 32p.
facsim. ed. of 'Padwick I' 1019 with a new introduction by Gerald Brodribb.

0472 Warner, *Sir* Pelham Francis
■ Lord's 1787-1945. Pavilion Books, 1987. 324p. illus. scores, stats. bibliog. index.
reprinted ed. of 'Padwick I' 1021 with a new introduction by Roy Hattersley.

Manchester: Old Trafford

0473 The Old Trafford story 1884-1984: centenary brochure.
■ [Manchester, Lancashire County Cricket Club, 1984]. 81p. incl. inside back cover. illus. (some col.) diagr. scores, stats.

Nottingham: Trent Bridge

0474 Seward, David *and* Wynne-Thomas, Peter, *compilers*
■ Memories of Trent Bridge, 1838-1988. Nottingham, Nottinghamshire C. C. C., 1987. 40p. illus. (some col.)
cover title: 'Memories of Trent Bridge: the story in words and pictures of famous cricketers and events of the past 150 years'.

0475 Wynne-Thomas, Peter
□ Trent Bridge: a history of the ground to commemorate the 150th anniversary (1838-1988). Nottingham, Nottinghamshire County Council in association with Nottingham County Cricket Club, 1987. x, 246p. illus. stats. index.
8pp. supplement 'The double champions of 1987' inserted to bring the book up to date to end of 1987 season.
——limited gold-leaf ed. of 600 copies, 1987.

ANNUALS AND PERIODICALS

ANNUALS

0476 Association of Cricket Statisticians
■ ACS cricket yearbook. Newnes Books. illus. stats.
1986 to date.
from 1987 with title 'ACS international cricket yearbook'.
1986-88 compiled by Peter Wynne-Thomas, Philip Bailey and John Stockwell.
1989 compiled by Philip Bailey.

0477 Benson and Hedges cricket year; edited by David Lemmon. Pelham Books. *annual*. illus. (some col.)
■ scores, stats.
first ed. Sep. '81 - Sep. '82 to date.

0478 The *Daily Telegraph* cricket year book; edited by Norman Barrett; consultant editor, Michael Melford. Daily Telegraph. *annual*. illus. scores, stats.
■ *1982 to date.*
1982 ed. covered 1982 season; 1984 covered 1983 season; continued in this sequence to date.
1990 pub. by Pan in association with 'Daily Telegraph'.

0479 Official tour guide: edited by David Lemmon. Test & County Cricket Board. *annual*. illus. (mostly col.) stats.
■ *1986 to date.*

0480 **Pelham** cricket year: a chronological record of first-class cricket throughout the world; edited by David Lemmon. Pelham Books. *annual.* illus. scores, stats.
continues 'Padwick I' 1095-2.
2nd ed. Sep. 1979 - Sep. 1980, 1980.
3rd ed. Sep. 1980 - Sep. 1981, 1981.
continued as 'Benson and Hedges cricket year'.

0481 **Playfair** cricket annual. Queen Anne Press. scores, stats.
1980-85 edited by Gordon Ross.
1986 to date edited by Bill Frindall.
continues 'Padwick I' 1098 to date.

0482 **Test and County Cricket Board**
Cricket. The Board. illus. (some col.) stats.
continues 'Padwick I' 1120.
1980-82 edited by R. J. Roe.
1983 edited by Reg Hayter.
1984-85 edited by David Lemmon with cover sub-title 'The official Test and County Cricket Board guide to the season'.
From 1986 incorporated in 'Official tour guide'.

0483 **World** of cricket; edited by Trevor Bailey; compiled by Bill Frindall. Queen Anne Press. *annual.* illus. scores, stats.
continues 'Padwick I' 1131-1 to 1980.

ANNUALS - WISDEN

0484 **Barnard, Derek,** *compiler*
An index to Wisden cricketers' almanack 1864-1984. Queen Anne Press, 1985. [viii], 645p.
updates 'Padwick I' 1053.

0485 **Green, Benny,** *compiler*
The Wisden book of obituaries: obituaries from Wisden Cricketers' Almanack, 1892-1985. Queen Anne Press, 1986. [x], 1029p.
——*reprinted with title 'The Wisden book of cricketers' lives', 1988.*

0486 **Green, Benny,** *editor*
The illustrated Wisden anthology 1864-1988. Macdonald & Co. for Marks and Spencer, 1988. 400p. illus. (some col.) scores, stats. index.

0487 Wisden anthology 1900-1940. Queen Anne Press, 1980. [viii], viii, 1177p. illus. scores, stats. index.
see also 'Padwick I' 1054-1.

0488 Wisden anthology 1940-1963. Queen Anne Press, 1982. [vii], vi, 1009p. scores, stats. index.

0489 Wisden anthology 1963-1982. Queen Anne Press, 1983. xiv, 978p. scores, index.

0490 The Wisden papers of Neville Cardus. Stanley Paul, 1989. [iv], 155p. illus.
a collection of articles contributed to 'Wisden cricketers' almanack' by Neville Cardus between 1927 and 1975.

0491 The Wisden papers, 1888-1946. Stanley Paul, 1989. [viii], 311p. illus.
anthology of essays appearing in 'Wisden cricketers' almanack'.

0492 † **Roberts, Edward Lamplough,** *compiler*
What's in Wisden? 1889-1937. The Author, 1937. [i], 45 leaves. *typescript.*
an index of the special articles, 'Cricketers of the Year', principal obituaries and statistical records.

0493 **Wisden** cricketers' almanack. Queen Anne Press. *annual.* illus. (some col. since 1988), scores, stats, index.
1985 to date pub. by John Wisden & Co.
1980 edited by Norman Preston.
1981-86 edited by John Woodcock.
1987 to date edited by Graeme Wright.
continues 'Padwick I' 1052 to date.

0494 † **Wisden** cricketers' almanack. (reprints).
1864-1878 second facsimile ed. [Sporting Handbooks, 1974].
1880 Stoke-on-Trent, Willows Publishing Co., 1987.
1881 Stoke-on-Trent, Willows Publishing Co., 1985.
1882 Stoke-on-Trent, Willows Publishing Co., 1988.
1883 Stoke-on-Trent, Willows Publishing Co., 1988.
1884 Stoke-on-Trent, Willows Publishing Co., 1984.
1885 Stoke-on-Trent, Willows Publishing Co., 1983.
1886 Stoke-on-Trent, Willows Publishing Co., 1985.
1887 Stoke-on-Trent, Willows Publishing Co., 1989.
1888 Stoke-on-Trent, Willows Publishing Co., 1989.
each of the Willows reprints limited to 500 copies; numbered except for the 1885 ed.

JUNIOR ANNUALS

0495 **Botham, Ian Terence**
Ian Botham sports annual. Purnell, [1983]. 64p. illus.
the only issue.

0496 **Ross, Gordon John,** *editor*
The young cricketers' yearbook. Queen Anne Press, 1984. 159p. illus. stats.
the only issue.

PERIODICALS

0497 † The **Badminton** magazine of sports and pastimes.
vols. 1-59, Aug. 1895 - Jan. 1923.
cricket content in most vols.

0498 **British** journal of sports history. Frank Cass. *three issues per year - May, Sept, Dec.*
vol. 1, no. 1, May 1984 to date.
from vol. 4, no. 1, May 1987 with title 'The international journal of the history of sport'.
contains cricket articles in most issues.

0499 The **Brooklane** browse-around; edited by Kieron Porter. [Ormskirk]. illus. scores. *typescript.*
fanzine; 2 issues pub. in 1985.

0500 **Christians in Sport**
Newsletter. Oxford. *quarterly.* illus.
cricket interest in most issues.
?/1985 to date.

0501 The **club** cricketer; edited by J. Nagenda. Club Cricketer Ltd. *weekly during season.* illus.
newspaper format 1983-84.
/vol. 1, no. 1, April 1983 - 1987/
continued as 'Cricket world and the club cricketer'.

0502 **Cricket** fanfare: a review of world cricket; editor David Lemmon. Fanfare Publications. *quarterly?* illus. (mainly col.) scores, stats.
vol. 1, no. 1 Spring 1986; other issues pub.?
special emphasis on cricket in Sharjah and the Indian sub-continent.

0503 **Cricket** life international; editor-in-chief Imran Khan, editor Bernard Halloran. South Publications (UK). *monthly.* illus. (some col.) scores, stats.
first issue July 1989 - last issue June 1990.

0504 **Cricket** world and the club cricketer: the official journal
■ of the National Cricket Association; edited by Michael
Blumberg. Windlesham (Surrey), Club Cricketer.
monthly. illus. (some col.) scores, stats.
/vol. 1, no. 1, June 1987 to date/
from vol. 3, no. 2, Feb. 1989 entitled 'Cricket World'.

0505 The **cricketer** international. Ashurst (Kent), *monthly.*
■ illus. (some col.) scores, stats.
editor: R.J.Hayter to April 1981 (vol. 62, no. 4).
*editor: Christopher Martin-Jenkins, May 1981 to Feb.
1988 (vol. 69, no. 2).*
*editorial director: Christopher Martin-Jenkins, March
1989 to date.*
executive editor: Peter Perchard, March 1989 to date.
continues 'Padwick I' 1199 to date.

0506 The **cricketer** quarterly facts and figures. Ashurst
■ (Kent), *The Cricketer.* illus. scores, stats.
to vol. 12, no. 4 Spring 1985, edited by Gordon Ross.
*vol. 13, no. 1, Summer 1985 - vol. 14, no 1, Summer
1986, edited by Bill Frindall.*
*vol. 14, no. 2, Autumn 1986 - vol. 14, no. 3, Winter
1986-87, edited by Richard Lockwood and Andrew
Longmore.*
*vol. 14, no 4, Spring 1987 to date, edited by Richard
Lockwood.*
continues 'Padwick I' 1200-1 to date.

0507 † **Fores's** sporting notes and sketches: a quarterly
magazine of British, Indian, colonial and foreign sport.
vols. I-XXIX, 1884-1912.
cricket in some issues.

0508 **Hayter, Reginald James,** *editor*
■ The best of *The Cricketer,* 1921-1981. Cassell, 1981. ix,
188p. illus. index.

0509 The **illustrated** encyclopedia of cricket; edited by Raj
■ Sacramie. Orbis. *weekly.* illus. (some col.) stats.
3 issues pub. in 1983.

0510 **Johnny** Miller 96 not out; edited by David Lewis.
■ Eastbourne. *irregular.* illus.
fanzine; issues 1-4, May, June, Aug. and Nov. 1989.

0511 **National Cricket Association**
■ Cricket: the official quarterly magazine of the National
Cricket Association; edited by Ralph Dellor. Sportsline
for the Association. *quarterly.* illus.
/Jul. 1983 - Summer 1986/

0512 † The **Sheffield** portrait gallery: an illustrated magazine of
□ literature, criticism and satire. Sheffield, Martin Hurst.
monthly. illus.
/vol. I, no. 1, Nov. 1874 - vol. II, no. 27, Jan. 1877/
cricket in some issues.

0513 **Sports** history; edited by John Goulstone. Bexleyheath,
□ the Editor. *biannual.* typescript.
/no. 1, 1982 - no. 10, 1987/
much cricket.

0514 **Sports** quarterly magazine; edited by John Goulstone.
□ Bexleyheath, the Editor. *quarterly.* typescript.
continues 'Padwick I' 1211-2 to no. 20, winter 1981.
continued as 'Sports history'.

0515 † **Sportsman's Book Club**
□ Sports news: the magazine of the Sportman's Book Club;
edited by Reginald Moore. The Club. *monthly.* illus.
scores.
/vol. 1, no. 1, March 1953 - vol. III, no. 12, Feb. 1956/?
*includes cricket book reviews by John Arlott and scores of
SBC matches v Indian Gymkhana.*

0516 † The **sportsman's** magazine of life in London and the
country: containing ... cricket. illus.
vol. I to vol. III, 1854-1857.
*cricket in each volume including articles on Lillywhite,
Nyren, Pilch, Felix and Mynn.*

0517 **Sticky** wicket: alternative cricket magazine; edited by
■ Peter Hardy. John Brown Publishing. *bi-monthly.* illus.
issue 1, April/May 1988 - issue 13, [April/May 1990].

0518 **Wisden** cricket monthly; edited by David Frith. Wisden
■ Cricket Magazines. illus. (some col.) scores, stats.
continues 'Padwick I' 1213-1 to date.

FIXTURES

0519 † **Bristol United Breweries Ltd.**
Fixtures 1946: laws of cricket and a few records -
Gloucester, Somerset, India. Bristol, 1946. [24]p.
earlier ed. of 'Padwick I' 1152.
——another ed. 1956.

0520 † **Principal** cricket fixtures. Cricket Press. *annual.* illus.
?/1902-1913/?
*includes portrait of notable contemporary cricketer on
front cover; two issues noted for 1910.*

ENGLISH CLUBS

MARYLEBONE C. C.

0521 **Bailey, Jack Arthur**
■ Conflicts in cricket. Kingswood Press, 1989. [ix], 193p.
illus.
*includes memories of thirteen years as Secretary of the
M.C.C.*

0522 **Doggart, [George] Hubert Graham** *and* **Woodcock,**
■ **John Charles**
Lord be praised: the story of MCC's bicentenary year.
Derby, English Life Publications, 1988. 28p. illus.
(some col.)
includes account of MCC v Rest of World.

0523 **Lewis, Anthony Robert ('Tony')**
■ Double century: the story of MCC and cricket. Hodder
& Stoughton, 1987. 375p. illus. (some col.) facsims.
scores, bibliog. index.
the bicentenary history.
*——limited members ed. of 100 leather-bound copies,
1987.*
——pbk. ed. Coronet Books, 1989.

0524 † **Mary-le-bone Club**
■ Alphabetical list of the members at the conclusion of the
season 1833. Printed by M. G. Duke, [1833]. 8p.

0525 **Marylebone Cricket Club**
■ Marylebone Cricket Club bicentenary ball, Friday 27th
March 1987 at Lord's. [The Club, 1987]. 68p. incl.
adverts. illus. (some col.)

0526 The MCC bicentenary match, 20th - 25th August at
■ Lord's: official souvenir programme. Programme
Publications [for the Club], 1987. 80p. illus. (mostly
col.) stats.
edited by Alan Lee; pre-match.

0527 MCC commemorative brochure. The Club, 1987.
■ *folder containing MCC bicentenary year official
catalogue and sheets promoting individual sale items.*

0528 MCC newsletter. The Club. *biannual.* illus.
□ */no. 1, Dec 1987/ to date?*

0529 MCC yearbook 1988-89. Harrington, Kilbride &
■ Partners, 1989. 280p. incl. adverts. illus. (some col.)
scores.
1988-89 first issue.

0530 **Slatter, William H.**
■ Recollections of Lord's and the Marylebone Cricket
Club. [Ewell], J. W. McKenzie, 1989. [vi], 32p.
*facsim. ed. of 'Padwick I' 1238 with a new introduction
by Gerald Brodribb.*

WANDERING CLUBS

Arabs

0531 † E.W. Swanton's XI: the Arabs Kenya tour 1980. [The
■ Club, 1979?]. [24]p. illus.
pre-tour; Jan 1980.

Arcadians

0532 **Smith, Tom**
■ Arcadians Cricket Club 1932-1982: a collection of essays
to commemorate the first fifty years. [Gloucester, the
Club, 1982]. [32]p. illus. scores, stats.

Bohemians

0533 **Bohemian** 1987. The Club, [1987]. [16]p. illus. stats.
*humorous summary of matches played in London and
the South of England.*

Buccaneers

0534 **Buccaneers** Cricket Club South African tour 1982. [The
■ Club, 1982]. 20p. incl. adverts. illus.
February-March 1982; pre-tour.

Devon and Somerset Wanderers

0535 † The **Devon** and Somerset Wanderers Cricket Club
1894-1914, 1921-1933. Taunton, P. J. Barnicott, 1934.
140p. frontis.

Forty Club

0536 **The Forty Club**
□ [Handbook]. The Club, *annual.*
continues 'Padwick I' 1258 to date?

0537 **Gabriel, Harold Edward Hammond**
■ 76 not out - my cricketing life. The Author, [1980]. [v],
49p. illus. *typescript.*
*limited ed., each copy signed by the author. Harold
Gabriel was a stalwart of the Forty Club.*

0538 **[Hunter, Herbert F. M.]**
■ XL - the first fifty years 1936-1986. Hunter Bureau of
Publications, [1986]. 84p. incl. adverts. illus.

Halifax Nomads

0539 **Halifax** Nomads Cricket Club 1939-1989. [The Club,
■ 1989]. 28p. illus. stats.

Hants & Sussex Borderers

0540 The **Hants** & Sussex Borderers Cricket Club: the first
■ fifty years - 1933-1983. [The Club, 1983]. [48]p. illus.
stats.
*includes season by season account since 1947; the club
plays annually in Devon and Cornwall.*

Hull Zingari

0541 † **Hull Zingari Cricket Club**
□ Handbook. [Hull, the Club]. *annual.* illus.
*club formed 1896.
/1969,70,75/ to date?*

I Zingari

0542 **Arrowsmith, Robert Langford** *and* **Hill, Barrington**
□ **Julian Warren**
The history of I Zingari. Stanley Paul, 1982. xii, 144p.
illus. (some col.) scores.
includes list of members as at 31 Dec 81.
——*de luxe ed. of 100 numbered copies signed by Lord
Home, 1982.*

Maltamaniacs

0543 **Maltamaniacs** cricket tour: Cape Province - South
■ Africa, February 1980. The Club, 1980. 20p. incl.
adverts. illus.
pre-tour.

0544 **Maltamaniacs** cricket tour: Malaysia and Singapore -
■ April 1982. The Club, 1982. 20p. incl. adverts. illus.
pre-tour.

Northants Bedouins

0545 **Larcombe, John** *and* **Larcombe, Peter,** *editor*
■ Bedouins down south. Northants Bedouins Cricket
Club, 1988. 28p. incl. adverts. illus. scores.
*cover sub-title: 'Northants Bedouins Cricket Club silver
jubilee 1988'.*

Optimists

0546 **Abbott, Martin ('Joe')**
■ The Optimists 40 years 1950-1989. [The Club, 1989].
[12]p. illus. stats.
*the Optimists commenced as a Purley Grammar School
team; its only matches are played on tour in
Worcestershire.*

Somerset Wanderers

0547 † **Englische** Kricketer in Berlin. 1938. 7p. illus.
*official programme of the Somerset Wanderers C. C. visit
to Berlin, August 1938.*

South Oxfordshire Amateurs

0548 **[Money, David C.]**
■ Fifty years of the SOA: seasons 1934-1983. [The Club,
1983]. 22p. illus.

South Wales

0549 **Smith, David T.** *and* **Smith, Jonathan B.**
■ South Wales Cricket Club 1859-1886. Corsham, the
Authors, [1987]. 53p. illus. scores, stats.
*limited ed. of 35 numbered copies, the first 10 of which
are hardback.*

Swallows

0550 The **Swallows** Australasia and India tour 1980. [32]p.
■ incl. adverts.

York Nondescripts

0551 **York** Nondescripts Cricket Club Far East tour 12 Feb - 5
March 1980. [The Club]. [16]p. incl. covers and adverts.
Singapore - Penang - Hong Kong - Bangkok; pre-tour.

Yorkshire Ramblers

0552 **Yorkshire** Ramblers New Zealand tour '86, February 10
■ - March 3. [The Club, 1986]. [12]p. incl. covers, illus.
map.
pre-tour.

PRIVATE CLUBS

Bill Frindall's XI

0553 **Bill** Frindall's XI tour of New Zealand and Australia.
Newmans Tours, 1985. 36p. illus.

Blue Mantles

0554 † **Blue Mantles Cricket Club**
■ [Season 1899]. Tunbridge Wells, [1900]. 99p. scores,
stats.
*as well as full details of previous season, includes rules of
the Club and accounts for the year ending 31 Dec 1899.
other years pub.?*

Heartaches

0555 **Rice, Timothy Miles Bindon,** *editor*
□ Heartaches cricketers' almanack. [Great Milton, the
Club]. *annual.* illus. scores, stats.
*each issue is limited ed. of 100 signed copies.
continues 'Padwick I' 1302-3 to date.*

Hudson's Hollywood XI

0556 **Birtles** Bowl bulletin; edited by Bernard Jordan.
■ Macclesfield. *annual.* illus. scores. *tabloid format.*
*Tim Hudson's team based at Birtles Hall, Macclesfield.
pub. 1987 and 1988.*

Kensington

0557 **Kensington** Cricket Club 1983/84. [The Club, 1984].
■ [12]p. col. illus. stats.
principally a review of the 1983 season; other years pub.?

Lords and Commons

0558 **Orr-Ewing, [Charles] Ian** *and* **Longmore, Andrew,**
■ *editors*
A celebration of Lords and Commons cricket 1850-1988.
Kingswood Press in association with Courage Limited,
1989. xi, 212p. illus. (some col.) scores, stats. index.

Sir Julien Cahn's Team

0559 † **Tour** of Malaya by Sir Julien Cahn's XI 1937. 13p.
■ *cover title; pre-tour.*
see also 'Padwick I' 4952.

COUNTRY HOUSE CRICKET

0560 A **cricket** match at Althorp. Burford (Oxon), Cygnet
■ Press, 1980. 12 leaves. score.
*cover title: 'The Earl Spencer's XI versus The Master of
Christ's XI, 1 June 1980'; limited ed. of 70 copies.*

CLUBS OF FIRMS, PROFESSIONS, ETC.

Admiralty Research Establishment

0561 **Warner, Guy**
■ ARE cricket almanack 1988. Portland, Admiralty
Research Establishment Sports & Social Club (Cricket
Section), 1988. [iv], 31p. illus. stats.

Bath Civil Service

0562 † **Bath** Civil Service Cricket Club. [The Club, 1976]. [iv],
■ 60p. illus. scores, stats.
celebrates 30th anniversary of the club.

British Aerospace

0563 **Kaye, David,** *compiler*
■ Planemen's cricket: British Aerospace Cricket Club
1938-1988: 50 years of cricket at Lostock. [Bolton, the
Club, 1988]. [iv], 123p. incl. adverts. illus. stats.

British Railways

0564 **Swindon British Railways Cricket Club**
■ Golden jubilee yearbook. Swindon, the Club, [1983].
[32]p. illus.

Coutts

0565 **Atkinson, D. K.**
■ Coutts Cricket Club 1960-1984: a history. [The Club],
1985. [360]p. scores, stats. *typescript.*

Kensington Griffins

0566 **Kensington Griffins**
Tour of Kent 1986.
banking team founded in 1984.

Lloyd's Register

0567 **Kidd, Denis**
■ 'A happy memory of cricket': 100 years of cricket at
Lloyd's Register. Lloyd's Register Cricket & Tennis
Club, 1982. [iv], 44p. illus.

Ordnance Survey

0568 **Harris, D. G.,** *editor*
■ Ordnance Survey Cricket Club 1882-1982.
[Southampton, the Club, 1982]. 64p. incl. adverts.
illus. stats.

Pearl Assurance Co.

0569 **Gray, Norman,** *compiler*
A century of Pearl cricket (1883-1983); with
contributions from Derek [J.] Underwood and Douglas
Eldridge; designed and edited by John Bishop. Pearl
Assurance Sports Club, 1983. 37p. incl. cover, illlus.
stats.

0570 **Underwood, Derek J.**
Uphill into the breeze; illustrations by Martyn Lucas.
Autolycus Press, 1984. 152p. illus.
*personal memories of London club cricket; the author
played for Pearl Assurance C. C.*

Prudential Assurance Co. (Ibis)

0571 † **Watson, T.**
A hundred years of Ibis cricket 1870-1969: (with some
notes on seasons 1962-68 by J. N. Earnshaw). [The Club,
1969]. [iv], 45p. illus. stats.

United London Banks

0572 **United London Banks Cricket Association**
Rules. [The Association], 1985. [8]p.
new ed. of 'Padwick I' 1332.

0573 The Sir Cyril Hawker Cup Competition playing
conditions. [The Association, n.d.] 2p.

SCHOOLS CRICKET

GENERAL

0574 The **Bunbury** English Schools cricket festival, July 1988.
56p. incl. adverts. illus.
*organised by Kent Schools Cricket Association; sponsored
by The Carphone Group Plc.
pre-tournament.*

0575 The **Bunbury** English Schools cricket festival, July 31st -
August 4th 1989. 72p. incl. adverts. illus.
*organised by the Somerset Schools Cricket Association.
pre-tournament.*

0576 **English Schools' Cricket Association**
Handbook. The Association. *annual.* illus. stats.
*continues 'Padwick I' 1339 to date.
1989 ed. produced 'in conjunction with Wrigley's
Chewing Gum'.*

0577 United Friendly Insurance cricket festival 1984: English
Schools (under 15). The Association, [1984]. [7]p. incl.
inside cover, illus.
pre-festival.

0578 **English** Schools' Cricket Association North of England
under 19 XI cricket festival. [Humberside S. C. A.,
1986]. [12]p. illus.
*21st to 25th July, 1986 - organised by the Humberside
Schools' Cricket Association.
pre-tournament.*

INDEPENDENT SCHOOLS

0579 **Mangan, James Anthony**
Athleticism in the Victorian and Edwardian public
school: the emergence and consolidation of the
educational ideology. Cambridge, Cambridge
University Press, 1981. xv, 345p. illus. facsims.

Bedford

0580 **Bedford** School Cricket Club Australian tour, Easter
1982. [Bedford, the School, 1981]. 80p. incl. adverts.
illus.

Bishop's Stortford College

0581 **Bishop's** Stortford College Sri Lanka cricket tour 1985/6.
[The College, 1985]. 32p.
pre-tour; Dec. 1985 - Jan. 1986.

Bradfield College

0582 **Bradfield** College Cricket Club: Sir Garfield Sobers
International Cricket festival, Barbados 1988. [The
College, 1988]. 28p. incl. adverts. illus.
pre-tournament.

0583 **Bradfield** College cricket tour to Bermuda, 9th - 22nd
July 1981. The College, 1981. 21p. illus.
pre-tour.

0584 **Bradfield** College tour to Bermuda 17-31 July 1984.
[The College, 1984]. 20p. illus. scores, stats.
pre-tour.

Charterhouse

0585 **Defriez, Philip**
Charterhouse School cricket, 1794-1914. St Albans, the
Author, [1987]. 30p. stats. *typescript.*

0586 **Raven, Simon Arthur Noel**
The old school: a study in the oddities of the English
public school system. Hamish Hamilton, 1986. xi, 139p.
illus. index.
many cricket references, especially pp. 45-49, 60-65.

Cheltenham College

0587 **Defriez, Philip**
Cheltenham College cricket, 1856-1914. The Author,
[1987]. 37p. stats. *typescript.*

Christ College, Brecon

0588 † **Cricket** centenary: Llandovery/Brecon. Llandysul,
Gomer Press, 1974. 11p. illus. stats.

Clifton College

0589 **Defriez, Philip**
Clifton College cricket, 1865-1914. The Author, [1987].
28p. stats. *typescript.*

Colfe's School

0590 **Anthony, Vivian S.**
150 years of cricket at Colfe's. Colfe's School, 1986.
96p. illus. score, stats.

Dulwich College

0591 ■ **Defriez, Philip**
Dulwich College cricket, 1874-1914. The Author, [1984]. 16p. stats. *typescript.*

0592 ■ **Dunnett, Harding McGregor**
Eminent Alleynians. Benenden (Kent), Neville & Harding, 1984. 48p. illus.
cricket pp. 18-21.
A. E. R. Gilligan; A. H. H. Gilligan; F. W. Gilligan; R. K. Nunes; C. M. Wells; S. C. Griffith; T. E. Bailey.

Durham School

0593 ■ **Durham** School Cricket Club. [Durham, the School], 1983. 40p. incl. adverts. illus. scores.
pub. to celebrate school tour to Barbados, 1983; includes a history of Durham School cricket.

Epsom College

0594 ■ **Gearing, Brian,** *editor*
Epsom College cricket tour to Barbados. [Epsom, the College, 1989]. 24p. illus.
pre-tour; participated in the Sir Garfield Sobers International Cricket tournament, 20th July - 9th August 1989.

Eton College

0595 ■ **Defriez, Philip**
Eton College cricket 1796-1914. St Albans, the Author, [1989]. 51p. stats. *typescript.*

0596 ■ **Eton** College tour of Hong Kong & Australia, December 1987 - January 1988. [The College, 1987]. 33p. illus. score.
pre-tour.

Felsted

0597 ■ **Felsted** School Australian tour 1985. [Felsted, the School, 1985]. 68p. incl. adverts. illus.
pre-tour.

Haileybury College

0598 ■ **Defriez, Philip**
Haileybury College cricket, 1840-1914. The Author, [1984]. 35p. stats. *typescript.*

Harrow School

0599 † ■ **[Cricket** rhymes]. 1877. [4]p.
dedicated to the Harrow Colts of 1877; contains 'Batting', 'Bowling and Fielding' and 'Fielding'.

0600 ■ **Defriez, Philip**
Harrow School cricket, 1805-1914. St Albans, the Author, [1989]. 40p. stats. *typescript.*

0601 † **Harrow** School song book: complete edition 1862-1904. Harrow School Musical Society, [1904]. 166p.
consolidated ed. of 'Padwick I' 1475.

0602 † The **tyro.** (by members of the Harrow School). *monthly.* scores.
/vols. I and II, nos. 1-19, 1 Oct., 1863 to 1 Aug., 1865/? cricket scores throughout; listed in Goldman ('Padwick I' 20).

Ipswich School

0603 ■ **Clayton, Roderick**
A century of cricket: Ipswich School versus Norwich School 1885-1985. [Ipswich, the School], 1985. [28]p. illus. stats.

King's School, Canterbury

0604 ■ The **King's** School, Canterbury Sri Lanka cricket tour 1986/87. [Canterbury, the School, 1986]. 36p. incl. adverts. illus. map.
pre-tour.

Llandovery College

0605 † **Cricket** centenary: Llandovery/Brecon. Llandysul, Gomer Press, 1974. 11p. illus. stats.

Malvern College

0606 ■ **Defriez, Philip**
Malvern College cricket 1871-1914. The Author, [1987]. 25p. stats. *typescript.*

Marlborough College

0607 ■ **Defriez, Philip**
Marlborough College cricket 1855-1914. The Author, [1987]. 36p. stats. *typescript.*

Norwich School

0608 ■ **Clayton, Roderick**
A century of cricket: Ipswich School versus Norwich School 1885-1985. [Ipswich, Ipswich School], 1985. [28]p. illus. stats.

Oakham School

0609 ■ **Needham, Brian**
Oakham School Cricket Club: 1st XI statistical records, 1884-1983. [Oakham, the Author], 1984. 68p. illus. stats.

Prebendal School, Chichester

0610 **Ollerenshaw, Neville**
A history of the Prebendal School (Chichester). Chichester, Phillimore, 1984. xviii, 88p. illus.
cricket references pp. 19, 23-25, 27, 33, 37, 54-55.

Repton School

0611 ■ **Defriez, Philip**
Repton School cricket, 1865-1914. The Author, [1987]. 27p. stats. *typescript.*

0612 ■ **Eric Marsh,** Repton coach 1950-80. [Repton, the School], 1980. 28p. illus.
Eric Marsh's testimonial brochure.

0613 ■ **Repton** School: Barbados tour 1984. [Repton, the School, 1984]. 52p. incl. adverts. illus. (one col.)
pre-tour.

Rossall

0614 ■ **Defriez, Philip**
Rossall school cricket 1863-1914. St Albans, the Author, [1988]. 17p. stats. *typescript.*

Rugby

0615 ■ **Defriez, Philip**
Rugby school cricket 1845-1914. St Albans, the Author, [1987]. 29p. stats. *typescript.*

Sherborne

0616 ■ **Defriez, Philip**
Sherborne school cricket 1865-1914. St Albans, the Author, [1988]. 18p. stats.

0617 ■ **Gibbs, D. F.**
A history of cricket at Sherborne School. The Author?, 1980? [iv], 43p. stats.

Shrewsbury

0618 ■ **Defriez, Philip**
Shrewsbury school cricket 1871-1914. St Albans, the Author, [1988]. 17p. stats. *typescript.*

St Dunstan's College

0619 ■ **Scovell, Brian,** *editor*
St Dunstan's College centenary tour of Australia. [The College, 1988]. [48]p. incl. adverts. illus. maps.
1988-89 tour celebrating centenary of College and Australian bicentenary.
pre-tour.

St George's College, Weybridge

0620 † ■ **Cricket** at St George's College. [The College, n.d.]
[12]p. incl. covers. stats.
mostly an anthology of cricket items from the College magazine.

0621 **St** George's College Weybridge 1984 centenary tour to Zimbabwe. The College, 1984.

Tonbridge

0622 ■ **Defriez, Philip**
Tonbridge School cricket, 1874-1914. The Author, [1983]. 18p. stats. *typescript.*

Trent College

0623 ■ **Trent** College Australian tour 1989/90. [The College, 1989]. [28]p. incl. adverts. illus.
pre-tour; Dec 1989 - Jan 1990.

Uppingham

0624 ■ **Defriez, Philip**
Uppingham School cricket, 1863-1914. The Author, [1983]. 30p. stats. *typescript.*

0625 **Matthews, Bryan**
Eminent Uppinghamians. Benenden (Kent), Neville and Harding, 1987. illus.
includes A. P. F. Chapman, S. Christopherson, C. Hurst and G. MacGregor.

0626 ■ **Uppingham** School Cricket Club Australian tour 1981/82. [The School, 1981]. 40p. incl. adverts. illus.
pre-tour.

Wellington College

0627 ■ **Defriez, Philip**
Wellington College cricket, 1866-1914. St Albans, the Author, [1984]. 28p. stats. *typescript.*

0628 ■ **Wellington College Cricket Club**
Hong Kong & Australia tour 1989-90. [The Club, 1989]. 40p. incl. adverts. illus.
pre-tour; Dec 1989 - Jan 1990.

Westminster

0629 ■ **Defriez, Philip**
Westminster School cricket, 1794-1914. St Albans, the Author, [1987]. 13p. stats. *typescript.*

Winchester College

0630 ■ **Defriez, Philip**
Winchester College cricket 1825-1914. St Albans, the Author, [1988]. 37p. stats. *typescript.*

Worksop College

0631 ■ **Worksop** College Australian cricket tour 1988-89. [The College, 1988]. 32p. incl. adverts. illus.
Dec 1988 - Jan 1989.
pre-tour.

OTHER SCHOOLS

Aston Comprehensive

0632 ■ **Aston** Comprehensive School cricket tour to the West Indies, Easter 1984. The School, [1984]. 48p. incl. adverts. illus.
pre-tour.

Bath Schools

0633 ■ **Bath** schools Australian cricket tour. 1988. 12p. incl. covers, illus.
tour made by representatives from Beechen Cliff School, King Edward's School, Kingswood School, Monkton Combe School and Prior Park College as part of Australia's bicentennial celebrations.
pre-tour.

0634 ■ **Bath** schools cricket tour of Kenya & Zimbabwe, March - April 1989. Bath, 1989. [10]p. illus.
pre-tour.

Berkshire Schools

0635 ■ **Berkshire Schools Cricket Association**
Tour of Sri Lanka, December 1984 - January 1985. [The Association, 1984]. [36]p. incl. adverts. illus.
pre-tour; tour eventually took place March - April 1985.

0636 ■ Tour report: Sri Lanka, March & April 1985. The Association, [1985]. [8]p. scores, stats. *typescript.*

0637 ■ **Sri Lanka Schools Cricket Association**
Berkshire Schools Cricket Association tour of Sri Lanka. [The Association, 1985]. [24]p. incl. adverts.
dedicated to International Youth Year 1985; pre-tour.

Castle School, Taunton

0638 **Castle School, Taunton**
Barbados tour 1989. [Taunton, the School, 1989]. 32p. *typescript.*
pre-tour.

Cornwall Schools

0639 □ **Cornwall Schools' Cricket Association**
Handbook. [The Association]. *annual.* stats.
?/1981, 1985, 1989/

0640 Tesco Stores cricket festival. The Association, [1989].
■ [8]p.
festival for under fourteen teams; held at Truro Cricket Club, July 26-28 1989.

Dyfed Schools

0641 **Dyfed Schools' Cricket Association**
Handbook. The Association. *annual.* illus. scores.
/1988 to date/

Essex Schools

0642 **Essex County Schools Cricket Association**
■ Barbados cricket tour 1982: report. [The Association, 1982]. 16p. incl. covers, illus. stats.
7th Aug to 22nd Aug; post tour.

0643 Golden Jubilee tour, March & April 1985: Australian tour - official tour brochure. The Association, [1985]. 20p. incl. covers and adverts. illus.
post tour.

0644 Report. The Association. *annual.* scores, stats.
□ *?/1989/*

Lancashire Schools

0645 † **Lancashire Schools Cricket Association**
Official programme and score card. Manchester, the Association. illus.
matches played by Lancashire Boys:
v Nottinghamshire Boys, 4 July 1959.
v Essex Boys, 23 July 1966.
v Durham Boys, 15 July 1967.
v Nottinghamshire Boys, 19 July 1969.
additional to those listed in 'Padwick I' 1587 - 1595 inclusive.

Lincolnshire Schools

0646 **Lincolnshire Schools' Cricket Association**
■ Tour to Zimbabwe 19 August to 11 September 1989. The Association, [1989]. 26p. illus.
pre-tour; includes short history of Lincolnshire schools cricket 1961-89 by Reg Woodward.

0647 **Lincolnshire Schools' Sports Federation**
■ Cricket tour of Sri Lanka, August 1982. 1982. [12]p. illus. *typescript.*
pre-tour.

0648 Cricket U. 15. 21st year. The Federation, [1981]. 26p.
■ stats. *typescript.*
celebrating 21st birthday of under-15 section of the Federation.

London Schools

0649 **London Schools' Cricket Association**
■ 1925-1985: history of the London Schools' Cricket Association to date. The Association. [1985]. 10p.
cover title: 'Diamond Jubilee 1925-1985'.

0650 Handbook. The Association. *annual.*
□ *?/1981, 1983/ to date?*

0651 Winter tour to Barbados 1986-87: tour brochure. The
■ Association, 1986. 24p. illus.
pre-tour; October 1986.

Netherhall School, Cambridge

0652 **Grey, Duncan S.**
■ A short history of Netherhall School staff cricket 1933-1982. Cambridge, Golden Bustard Press, 1983. [28]p. stats.
includes brief list of all matches.
limited ed. of 50 signed and numbered copies.

Newcastle Royal Grammar School

0653 **Stevens, B. D. R.**
■ Newcastle Royal Grammar School Cricket Club, 1861-1979. Newcastle, [the School], 1981? [viii], 133p. illus. stats.

Northamptonshire Schools

0654 **Northamptonshire Schools Cricket Association**
■ [Brochure]. The Association, 1985. [14]p. scores, stats. *typescript.*
pub. annually?

Nottinghamshire Schools

0655 † **City of Nottingham Schools' Cricket Association**
□ Nottingham schoolboys' cricket handbook. The Association. *annual.* illus. diagrs. in various years.
continues 'Padwick I' 1610.
/1963-1969/ to date?

Queen Mary's Grammar School, Clitheroe

0656 **Green, Dudley** *and* **Harwood, Keith**
■ Queen Mary's Grammar School Clitheroe: a history of Clitheroe Royal Grammar School 1554-1983. Chorley, Countyside Publications, 1983. 112p. illus.
scattered references to school cricket.

Reading School

0657 **Haines, J. W.** *et al*
■ A history of cricket at Reading School. Reading, the School? [1986]. 80p. illus. stats.

Sussex Schools

0658 **Sussex Schools' Cricket Association**
□ Annual report. The Association. stats. *typescript.*
?/1987/ to date?

Walthamstow Schools

0659 † **Birmingham, L. F.**
Walthamstow Schools' Cricket and Football Association diamond jubilee handbook. [The Association]. 1958.

Welsh Schools

0660 [**Davies, R. G.,** *compiler and editor*]
■ Tour of Barbados: 1984. Welsh Schools' Cricket Association, 1984. [12]p. illus.
pre-tour; Oct.-Nov. 1984.

0661 **Welsh Schools Cricket Association**
□ Handbook. The Association. *annual.* illus. stats.
1979?/1985-86, 88-89/

0662 Tour to Australia 1986-87: official souvenir. The
■ Association, 1986. [20]p. illus.
pre-tour; Dec. 86 - Jan. 87.

0663 Tour to Sri Lanka 1988: official tour brochure. The
■ Association, 1988. 24p. incl. adverts. illus.
pre-tour; Oct. 1988.

West Leeds High School

0664 † **Harland, Oswald H.**
■ West Leeds High School for Boys: a chronicle history 1907-1957. [Leeds], the School, 1957. 80p. illus.
cricket pp. 38-41 and other scattered references.

Yorkshire Schools

0665 † **Sowerby, Brian,** *compiler*
■ 50 not out: a brief history of the Yorkshire Schools Cricket Association. [The Association], 1975. [i], 26p.
typescript.

OLD SCHOOL CLUBS

0666 *The Cricketer* Cup: a statistical summary. Ashurst
■ (Kent), *The Cricketer*, 1989. 16p. stats.
Old Boys tournament.

0667 **Huskinson, T. A. L.,** *compiler*
■ *The Cricketer* Cup 1967-1985: a statistical summary ... The Author?, 1986. 18p. scores, stats.
Old Boys tournament.

Old Askeans

0668 The **Old** Askean Cricket Club centenary year 1887-1987.
■ [The Club], 1987. [20]p. incl. adverts. illus.
includes a brief history of the Club by John Grant and a preview of the Club's 1987 Barbados tour.

Old Carthusians

0669 † **Old Carthusians Cricket & Football Club**
Rules, list of members and results of matches. Godalming, the Club, 1890. 104p.
earlier ed. of 'Padwick I' 1674.

Old Emanuel

0670 **Old** Emanuel Cricket Club ... diamond jubilee tour,
■ Barbados 1986. The Club, 1986. [28]p. incl. adverts. illus.
March - April 1986.
pre-tour.

Old Fullerians

0671 **Walters, Mike** *and* **Gardner, David,** *editors*
■ Old Fullerians' Cricket Club: fortieth anniversary official club brochure. [Watford, the Club, 1987]. [14]p. illus.

Old Gravesendians

0672 **Latham, Paul** *and* **Haines, Jack,** *editors*
■ Old Gravesendians' Cricket Club diamond jubilee 1927-1987. Chalk, Old Gravesendians Cricket Club, [1987]. [32]p. incl. adverts. illus.

Old Higher Grade, Cambridge

0673 † **Old Higher Grade Cricket Club**
■ Annual meeting 1895. [Cambridge, the Club, 1895]. [4]p.
only issue?

0674 † Minute book.
■ *original minute book in Cambridgeshire Collection, Cambridge Central Library.*
Club formed March 12 1887 as old boys club of Higher Grade Boys School, Cambridge.

0675 † Results of matches and batting and bowling averages.
□ [Cambridge, the Club]. *annual.* [4]p. folded card, stats.
?/1889-1894/?

0676 † Rules. [Cambridge, the Club]. *annual*? [4]p. folded
□ card.
?/1890, 1891/?
1891 with title 'Rules and fixtures'.

St Peter's Old Boys

0677 † **'Ourselves'** 1927-1930. n.p. [1930]. [vi], 40p. scores,
■ stats.
scores and descriptions of matches played by the Old Boys of St Peter's Preparatory School, Seaford, 1927-30.

YOUTH CRICKET

0678 **National Association of Young Cricketers**
■ Year book. The Association. illus. scores, stats.
continues 'Padwick I' 789 to date.

0679 **National Cricket Association**
■ Eighth international youth tournament at Radley College, Oxford, July 1989. [The Association, 1989]. [28]p. illus.
pre-tournament.

0680 Youth representative cricket in the British Isles. *annual.*
□ *complete fixture list of all representative youth cricket at county, regional and national level.*
1987/1989/
1989 edited by Brian Aspital.

0681 The **young** cricketer: a plan for the future; the report of
■ the Cricket Council enquiry into junior and youth cricket, 1980. The Cricket Council, 1980. 30p.

Berkshire Youth

0682 **Berkshire Cricket Association**
■ Tour of Australia, December 1986 - January 1987. The Association, [1986]. [36]p. incl. adverts. illus.
under eighteen tour; pre-tour.

0683 Tour to Barbados, 23 March - 6 April 1989. The Association, 1989. [8]p. incl. covers, illus.
youth tour; pre-tour.

Derbyshire Youth

0684 **Looking** to the future: the Loundsley Green youth
■ cricket tour of Barbados, October 1981. [1981]. 24p.
illus.
pre-tour.

0685 **Suttle, Charles Richard William**
■ Caribbean mission accomplished. [Chesterfield, the
Author, 1984?]. [v], 95p. illus. scores, stats.
*report of Loundsley Green Youth Cricket Club tour to
Barbados, October 1981.*

Kent Youth

0686 The **Young** Kentish cricketer. [Maidstone District of the
■ A. K. C. C.]. *irregular.* illus. scores.
two issues pub. in 1986.

Leicestershire Youth

0687 **Leicestershire Cricket Association**
☐ Youth cricket programme. The Association. *annual.*
scores in v.y.
?/1981 ... 1989/

Middlesex Youth

0688 **Middlesex Colts Association**
☐ Official cricket handbook. The Association. *annual.*
illus.
continues 'Padwick I' 2342-2 to date

Staffordshire Youth

0689 **Kidsgrove and District Junior Cricket League**
[Handbook]. Kidsgrove, the League. *annual.*
includes teams from Cheshire.
continues 'Padwick I' 2578 to date

0690 Report. Kidsgrove, the League. *annual.* stats.
report on the season.
continues 'Padwick I' 2577 to date.

Surrey Youth

0691 **Surrey** youth Australian tour 1989. [Surrey County
■ Cricket Club / Surrey Cricket Association & Surrey
Schools], 1989. 28p. incl. adverts. illus.
pre-tour; Dec. 89 - Jan. 90.

0692 **Surrey** youth [in] Australia 1985. [National Cricket
Association, 1985]. 32p. incl. adverts. illus.
pre-tour.

Welsh Youth

0693 **South Wales Junior Cricket League**
Official handbook. The League. *annual.*
?/1989/

Yorkshire Youth

0694 **Airedale Junior Cricket League**
■ Golden jubilee 1939-1989: jubilee cricket match
programme - East v West at Guiseley, 23 July 1989. The
League, 1989. 16p. incl. covers, illus.
includes history of the League.

0695 † Official rules and fixtures. The League, *annual.*
☐ *?/1978 to date.*
golden jubilee ed. 1989.

0696 **Batley & Dewsbury Area Boys Cricket League**
☐ General information. *annual. typescript.*
league founded 1973.
?/1981,83,85/ to date?

0697 **Bradford Junior Cricket League**
■ B.J.C.L. Caribbean tour to Barbados, April 1986. [The
League, 1985]. [48]. incl. adverts. illus.
pre-tour.

0698 † [Handbook]. The League, *annual.*
☐ *?/1978 to date.*

0699 **Huddersfield & District Under 13 Cricket League**
☐ [Handbook]. The League. *annual.*
?/1980-82,87/ to date.

0700 † **Huddersfield Junior Cricket League**
☐ Rules & fixtures. The League. *annual.*
?/1979-81,83,85/ to date.

0701 **Jessop, Ben**
■ The first 38 years; a history of Sheffield & District Junior
Cricket League. [The League, 1988]. 128p. incl.
adverts. illus. scores.

0702 † The **Joe** Lumb cricket competition. *annual.*
☐ *Yorkshire-wide under 18's competition.*
?/1971,73/ to date.

0703 † **Kirklees** Junior Sunday Cricket League souvenir
■ brochure, Spring tour 1979 - Isle of Man, May 8th-15th.
1979. [28]p. incl. adverts. illus.
pre-tour.

0704 **Leeds and District Junior Cricket League**
☐ [Handbook]. The League. *annual.* stats.
?/1980 to date.

0705 † **Leeds Cricket Club**
■ Leeds Cricket Club under XV Fylde coast tour 1978.
[The Club, 1978]. 20p. illus. *typescript.*
pre-tour.

0706 **Pontefract & District Junior Cricket League**
☐ Brochure. The League. *annual. typescript.*
?/1983-85/ to date?

0707 † **York and District Under 16 Cricket League**
☐ Fixtures and rule book. The League. *annual.*
?/1979-80/ to date?

UNIVERSITY AND COLLEGE CRICKET

0708 † **Oxford** - Cambridge cricket tour of Malaysia, 20th July -
6th August 1972. [1972]. 32p. incl. adverts. illus. stats.
Penang vs Oxford - Cambridge, 29th & 30th July 1972.

0709 **Oxford** and Cambridge Universities cricket tour of Hong
■ Kong and Australia, December 1985 - January 1986.
[1985]. [20]p. incl. adverts. illus.
pre-tour.

Brighton

0710 **Brighton Polytechnic Cricket Club**
☐ Handbook. Brighton, the Club. illus. scores, stats.
typescript.
1986/87 the only issue?

Cambridge

0711 † **Cambridge University**
■ The Cambridge University general almanack and
register. Cambridge, J. Webb & Co; London, Clive &
Co. *annual.* scores, stats.
1895-1897.
continues 'Padwick I' 1624.

0712 **Cambridge University Cricket Club**
■ Fenner's '83. [Cambridge, the Club, 1983]. [24]p. incl.
adverts. illus.

Exeter

0713 **Fisher, Stephen,** *editor*
■ The Erratics: fifty not out: a history of the University of
Exeter Staff Cricket Club 1934-1984. Exeter, the Club,
1987. xiii, 209p. illus. facsims. stats.

London

0714 † **Catt, Frederick Charles**
■ Report on the first hundred years of the Maurice Cricket
Club. Working Men's College, 1957. 11p.
*history of the Working Men's College Cricket Club,
founded 1857, and subsequently re-named after F. D.
Maurice, founder of the College.*

0715 **Haringey Cricket College**
■ Annual report 1985 / Caribbean tour brochure. The
College, [1986]. [48]p. incl. covers and adverts. illus.
scores.
*record of 1985 season and first year of opening; preview
of tour to West Indies, March 1986.
other years pub?*

Oxford

0716 † **An undergraduate,** *pseud.*
■ Reminiscences of Oxford varsity life. Oxford, T. and G.
Shrimpton, [1862]. [20]p. illus.
*pen and ink drawings including two cricket scenes 'A
drive for six' and 'Waiting for the verdict'.*

Oxford: Magdalen College

0717 † **Wright, F. B.**
Magdalen Cricket Club 1827-29 scorebook.
ms. at Lord's according to 'Allen EBC'.

Reading

0718 **Giles, Anthony Kent**
■ About twenty five years of cricket: a history of Reading
University Academic Staff Cricket Club. Reading, the
Club, 1983. 185p. illus. stats. index.

Oxford v Cambridge Matches

0719 † The **blue** book: a record of Oxford and Cambridge
inter-university competitions 1913-1914. Cambridge, F.
W. Talbot, [1914]. 20p.
cricket on p. 8.

0720 **Chesterton, George Herbert** *and* **Doggart, [George]**
■ **Hubert Graham**
Oxford and Cambridge cricket. (The MCC Cricket
Library). Willow Books, 1989. 319p. illus. stats.
scores, bibliog. index.

SERVICES CRICKET

0721 † **[Garrison Cricket Club]**
■ [Rules]. Valenciennes, 1816. 4p.
*Club formed for English officers in France during
Napoleonic War. Rules drawn up 4 Aug. 1816. Rule 4
requires that 'The game will be played upon the Plain of
Mons'.*

0722 † **Hesketh-Prichard, Hesketh Vernon**
Sniping in France: with notes in the scientific training of
scouts, observers and snipers; illustrations by Ernest
Blaikey. Hutchinson, [1920]. 268p.
*contains several references to cricket played in
France/Belgium during the 1914-18 War.*

0723 † The **journal** of the Household Brigade; edited by I.E.A.
☐ Dolby. W. Clowes & Sons. illus. scores.
*1862/1870, 1876, 1877/?
contains reports and scores of Brigade matches.*

0724 **Reese, Anna**
Cricket tours, the Midlands and East Anglia. Upper
Heyford (Oxon.), RAF Upper Heyford, [1981]. 48p.
illus. bibliog. index.
RAF Upper Heyford C.C. tours.

LEAGUE, CLUB AND VILLAGE CRICKET

LEAGUE CRICKET

(For most leagues see under names of counties, towns etc.)

0725 † **All** England law reports 1955, vol. 1. Butterworths, 1955.
■ *pp. 93-107 contain Court of Appeal judgment in the case of Moorhouse v Dooland concerning taxation of collections made at league matches for meritorious performances.*

0726 **The County Alliance of Cricket Clubs**
Handbook. [Bristol], the Alliance. *annual.* maps. stats.
founded 1985.
includes teams from Gloucestershire and surrounding counties.
1986? to date.

0727 **The Famous Grouse Inter-League Trophy**
■ Rules. [1989]. *typescript.*
copy seen amended to Nov. 1989.

0728 **Hetheringtons, Pretty & Ellis Thames Valley Cricket**
□ **League**
Handbook. The League. *annual.* illus. stats.
founded 1970.
includes teams from Berks, Bucks, Hants, Herts and Middx.
1972/1985/ to date.

0729 **Home Counties Cricket League**
□ Handbook. The League. *annual.*
includes teams from Beds, Herts and Greater London.
1981?/1988/ to date?

0730 **League Cricket Conference**
■ Handbook. Nantwich, Rob Sproston Sports. *annual.* illus.
pub. 1984, 85, 88 and 89.
compiled and edited by Neil Edwards.

0731 **Lee 1975 Cricket League**
■ Handbook. The League. *annual.* illus. stats.
founded 1973.
sponsored by Truman 1975-83; includes clubs from Berks, Bucks, Middx and Surrey.
1987 to date

0732 **Mangan, James Anthony** *and* **Small, R. B.,** *editors*
Sport, culture, society: international, historical and sociological perspectives. Andover, Spon, 1986. xi, 348p. illus. bibliog. index.
includes 'The development of professionalism in English league cricket, c. 1900-40' by J. Hill pp.109-116.

0733 **Three Counties League**
Handbook. The League. *annual.*
Gloucs., Herefordshire and Monmouthshire.
?/1988 to date.

0734 **Touche** Ross Trophy. Bristol, Touche Ross & Co.
□ *biannual.*
60 over Sunday League cricket tournament based in West Country.
with title 'TNT Trophy' to 1986.
1984, 1986/1988/

CLUB CRICKET

0735 **Burgess, Martin** *and* **Allen, Patrick,** *editors*
■ Rothmans club cricket yearbook 1982. Aylesbury, Rothmans Publications, 1982. xiv, 322p. illus. stats.
the only issue.

0736 **Club Cricket Conference**
□ League newsletter. New Malden (Surrey), the Conference. *irregular.*
sponsored by Schweppes.
1988? to date.

0737 Official handbook. New Malden (Surrey), the
■ Conference. *annual.* illus.
continues 'Padwick I' 1713 to date.

0738 **Midlands Club Cricket Conference**
■ Yearbook. [Birmingham], the Conference. illus. scores, stats.
1980-82 edited by J.W.Jones and Miss M.V.Wheeldon.
1983-88 edited by Brian F. Jones and Miss M.V.Wheeldon.
1989 edited by N.C.Pollock and Miss M.V.Wheeldon.
continues 'Padwick I' 1721 to date.

VILLAGE CRICKET

0739 † **Archer, Fred**
The distant scene; illustrations by James Moss. Hodder & Stoughton, 1967. 192p. illus.
ch. 16: 'Village cricket and umpires'.

0740 **Bailey, Brian**
■ The English village green. Robert Hale, 1985. 223p. illus. (some col.) bibliog. index.
some cricket.

0741 † **Grey, Julian,** *pseud. [i.e. Glover, C. Gordon]*
Parish pump; illustrated by Michael Bell. Kineton, Roadwood Press, 1975. xii, 124p. illus.
collection of articles from 'The country gentleman's magazine'; cricket in chs. 12, 15 and 17.

0742 **Howat, Gerald Malcolm David**
■ Village cricket. Newton Abbot, David & Charles, 1980. 160p. illus. bibliog. index.

0743 **Jenkins, Alan C.**
■ A village year. Exeter, Webb & Bower, 1981. 160p. illus. (some col.) bibliog. index.
cricket pp. 98-104 and 115-116.

0744 **Norsk** Hydro village cricket annual; edited by Tony
■ Huskinson. Ashurst (Kent), *The Cricketer.* illus. scores, stats.
1986-88.
1988 ed. with title 'Hydro village cricket annual'.

0745 **Radcliffe, H. Talbot**
■ The power of the game. [Holyhead], the Author, [1988]. 56p. illus. diagrs.
all aspects of forming and running a village cricket club.

0746 **Whitbread** village cricket handbook; edited by Findlay
☐ Rea. Ashurst (Kent), *The Cricketer* for Whitbread &
Co. *annual*. illus. stats.
continues 'Padwick I' 1731-1 to 1985?
continued as 'Norsk Hydro village cricket annual'?

CRICKET IN THE COUNTIES

(for Junior cricket leagues, see Youth Cricket)

COUNTY CRICKET

0747 † **All** England law reports reprint: being a selection from
■ the *Law Times* reprints 1843-1935: revised and annotated
1927. Butterworth & Co., 1959. [vi], 753p.
*pp. 294-304 contain final ruling by House of Lords on
Seymour v Reed case; see also 'Padwick I' 942.*

0748 **Association of Cricket Statisticians**, *compiler*
■ The first class counties' second XI annual. Haughton
(Notts.), the Association. scores, stats.
1985-87.
*1988-89 with cover title 'ACS first class counties' second
eleven annual'.*

0749 † **British Broadcasting Corporation**
■ Taking stock: 'problems of county cricket'; broadcast 24
April 1952; chairman: John Arlott, speakers:
H.S.Altham, R.W.V.Robins, Bill Bowes, H.L.V.Day.
15p. *typescript*.
transcript of radio broadcast.

0750 **Coleman, Vernon**
■ Diary of a cricket lover: around the counties. Enigma
Books, 1984. 159p.
the 1984 season.

0751 **County** champions. Quixote Press, 1982. [viii], 198p.
■ illus.
*seventeen well-known cricket enthusiasts write about an
aspect of the county they support.*

0752 **Finch, J. S.**
■ 'Game in season': 'Mr Abbott's sporting tour'. The
Author, 1984. [xii], 134p. illus. index.
*personal reminiscences of 1981 county cricket.
limited ed. of 150 copies in slip case.*

0753 Three men at the match: a journey through the English
■ county cricket season. Queen Anne Press, 1989. 220p.
illus. index.
1988 season.

0754 **Kirkby, Donald**
■ The financing of county cricket clubs. Huddersfield,
Huddersfield Polytechnic, n.d. 14p.
covers seasons 1981 and 1982.

0755 **Martin-Jenkins, Christopher Dennis Alexander**
■ The Wisden book of county cricket; with statistics edited
by Frank Warwick. Queen Anne Press, 1981. 447p.
illus. stats.

0756 **Martin-Jenkins, Christopher Dennis Alexander**, *editor*
■ County championship review. Ashurst (Kent), *The
Cricketer* for Britannic Assurance. *annual*. illus. (some
col.) scores, stats.
*includes full scores and summaries of all County
championship matches.
pub. in 1985 and 1986 only.*

0757 **Reddie, Richard**
County cricket clubs and personalities. [Bradford, the
Author, 1985]. 37p. col. illus.

0758 **World** of cricket 83. Minicards, 1983. 40p. col. illus.
■ *a 'Figurine Panini' sticker album containing portraits of
all county cricketers.*

MINOR COUNTIES CRICKET

0759 **Minor** Counties cricket annual and official handbook.
■ West Bridgford (Notts.), Association of Cricket
Statisticians in conjunction with Minor Counties Cricket
Association. illus. scores, stats.
*1980-83 with title 'Minor Counties Annual'.
1980 edited by Brian Hunt.
1981-83 edited by Brian Hunt and Robert Brooke.
1984 to date edited by David Armstrong.
continues 'Padwick I' 1756 to date.*

0760 **Minor Counties Cricket Association**
■ Souvenir brochure October/November 1982 in support
of the M.C.C.A. tour of East Africa. [The Association,
1982]. 52p. illus.

0761 **Minor** Counties quarterly; edited by Mike Berry.
■ Frankton (Warwicks.), Berrys Sports Agency. *irregular*.
illus. scores, stats. plans.
no. 1 June 1987 - no. 7 winter 1990 (i.e. 1989?).

BEDFORDSHIRE

Southill

0762 **Massey, Arthur** *et al*
■ Southill Park Cricket Club: 100 years of cricket
1884-1984 centenary souvenir booklet. [Southill, the
Club, 1984]. 46p. incl. adverts. illus. stats.

BEDFORDSHIRE C. C. C.

0763 **Bedfordshire County Cricket Club**
☐ Annual report. Bedford, the Club. stats.
continues 'Padwick I' 1764 to date.

BERKSHIRE

0764 **Chilterns Cricket League**
Handbook. The League. *annual*. stats.
*league formed 1975.
1982-85 sponsored by Grasshopper.
1985-86 sponsored by Bryan.
1987-89 sponsored by Prudential.*

0765 The Lafford & Leavey Berkshire League
☐ League handbook. The League. *annual.* illus. scores, stats.
founded 1977.
?1978/1979-82,84 to date/
1977-80 Berkshire Mercury County Cricket League.
1981-83 Mercury Berkshire County Cricket League.
1984 Berkshire County Cricket League.

Ascot

0766 Anderson, Bert
■ Royal Ascot Cricket Club 1883-1983 centenary. [Ascot, the Club, 1983]. 28p. illus. map, scores.

Bracknell

0767 Harman, John *and* Taylor, Eric
■ Bracknell & District Cricket Club: 1880-1980 centenary handbook. [The Club], 1980. [36]p. illus. facsims. stats.

Datchet

0768 Datchet C.C. v Derek Underwood XI, Friday 12
■ September '86. [40]p. incl. adverts. illus. stats.
played for Derek Underwood's benefit; includes history of Datchet Cricket Club.

Newbury

0769 Church, David
■ Falkland Cricket Club 1884-1984. [Newbury, the Club, 1984]. 72p. incl. adverts. illus. map.

BERKSHIRE C. C. C.

0770 Berkshire County Cricket Club
■ Berkshire cricket yearbook. [Reading, the Club]. illus. scores, stats.
also includes club and school cricket in Berkshire.
1987 to date.
edited by Ralph Dellor.

0771 Official New Zealand tour 1988/89. Harrow, Directory
■ of Training Limited, [1988]. [20]p. incl. adverts. illus.
pre-tour.

BUCKINGHAMSHIRE

0772 Chilterns Cricket League
Handbook. The League. *annual.* stats.
league formed 1975.
1982-85 sponsored by Grasshopper.
1985-86 sponsored by Bryan.
1987-89 sponsored by Prudential.

Aylesbury

0773 Aylesbury and District Mid-Week Cricket League
☐ Handbook and fixtures. [Aylesbury, the League].
annual.
founded 1974.
?/1985 to date.
sponsored by 'The Bucks Herald' from 1988.

Chesham

0774 Mike Taylor's Hampshire C. C. C. XI v Chesham C. C. ...
■ Friday 7th July. 1989. [24]p. incl. adverts. illus. stats.
includes a short history of Chesham Cricket Club by Edwin Webb.

Gerrards Cross

0775 Russell, J. F. S., *editor*
■ Gerrards Cross Cricket Club - 100 years [1882-1982].
[Gerrards Cross, the Club, 1982]. [32]p. incl. adverts. illus.

Milton Keynes

0776 Volkswagen Milton Keynes Midweek Cricket League
■ Constitution. Milton Keynes, the League, 1986. [6]p.
typescript.
the League does not publish a handbook.

Soulbury

0777 Dilley, J.
■ A short history of Soulbury Village Cricket Club. [The Club, 1984]. [ii], 22p. illus.

Stewkley

0778 Stewkley Vicarage Cricket Club centenary brochure.
■ [Stewkley, the Club, 1982]. 26p. illus.

Winslow

0779 Winslow Town Cricket Club 1886 1986: centenary year
■ brochure 1986. [The Club], 1986. 32p. incl. adverts. illus. stats.

BUCKINGHAMSHIRE C. C. C.

0780 Buckinghamshire County Cricket Club
☐ [Handbook]. The Club, *annual.* illus. stats. scores.
continues 'Padwick I' 1784 to date.

0781 Tour of Australia 1989. [The Club, 1988]. [40]p. incl.
■ adverts. illus. map.
pre-tour; Jan.-Feb. 1989.

CAMBRIDGESHIRE

0782 Beach Villas Cambridgeshire Cricket League
■ Handbook. Cambridge, the League. *annual.* illus. stats.
formed 1979.
/1985-89/
sponsored previously by TSB.

0783 † Cambridgeshire Cricket Association
☐ Constitution. Cambridge, the Club. *annual.*
/1889...1902/?

0784 Official handbook. Cambridge, the Association. *annual.*
■ *continues 'Padwick I' 1786 to date.*

Bluntisham

0785 Bluntisham Cricket Club
■ Village cricket is back. The Club, 1989. [8]p. incl.
covers and adverts.
inaugural match programme celebrating return of cricket to Bluntisham; includes a brief history of cricket in Bluntisham.

Burrough Green

0786 Davis, Tony *and* Freedland, Jeremy
■ A village cricket team called Burrough Green: history of Burrough Green Cricket Club. [The Club, 1987]. [36]p. illus. scores.

Cambridge

0787 † **Booksellers Cricket Club**
■ Minute book.
original minute book in Cambridgeshire Collection in Cambridge Central Library.
Club formed March 1886 and dissolved April 1889.
Minute book includes rules etc.

0788 **Gray, P. C.**
■ History of Camden Cricket Club, Cambridge 1881-1981. [Cambridge, the Club, 1981]. [ii], 58p. illus. stats.

0789 † **St Giles Cricket Club**
■ Annual dinner on Thursday, September 30th, 1926 ... [The Club, 1926]. [3]p. stats.
includes club records for the season.
Club later moved to Dry Drayton.

0790 † **Town and Country Cricket Club**
■ Annual report. 1846. 8p. stats.
only issue?
reprinted from 'Cambridge Independent Press' of Nov 28, 1846.

Over

0791 **Over Cricket Club**
□ Newsletter. *annual?*
?/1983-1985/ to date?

Whaddon

0792 † **Pearce, G.** *et al*
■ Memories of Whaddon cricket. [The Author?]. 1977. [5]p. frontis.

CAMBRIDGESHIRE C. C. C.

0793 † **Cambridgeshire County Cricket Club**
■ Annual report. Cambridge, the Club.
first ed. 1892 with title 'First annual report, rules and list of subscribers with the officers for 1891 and 1892'. 11p.
1893 with title 'Second annual report and list of subscribers with the officers for 1893' 14p.

0794 † Official handbook. [The Club]. *annual.* illus. scores,
□ stats.
?/1975,1978-81,87,89/

CHESHIRE

0795 † **Cheshire County Cricket League**
□ Handbook. illus. stats.
1975 to date.
edited by Mike Talbot-Butler.
1980-83 entitled Sondico C. C. C. League.
1987-88 entitled Henderson C. C. C. League.
1989 entitled Boddingtons C. C. C. League.

0796 **Cheshire Cricket Association**
[Handbook]. The Association. *annual.*
continues 'Padwick I' 1791 to date.

0797 † **Cheshire Cricket Competition**
[Handbook]. [The League]. *annual.*
/1977 to date/

0798 **Derbyshire & Cheshire Cricket League**
□ [Handbook]. The League. *annual.*
?/1985-87, 1989/

0799 **Lancashire and Cheshire Cricket League**
[Handbook]. [The League]. *annual.*
continues 'Padwick I' 1793 to date.

0800 † **Meller Braggins Cheshire Cricket League**
Handbook. The League. *annual.*
league founded 1974.
/1974 to date/

0801 **North Staffordshire and South Cheshire Cricket League**
Official handbook. [The League]. *annual.*
continues 'Padwick I' 1796 to date.

0802 **South Cheshire Cricket Alliance**
□ [Handbook]. The Alliance. *annual.* scores, stats.
continues 'Padwick I' 1796-1 to date.

Alvanley

0803 **Alvanley Cricket Club**
■ Centenary brochure 1884-1984. [The Club, 1984]. 36p. incl. covers and adverts. illus. scores.

Ashley

0804 **Turton, G. F.**
■ Ashley Cricket Club: a history 1888-1988. [The Club, 1988]. 52p. illus. stats.

Barnton

0805 **Barnton** Cricket Club centenary brochure 1880-1980.
■ [Barnton, the Club, 1980]. 94p. incl. covers and adverts. illus. scores, stats.

Birkenhead

0806 **McInnis, Jean**
Birkenhead Park. 1984. 61p. illus.
includes information on Birkenhead Park C. C. and other cricket clubs which use the Park.

Bramhall

0807 **Bramhall Cricket Club**
■ 100 not out: Bramhall AFC, Bramhall CC centenary year 1986. [The Club, 1986]. 85p. incl. adverts. illus. stats.
cricket pp. 5-41.

0808 Extra cover. The Club. *monthly during season.*
pub. 1981 only?

Cheadle

0809 **Cheadle** Kingsway Sports Club Ltd: Cheadle Cricket Club 1887-1987. 60p. incl. adverts. illus.
some cricket.

Cheadle Hulme

0810 **Cheadle Hulme Cricket Club**
Centenary souvenir 1881-1981. [The Club, 1981]. 96p. incl. adverts. illus.

Cholmondeley

0811 **Cholmondeley Cricket Club**
Centenary week 6-13 July 1986 official programme. [The Club, 1986]. 20p. *typescript.*
includes history of the Club and records 1962-85 compiled by M.J.Boulane.

Crewe

0812 **Crewe** Vagrants 1932-1982 celebration brochure.
■ [Crewe, the Club, 1982]. [24]p. incl. adverts. illus.

Davenham

0813 **Davenham Cricket Club**
■ Centenary brochure 1885 to 1985. [Davenham, the Club, 1985]. [xiv], 50p. incl. adverts. illus.

Flowery Field

0814 **Beard, A. M.**
■ Flowery Field Cricket Club anniversary brochure. [The Club, 1988]. 32p. incl. adverts. illus. score.
150th anniversary, 1838 to 1988.

Lymm

0815 **McIntosh, S. A.,** *editor*
□ Following on ... reminiscences from the history of Lymm Oughtrington Park Cricket Club 1884-1989; statistics compiled by J.H.Pye. [Lymm], Blind Eye Publications, 1989. 36p. illus. stats.
—— *1st ed. pub. 1984.*

Mobberley

0816 † **Mobberley** Cricket Club: 100 years of cricket 1876-1976: souvenir centenary brochure. [The Club, 1976]. 51p. illus.

Sale

0817 **Brooklands** Sports Club centenary 1883-1983. [The Club, 1983]. 40p. incl. adverts. illus.
some cricket.

0818 **Cowan, Gordon**
■ A centennial history of Sale Moor Cricket Club 1887-1987. [Sale, the Club, 1987]. [ii], 42p. illus. maps.

Sandbach

0819 **Sandbach Cricket Club**
Official brochure centenary year 1986. [The Club, 1986]. 76p. incl. adverts. illus. stats.

Stalybridge

0820 † The **Incorporated** Stalybridge Cricket and Athletic Club centenary brochure. [Stalybridge, the Club, 1979]. 40p. incl. adverts. stats.

Stockport

0821 † **Heaton** Mersey Cricket, Tennis & Lacrosse Club centenary 1879-1979. [The Club, 1979]. 36p. illus. stats.

Tattenhall

0822 **Wilson, Dave**
One hundred not out: the story of Tattenhall C. C. - centenary year 1989. [The Club, 1989]. 118p. illus. scores.

Timperley

0823 † **Timperley** Cricket Club, 1877-1977. [Timperley, the Club, 1977].

Toft

0824 **Toft Cricket Club**
■ The road to Lord's. [The Club, 1989]. [8]p. incl. covers, illus. score.
winners of 1989 Hydro Village Championship.

Weaverham

0825 **Livesley, B.** *and* **Goodier, T. R.,** *editors*
■ Weaverham Cricket Club 1883-1983. [Weaverham, the Club, 1983]. 44p. incl. adverts. illus.

CHESHIRE C. C. C.

0826 **Cheshire County Cricket Club**
□ Annual report. The Club. scores, stats.
continues 'Padwick I' 1810 to date.

CORNWALL

Perran-ar-Worthal

0827 **Richards, R. E.,** *compiler*
■ 100 not out: a history of Perran-ar-Worthal Cricket Club. [The Club, 1983]. 75p. illus. stats.
sub-title on cover: '1883-1983'.

CORNWALL C. C. C.

0828 **Cornwall County Cricket Club**
□ Notice of the Annual General Meeting. Truro, the Club. stats.
continues 'Padwick I' 1816 to date.

CUMBERLAND

0829 **Eden** Valley Cricket League: 25 years silver jubilee. [Penrith, the League], 1985. [104]p. incl. adverts. stats.

0830 † **Cumberland Senior Cricket League**
□ [Handbook]. The League. *annual.* stats.
?/1967-69/ to date?

Cleator

0831 The **history** of Cleator Cricket Club. 1987. [ii], 14p.
■

Whitehaven

0832 **Jackson, Herbert** *and* **Jackson, Mary**
■ Whitehaven 158 not out. [Whitehaven, Whitehaven Cricket Club, 1982]. 136p. illus. stats.

CUMBERLAND C. C. C.

0833 **Craven, Nico**
■ One good season deserved another; illustrations by Frank Fisher. [Seascale, the Author], 1987. 100p. illus. scores.
includes Cumberland's winning of Minor Counties Championship in 1986.

0834 **Cumberland County Cricket Club**
■ [Handbook]. [Penrith], the Club. *annual.* illus. scores.
1986 to date.
1986-88 edited by Ted Roberts and John Hurst.
1989 edited by Ted Roberts.

0835 **Hurst, John**
■ Cumberland County Cricket Club: a history; with statistics by Keith Barnett. Penrith, the Club, 1982. [iv], 118p. illus. stats.

DERBYSHIRE

0836 Derbyshire & Cheshire Cricket League
□ [Handbook]. The League. *annual.*
?/1985-87, 1989/

0837 Derbyshire County Cricket League
□ [Handbook]. The League. *annual.*
league founded 1981 as successor to Nottinghamshire and Derbyshire Border Cricket League.
1981/1985,86/ to date?

0838 Fox, S. B., *compiler*
■ A pot-pourri of sport in North East Derbyshire 1834-1981. Bolsover, the Author, 1982? 52p. illus.
mainly cricket and soccer.

0839 Nottinghamshire and Derbyshire Border Cricket League
[Handbook]. [The League]. *annual.*
continues 'Padwick I' 1823 to 1980.
League re-formed in 1981 as Derbyshire County Cricket League.

Alfreton

0840 Alfreton Miners Welfare v Derbyshire. 1985.
match played for Geoff Miller testimonial; includes information on cricket in Alfreton.

Chesterfield

0841 Chesterfield and District cricket touring team,
■ Barbados, 20th October - 5th November 1988.
[Chesterfield, 1988]. 24p. illus.
pre-tour.

Derby

0842 † Henderson, Harry G. M.
■ The Midland Cricket Club: a Derby cricket ditty.
Elvaston (Derbys.), the Author, 1899. [4]p.
song dedicated to Hadyn A. Morley and the members of the Derby Midland C. C.

Grassmoor

0843 Grassmoor Cricket Club 1884-1984: centenary souvenir
■ brochure. [The Club, 1984]. 52p. incl. adverts. illus.
scores, stats.

Spondon

0844 Spondon Cricket Club centenary 1883-1983. [Spondon,
■ the Club, 1983]. 80p. illus.

DERBYSHIRE C. C. C.

0845 Barrett, Idris
■ Derbyshire's England cricketers. [Burton-on-Trent, the Author], 1983. [i], 58p. map. stats. index. *typescript*

0846 Derbyshire County Cricket Club
□ Annual report and statement of accounts ... Derby, the Club.
?/1986/ to date.

0847 † Derbyshire '79. [Derby, the Club], 1979. 24p. illus.
stats.
issue no. 1, Summer 1979. only issue published.

0848 Derbyshire County Cricket Club 1989 benefit book.
■ [Derby, the Club], 1989 40p. illus.

0849 Derbyshire County Cricket Club news. [Derby, the Club]. 12p. illus. stats.
April 1980 only issue.

0850 Derbyshire cricketer. [Derby, the Club], *irregular during season.* illus. stats.
seven issues pub. between April 1984 and July 1985.

0851 Refuge Assurance League programme and scorecard.
■ Derby, the Club. *for each home match.* illus. scores.
pub. in 1987 and 1988.

0852 Year book. [Derby], the Club. illus. scores, stats.
■ *1980-82 edited and compiled by F. G. Peach and A. F. Dawn.*
1983 to date edited by S. W. Tacey.
continues 'Padwick I' 1846 to date.

0853 † [Derbyshire County Cricket Club]
Souvenir. [The Club, 1920?]. 32p. incl. adverts. illus.

0854 Peach, Frank G. *and* **Bailey, Philip Jonathan,** *compilers*
■ Derbyshire cricketers 1871-1981. Haughton Mill (Notts.), Association of Cricket Statisticians, [1982]. 38p. map. stats.

0855 Rippon, Anton *and* **Grainger, John**
■ Derbyshire County Cricket Club: a pictorial history. Derby, Breedon Books, 1982. 46p. incl. covers, illus. scores.

0856 Shawcroft, John
■ Derbyshire bowlers: a cricket history of Derbyshire bowlers (Derbyshire Heritage series). Derby, J. H. Hall & Sons, 1986. 57p. illus. bibliog.

0857 The official history of Derbyshire County Cricket Club;
■ with a personal view by Bob Taylor. Bromley, Christopher Helm, 1989. viii, 327p. illus. stats. scores. bibliog. index.
——*autographed ed., 1989, limited to 200 numbered copies in slip case and signed by all the living Derbyshire captains.*

DEVON

0858 Devon Cricket Association
■ Newsletter. The Association. *eleven issues per year.*
typescript.
continues 'Padwick I' 1855-2 to date.

0859 Rules. The Association, n.d. 2p. *typescript.*
■

Barnstaple

0860 † Rules of the North Devon Cricket Club. Barnstaple, the Club, 1849. *bs.*
pub. 26 April 1849.

Hatherleigh

0861 Hatherleigh Cricket Club
■ Centenary 1888-1988. [Hatherleigh, the Club, 1988]. 19p. illus. facsims. scores.

Lustleigh

0862 Lustleigh Cricket Club
■ A glorious half century. [The Club, 1988]. 28p. incl. adverts. stats.
cover sub-title: '50th anniversary programme'.

Sidmouth

0863 **Haffenden Ian**
■ Cricket menopause: a diary. Sidmouth, Haf
Publications, 1989. x, 89p. illus.
a season's reminiscences by Sidmouth C.C. groundsman.

Torquay

0864 **Carne, Aubrey**
■ Brockman Cricket Cup Competition: golden jubilee
souvenir brochure 1933-1982 inclusive. [Torquay, the
Competition, 1982]. [16]p. incl. adverts. illus.

DEVON C. C. C.

0865 **Devon County Cricket Club**
□ Year book. [Exeter, the Club]. illus. scores, stats.
continues 'Padwick I' 1866 to date.

DORSET

0866 **Save & Prosper Southern Cricket League**
□ Year book. The League. illus. stats.
*to 1984 was entitled 'Town and Country Southern Cricket
League year book'.*
continues 'Padwick I' 1866-2 to date.

Broadstone

0867 **Richards, Jerry**
■ 100 years of Broadstone cricket (1888-1988). The Club,
[1988]. [80]p. illus.

Dorchester

0868 **Dorchester and District Evening Cricket League**
■ Takin' fresh guard: the golden anniversary of Dorchester
and District Evening Cricket League. Dorchester, the
League, 1983. [52]p. illus.
*special ed. of annual handbook compiled by D. Read;
other eds. not seen.*

Weymouth

0869 † **Weymouth Cricket Club**
■ Report. 1894. [4]p. stats.
statistical report for 1894 season; other years pub?

DORSET C. C. C.

0870 **Dorset County Cricket Club [and] Dorset Cricket**
□ **Association**
Yearbook. The Club and the Association. illus. scores,
stats.
continues 'Padwick I' 1871 to date.

DURHAM

0871 † **Cleveland and Teesside Cricket League**
□ Handbook. The League, *annual*.
*1985 pub. as special centenary ed. with title '100 not out:
the history of the Cleveland & Teesside Cricket League
1885-1985' [compiled by Frank Jewitt and Steve Oakey].
?/1979-83, 85/ to date?*

0872 † **Durham County Cricket Association**
Newsletter. [The Association]. *annual*.
1975 to date.

0873 † **Durham County Cricket League**
□ Fixtures. The League. *annual*.
*1948/1986 to date/.
1985 to date with title Whitbread Durham County
Cricket League.*

0874 **Durham Senior Cricket League**
□ Rules and fixtures handbook. stats.
*1986 TNT Durham Senior Cricket League.
1987 Greenalls Brewery Durham Senior Cricket League.
1988 to date, Vaux Durham Senior Cricket League.
continues 'Padwick I' 1875 to date.*

0875 **Girobank North Yorkshire and South Durham Cricket**
□ **League**
[Handbook]. The League, *annual*. stats.
*continues 'Padwick I' 1880 to date.
sponsored by Girobank since 1986.*

0876 † **[Trenholm, Herbert,** *compiler***]**
■ North Yorkshire and South Durham Cricket League
statistics 1956-68. The League, c.1969. 104p. stats.
supplement to 'Padwick I' 1881.

0877 **Tyneside Senior Cricket League**
[Handbook]. Newcastle, the League. *annual*.
*also includes team from Northumberland.
continues 'Padwick I' 2470 to date.*

0878 † **Vaux Durham Coast Cricket League**
Handbook. [The League]. *annual*.
*League formed 1925.
1979? to date.*

Billingham

0879 **[Baker, Ray],** *compiler*
■ Billingham Synthonia Cricket Club. The Club, 1987.
48p. stats.
includes concise history of the Club.

Darlington

0880 † **Darlington & District Cricket League**
Rules & fixtures. [The League]. *annual*
*league founded in 1961;
?/1978-1983/ to date?*

Durham

0881 † **Durham** City Cricket Club 150 years, 1829-1979:
■ souvenir brochure. [The Club, 1979]. [28]p. incl.
adverts. illus. scores, stats.

Lintz

0882 † **All** England law reports 1977, vol. 3. Butterworths, 1977.
■ *pp. 339-351 contain Court of Appeal judgement in the
case of Miller v Jackson concerning the injunction
granted to Mr and Mrs Miller, who lived next door to the
Lintz Club ground, preventing the Club from using their
ground. The injunction was suspended for one year to
enable the defendants to find another ground.*

South Shields

0883 **Crickmer, Clive**
■ Grass roots: a history of South Shields Cricket Club
1850-1984; drawings by Ron Emmerson. [South Shields,
the Club, 1985]. 359p. illus. scores, stats. bibliog.

Swalwell

0884 **Wilkinson, Jack** *and* **Lumley, Clive**
■ Swalwell C. C.: centenary brochure 1880-1980. [The
Club], 1980. 48p. incl. adverts. illus. stats.

DURHAM C. C. C.

0885 **Durham County Cricket Club**
☐ Annual report. Durham, the Club. scores, stats.
continues 'Padwick I' 1891 to date.

0886 **Hunt, Brian**
■ 100 years of Durham County Cricket Club.
Chester-le-Street, Casdec, 1983. xii, 186p. incl. adverts.
illus. scores, stats.
——*supplement*, 1986.

ESSEX

0887 **Anglo Two Counties Cricket Championship**
■ Official handbook. The Championship. *annual*. stats.
founded 1971; also includes teams from Suffolk.
1987 with title 'Bulldog Two Counties Cricket
Championship'.
1987 to date.

0888 **Chargecrest Security Invitation League**
☐ [Handbook]. [Romford], the League, *annual*. illus.
stats.
formed 1985.
/1987,89/

0889 † **Essex Cricket Association**
☐ Annual report. The Association.
1969/1987 to date/

0890 Directory and handbook 1982. [The Association, 1981].
■ 19p.
information about all levels of cricket in Essex.

0891 **Morrant Essex Cricket League**
■ Official handbook. The League. *annual*. stats.
1986 to date.

0892 **Paladin Plastics Essex League**
☐ Official handbook. The League. *annual*. illus. scores,
stats.
formerly known as Truman Essex League.
continues 'Padwick I' 1892-2 to date.

0893 † *Walthamstow, Leyton, Chingford & Woodford Guardian*
■ cricket annual 1948; edited by C. E. Waller. 88p. illus.
stats.
Essex county and club cricket, 1947.
the only issue?

Abridge

0894 **Ferguson, Derrick** *and* **Lister, Alan**
■ Abridge Cricket Club: a celebration of 150 seasons.
Abridge, the Club, 1987. 110p. illus. (one col.)
facsims. map, stats.

Brentwood

0895 **[Adams, Paul,** *editor***]**
■ Brentwood Cricket Club 1881-1981. [The Club, 1981].
36p. incl. adverts. illus. stats.

Chelmsford

0896 † **Chelmsford Cricket Club**
■ Rules and regulations of the Chelmsford Cricket Club.
Chelmsford, printed by Meggy and Chalk, 1825. 8p.
Club established 30 April 1825.

Chingford

0897 **[Blake, Michael,** *editor***]**
■ Chingford Cricket Club centenary 1884-1984. [The Club,
1984]. [88]p. incl. adverts. illus. facsims. scores.

0898 **Chinghoppers** Cricket Club 1932-1982. [The Club,
■ 1981]. 40p. scores, stats.

Clacton

0899 **Clacton** cricket centenary 1982. Clacton Cricket Club,
■ 1982. 28p. illus. scores, map.

Copford

0900 **Copford** Cricket Club v Samuel Whitbread's Old
■ England ... July 10th 1988. The Club, 1988. 24p. incl.
covers and adverts. illus.
includes a brief history of the Club.

Galleywood

0901 **Galleywood** Cricket Club 1931-1981. [The Club], 1981.
■ iv, 52p. illus. stats.

Halstead

0902 **Halstead** Cricket Club 1885-1985. [Halstead, the Club,
■ 1985]. 87p. illus. scores, stats.

Hornchurch

0903 **Hornchurch** Cricket Club 1783-1983. [Hornchurch, the
■ Club], 1983. 36p. incl. adverts. illus.

Ilford

0904 † **Ilford and District Cricket Association**
■ Brochure. [Ilford], the Association, 1979. maps, stats.
Association formed 1964; brochure produced for 15th
anniversary.

0905 † Newsletter. [Ilford, the Association.]
1977 - ?

Langley

0906 **Smith, Clive,** *editor*
■ Langley Cricket Club: to mark the centenary 1885-1985.
[The Club], 1985. 40p. incl. adverts. illus. score.

Leigh-on-Sea

0907 † **Leigh-on-Sea Cricket Club**
☐ Annual report. The Club. stats. *typescript*.
?/1973-76/ to date?

Loughton

0908 **Shields, Andrew**
■ South Loughton Cricket Club: 50 years, 1938-1988. [The
Club, 1988]. [88]p. incl. adverts. illus. stats.

South Woodford

0909 **Hubbard, W. J. A.,** *compiler*
South Woodford Cricket Club: results and averages.
Leytonstone, the Author. *annual*. stats.
continues 'Padwick I' 1914-3 to date?

Stanford-le-Hope

0910 The **maiden** century: a celebration of Stanford cricket
■ and cricketers. [Stanford-le-Hope, the Club, 1987].
[50]p. incl. covers, illus. scores, stats.
centenary year 1887-1987.

Stebbing

0911 **Holles, Robert**
■ The guide to real village cricket; illustrated by Roy Raymonde. Harrap, 1983. 96p. illus.
——*pbk. ed.* Unwin, 1984.
includes memories of Stebbing CC.

Wickford

0912 **Crook, Lester**
■ The first hundred years: Wickford Cricket Club 1887-1987. Crook Academic Publishing with Wickford Cricket Club, 1987. 79p. illus.

ESSEX C. C. C.

0913 **Edwards, Peter**
■ Champions! A pictorial souvenir of Essex County Cricket Club's triumphant 1983 season. Chelmsford, the Club, [1984]. 61p. incl. covers. illus. diagr.

0914 **Essex** County Cricket Benefit Association 1987. [Benefit
■ Committee, 1987]. 80p. incl. adverts. illus. (some col.)

0915 **Essex** County Cricket Benefit Association 1988. [Benefit
■ Committee, 1988]. 64p. incl. adverts. illus. (some col.)

0916 † **Essex County Cricket Club**
□ Annual report and statement of accounts. Chelmsford, the Club.
?/1972-89/

0917 Handbook. [Chelmsford, the Club]. *annual.* illus.
■ scores, stats.
edited by Peter Edwards.
1989 entitled 'Yearbook'.
continues 'Padwick I' 1926 to date.

0918 † Leyton cricket festival 1969 ... souvenir programme. A.
■ E. Sedgwick, 1969. 24p. incl. adverts.
v Northants, Aug 2nd, 4th and 5th.
v Warwicks, Aug 6th, 7th and 8th.
v Surrey, Aug 9th, 11th and 12th.

0919 † List of members 1925. Leyton, the Club. 108p.
■ *another ed. of 'Padwick I' 1924.*

0920 † Westcliff-on-Sea cricket festival. Southend, Southend
■ News and Press Agency. *annual.*
1969: July 9, 10 & 11 v Middlesex; July 12, 13 & 14 v New Zealand. 27p. incl. adverts.
earlier ed. of 'Padwick I' 1929.

0921 **Lemmon, David Hector**
■ Summer of success: the triumph of Essex County Cricket Club in 1979. Pelham Books, 1980. 206p. illus. scores, stats. index.

0922 **Lemmon, David Hector** and **Marshall, Mike**
■ Essex County Cricket Club: the official history. Kingswood Press, 1987. xviii, 452p. illus. stats. bibliog. index.

0923 **Montgomery, Kevin**
■ Essex in the Benson and Hedges Cup. The Author, 1980. 68p. scores, stats.
detailed scoresheets of 1979 season and statistics for 1972-79.

0924 **Newnham, Leslie,** *compiler*
■ Essex cricketers 1876-1986. Haughton Mill (Notts.), Association of Cricket Statisticians, 1987. 36p. map. stats.

GLOUCESTERSHIRE

0925 **Avon** summer sports. Bristol, Sportsline Magazines, 1985. 16p.
issue no. 12, 26 July 1985, devoted entirely to cricket.

0926 † **Famous Grouse Western Cricket League**
□ Handbook. The League. *annual.* stats.
founded 1971 as Western Cricket League; also includes teams from Wales, Somerset and Wiltshire.
1972?/1983/ to date?

0927 **Gloucestershire Cricket Association**
□ Official handbook. The Association, *annual.* stats.
club and school cricket in Gloucestershire.
?/1982 to date/

Adlestrop

0928 **International** cricket at Adlestrop Park: Adlestrop v
■ Malaysia on Sunday, June 15th, 1986 ... [The Club], 1986. [12]p. incl. adverts. illus.
includes short history of the Club.

Bristol

0929 **Bristol and District Cricket Association** and **Bristol and District Cricket Umpires' Association**
Official handbook. Bristol, the Association. *annual.* stats.
sponsored successively by Halls, Bowdens and Sun Life.
continues 'Padwick I' 1939 to date.

0930 **Burrell, Jack F.,** *editor*
■ Sides & squares: Clifton Cricket Club 1819-1983. Henbury (Bristol), the Club, 1983. 83p. illus.

0931 **Clarke, Andy,** *editor*
■ Patchway Cricket Club 1913-1988: 75th jubilee handbook. [The Club], 1988. xv, 45p. illus. stats.

Cheltenham

0932 † **Snell, J.**
St Stephen's Cricket Club Cheltenham, 1884-1974: a history. Cheltenham, [the Club], 1975.

Chipping Sodbury

0933 **Edmonds, Tom** *et al, editors*
■ Chipping Sodbury Cricket Club 1860-1985: 125th anniversary handbook. [Chipping Sodbury, the Club, 1985]. 56p. incl. adverts. illus.

Coln Valley

0934 **Field, Dick**
■ Up and down the valley: growing up in the Cotswolds in the 1920's. Cirencester, Gryffon Publications, 1985. 112p. illus.
includes memories of Coln Valley Cricket Club pp. 79-82.

Dumbleton

0935 **Craven, Nico**
■ Dumbleton day: 'an August occasion'. [Seascale], the Author, 1988. 12p. score.
description of Dumbleton v Eton Ramblers, 9 August 1987.

0936 **Dumbleton** Cricket Club centenary year book 1985.
■ [The Club, 1985]. 48p. illus. facsims, scores.

Fairford

0937 The **story** of 100 years of cricket at Fairford. [Fairford, the Club], 1989. [48]p. incl. adverts. illus.

Hatherley

0938 A **history** of the Hatherley & Reddings Cricket Club. [The Club], 1986. xii, 117p. incl. adverts. illus. scores, stats.
limited ed. of 300 numbered copies.

Newnham

0939 † **Lucas, Don**
Cricket in Newnham. The Author, 1976. 10p. illus.

Pilning

0940 **Pilning** Cricket Club 100 years history 1883-1983. [Pilning, the Club, 1983]. [7]p. incl. covers.

Shirehampton

0941 **Shirehampton** Cricket Club 1858-1983: 125th anniversary. [Shirehampton, the Club, 1983]. 32p. illus. map, stats.

Thornbury

0942 **Thornbury Cricket Club (Bristol)**
Handbook. [Thornbury, the Club]. *annual.*
1988 to date.

GLOUCESTERSHIRE C. C. C.

0943 **Ball, Keith** *et al*
1889 when play began at Ashley Down: official souvenir. Bristol, Gloucestershire County Cricket Club, 1989. 18p. incl inside covers, illus. facsims. scores, stats.

0944 **Coley, Chris,** *editor*
Gloucestershire County Cricket Club 1980. [The Club], 1980. [28]p. incl. adverts. illus. stats.

0945 **Craven, Nico**
A friend of the family; with illustrations by Frank Fisher. [Seascale, the Author], 1980. 131p. illus. scores.
Gloucestershire in 1979 season.

0946 One good season deserved another; illustrations by Frank Fisher. [Seascale, the Author], 1987. 100p. illus. scores.
Gloucestershire in 1985 and 1986 seasons.

0947 Playing a supporting role; with illustrations by Frank Fisher. [Seascale, the Author], 1981. 156p. illus. scores.
Gloucestershire memories, including 1980 season.

0948 Summer and sunshine; illustrations by Frank Fisher. [Seascale, the Author], 1985. 86p. illus. scores.
includes Cheltenham festivals, 1982 and 1983.

0949 Tea for twenty two. [Seascale, the Author], 1983. 131p. frontis. scores.
Gloucestershire in 1981 season.

0950 Waiting for Cheltenham; illustrations by Frank Fisher. [Seascale, the Author], 1989. 58p. illus. scores.
the Cheltenham festival, 1988.

0951 **Foot, David**
From Grace to Botham: profiles of 100 West Country cricketers. Bristol, Redcliffe Press, 1980. 123p. illus.

0952 **Gloucestershire County Cricket Club**
Bristol cricket festival. Bristol, the Club. *annual.* illus.
1987 festival sponsored by Halls.
?/1985-87/ to date?

0953 Cheltenham festival 1988 official souvenir programme. [Bristol, the Club], 1988. 28p. incl. covers and adverts. illus.
pre-festival; other years pub.?

0954 On the wicket. [Bristol, the Club]. *annual?* illus. stats.
?/1982, 1985/ to date?

0955 Year book. [Bristol], the Club. illus. scores. stats.
continues 'Padwick I' 1964 to date.

0956 **Gloucestershire Exiles**
Outside-edge: the newsletter of Gloucestershire Exiles. *irregular.* stats.
organisation to support and promote the interests of Gloucestershire C.C.C.; founded 1971.
Autumn 1988 was issue no. 44.

0957 **Parker, Grahame Wilshaw**
Gloucestershire road: a history of Gloucestershire County Cricket Club. Pelham in association with National Westminster Bank, 1983. 256p. illus. scores, stats. index.

HAMPSHIRE

0958 **Hampshire Cricket League**
Handbook. The League. *annual.* illus. stats.
continues 'Padwick I' 1975 to date.

0959 **Save & Prosper Southern Cricket League**
Year book. The League. illus. stats.
to 1984 was entitled 'Town and Country Southern Cricket League year book'.
continues 'Padwick I' 1980-2 to date.

0960 † *Southern Evening Echo* **League**
Playing conditions. The League, [1969]. [2]p. *typescript.*

Bournemouth

0961 **Bournemouth** and South Hampshire Cricket Club tour of Canada & Nevada, September / October 1989: souvenir brochure. [The Club, 1989]. 36p. incl. adverts. illus.
pre-tour.

Cadnam

0962 **Biddlecombe, R. W.,** *editor*
Cadnam Cricket Club 1880 1980. [The Club, 1980]. [ii], 51p. incl. adverts. illus. scores, stats.

Christchurch

0963 **Kelly, Tom**
The cricket clubs of Christchurch: a history. [Christchurch, the Club, 1988]. [163]p. incl. adverts. illus. scores.

Eversley

0964 **Renshaw, Andrew James**
Cricket on the green: celebrating 200 years of cricket at Eversley, Hampshire. [The Club], 1987. 48p. incl. adverts. illus.

Gosport

0965   **Brown, Ron**
This sporting life: a light-hearted reminder of Gosport's sporting past. Horndean, Milestone Publications, 1984. 74p. illus.
contains chapter 'Knocking the ball around' about Gosport cricket.

Hambledon

0966 †   **British Broadcasting Corporation**
■   'Bat and Ball'; TV broadcast, 26 August 1954. v.p.
typescript.
rehearsal transcripts including directions for re-enactment of Hambledon v All England.

0967 †   **Hambledon** v All England 1908: illustrated souvenir of the cradle of cricket. 1908. 12p. illus.

0968   **Knight, Ronald D.**
■   Hambledon's cricket glory. Weymouth, the Author, Bat & Ball Press. illus. facsims. diagrs. scores, bibliog.
typescript.
vol. 7. 1772. 1981. 50p.
vol. 8. 1773-1774. 1982. 80p.
vol. 9. 1775-1776. 1982. 66p.
vol. 10. 1777-1778. 1983. 72p.
vol. 11. 1779-1780. 1984. 72p.
continues 'Padwick I' 1997-1.

0969   **Millson, Cecilia**
■   Tales of old Hampshire. Newbury, Countryside Books, 1980. 96p. illus.
'Cricket at Hambledon' pp. 14-16.

Hursley

0970   **200** years of cricket in Hursley: bi-centenary booklet
■   1785-1985. [Winchester, Hursley Park Cricket Club], 1985. [53]p. incl. adverts. illus. scores.

Lymington

0971   **Gannaway, Norman Major**
The Barfield: one hundred and fifty years of cricket at Lymington Sports Ground 1836-1986. Highcliffe (Dorset), Eon Graphics, 1986. 92p. illus.

0972   The history of Lymington Cricket Club 1807-1982.
■   Highcliffe (Dorset), Eon Graphics, [1982]. 219p. illus. scores, stats.

New Forest

0973   **New Forest Club Cricket Association**
□   Handbook. The Association. *annual.* illus. scores, stats.
continues 'Padwick I' 2013 to date?
latterly sponsored by Wadham Stringer.

Southampton

0974 †   **Southampton Public Grounds Cricket Association**
□   Rules. Southampton, the Association. *annual.*
?/1969/?

Warnford

0975   **Bazalgette, Christopher**
■   Hampshire Hogs C. C.: a centenary history 1887-1987. Warnford, the Club, 1987. 64p. illus. scores, stats. index.
Club has played on a number of grounds in Hampshire - now based at Warnford.

HAMPSHIRE: ISLE OF WIGHT

0976   **Isle** of Wight County Cricket Association handbook.
□   The Association. *annual.* illus. stats.
1982 to date.

HAMPSHIRE C. C. C.

0977   **Cricket.** Southampton, *Southern Evening Echo. annual.* col. illus. stats.
pre-season brochure.
?/1987 to date/

0978   **Cricket** grounds of Hampshire. West Bridgford
■   (Notts.), Association of Cricket Statisticians, 1988. 28p. illus. stats.

0979   **Edwards, Alan**
■   Milestones of Hampshire cricket. Chandler's Ford, Hampshire Cricket Society, 1983. 19p.

0980   **Hampshire County Cricket Club**
■   Handbook. Southampton, the Club. *annual.* illus. scores, stats.
to 1986 entitled 'Illustrated handbook'.
1980-85 edited by Peter Marshall.
1986 to date edited by Tony Mitchener.
continues 'Padwick I' 2027 to date.

0981   Report and accounts ... Southampton, the Club. *annual.*
□   *?/1986/ to date?*

0982   **Hampshire Exiles**
Newsletter. *4 issues per year.*
? to date.

0983   **Isaacs, Victor H,** *compiler*
■   Hampshire County Cricket Club: first-class records 1864-1986. Southampton, the Author, 1987. 72p. stats.
cover title; limited ed. of 20 copies.

0984   **Isaacs, Victor H** *and* **Thorn, Philip R.,** *compilers*
■   Hampshire cricketers 1800-1982. Haughton Mill (Notts.), Association of Cricket Statisticians, [1983]. 46p. map, stats.

0985   **Nicholas, Mark Charles Jefford,** *[editor]*
■   Hampshire County Cricket Club: 100 years at Southampton. Basingstoke, J. B. Shears & Sons, 1985. 76p. incl. adverts. illus. (some col.)
pub. with a cassette of John Arlott recalling his favourite tales from the past 100 years.

0986   **Wynne-Thomas, Peter**
■   The history of the Hampshire County Cricket Club; with a personal view by John Arlott; statistics by Victor Isaacs. Bromley, Christopher Helm, 1988. 275p. illus. stats. bibliog. index.

HEREFORDSHIRE

Canon Frome

0987   **50** golden years of Canon Frome Cricket Club,
■   1938-1988. [The Club], 1988. 72p. incl. adverts. illus.
limited ed. of 500 signed and numbered copies.

Ledbury

0988   **Cartwright, Peter**
■   Ledbury 150: the story of cricket in a famous market town since 1837. Ledbury, the Author for Ledbury Cricket Club, [1987]. [x], 103p. illus.

HERTFORDSHIRE

0989 † **Bryan Hertfordshire Cricket League**
☐ Handbook. The League. *annual.* illus. scores, stats.
founded 1973; previously sponsored by Truman.
/1974,78,82-83,85-87/ to date.

0990 **Hertfordshire County Cricket Association**
☐ Official handbook. The Association. *annual.* illus.
scores, stats.
county, youth, school and club cricket.
?/1982 to date/

0991 Presentation on the activities of Hertfordshire County
■ Cricket Association. The Association, [1987]. 12 leaves.
for potential sponsors and advertisers.

0992 **Hertfordshire Cricket Competition**
☐ Official handbook. The Competition. *annual.* stats.
*sponsors of the Competition have included Selectaglaze
and Laing Homes.*
continues 'Padwick I' 2037 to date.

Haileybury

0993 † **Haileybury Cricket Club**
Matches played by the Haileybury Cricket Club 1840-51.
Hertford, 1852. 82p.
mentioned in 'Allen EBC'.

Hertford

0994 † **Catt, Frederick Charles**
■ Report on the first hundred years of the Bengeo
Working Men's Club 1878-1978. [1978]. [48]p. illus.
some cricket.

0995 **Fairhall, Alan G.,** *compiler*
■ Bayford and Hertford Nondescripts Cricket Club 1988
end of season reports. [The Author, 1988]. [185]p.
stats.
*comprehensive statistical report for all teams in the Club
for 1988 season, and individual career records.*

0996 **Hertford Cricket Club**
■ One hundred years of cricket at Balls Park. [Hertford,
the Club, 1983]. 38p. incl. adverts. illus.

Kings Langley

0997 **Kings Langley Cricket Club**
■ 1983 handbook. The Club, 1983. 28p. incl. adverts.
illus.
*includes brief history of the Club by C.E.Holroyd.
not pub. in other years.*

North Mymms

0998 **North Mymms Cricket Club**
■ New pavilion appeal programme. 1985? [24]p. incl.
covers and adverts. illus.
*featuring Greene King six-a-side tournament, 3rd-7th
August.*

Northchurch

0999 **Northchurch Cricket Club**
■ 1885-1985: one hundred not out. [Northchurch, the
Club, 1985]. [38]p. incl. covers and adverts. illus. stats.

Preston

1000 **Smith, Tony**
■ Preston Cricket Club 1882-1982: a review of the first 100
years. [Preston, the Club, 1982]. [36]p. incl. adverts.
illus.

Radlett

1001 **Doughty, Richard,** *editor*
■ Radlett Cricket Club centenary year 1884-1984. [The
Club, 1984]. 64p. incl. adverts. illus. stats.

Rickmansworth

1002 **Rickmansworth** Cricket Club bi-centennial 1787-1987.
■ [Rickmansworth, the Club, 1987]. [48]p. incl. covers
and adverts. illus. scores.

Stanstead Abbots

1003 **[Edge, R. W. O.]**
■ St Margaretsbury Cricket Club: 250th anniversary,
1737-1987. The Club, 1987. 20p. incl. adverts. illus.
formerly Stanstead Abbots C. C.

Tring

1004 **Kempster, David J.**
■ Tring Park Cricket Club sesquicentennial 1836-1986.
[Tring, the Club, 1986]. 56p. illus. scores.

Watford

1005 **West Herts Cricket Club**
☐ Handbook. [Watford, the Club]. *annual.* stats.
typescript.
?/1983/ to date.

HUNTINGDONSHIRE

Huntingdon

1006 **Swift, E. M.**
Huntingdon Cricket Club: 1880-1980 centenary. St Ives,
Cambridgeshire Life, 1980. 32p.

KENT

1007 **Association of Kent Cricket Clubs**
☐ Cricket in Kent: the official handbook of the Association
of Kent Cricket Clubs. The Association. *annual.* illus.
scores, stats.
continues 'Padwick I' 2058 to date.

1008 **Colmore Kent Metropolitan Cricket League**
☐ Official handbook. The League. *annual.* scores, stats.
continues 'Padwick I' 2069 to date?

1009 † **[Duncombe, John]**
■ Surry triumphant or the Kentish-mens defeat: a new
ballad being a parody on Chevy-Chace. Bourne (Kent),
Bourne End Paddock Cricket Club, 1937. 16p. incl.
covers.
*Surrey v Kent, July 1773; reprint of the parody contained
in 'Padwick I' 2064, excluding the score.*

1010 **Mid Kent Cricket League**
☐ Official handbook. The League. *annual.* illus. stats.
League formed c. 1974.
/[1980], 86, 88/ to date.

1011 † **Morrant North Kent Cricket League**
■ Constitution. The League. 1977. 2p. *typescript.*
——*another ed.* 1985.
known as North Kent Cricket League to 1982.

1012 Facts and figures. The League. *annual.* stats.
■ */1982-84/*

1013 Official handbook. The League. *annual.*
■ *1988* to date.
includes playing conditions which were previously pub. separately.

1014 **Myers, Colin D.,** *editor*
■ The Kent Cricket League 1971-1982. [The League, 1982]. 72p. illus. stats.

1015 **Prudential East Kent League**
■ Handbook. The League. *annual.* stats.
League matches started in 1976; formerly known as Anglia East Kent League.
1988 to date.

1016 **South Thames Cricket League**
□ Yearbook. Pett's Wood, D. H. Roberts for the League. illus. scores, stats.
continues 'Padwick I' 2071 to date.

1017 † **University of Kent.** *Faculty of Social Sciences*
Leisure pursuits in Kent 1850-1914. Canterbury, the University, 1973.
group research project as part of a course on economic and social history of Kent; much cricket.

1018 **Woolwich Kent Cricket League**
□ Handbook. The League. *annual.* illus. stats.
formerly Kent Cricket League, now sponsored by Woolwich Equitable Building Society.
1984 with title 'Courage Kent Cricket League Handbook'.
1983/1984,1988/ to date; *not pub. 1985-87.*

Beckenham

1019 † **Beckenham Cricket Club**
□ [Handbook]. [Beckenham, the Club], *annual.* scores, stats.
review of previous season; contains rules, a list of members, fixtures and balance sheet.
?/1911, 1914/?

1020 **Christ** Church Institute Cricket Club Beckenham
■ centenary 1887-1987. [Beckenham, the Club, 1987]. [ii], 78p. illus. stats.

Bekesbourne

1021 † **Bekesbourne** Sports Club cricket annual 1972. [The
■ Club, 1972]. 24p. incl. covers, scores, stats.
post season; the only ed.?

Benenden

1022 A **cricket** match: Benenden v A.G.E. Ealham and D.L. Underwood. Benenden Cricket Club, 1984.
fund raising double wicket contest; includes notes on the Club and description of two earlier local double wicket contests in 1884 and 1936.

Blackheath

1023 † **Blackheath Cricket Club**
■ Rules and regulations of the Blackheath Cricket Club established 1839. Greenwich, printed by H. S. Richardson, [1839]. 1p.

Brenchley

1024 **Siegfried** Sassoon 1886-1967: a centenary celebration. Lewes, Beacon Press, [1986]. 22p. illus.
includes article on Brenchley C. C. by J. Young.

Bromley

1025 **Cannon, N. S.** *and* **Clarke, D. L.,** *editors*
■ Bromley Town & Old Bromleians Cricket Club 1885-1985. [Bromley, the Club], 1985. 36p. incl. adverts. illus. facsims.

1026 **Eames, Geoffrey Leonard**
Early Bromley cricket until 1847. [1980]. 82p. *typescript. copy in Bromley Library.*

Canterbury

1027 † **St.** Lawrence Cricket Club 1897. [The Club, 1897]. 8p.
■ incl. covers. stats.
statisticial record of 1897 season; other years pub?

Chislehurst

1028 **Chislehurst & West Kent C. C.**
■ 250 years of cricket at the Chislehurst Cricket Ground on the common: cricket week, July 4th-10th 1988. [The Club], 1988. [18]p. incl. adverts.
includes a brief history of the Club.

Dartford

1029 † **Dartford** Club and Ground. Dartford, the Club, 1907.
■ [4]p. illus.
appeal brochure for Hesketh Park; Club later became Dartford Cricket Club.

Dover

1030 † **Blanche, Robin**
M.C.C.: a survey of Maxton Cricket Club during the period 1964-74. Dover, the Author, 1975.

Folkestone

1031 **Hewson, William J.**
■ Folkestone Cricket Club 125th anniversary. Folkestone, the Club, 1981. [20]p. incl. covers, stats.

Gravesend

1032 † **Gravesend Cricket Club**
Gravesend Cricket Club - a brief history. [Gravesend, the Club, 1968].

Harvel

1033 † **Harvel** Cricket Club 1872-1972. Harvel, the Club,
■ [1972]. 40p. incl. adverts. illus.

Leigh

1034 † **Watson, T.**
The history of Leigh cricket to 1837. n.d. 32p. *typescript. copy in Maidstone Library.*

Linton

1035 **Linton** Park C. C. Linton, the Club, [1983]. 3p.
■ *formerly known as Coxheath Cricket Club.*

Locksbottom

1036 **Tolman, Roger C.**
A history of Locksbottom Cricket Club, together with facts and figures relating to the Club researched and compiled by Ian Lawless. [Locksbottom, the Club, 1980]. [iv], 101p. illus. stats.
cover title: 'The history of Locksbottom Cricket Club 1947-1980'.

Margate

1037 † **Margate Cricket Club**
Rules and regulations. Margate, the Club, 1864.
copy in Margate Library.

Meopham

1038 **Gunyon, William**
The Cricketers' Inn at Meopham: a celebration of the 250-year partnership between Meopham cricketers and their pub. [Meopham, Meopham Cricket Club, 1985]. 32p. illus. (some col.)

Rodmersham

1039 **Adams, John,** *compiler*
The history of Rodmersham Cricket Club 1885-1985. [The Club], 1985. vi, 56p. illus. facsims.

Sevenoaks

1040 **Hollamby, Guy,** *editor*
Sevenoaks Vine Cricket Club 1734-1984: 250 years of cricket in Sevenoaks. Sevenoaks, the Club, 1984. [68]p. incl. adverts. illus.

1041 **Sennocke Cricket Club**
The Reg Cheeseman memorial: a Kent County XI v Sennocke C. C. at Knole Park, Sevenoaks on Sunday, June 15th. Sennocke, the Club, 1980. [29]p. incl. adverts. illus.
contains brief history of Sennocke Cricket Club.

1042 **Smart, Kenneth John**
Cricket on the Vine 1734-1984. Sevenoaks, Sevenoaks Vine C. C., 1984. 62p. illus. map, scores.

Sidcup

1043 **Bennett, Walter,** *compiler*
Sidcup Cricket Club: another ten years 1977-1986. [Sidcup], the Author, 1988. 304p. illus. stats.
supplementary volume to 'Padwick I' 2118-1.

Sittingbourne

1044 **Gore Court Cricket Club**
1839-1989 150th anniversary: souvenir programme. Sittingbourne, the Club, 1989. 36p. incl. adverts. plan.
includes a brief history of the Club by Eric Ford, pp. 3-13.

Stone

1045 **Stone Cricket Club**
100 years of cricket in Stone 1888-1988. Stone, the Club, 1988. 64p. incl. adverts. illus. scores.

Tunbridge Wells

1046 **Openshaw, Carl F.,** *editor*
History of the Tunbridge Wells Cricket Club: bi-centenary 1782-1982. [Tunbridge Wells, the Club, 1982]. 128p. incl. adverts. illus.

West Malling

1047 **Town Malling Cricket Club** *[and]* **West Malling Chamber of Commerce**
Dickensian Gala Weekend July 7th, 8th, 9th [1989]: [souvenir programme]. West Malling, Town Malling Cricket Club, [1989]. [12]p. incl. adverts. illus.
dates in cricket history at Town Malling, pp.6-7.

Whitstable

1048 **Hewitt, George K.**
Nompere: odyssey of a cricket umpire. [The Author], 1984. [24]p. illus.
an umpire's memories of Whitstable Cricket Club; limited ed. of 300 copies.

Wilmington

1049 **Haylor, Peter**
Wilmington Cricket Club 1889-1989: a century of cricket. [The Club], 1989. 76p. incl. adverts. illus.

KENT C. C. C.

1050 † **Ashley-Cooper, Frederick Samuel**
Kent county cricket. George W. May, 1923. 40p. illus.
earlier ed. of 'Padwick I' 2131.

1051 **Barnsley, Peter Martyn**
The tenth wicket record: an account of the Worcestershire v Kent match at Stourbridge (Amblecote) in July 1909 ... West Hagley, Two Gates Publications, 1987. 16p. illus. score.

1052 **Brett, Brian**
Kent versus Somerset first-class matches 1884 to 1983. Macclesfield, the Author, [1983]. 45p. stats. index.

1053 † **County** cricket in Kent. Tonbridge, Quill Publications, 1979. [8]p. illus. stats.
Maidstone Week ed.; others pub. in 1979 to coincide with cricket weeks?

1054 **Harris, George Robert Canning,** *4th Baron, editor*
The history of Kent county cricket - Appendix I 1964-1984. Canterbury, The Canterbury Printers, [1985]. [iv], 163p. illus. stats.
compiled by Howard Milton and John F. Griffiths. continues 'Padwick I' 2141.

1055 **Kent County Cricket Club**
Annual. Canterbury, the Club. illus. (some col. from 1986), scores, stats.
1980-88 [edited by Cyril Garnham].
1989 edited by John Evans.
continues 'Padwick I' 2146 to date.

1056 Kent calling: the official newsletter of Kent County Cricket Club. Canterbury, the Club. *quarterly.* illus. scores, stats.
formerly 'K. C. C. C. newsletter' - one issue published, May 1983.
August 1983 to date.

1057 † Notice of annual general meeting ... reports and accounts. Canterbury, the Club.
1966 to date.

1058 Report on the affairs of the Club. [Canterbury], the Club, 1982. 16p.

1059 † Rules, balance sheet, list of subscribers and fixtures. Canterbury, the Club. *annual.*
[1873-77].
earlier eds. of 'Padwick I' 2143?

1060 Rules. Canterbury, the Club, 1984. [8]p.
■

1061 **Kent** indoor cricket: offer and subscription under the Business Expansion Scheme. Kent Indoor plc. n.d. 32p.

1062 † The **Kent** supporter: the official organ of the Kent
□ County Cricket Supporters' Club. Canterbury, the Club, *quarterly*.
January 1978? to date.

1063 **Milton, Howard Roy,** *compiler*
■ Kent cricketers 1834-1983. Haughton Mill (Notts.), Association of Cricket Statisticians, 1983. 56p. maps, stats.

1064 **Moore, Dudley**
■ The history of Kent County Cricket Club; with a personal view by Derek Underwood. Bromley, Christopher Helm, 1988. 300p. illus. stats. index.
——*rev. and updated ed.,* 1989.

1065 **Porter, Clive Willoughby**
■ The white horse and the kangaroo: Kent v the Australians 1882-1977. Rainham (Kent), Meresborough Books, 1981. 128p. illus. scores, stats.

1066 **Russ, George,** *compiler*
■ Kent versus Surrey. West Bridgford (Notts.), Association of Cricket Statisticians, 1987. 16p. incl. covers, stats.
records 1828-1986.

1067 **Swanton, Ernest William** *and* **Taylor, Christopher H.**
■ Kent cricket: a photographic history 1744-1984. Ashford (Kent), Birlings, [1985]. [44]p. illus. (some col.) scores.
——*2nd. ed.* Geerings, 1988.

1068 **Team** up with Kent Larkfield, South Eastern
□ Newspapers, 1980. illus.
May 1980: a 'Living in Kent' cricket special.
June 1980: 'Tunbridge Wells Cricket Week special'.
other months pub?

LANCASHIRE

1069 **Aspin, Chris**
■ Surprising Lancashire. Helmshore, Helmshore Local History Society, 1988. [vi], 74p. illus.
'Brighter cricket' pp. 33-34; 'Littleborough to Lord's'
[Leslie Warburton], p.65.

1070 **Central Lancashire Cricket League**
□ [Handbook]. Rochdale, the League. *annual.* stats.
continues 'Padwick I' 2153 to date.

1071 **Lancashire and Cheshire Cricket League**
[Handbook]. [The League]. *annual.*
continues 'Padwick I' 2156 to date.

1072 **Lancashire Cricket Association**
□ Handbook. The Association. *annual.* illus.
continues 'Padwick I' 2158-1 to 1981; subsequently
incorporated in Lancashire C. C. C. year book.

1073 **Lancaster Garages Cricket League**
□ Handbook. The League. *annual.*
?/1984, 1986/ to date?

1074 **Matthew Brown Lancashire Cricket League**
□ Official handbook. The League. *annual.* illus. stats.
continues 'Padwick I' 2161 to date.

1075 **Matthew Brown Northern Cricket League**
□ Official handbook. The League. *annual.* stats.
continues 'Padwick I' 2168 to date.

1076 **North Lancashire and District Cricket League**
Rules and fixtures. [The League]. *annual.*
continues 'Padwick I' 2165 to date.

1077 **South Lancashire Cricket League**
□ Rules and fixtures. The League. *annual.* stats.
successively known as South Lancashire Cricket League,
South Lancashire Industrial League, and South
Lancashire Cricket League.
continues 'Padwick I' 2174 to date.
see also 'Padwick I' 2173.

1078 **Thwaites Ribblesdale Cricket League**
□ Official handbook. The League. *annual.* stats.
continues 'Padwick I' 2979 to date.
includes teams from Yorkshire.

Blackburn

1079 † **Blackburn and District Cricket Annual and Sunday**
■ **School League**
Official handbook. Blackburn, *The Blackburn Herald.*
annual? 96p. stats.
season 1932.
other years pub.?

1080 † **East Lancashire Club**
■ Souvenir handbook of the 'Merrie England' bazaar on March 6th, 7th, 8th and 9th 1929 ... Blackburn, [the Club], 1929. 120p. incl. adverts. illus.
includes 'A history of East Lancashire Cricket Club' by
'Purr C. Doubleyou', pp. 33-103.

Blackpool

1081 **Blackpool** Cricket Club centenary 1888-1988:
■ commemorative brochure. [Blackpool, the Club, 1988]. 64p. incl. adverts. illus. stats.

Bolton

1082 **Bolton Cricket League**
[Handbook]. Bolton, the League. *annual.* illus. stats.
continues 'Padwick I' 2191 to date.

1083 **Cavanagh, Roy**
■ Cotton town cricket: the centenary story of Lancashire's oldest cricket league. Bolton, Vimto Bolton & District Cricket Association, [1988]. [iv], 143p. incl. adverts. illus.

1084 **Cleworth, Geoffrey**
■ Cricket at Eagley: the story of Eagley Cricket Club 1837-1987. [Eagley, the Club], 1987. [ii], 49p. illus. scores, stats.

1085 **Hargreaves, Arthur L.**
■ Cricket in my life: a story of cricket in the Bolton District 1917-83. Swinton, Neil Richardson, [1984]. 88p. incl. covers, illus.

1086 Cricket in my life (second innings): another story of
■ cricket in the Bolton District. [Bolton, the Author], 1987? [88]p. illus.

1087 **Kaye, David,** *compiler*
■ Planemen's cricket: British Aerospace Cricket Club 1938-1988: 50 years of cricket at Lostock. [Bolton, the Club, 1988]. [iv], 123p. incl. adverts. illus. stats.
the Club plays in Bolton & District Cricket Association.

1088 † Kearsley Cricket Club
Centenary brochure 1875-1975. Bolton, the Club, 1975.

1089 † McNeil, M. J. and Battersby, R., editors
Bolton Cricket Club: 100 years at Green Lane, 1875-1975. [1975]. 65p.

1090 Sporting buff cricket review. Bolton, *Bolton Evening News*, 1983. 60p. illus. scores, stats.
souvenir of 1983 season in the Bolton League, Bolton Association and other local competitions.

1091 Vimto Bolton & District Cricket Association
Annual handbook. Bolton, the Association. illus. stats.
centenary ed. 1988.
continues 'Padwick I' 2190 to date.

Bootle

1092 † Bootle Cricket Club
Souvenir handbook, seasons 1948-1950. The Club, 1950. 16p. illus.

1093 † Brown, H. S.
The history of Bootle Cricket Club. 1942.
unpublished; listed in bibliog. in Walker's 'The Liverpool competition' (item 1111).

1094 Massen, P. C., [editor]
Bootle Cricket Club 150th anniversary 1833-1983: souvenir book. [Bootle, the Club, 1983]. [72]p. incl. adverts. illus.

Bradshaw

1095 Taylor, J. Barry, compiler
Bradshaw Cricket Club 1884-1984: a publication ... to mark the centenary year of Bradshaw Cricket Club. Bradshaw, the Club, 1984. 97p. incl. adverts. illus. stats.

Crosby

1096 Price, David C.
History of the Northern Cricket Club 1859-1961. Crosby, the Club, 1985. [ii], 81 leaves, illus. scores, stats.
pub. after the Club's 125th anniversary year, 1984.

Egerton

1097 Egerton Cricket Club souvenir brochure 1864-1989. [Bolton, the Club, 1989]. [iv], 116p.

Fylde

1098 Brown, Enid L.
A history of the Fylde Cricket League. [1988]. 5p.

Heywood

1099 † Heywood Cricket Club, Crimble, souvenir brochure. [The Club], 1956. [16]p. incl. adverts.

Lancaster

1100 Alderson, Tom
Cricket by the Lune: a history of Lancaster Cricket Club. [Lancaster, the Club, 1985]. [iv], 120p. illus. scores, stats.

1101 † Lancaster and District Cricket League
Handbook. The League. *annual*. stats.
?/1952 ... 1965/ to date?

1102 † Lancaster Cricket and Lawn Tennis Club
Handbook of a grand bazaar ... May 5th, 6th & 7th 1892. [Lancaster, the Club, 1892]. [128]p. illus. plan.
includes history of the Club.

Lindal-in-Furness

1103 McKeever, Michael
Lindal Moor C. C. centenary brochure. Lindal-in-Furness, Sawmill Publications, 1983. [142]p. incl. adverts, illus. stats.

Littleborough

1104 Colligan, A. W.
A short history of Littleborough Cricket Club. Littleborough, the Author, 1980. 40p. illus. bibliog.

Liverpool

1105 Bowman, Peter and Bowman, Derek, editor
The Bowmans: a Liverpool family history. Liverpool, the Author, 1983. 88p. illus. facsims.
memories of the Liverpool Licensed Victuallers' Cricket & Athletics Club, pp. 34-43.

1106 † Lancashire Association of Schoolmasters. Sports Committee
Sports handbook. Liverpool, the Association. *annual*.
much cricket.
?/1953,1954/?

1107 † Liverpool Cricket Club
Memorandum and articles of association of the Liverpool Cricket Ground Company, Limited, July 24th 1877. The Company, 1877. 6p.

1108 † [Score book]. 1822. [166]p. scores, stats.
ms. in the Tony Laughton collection.

1109 Merseyside Cricket Competition
Official handbook. The Competition. *annual*. stats.
Competition founded in 1936.
history of the competition pub. in Lancs. C. C. C. Sunday League programme for match v Leics., 12 July 1987.
/1985 to date/

1110 Ross, Alan J.
Cricket and the establishment: a social history of cricket in Lancashire with specific reference to the Liverpool Competition, 1775-1935. Ohio State University, 1987.
unpublished thesis.

1111 Walker, Peter N.
The Liverpool competition: a study of the development of cricket on Merseyside. Birkenhead, Countyvise, 1988. 87p. illus. maps, bibliog.
originally researched as a dissertation for a Diploma in Local History at the University of Liverpool, 1983.

1112 † A week's cricket: a rhyming record of the doings of a Liverpool eleven in Shropshire and neighbouring counties. Liverpool, [c. 1865]. 33p. scores.
mentioned in 'Allen EBC'.

1113 Youngers Liverpool & District Cricket Competition
Official handbook. The Competition. *annual*. illus. stats.
from 1989 with title 'Kidsons Liverpool & District Cricket Competition'; edited by Harold A. Wolfe.
1986 to date.

Manchester

1114 **Manchester and District Cricket Association**
Handbook. Manchester, the Association. *annual*. stats.
continues 'Padwick I' 2222 to date.

Morecambe

1115 **Mosey, Derek,** *compiler*
Morecambe Cricket Club centenary 1889-1989:
commemorative brochure. [The Club, 1989]. [44]p.
incl. adverts. illus. scores.

Ormskirk

1116 **Ormskirk** Cricket Club 1835-1985: 150 not out.
[Ormskirk, the Club, 1985]. 52p. incl. adverts. illus.

1117 † **Stretch, Walter,** *compiler*
Ormskirk Cricket Club 1835-1935. Ormskirk, *Ormskirk Advertiser*, [1935]. 32p. illus. stats.

Poolstock

1118 **[Melling, David]**
Poolstock Cricket Club 100 not out: centennial
programme 1888-1988. [The Club], 1988. 40p. incl.
adverts. illus. stats.

Preston

1119 **Dutton-Forshaw** Cricket & Hockey Club golden jubilee
celebration and grand opening of new ground ... 2nd May
1983. The Club, 1983. 40p. incl. covers & adverts. illus.
includes a brief history of the Club.

1120 **Penwartham Cricket Club**
Centenary, 1880-1980: souvenir brochure. Preston, the
Club, 1980.

Prestwich

1121 † **Prestwich Cricket, Tennis and Bowling Club**
The story of Prestwich Cricket, Tennis and Bowling
Club: souvenir handbook, 1840-1946. Prestwich, the
Club, 1947.

Rawtenstall

1122 **Cottrell, Chris**
Rawtenstall Cricket Club 1886-1986: centenary souvenir
brochure. [The Club, 1986]. 48p. incl. adverts. illus.
map, stats.

1123 † **Rawtenstall Cricket Club**
Bazaar ... on Sept 22nd to Sept 25th, 1926. [The Club],
1926. 128p. incl. adverts. illus.
*includes 'History of Rawtenstall Cricket Club' compiled
by W. H. Hamer, pp. 65-107.*
See also 'Padwick I' 2241-1.

Rochdale

1124 † **Allen, A. G.,** *editor*
Castleton Moor Cricket Club Norwegian scenic bazaar ...
April 5th, 6th and 7th, 1923. 1923. 72p. incl. adverts.
illus.
*includes 'The history of the Castleton Moor Cricket Club'
pp. 31-53.*

1125 † **Fielding, James L.**
A history of Norden Cricket Club 1875-1950. [The
Author, 1950]. 91p. illus. *typescript.*

1126 † **Rochdale Cricket Club**
Rochdale cricket guide. Rochdale, the Club, 1950. 80p.
incl. adverts. illus. stats.
record of 1949 season.
other years pub?

Southport

1127 **Porter, K. H.**
Twelve decades of cricket 1859-1979: being the story of
Southport and Birkdale Cricket Club. 1980.
*unpublished; listed in bibliog. in Walker's 'The Liverpool
competition' (item 1111).*

Westhoughton

1128 † **Westhoughton Cricket Club**
Magazine. The Club. *monthly during season?*
May? 1973 to date?

Widnes

1129 † **Widnes Cricket Club**
Centenary year: 1865-1965. Widnes, the Club, 1965.

Wrea Green

1130 † **Withington, Neil,** *editor*
50 golden years, 1929-1979: Dick Wilson - fifty years with
Wrea Green Cricket Club: official souvenir brochure.
1979. 8p. incl. covers. illus.

LANCASHIRE C. C. C.

1131 **Cardus,** *Sir* **[John Frederick] Neville**
The roses matches 1919-1939. Souvenir Press, 1982.
520p. illus. scores.

1132 **Else, David,** *compiler*
Farndale book of one-day cricket: Lancashire edition
1982. Chester, Farndale Publications, 1982. 45p. stats.
Lancashire records in one-day cricket 1963-1981.
no other editions published?

1133 **Hayes, Dean P.**
Lancashire cricketing greats: 57 of the best cricketers for
Lancashire, 1864-1989. Preston, Carnegie Press, 1989.
124p. illus. stats.

1134 **Hodcroft, Gerald A.**
My own red roses. Lewes, Book Guild, 1984. viii, 155p.
illus. scores, index.
*portraits of 25 Lancashire cricketers from Hornby to Clive
Lloyd.*

1135 **Lancashire County Cricket Club**
Official match programme and scorecard. Langwood for
the Club. *pub. for Sunday League matches.* col. illus.
score, stats.
vol. 1, no. 1, 1983? to date.

1136 Old Trafford ground development appeal. Manchester,
the Club, 1982. [20]p. incl. adverts. illus.
*programme for Lancashire C. C. C. v Clive Lloyd's
International XI at Southport & Birkdale C. C., 27 July
1982.*

1137 Pavilion restoration appeal. [Manchester, the Club,
1989]. [60]p. mostly adverts. illus.

1138 Red rose news: the official newsletter of Lancashire C.
C. C. Manchester, the Club. *irregular*. illus.
[no. 1], April 1988 to date.

1139 Year book. Manchester, the Club. illus. scores, stats.
■ *edited by R. Warburton; statistics 1980-86 by Charles Oliver, 1987 to date by Malcolm G. Lorimer. continues 'Padwick I' 2260 to date.*

1140 **Lorimer, Malcolm George,** *compiler*
■ Lancashire cricketers 1865-1988. West Bridgford (Notts.), Association of Cricket Statisticians, 1989. 50p. maps, stats.
Liverpool & District XI compiled by Don Ambrose.

1141 **Lorimer, Malcolm George** *and* **Warburton, Bob**
■ The Lancashire cricket quiz book. Edinburgh, Mainstream Publishing, 1989. 142p. illus.

1142 **Midwinter, Eric Clare**
■ Red roses crest the caps: the story of Lancashire C. C. C. Kingswood Press, 1989. [vi], 248p. illus. stats. index.

1143 **Wynne-Thomas, Peter**
■ The history of Lancashire County Cricket Club; with a personal view by Brian Statham. Bromley, Christopher Helm, 1989. [v], 290p. illus. stats. bibliog.

LEICESTERSHIRE

Ashby de la Zouch

1144 **Ashby** Hastings Cricket Club: a concise history. [Ashby
■ de la Zouch, the Club, 1980]. 24p. illus. facsims. scores.

Lutterworth

1145 **Payne, Sheila**
■ A history of Lutterworth Cricket Club 1789-1989. [The Club], 1989. [24]p. incl. adverts. illus. score.

Market Harborough

1146 **Market** Harborough Cricket Club cricket handbook 1986
■ season featuring I.C.C. Trophy Match, 13th June, Papua New Guinea v U.S.A. [The Club], 1986. [28]p. incl. adverts.
includes a brief history of the Club.

Melton Mowbray

1147 **Irving, David**
■ A celebration of one hundred years of Egerton Park Cricket Club from its inaugural meeting on August 4th 1882. [Melton Mowbray, the Club, 1982]. [104]p. incl. adverts. illus.

LEICESTERSHIRE C. C. C.

1148 **Leicestershire County Cricket Club**
□ Annual report and statement of accounts. Leicester, the Club. illus.
continues 'Padwick I' 2311 to date.

1149 † Leicestershire cricket season 1936. Leicester, the Club, 1936. 16p. illus.

1150 Yearbook. Leicester, Polar Publishing. illus. (some
□ col. since 1989), scores, stats.
continues 'Padwick I' 2309 to date; (1984-87 not pub.)

1151 **Paul, David** *and* **Tilley, Peter,** *compilers*
Representative cricket at the Leicester Road Ground, Hinckley: commemorative souvenir brochure. The Authors for Leicestershire County Cricket Club, [1981]. 28p. incl. adverts. illus. stats.

1152 **Snow, Edward Eric**
■ Cricket grounds of Leicestershire. Haughton Mill (Notts.), Association of Cricket Statisticians, [1987]. 40p. illus. stats.

LINCOLNSHIRE

1153 **Harcros Lincolnshire County Cricket League**
□ [Handbook]. [The League]. *annual.* stats. *typescript.*
1986-7 : sponsored by Wintringhams.
1988 to date sponsored by Harcros.
continues 'Padwick I' 2318 to date.

1154 **Lincolnshire and South Humberside Cricket**
□ **Association**
Newsletter. The Association. *2 issues per year.*
1988? to date.

1155 **South Lincs and Border League**
□ Year book. The League. *annual.* stats.
founded c. 1970; includes clubs from adjacent counties.
?/1988 to date/

Cleethorpes

1156 **Cleethorpes** Cricket Club 1931-1981: golden jubilee
■ anniversary of the ground. [The Club, 1981]. 48p. incl. adverts. illus. stats.

Sleaford

1157 **Sleaford Cricket Club**
□ Official handbook. Sleaford, the Club. *annual.* illus. scores in v.y. stats.
continues 'Padwick I' 2325-2 to date.

LINCOLNSHIRE C. C. C.

1158 **Lincolnshire County Cricket Club**
■ Year book. [Lincoln, the Club]. illus. scores, stats.
continues 'Padwick I' 2327 to date.

LONDON

1159 **London Community Cricket Association**
■ Constitution. The Association, 1987? 11p. *typescript.*

1160 Friends of London cricket newsletter. The Association.
■ illus.
Autumn 1989 was first issue.

1161 London cricketer. The Association. *quarterly.* illus.
■ (some col.)
pub. Summer 1987 and Winter 1987-88 only.

MIDDLESEX

1162 **McKenzie Bookseller Thameside Cricket League**
□ Handbook. [The League]. *annual.* illus. stats.
founded 1970.
1982-87 sponsored by Morrant.
1972?/1987 to date/

1163 **Middlesex County Cricket Development Association**
Sunday League
Fixtures, constitution and rules. The Association. *annual.*
League founded 1987.
1987? to date.

1164 † **Middlesex County Cricket League**
■ The first years 1972-1976. The League, 1976. 11p. stats.
statistical review.

1165 **Middlesex Cricket Union**
■ Handbook. [The Union]. *annual*. illus. stats.
1989 was first issue.

1166 Scorecard. [The Union]. *irregular*. illus. stats. *typescript*.
□ *M.C.U. newsletter.*
1984?/1989/

1167 **Nixdorf Computer's The 1987 Cricket League**
■ League handbook. The League. *annual*.
1988 to date.

Alexandra Park

1168 **Alexandra** Park Cricket Club centenary souvenir
■ programme. [The Club, 1988]. 12p. illus.

Cockfosters

1169 **Cockfosters Cricket Club**
■ New Zealand tour: November 1981. The Club, 1981.
64p. incl. adverts. illus. scores, map.
pre-tour.

Ealing

1170 **Brentham** Cricket Club fixtures handbook 1983: 75th
■ season. [The Club], 1983. 43p. illus. scores, stats.
includes a history of the Club, pp. 22-34.

Enfield

1171 † **Enfield Amateur Cricket Club**
■ [List of members and statement of accounts]. [Enfield,
the Club]. *annual*.
?/1878,1902/?
subsequently became Enfield Cricket Club.

1172 † [List of results for the season of 1875]. [Enfield, the
■ Club]. [4]p. incl. covers.
other years pub?

1173 † **Enfield Cricket Club**
■ Military assault-at-arms at the Bycullah Athanaeum, on
Thursday, January 23rd, 1902. [Enfield, the Club, 1902].
[4]p. incl. covers.
programme for a Club fundraising event.

1174 **One** hundred years to remember: a history of the North
■ Enfield Cricket Club 1886-1986. [Enfield, the Club,
1986]. v, 66p. illus. scores.

Finchley

1175 **Finchley Cricket Club**
□ [Handbook]. The Club. *annual*. stats.
?1982/1988 to date/

Hampstead

1176 † **Gospel Oak and Hampstead Cricket League**
□ Official handbook. [The League]. *annual*. scores, stats.
instituted 1895.
?/1934-37,39/?

Hampton Wick

1177 **Hampton Wick Royal Cricket Club**
■ [125th anniversary season brochure, 1863-1988]. [The
Club, 1988]. [32]p. incl. adverts. illus. stats.
brochure for 1989 also produced.

Harrow

1178 **Harrow** Cricket Club, 1888-1988. [The Club, 1988]. 74p.
■ incl. end covers and adverts. illus. map.

Hatch End

1179 **Roe, Ron**
■ Hatch End Cricket Club 50th anniversary brochure.
[Hatch End, the Club], 1983. [23]p. incl. covers, illus.
scores, stats.

Hillingdon

1180 **Hillingdon** Cricket Club ... 150 years souvenir. [The
■ Club], 1984. [32]p. illus.

Mill Hill

1181 † **Mallatratt, Howard**
■ The story of cricket at Mill Hill Village 1852-1952. [The
Author], 1977. [v], 146p. scores, stats. *typescript*.

Osterley

1182 **Wycombe** House Cricket-Tennis and Social Club
■ founded 1889: centenary brochure. [Osterley, the Club,
1989]. 50p. incl. adverts. illus.

Shepherds Bush

1183 **Shepherds** Bush Cricket Club 1882-1982. [The Club],
■ 1982. 52p. incl. adverts. illus. scores.

Southgate

1184 † **Southgate Cricket Club**
□ Review. [Southgate, the Club]. *annual*. illus. stats.
1973 ... /1989/ with various titles;
edited by Ricky Gunn.

1185 **Walker** Ground, Southgate. [Southgate, the Club,
■ 1984]. 4p. illus. map.
notes on the history of the ground.

Totteridge

1186 **Hughes, Ken** *et al*
■ A history of Totteridge Cricket Club. [Totteridge, the
Club], 1980. [v], 94p. illus.
'Totteridge CC 1881-1981'.

1187 **Totteridge** Cricket Club tour of Kenya 1986-1987. [The
■ Club], 1986. 46p. incl. adverts. illus.
pre-tour; includes a brief history of the Club, p18.

Uxbridge

1188 **Griffiths, Dennis M.**
■ 200 not out: Uxbridge Cricket Club 1789-1989.
[Uxbridge, the Club], 1989. ix, 112p. illus. facsims.
scores.

1189 **Uxbridge** Cricket Club 1789-1989: bicentenary
■ handbook. [Uxbridge, the Club, 1989]. [iii], 61p. incl.
adverts. illus. scores.

Wembley

1190 **Seers, Bill**
■ Wembley Cricket Club 1860-1985. [The Club], 1985. [i],
43p. stats.

Winchmore Hill

1191 **Bath, Tony** *and* **Bath, Jennifer**
■ Winchmore Hill Cricket Club: the first hundred years 1880-1980. The Club, 1980. 65p. illus.

MIDDLESEX C. C. C.

1192 **Lemmon, David Hector**
■ The official history of Middlesex County Cricket Club; with a personal view by Denis Compton. Bromley, Christopher Helm, 1988. 365p. illus. scores, stats. bibliog. index.

1193 **Middlesex County Cricket Club**
■ Middlesex and Seaxe cricketers' companion 1980. [The Club, 1980]. 16p. incl. covers. maps.
pre-season; the only issue.

1194 Middlesex matters: Middlesex County Cricket Club
■ newsletter. The Club. *irregular.* illus. stats.
changed to present name, June 1982.
continues 'Padwick I' 2418-1 to date.

1195 Review ... containing the annual report. The Club.
■ *annual.* illus. scores, stats.
1980/81 to date.

1196 † Rules. The Club, 1976. [8]p. *typescript.*
■ *rev. ed. of 'Padwick I' 2415.*

1197 **Middx.** monthly. stats. *typescipt.*
■ *no. 1, May 1983, was only issue.*

1198 **Rippon, Anton**
■ The story of Middlesex C. C. C. Ashbourne, Moorland Publishing, 1982. 141p. illus. stats.

1199 **Seaxe Club**
■ Constitution and rules. [4]p. folded sheet. n.d.
affiliated to Middlesex C.C.C.

1200 Seaxe news. The Club. *quarterly. typescript.*
□ *Middlesex C.C.C. Supporters' Club newsletter.*
edited successively by Stan Wignall, Dave Silver, Kate Woodruff, Tony Cliff and Frank Butterfield.
?1978 to date.

NORFOLK

1201 **Norwich Union Norfolk Cricket Alliance**
Handbook. The Alliance. *annual.* stats.
Alliance formed in 1971.
1981 to date.

NORFOLK C. C. C.

1202 **Norfolk County Cricket Club**
□ Annual report; batting and bowling averages; full match scores ...; financial statement; list of members. [Norwich, the Club]. illus. scores, stats.
1989 ed. with titile 'Handbook'.
continues 'Padwick I' 2446 to date.

NORTHAMPTONSHIRE

1203 **Blower, John L.**
■ South Northants Cricket League diamond jubilee 1920-1980. [Culworth], the League, 1980. 88p. illus.

1204 † **South Northants Cricket League**
■ Souvenir jubilee year book 1920-70. [The League, 1970]. 43p. illus.
other yearbooks pub?

Barnack

1205 **Palmer, Brian**
■ Cricket in Barnack 1847-1983: a history of Walcot Park and Barnack Cricket Club. [Barnack, the Club, 1984]. [viii], 128p. illus. maps, scores, stats.

Cogenhoe

1206 **Street, Tim**
■ Cogenhoe Cricket Club: a centenary history. Cogenhoe, the Club, 1982. 44p. incl. adverts. illus.

Kettering

1207 **Larcombe, Peter**
■ A century of cricket at Kettering 1885-1985. [Kettering, the Club, 1985]. 44p. incl. adverts. illus. scores.

Northampton

1208 **Sibley, Gil** *et al*
■ The Northampton Town Cricket League centenary year 1886-1986. [Northampton, the League, 1986]. 108p. incl. adverts. illus. stats.
formerly Northampton Cricket League.

Weldon

1209 **Weldon** Cricket Club 125 not out, 1863-1988. [The
■ Club], 1988. 16p. incl. covers. illus.

NORTHAMPTONSHIRE C. C. C.

1210 **Association of Cricket Statisticians**
■ Northamptonshire cricketers 1905-1984. Haughton Mill (Notts.), the Association, 1984. 24p. map, stats.

1211 **Clifton, Peter,** *compiler*
■ Northants '87: a complete review of the county's year. Northampton, Northampton Mercury, [1987]. 72p. incl. covers and adverts. illus. (some col.) stats.

1212 **Northamptonshire County Cricket Club**
□ Annual report and statement of accounts. Northampton, the Club. illus. scores, stats.
continues 'Padwick I' 2463 to 1987?
1988 to date continued as 'Official yearbook', edited by J. B. Baskcomb and S. P. Coverdale, pub. Leicester, Polar Publishing.

1213 **Northamptonshire County Cricket Supporters Club**
■ Newsletter. The Club. *irregular.*
1st issue Sep/Oct 1988 with title Northamptonshire County Cricket Supporters' Club Northampton Branch newsletter.
7 issues to date.

NORTHUMBERLAND

Corbridge

1214 **Pickworth, Gillian** *et al*
■ Corbridge Cricket Club 1886-1986 centenary brochure. Corbridge, the Club, 1986. 61p. incl. adverts. illus. scores.

Hexham

1215 **Wood, Robert E.**
■ A Tynedale centenary 1888-1988: Prior's Flat, Hexham. [Hexham, Tynedale Athletic Association, 1988]. 137p. incl. adverts. illus. stats.

Ponteland

1216 **Robinson, Ken**
■ Ponteland Cricket Club 1880-1980. [Ponteland, the Club, 1980]. [56]p. incl. adverts. illus.

NORTHUMBERLAND C. C. C.

1217 **Jude, J. H. ('Harry')**
■ Northumberland: a history of county cricket. [Morpeth, the Author, 1989]. [ii], v, 170p. illus. scores, stats.

1218 **Northumberland County Cricket Club**
□ Year book. [Newcastle], the Club. illus. scores, stats.
continues 'Padwick I' 2471 to date.

NOTTINGHAMSHIRE

1219 **Bassetlaw and District Cricket League**
□ Official handbook. The League. *annual.* stats.
continues 'Padwick I' 2480 to date

1220 **Nottinghamshire and Derbyshire Border Cricket League**
[Handbook]. [The League]. *annual.*
continues 'Padwick I' 2474 to 1980.
League re-formed in 1981 as Derbyshire County Cricket League.

1221 **Notts Cricket Association**
■ Official handbook. [Nottingham, the Association].
annual. illus. scores.
continues 'Padwick I' 2476 to date.

1222 **The Save & Prosper South Notts Village Cricket League**
□ Handbook. The League. *annual.* stats.
league formed 1972.
?/1989/

Hucknall

1223 **[Silverwood, Richard, *editor*]**
■ Hucknall Ramblers Cricket Club: 50 not out: golden jubilee year 1981. [Hucknall, the Club, 1981]. 24p. incl. adverts. illus.

Mansfield

1224 † **Mansfield & District Cricket League**
■ Rule and fixture book. [The League]. *annual.*
/1947 to date/
1949-1951 with title 'Fixture book'.
from 1977 with title 'Handbook'.
illus. from 1985.

Newark

1225 **Newark** Cricket Club, 1830-1980. Newark, *Newark Advertiser*, 1980.

1226 **Vernon, Rolf**
■ Newark before Victoria [1827-1837]. Newark, Newark District Council, 1984. 217p. illus. map.
cricket pp. 163-172.

Nottingham

1227 The **30th** anniversary of the West Indies Carib Cricket
■ Club. [The Club, 1981]. [16]p. illus. stats.
club set up for West Indians living in the Nottingham and Derby areas; plays in the Nottingham Amateur Cricket League.

1228 † **Iliffe, Richard *and* Baguley, Wilfred**
■ Victorian Nottingham: a story in pictures, volume 18. Nottingham, Nottingham Historical Film Unit, 1977. 100p. illus. facsims.
cricket pp. 5-52.

1229 **Nottingham Evening Cricket League *[and]* Nottingham**
□ **Evening (Youth) Cricket League**
[Handbook]. [Nottingham, the Leagues]. *annual.* stats.
typescript.
records of the previous season and fixtures for the coming season.
continues 'Padwick I' 2485-1 to date.

Retford

1230 **Bridon** (Retford) C. C. golden jubilee 1987: souvenir
■ brochure. [The Club, 1987]. [15]p. illus.

Ruddington

1231 **Turner, David**
■ Ruddington Cricket Club, season 1984: a souvenir booklet to celebrate promotion. [The Club, 1984]. [19]p. stats.
runners up in first division of Notts Amateur League 1984.

Southwell

1232 **Hodson, Richard, *editor***
■ Southwell Cricket Club 1787-1987. The Club, 1987. 24p. incl. adverts. illus.

Worksop

1233 **Langdale, George Richmond, *editor***
■ Notts County Cricket Club and Worksop Cricket Club. [Worksop, the Club, 1989]. [12]p. incl. covers and adverts. stats.

NOTTINGHAMSHIRE C. C. C.

1234 † **Ashley-Cooper, Frederick Samuel**
■ Nottinghamshire cricket and cricketers. [1923]. viii, 410p. stats. bibliog.
de luxe ed. of 'Padwick I' 2498 limited to 20 copies of which nos. 1-4 presented to Royalty and nos. 5-20 presented to friends of the author.

1235 **Dalling, Harry William *in conversation with* Lucy, Nick**
■ Nottinghamshire County Cricket Club. Urmston (Manchester), Archive Publications in association with Nottingham Evening Post, 1988. [126]p. illus. (some col.)
cover title: 'Nottinghamshire County Cricket Club: a man for 40 seasons'.

1236 **Langdale, George Richmond, *editor***
■ Notts County Cricket Club and Worksop Cricket Club. [Worksop, the Club, 1989]. [12]p. incl. covers and adverts. stats.

1237 **Lawson, John *and* Bowles, Terry, *editors***
■ Champions ... official souvenir brochure to mark Nottinghamshire's Schweppes Championship success in 1981. [The Club, 1981]. [44]p. incl. adverts. illus. stats.

1238 **Lucy, Nick**
Nottinghamshire County Cricket Club: bridging 150 glory years. Nottingham, *Nottingham Evening Post*, 1988. [8]p. illus. (some col.) stats.
special souvenir ed., 12 April 1988.

1239 **Nottinghamshire County Cricket Club**
■ Annual report. Nottingham, the Club. illus.
1980 with title 'Annual report and handbook'.
continues 'Padwick I' 2510 to date.

1240 A pictorial history of Nottinghamshire cricket.
■ Nottingham, the Club, 1982. 20p. illus. maps.

1241 Trent Bridge juniors newsletter. Nottingham, the Club.
■ *irregular*. illus.
1988? to date.

1242 Trent Bridge monthly: official newspaper of
■ Nottinghamshire C. C. C. Lawson & Bowles / The Club,
monthly, May - September. illus. *tabloid format.*
no. 1 May 1979.
special 'Trent Bridge 150' ed. pub. 1988.
special youth ed. pub. Sept. 1989.
continues 'Padwick I' 1027-4 to date.

1243 A unique setting for entertaining ... [13] leaves. illus.
■ map.
cover title; brochure for sponsors and local businesses.

1244 Yearbook. Nottingham, the Club. illus. scores, stats.
■ *[edited by John Lawson and Terry Bowles].*
1981, 1984 to date.

1245 **Nottinghamshire** cricket cards. West Bridgford
■ (Notts.), Sport-in-Print, [1989].
pub. in four albums: 'Batsmen', 'Bowlers', 'All-rounders',
'In the field'; each album contains 16p. with spaces
provided for cards to match accompanying text.

1246 **Nottinghamshire** means business in '85. 1985. [8]p.
■ illus.
a 'Nottinghamshire Business and You' special supplement.

1247 **Seward, David** and **Wynne-Thomas, Peter**, *compilers*
■ Memories of Trent Bridge, 1838-1988. Nottingham,
Nottinghamshire C. C. C., 1987. 40p. illus. (some col.)
cover title: 'Memories of Trent Bridge: the story in words
and pictures of famous cricketers and events of the past
150 years'.

1248 **Tennant, Dick**
■ Trent Bridge '84'. Nottingham, the Club, 1984. 64p.
incl. covers and adverts. illus.
pub. for the Club's benefit year.

1249 **Wynne-Thomas, Peter**
■ A chronological history of cricket in Nottinghamshire.
[The Author], 1981. 16p.
cover title: 'Milestones of Nottinghamshire cricket'.

1250 **[Wynne-Thomas, Peter]**
■ Cricket grounds of Nottinghamshire Haughton Mill
(Notts.), Association of Cricket Statisticians, 1984. 32p.
illus. stats.

1251 **Wynne-Thomas, Peter**
■ Nottinghamshire champion county 1981: a souvenir
booklet to commemorate the winning of the
Championship. Haughton Mill (Notts.), [the Author],
1981. 56p. illus. scores, stats.
incorporates 'The Nottinghamshire Scorebook', vol. 2 no.
4.

1252 Nottinghamshire: cricket's double champions 1987.
■ Heinemann, Kingswood, 1988. [xi], 131p. illus. scores,
stats.
County Champions and Nat. West Trophy winners.

1253 Trent Bridge: a history of the ground to commemorate
□ the 150th anniversary (1838-1988). Nottingham,
Nottinghamshire County Council in association with
Nottingham County Cricket Club, 1987. x, 246p. illus.
stats. index.
8pp. supplement 'The double champions of 1987'
inserted to bring the book up to date to end of 1987
season.
——limited gold-leaf ed. of 600 copies, 1987.

1254 **Wynne-Thomas, Peter**, *compiler*
■ Nottinghamshire scorebook. Nottingham, [the Author].
monthly during season. scores, stats. bibliog.
vol. 1 no. 1, June 1980 - vol. 2 no. 4, September 1981.
part of an extended essay on the bibliography of
Nottinghamshire cricket books is included in each issue.

OXFORDSHIRE

1255 **Grant Thornton Cherwell League**
■ [Handbook and fixtures]. [Oxford, the League].
annual. illus. stats.
founded 1974 as Cherwell League.
1980-87 known as Buckell & Ballard Cherwell League.
includes clubs from adjacent counties.
1980 to date.

1256 **Oxfordshire** cricket handbook: representative cricket in
■ Oxfordshire. 1989. illus. scores, stats.
a joint publication by Oxfordshire County Cricket Club,
Oxfordshire County Cricket Association and Oxfordshire
Cricket Umpires Association;
first year of publication.

Cowley

1257 **Ricks, Clive**, *compiler*
■ Cowley St. John Cricket Club centenary handbook. [The
Club, 1987]. 40p. incl. covers and adverts. illus.
facsims. stats.

Moreton

1258 **Howat, Gerald Malcolm David**, *editor*
■ Bud Finch remembers North Moreton over eighty years.
North Moreton, North Moreton Press, 1989. 80p. illus.
map.
includes memories of sixty years connection with Moreton
Cricket Club.

Tiddington

1259 **Tiddington** Cricket Club 1886-1986. centenary handbook
■ and fixture list. [Tiddington, the Club, 1986]. [24]p.
incl. adverts. illus.

SHROPSHIRE

Claverley

1260 **Ashton, J.**
Claverley Cricket Club 1932-82. 1982. 83p.

Madeley

1261 **Madeley (Salop) Cricket Club**
■ 125 years of cricket at Madeley, 1855-1980. [The Club,
1980]. [ii], 42p. incl. adverts. illus. scores, stats.

Shrewsbury

1262 **Arthan, John,** *editor*
■ Shrewsbury at Lord's. Shrewsbury, Shrewsbury Cricket Club, 1984. 104p. incl. adverts. illus. scores.
celebrates Shrewsbury Cricket Club's winning of the William Younger Cup (Club Cricket Championship) in August 1983.

SHROPSHIRE C. C. C.

1263 **Shropshire County Cricket Club**
□ Handbook. [Shrewsbury, the Club]. *annual*. illus. scores, stats.
continues 'Padwick I' 2542 to date?
silver jubilee ed. 1981.

SOMERSET

1264 † **'Lycaon',** *pseud.*
Saunters in Somerset. Buckenham & Co., [1924]. [x], 161p.
cricket, pp. 80-85.

1265 **Somerset Cricket League**
□ Official handbook; edited by Brian Morris. The League. *annual*? stats.
League founded 1973.
?/1983/ to date?

Abbots Leigh

1266 **Wheare, Robert C.** *and* **Nottingham, Jack**
■ The identification of James Flower Fussell & his connection with cricket in Abbots Leigh. Abbots Leigh Cricket Club, 1986. 20p. illus.
cover title: 'The background to cricket in Abbots Leigh'.

Bath

1267 **Bath Cricket Club**
■ 125th anniversary: 1859-1984 souvenir programme. [Bath, the Club, 1984]. [12]p. incl. adverts. and covers, illus. score.

1268 † The **Lansdown** letter 1825-1975. [Lansdown Cricket Club, 1975]. [20]p.
■ *magazine started to commemorate the Club's 150th anniversary; the only issue?*

Castle Cary

1269 **Castle** Cary Cricket Club 1837-1987: a collection of memorabilia from the Club archives to celebrate 150 years of cricket in Somerset. [Castle Cary, the Club, 1987]. 52p. incl. covers and adverts. illus. facsims.

SOMERSET C. C. C.

1270 **Brett, Brian**
■ Kent versus Somerset first-class matches 1884 to 1983. Macclesfield, the Author, [1983]. 45p. stats. index.

1271 **Crampsey, Robert Anthony**
■ The Somerset cricket quiz book. Edinburgh, Mainstream Publishing, 1988. 160p. illus.

1272 **Foot, David**
■ From Grace to Botham: profiles of 100 West Country cricketers. Bristol, Redcliffe Press, 1980. 123p. illus.

1273 Sunshine, sixes and cider: the history of Somerset cricket. Newton Abbot, David & Charles, 1986. 224p. illus. stats. bibliog. index.

1274 **Marks, Victor James**
■ Somerset county cricket scrapbook. Souvenir Press, 1984. 128p. illus. scores.

1275 **Mills, David,** *editor*
■ Memories of Somerset cricket: people, matches, grounds. [Taunton], Somerset County Cricket Club, 1989. [vii], 128p. illus. scores, stats.

1276 **Somerset County Cricket Club**
□ Annual report and statement of accounts. Taunton, the Club.
/1986/ to date?
previously incorporated in Handbook.

1277 Somerset cricket news and scorecard. [Taunton, the Club], *pub. for Sunday League matches*. scores, stats.
■ *vol. 1 no. 1 1986 to date.*

1278 Yearbook. [Taunton], the Club. illus. scores, stats.
■ *with title 'Handbook' until 1985.*
1980-85 edited by Eric Coombes.
1986 edited by Tony Williams.
1987 to date edited by Michael Hill.
continues 'Padwick I' 2561-3 to date.

1279 **Somerset** cricket '85. Taunton, South West Counties Newspapers, 1985. 24p. illus. (some col.)
■ *pre-season.*

1280 **Somerset Old County Cricketers Association**
Newsletter. Taunton, the Association. *biannual*.
1982 to date.

1281 **Somserset Wyverns**
□ Newsletter. Taunton, the Club. *biannual*. stats.
continues 'Padwick I' 2562-1 to date.

STAFFORDSHIRE

1282 **Hodson, Arthur**
■ A history of the James and Tatton North Staffordshire and District Cricket League, 1889-1989. [The League], 1989. 36p. illus. stats.

1283 **James and Tatton North Staffordshire and District**
□ **Cricket League**
[Handbook]. The League. *annual*. stats.
continues 'Padwick I' 2564 to date.

1284 Report. The League. *annual*. stats.
continues 'Padwick I' 2564 to date.

1285 **North Staffordshire and South Cheshire Cricket League**
Offical handbook. [The League]. *annual*.
continues 'Padwick I' 2566 to date.

1286 † **'Recorder'**
An historical survey of the North Staffordshire and District Cricket League since its inception. Longton, Hughes & Harber Ltd, [1950]. 16p. illus.

Bignall End

1287 † **Burgess, A.**
A history of Bignall End Cricket Club. 1975. 125p.

Bloxwich

1288 **Jenkinson, T. H.**
■ The history of Bloxwich Cricket Club. Bloxwich, the Club, 1986. 144p. incl. adverts. illus. stats.
celebrating 125th anniversary.

Himley

1289 Brandrick, Kevan
■ Himley to Lord's '88: souvenir brochure. 1988. 52p. incl. adverts. illus. scores.
to celebrate Himley's appearance in the Hydro Village Cricket Championship, August 1988. The match was abondoned halfway and Himley lost the re-arranged final played at Beckenham.

1290 Himley Cricket Club
■ Centenary year 1983: centenary year book. Himley, the Club, [1983]. 48p. incl. adverts. illus.

Leek

1291 † Leek Cricket Club
Bazaar handbook. [Leek, the Club], 1955. 32p. illus.

Pelsall

1292 [Dolphin, B. *and* Bennett, L., *compilers*]
■ One hundred not out: Pelsall Cricket & Sports Club 1885-1985. [The Club], 1985. 76p. incl. adverts. illus.

Walsall

1293 † Walsall Cricket Club
■ Minute book. 1846-48.
ms. in the Tony Laughton collection.

1294 † Rules. n.d. 1p.
■ *club founded in 1846; reprint of 1847 rules.*

1295 Yearbook. [Walsall, the Club]. *annual.* stats.
■ *1989 was first issue.*

Wolverhampton

1296 † Wolverhampton Cricket Association
Tour of West Indies, Easter 1976: official brochure. Wolverhampton, the Association, [1976]. [26]p. incl. adverts. illus.
pre-tour.

STAFFORDSHIRE C. C. C.

1297 Staffordshire County Cricket Club
□ [Yearbook]. [Stoke-on-Trent, the Club]. illus. scores, stats.
continues 'Padwick I' 2588 to date.

SUFFOLK

1298 Anglo Two Counties Cricket Championship
■ Official handbook. The Championship. *annual.* stats.
*founded 1971; also includes teams from Essex.
1987 with title 'Bulldog Two Counties Cricket Championship'.
1987 to date.*

1299 Mick McNeil Suffolk Cricket League
■ Constitution. The League, 1988. 3p. *typescript.*
League re-formed 1986.

1300 Suffolk County Cricket Association
□ Handbook. Ipswich, the Association. *annual.* illus. scores, stats.
*?1985 to date with title 'Suffolk cricket: Suffolk County Cricket Association handbook'.
continues 'Padwick I' 2591-1 to date.*

Copdock

1301 Copdock Cricket Club 150th anniversary souvenir
■ brochure, 1839-1989. [The Club], 1989. 56p. incl. covers and adverts. illus.
Club history plus review of 1988 season.

Hadleigh

1302 Hadleigh Cricket Club
□ Year book. The Club. illus. stats.
?/1985-86/ to date.

Sudbury

1303 Cocksedge, Alan
■ 1787-1987: cricketers of Sudbury, incorporating the history of Friars Street Sports Ground, Sudbury. Sudbury, Sudbury C. C., 1987. 28p. illus. scores.

SURREY

1304 Collyer, Graham
The Surrey village book; with illustrations by Christopher Howkins. Newbury, Countryside Books, 1984. 168p. illus.
many cricket references.

1305 † [Duncombe, John]
■ Surry triumphant or the Kentish-mens defeat: a new ballad being a parody on Chevy-Chace. Bourne (Kent), Bourne End Paddock Cricket Club, 1937. 16p. incl. covers.
Surrey v Kent, July 1773; reprint of the parody contained in 'Padwick I' 2597, excluding the score.

1306 McKenzie Bookseller Thameside Cricket League
□ Handbook. [The League], *annual.* illus. stats.
*founded 1970.
1982-87 sponsored by Morrant.
1972?/1987 to date/*

1307 The Morrant Three Counties Cricket League
□ Handbook. The League. *annual.* illus.
*founded 1972; based in Surrey; also includes teams from Berks and Hants.
1985/1986 to date/*

1308 Slazenger Surrey Cricket League
□ Handbook & fixtures. Chessington, the League. *annual.* illus. scores, stats.
*founded 1975?
?/1986/ to date.*

1309 South Thames Cricket League
□ Yearbook. Pett's Wood, D. H. Roberts for the League. illus. scores, stats.
continues 'Padwick I' 2603 to date.

1310 The Surrey Championship
■ Yearbook. Surrey Championship Association. illus. scores, stats.
continues 'Padwick I' 2607 to date.

1311 Surrey Cricket Association
□ Year book. The Association. illus. stats.
*junior and club cricket throughout the county.
1984/1985/ to date?*

Barnes

1312 Turner, E. Graham
■ Barnes Cricket Club, 1919/1980. [The Club, 1980]. [7]p.
updated ed. of 'Padwick I' 2614.

Dorking

1313   A **history** of sports in Dorking. Dorking, Dorking Local
History Group and Leith Hill District Preservation
Society, 1985. 138p.
some cricket.

Farncombe

1314   **[Newman, Barry]**
■   A history of Farncombe Cricket Club: 1938-1988 at
Broadwater Park. [The Club, 1988]. 64p. incl. adverts.
illus. scores.
cover title '50 years to remember'.

Farnham

1315   **Collyer, Graham**
■   Farnham Cricket Club 1782-1982: a bi-centenary history,
also featuring the life of William 'Silver Billy' Beldham
and cricket in the village. Farnham, Farnham Castle
Newspapers, 1982. 96p. illus. scores, stats.

1316   **Farnham** Cricket Club bi-centenary 1782-1982. [The
■   Club], 1982. 48p. incl. adverts. illus.

Godstone

1317   **Dumbrill, Reg**
■   Cricket on the green 1749-1983: Godstone Cricket Club
founded 1868. [Godstone, the Club, 1983]. [12]p. illus.

Guildford

1318   **Frith, David Edward John,** *editor*
■   Guildford jubilee: fifty years of county cricket 1938-1988.
Guildford, Guildford Cricket Club, 1988. 44p. illus.
includes short history of cricket in Guildford.

Ham

1319   **Philpot, Peter**
■   One hundred and seventy not out: a history of Ham and
Petersham Cricket Club 1815-1985. [Ham, the Club],
1985. ix, 48p. illus. map.

Honor Oak

1320   **Alexander, Maurice Benjamin**
■   A short history of Honor Oak Cricket Club 1866-1982.
[1982]. 14p. illus.

Hook

1321 † **[Hickman, Derek,** *editor***]**
■   Hook and Southborough Cricket Club 1870-1970. [The
Club, 1970]. [ii], 36p. scores.

Kenley

1322   A **centenary** history of the Kenley Cricket Club
■   1880-1980. [The Club], 1980. [12]p. incl. adverts. illus.

Kew

1323   **Burgess, Martin,** *editor*
■   Kew Cricket Club 1882-1982. [Kew, the Club, 1982].
32p. incl. adverts. illus.

Mitcham

1324   **Higgs, Tom**
■   300 years of Mitcham cricket. [Mitcham, Mitcham
Cricket Club, 1985]. 48p. illus. score.

Newchapel

1325   **Newchapel** and Horne Cricket Club centenary cricket
■   week (1886-1986), Tuesday 1st July - Sunday 6th July
1986. [The Club], 1986. [16]p. incl. adverts.
includes a brief history of the Club.

Outwood

1326   **Nuklin, Frank,** *editor*
■   Centenary book. [Outwood, Outwood Cricket Club,
1987]. 72p. incl. adverts. illus. scores, stats.

Redhill

1327   **Barton, John**
■   The history of Frenches Cricket Club. Redhill, the
Author, [1987]. 200p. illus. scores, stats.
Frenches Manor in Redhill.

Sanderstead

1328   **Corderoy, Mike** *and* **Jones, Robert,** *editors*
■   Sanderstead Cricket Club centenary 1881-1981. [The
Club, 1981]. [72]p. illus. (some col.) stats.

Streatham

1329 † The **Osborne** journal: a magazine devoted to the affairs
□   of the Osborne Cricket Club and other matters; edited
by Leo Munro. The Editor. *monthly.* illus. scores, stats.
/vol. I, no. 1, May 1896 - vol. I, no 12, April 1897/?

Sunbury

1330   **Kincaid, Bill**
■   Half-century! the story of Sunbury Cricket Club,
1938-1988; statistics by Les Wood. Sunbury, the Club,
1988. 127p. illus. stats.

Tilford

1331   **Collyer, Graham**
■   Tilford Cricket Club 1885-1985: a history of the club.
[Tilford, the Club, 1985]. 99p. incl. adverts. and covers,
illus.

1332   **Collyer, Graham** *et al*
■   Tilford through the ages. [The Authors?], 1980. 48p.
illus. maps, bibliog.
cricket in the village pp. 34-37.

SURREY C. C. C.

1333   **Association of Cricket Statisticians**
■   Surrey cricketers 1839-1980. Cleethorpes, the
Association, [1981]. 50p. map. stats.

1334   **Crampsey, Robert Anthony**
■   The Surrey cricket quiz book. Edinburgh, Mainstream
Publishing, 1988. 156p. illus.

1335   **Frith, David Edward John,** *editor*
■   Guildford jubilee: fifty years of county cricket 1938-1988.
Guildford, Guildford Cricket Club, 1988. 44p. illus.
*contains potted scores of every county match played at
Guildford.*

1336   **Lemmon, David Hector**
■   The official history of Surrey County Cricket Club; with a
personal view by Peter May. Bromley, Christopher
Helm, 1989. [v], 373p. illus. stats. scores, bibliog.
index.

1337 **Russ, George,** *compiler*
■ Kent versus Surrey. West Bridgford (Notts.),
Association of Cricket Statisticians, 1987. 16p. incl.
covers, stats.
records 1828-1986.

1338 † S.C.C.C. scores 1872. n.d.
■ *reprinted scorecards for 30 first eleven and club and
ground matches played in 1872.*

1339 **Surrey County Cricket Club**
□ Around the Oval. The Club, *quarterly.* illus. (some col.)
from Spring 1989 'Around the Foster's Oval'.
continues 'Padwick I' 2695-2.

1340 The Oval: the home of Surrey County Cricket Club. The
■ Club, [1986]. [8]p. col. illus.
for sponsors and local businesses.

1341 † Souvenir of the Championship dinner at the Cafe Royal,
Wednesday 3rd December, 1952. [4]p. illus.

1342 Yearbook ... containing a record of the season, the
■ annual accounts, the Committee's report. The Club.
illus. scores, stats.
1980 compiled by Alan Hughes.
1981-83 edited by C.H.Burgess.
1984 to date edited by A.Bickerstaff.
1982 was the last issue to include list of members.
continues 'Padwick I' 2693 to date.

1343 **Surrey County Cricket Club Supporter's Association**
Oval world. The Association. *8 times per year.*
newsletter of the Association.

SUSSEX

1344 **Sussex Championship League**
■ Rules. The League. n.d. [6]p. folded card.
another ed. of 'Padwick I' 2710-1.

1345 **Sussex Cricket Association**
□ Handbook. The Association. *annual.* illus. stats.
continues 'Padwick I' 2712 to date.

1346 **Sussex Cricket League**
Handbook & fixtures. The League. *annual.*
founded 1970.

1347 **Sussex Invitation Cricket League**
□ Handbook. The League, *annual.* stats.
formed 1977; first match played 1979.
?/1984,87/ to date?

1348 **Swinfen, Warden** *and* **Arscott, David**
The BBC Radio Sussex guide to people of hidden
Sussex; with line drawings by John Whiting. Brighton,
BBC Radio Sussex, 1985. 166p. illus. map.
cricket references pp. 37, 42, 59, 101, 102 and 106.

1349 **Wales, Tony**
The West Sussex village book; with illustrations by David
Thelwell. Newbury, Countryside, 1984. 221p. illus.
map.
some cricket references.

Arundel

1350 **Arundel Cricket Club**
■ Pavilion centenary cricket week, June 17 to 23, 1984.
[The Club, 1984]. [12]p. incl. adverts.

Brighton

1351 † **Bridle, Bert**
Preston Nomads Cricket Club 1927-1977. [Hove, the
Club, 1977]. 20p.

1352 † **Brighton** Cricket Club matches for 1849 and 1850.
mentioned in 'Allen EBC'.

1353 † **Davies, William**
Brighton Cricket Club scorebook 1832-33.
ms. at Lord's according to 'Allen EBC'.

Burpham

1354 **Short** history of Burpham & Warningcamp Cricket Club
■ 1880-1980. [The Club], 1980. 7p.

1355 **Souvenir** programme: the centenary match, Sunday 14th
■ September 1980. Burpham & Warningcamp Cricket
Club versus Sussex County Cricket Club 1st XI. [The
Club], 1980. 56p. incl. adverts. illus.
includes a short history of the Club.

Crowborough

1356 **Crowborough** Cricket Club Times. [The Club]. stats.
■ *Nov 1988 the only issue.*

Ditchling

1357 St James's C. C. v Sussex C. C. C. XI, Saturday, 15th
■ September 1984. [The Club, 1984]. [32]p. incl. adverts.
illus. stats.
*includes history of St James's Cricket Club; match played
for Chris Waller's benefit.*

Easebourne

1358 Easebourne C. C. 1885-1985: centenary brochure. [The
■ Club], 1985. 36p. incl. covers and adverts. illus. stats.

Eastbourne

1359 **Armstrong, Robert**
Robert Armstrong's guide to Eastbourne. Eastbourne,
Sound Forum, 1984. 74p. illus.
*includes notes on The Saffrons and other Eastbourne
cricket grounds.*

Falmer

1360 **Williams, Doris**
Falmer Parish reflections. 1985.
references to Stanmer and Falmer C.C., pp.133-34.

Glynde

1361 **Glynde and Beddingham Cricket Club**
Boundary news. The Club. *quarterly?*
?/Autumn 1982/?

1362 Centenary handbook 1885-1985. Glynde, the Club,
■ [1985]. 88p. incl. adverts. illus. scores.

Groombridge

1363 **Hadley, Guy**
■ Cricket in Groombridge 1782-1982. [The Club?], 1982.
[i], 8p.

Hailsham

1364 **Cricket** in Hailsham since 1762: a short history of cricket played on Hailsham common and the early beginnings of the Hailsham Cricket Club. [The Club], 1984. [iii], 33p. illus.

Hastings

1365 The **history** of the Park Cricket Club: golden jubilee year 1936-1986. [Hastings, the Club, 1986]. 25p. incl. covers, illus. stats.

1366 **To** commemorate the centenary of Hastings cricket week: 'a history of cricket in Hastings'. [Hastings], Manpower Services Commission for the Hastings Museum, 1987. [14]p. illus. plan. stats.
includes plan of proposed new ground at Summerfields, St. Leonards.

Haywards Heath

1367 **Ford, Wyn K.** *and* **Gabe, A. C.**
The metropolis of mid Sussex: a history of Haywards Heath. 1981.
cricket references pp. 111-114.

Horsham

1368 † **Sussex Archaeological Society**
Sussex archaeological collections ... vol. 52. Lewes, Farncombe, 1909. illus.
includes 'Extracts from Mr John Baker's Horsham diary' covering the period 1771-1777 with cricket references throughout.

Newick

1369 **Newick** Cricket Club 1884-1984: a centenary celebration. [The Club, 1984]. 64p. incl. adverts. illus. scores, stats.

Poynings

1370 **Purkiss, Bill**
Poynings Cricket Club: memoir of a Sussex village; with drawings by Graham Jeffery. [The Club, 1986?]. 21p. incl. front cover, illus.

Slindon

1371 **Slindon Cricket Club**
250th anniversary of the noble sport at Slindon Cricket Club. Bognor Regis, Interscope, [1981]. 45p. incl. adverts. illus.

Storrington

1372 † **Greenfield, Florence M.**
Round about Old Storrington. [Storrington], the Author, 1972. [ii], 100p. illus.
'Cricket in the 19th century in Storrington' pp. 63-66.

Watersfield

1373 **Saer, Sandra**
Coldwaltham: a story of three hamlets. Pulborough, SMH Enterprises, 1987. xi, 228p. illus. maps. bibliog.
contains notes on Watersfield C.C., pp.179-180.

SUSSEX C. C. C.

1374 **Lee, Christopher**
From the sea end: the official history of Sussex County Cricket Club. Partridge Press, 1989. [xiv], 321p. illus. stats. index.

1375 **Sussex County Cricket Club**
Handbook. Hove, Caldra House for the Club. *annual.* illus. scores, stats.
edited by H.A. Osborne.
continues 'Padwick I' 2781 to date.

1376 **Sussex** County Cricket Club 1839-1989: 50th anniversary. [Hove, *Evening Argus*, 1989]. 44p. incl. covers, illus. (some col.)
an 'Evening Argus' souvenir special.

1377 The **Sussex** cricketer: the newspaper of Sussex County Cricket Club. Hove, CR Management Services on behalf of Sussex County Cricket Club.
/vol. 1. no. 1. 1980/ to date?

1378 **To** commemorate the centenary of Hastings cricket week: 'a history of cricket in Hastings'. [Hastings], Manpower Services Commission for the Hastings Museum, 1987. [14]p. illus. plan. stats.
includes plan of proposed new ground at Summerfields, St. Leonards.

WARWICKSHIRE

1379 † **Crompton** and Meesons reports, vol. 1. 1833.
pp. 797-806 contain Court of Exchequer judgement in the case of Hodson v Terrill concerning the illegality of a £20 bet on the result of a match between the Birmingham Union Club and the Warwick Club on 8 October 1832.

1380 **Warwickshire Cricket Association**
Handbook. Birmingham, Warwickshire Publishing. *annual.* scores.
?/1989/

Birmingham

1381 **Birmingham and District Cricket League**
Annual report, accounts and averages. Birmingham, the League. stats.
?/1989/

1382 Rules, fixtures and instructions to umpires. Birmingham, the League. *annual.* illus.
1988 was centenary ed.
continues 'Padwick I' 2795 to date.

1383 The **Birmingham** centenary cup 1889-1989: sixteen team knockout, Sunday May 14th 1989 at the Edgbaston Cricket Ground. [1989]. 80p. incl. adverts. illus. facsims.
tournament for Birmingham based firm's teams sponsored by Mitchells & Butlers and Warwickshire County Cricket Club.

1384 **Bryant, David C.**, *editor and compiler*
100 not out: 1888-1988. Birmingham, Birmingham and District Cricket League, 1988. 16p. illus.
souvenir brochure to celebrate the centenary of the Birmingham and District Cricket League.

1385 **Davis, Alexander Edward**
First in the field: the history of the world's first cricket league, the Birmingham and District Cricket League formed, 1888. Studley, Brewin Books, 1988. [viii], 232p. illus. stats. index.

1386 ■ Warwickshire C.C.C. Birmingham and District Cricket League: record of performances of the club in the first division - seasons 1975 to 1984 ... [Warwickshire C.C.C., 1985]. 48p. illus. stats.

1387 ■ **Goodyear, David William**
Bournville Cricket Club: the start of it all - a century of cricket 1882-1982. [The Club, 1982]. [24]p. incl. covers, illus. stats.

1388 ■ **Gross, Nicholas Clive**
Olton & West Warwickshire Cricket Club 1888-1988: commemorating 100 years of cricket at Olton. [The Club, 1988]. 108p. incl. adverts. illus. stats.

Coventry

1389 □ **Mitchells & Butlers Coventry and District Cricket League**
Official handbook. Coventry, the League. *annual*. stats. *1976?/1988 to date/*

Knowle

1390 ■ **Knowle** Village Cricket Club centenary: a souvenir history and programme of events and fixtures 1982 season. [The Club, 1982]. 22p. incl. adverts. illus. maps.

Leek Wootton

1391 ■ **Leek** Wooton C.C. centenary handbook. [The Club, 1989]. [ii], 87p. illus. stats.

Nether Whitacre

1392 ■ **Barnett, Maurice**
Cow pats and cricket bats: 100 years of Nether Whitacre Cricket Club. [The Club, 1987]. 40p. illus. facsims, scores.

Rowington

1393 ■ **Rowington** Cricket Club 1887-1987. [The Club], 1987. 48p. illus. facsims, stats.

Walmley

1394 ■ **Walmley** C.C.: the first 100 years: official centenary handbook. [The Club, 1986]. 32p. incl. adverts. illus.

Water Orton

1395 ■ **Appleyard, F. S.,** *compiler*
Water Orton: a hundred years of cricket. [Water Orton, Water Orton C. C., 1980]. [70]p. illus. facsims. scores, stats.

1396 ■ **Water** Orton Cricket Club: official opening of the new pavilion. [The Club], 1983. [16]p. incl. adverts. illus.

WARWICKSHIRE C. C. C.

1397 ■ **[Brooke, Robert William]**
Cricket grounds of Warwickshire. West Bridgford (Notts.), Association of Cricket Statisticians, [1989]. 36p. illus. stats.

1398 ■ **Brooke, Robert William,** *compiler*
Warwickshire cricket record book. [Haughton Mill (Notts.)], Association of Cricket Statisticians in conjunction with the Author, [1982]. 96p. illus. stats. *covers period 1894-1981.*

1399 ■ **Brooke, Robert William** *and* **Goodyear, David William**
A who's who of Warwickshire County Cricket Club. Robert Hale, 1989. xix, 220p. illus. stats.

1400 ■ **Griffiths, Barry**
A Warwickshire cricket chronicle. Lewes, Book Guild, 1988. 232p. illus. scores, bibliog. index.

1401 ■ **Walton, Timothy Michael Keith,** *compiler*
Warwickshire Sunday League records 1969-1988 incorporating both Refuge Assurance League and John Player. [Birmingham], the Author, 1989. 88p. stats.

1402 ■ The **Warwickshire** centenary story: 100 years of Warwickshire cricket. [Birmingham], Birmingham Post and Mail, [1982]. 58p. incl. adverts. illus. (some col.) stats.

1403 ■ **Warwickshire County Cricket Club**
Beyond the boundary: magazine of Warwickshire County Cricket Club. Birmingham, the Club. *irregular*. illus. (mostly col.)
issue [no. 1], Jan 1988 to date.

1404 ■ Official year book including annual report and statement of accounts. [Birmingham, the Club]. illus. (some col.) scores, stats.
with title 'Annual report and statement of accounts' until 1987.
continues 'Padwick I' 2822 to date.

1405 ■ Warwickshire newsletter. [Birmingham, the Club]. illus.
Winter 1986/87 was only issue.

WESTMORLAND

1406 □ **South Lakeland Cricket League**
Handbook. The League. *annual*. stats.
continues 'Padwick I' 2830-1? to date?

WILTSHIRE

1407 □ **Wiltshire County Cricket Club** *and* **Wiltshire Cricket Association**
Wiltshire cricket. Trowbridge, the Club and the Association. *annual*. illus. scores, stats.
sponsored by The Carphone Group.
?/1988 to date/

1408 ■ **Wiltshire Cricket League**
[Handbook]. [The League]. *annual*.
league formed 1981.
1986? to date.

Alderbury

1409 ■ **Alderbury** Cricket Club 1885-1985. [The Club, 1985]. 32p. illus.

Beckhampton

1410 † ■ **Beckhampton Cricket Club**
Rules of the Beckhampton Cricket Club [and list of members]. Devizes, printed by Smith, c. 1820. [4]p.

Broad Chalke

1411 ■ **Penn, Malcolm K.,** *compiler*
Broad Chalke Cricket Club silver jubilee, 1957-1982. [the Club, 1982]. 15p. stats. *typescript.*

Chippenham

1412 † **Chippenham Cricket Club**
Souvenir of the 60th season of cricket at Harden Huish Park. Chippenham, Chippenham Town Football Club, 1952.

North Bradley

1413 **Hobbs, Owen**
North Bradley: 100 years of cricket 1867-1967. North Bradley, Mrs Lanfear, 1982. 25p.

Swindon

1414 **Lenham, Alan P.** *and* **Brewer, B. H. ('Bert')**
■ Notes for a history of Swindon Cricket Club. [The Club], 1988. 73p. stats.
cover title: 'Swindon Cricket Club 1844-1988'.

1415 **Swindon Cricket Club**
■ 1985 Barbados tour. [Swindon, the Club, 1985]. 28p. incl. adverts. illus.
pre-tour; April-May.

1416 Fixture list. Swindon, the Club. *annual.* illus.
□ *includes historical and other editorial material. /1985-87/ to date?*

Warminster

1417 **Warminster Cricket Club**
■ Souvenir programme 1838-1988. [The Club, 1988]. 24p. illus.
includes a history of the Club by Andrew J. Pinnell.

WILTSHIRE C. C. C.

1418 **Wiltshire** County Cricket Club: centenary brochure
■ 1882-1982. [Trowbridge, the Club, 1982]. 44p. illus. stats.

1419 **Wiltshire County Cricket Club**
□ [Annual report]. [The Club]. scores, stats.
from 1988? incorporated in 'Wiltshire Cricket'. continues 'Padwick I' 2842 to date.

1420 **Wiltshire County Cricket Club** *and* **Wiltshire Cricket**
□ **Association**
Wiltshire cricket. Trowbridge, the Club and the Association. *annual.* illus. scores, stats.
sponsored by The Carphone Group. ?/1988 to date/

WORCESTERSHIRE

1421 **Worcestershire Cricket Association**
□ Year book. Worcester, the Association. illus. stats.
latterly with title 'Cricket in Worcestershire'. continues 'Padwick I' 2844-1 to date.

Barnt Green

1422 **Barnt** Green Cricket Club: 100 not out. [The Club],
■ 1989. 68p. incl. covers and adverts. illus.

Bransford

1423 † **[Anderton, H. S. Cliff** *et al, editors*]
■ Worcester Nomads club history 1927-1977. [The Club, 1977]. [28]p. illus. stats.
played as wandering club until 1959.

Broadway

1424 † **Andrews, Maurice**
■ 'A village remembered'. Eastbourne, the Author, 1971. viii, 56p. illus.
includes memories of the Broadway Cricket Club, pp. 35-38.

Elmley Castle

1425 **Elmley** Castle Cricket Club v Worcestershire County
■ Cricket Club souvenir programme. [The Club], 1989. [40]p. incl. adverts. illus. stats.
to celebrate the 125th year of Elmley Castle Cricket Club.

Tenbury Wells

1426 **Jones, Pip**
Sixty years at play on the Teme. 1985. 109p. illus.
cricket in Tenbury Wells.

WORCESTERSHIRE C. C. C.

1427 **Barnsley, Peter Martyn**
■ The tenth wicket record: an account of the Worcestershire v Kent match at Stourbridge (Amblecote) in July 1909 ... West Hagley, Two Gates Publications, 1987. 16p. illus. score.

1428 † **Catalogue** of an exhibition on the history of Worcestershire C. C. C. [Worcester, Worcester City Library], 1975.

1429 **[Hatton, Leslie Walter]**
■ Cricket grounds of Worcestershire. Haughton Mill (Notts.), Association of Cricket Statisticians, [1985]. 33p. illus. stats.

1430 **Hatton, Leslie Walter**
■ The Worcestershire cricket quiz book. Edinburgh, Mainstream Publishing, 1989. 144p. illus.

1431 **Lemmon, David Hector**
■ The official history of Worcestershire County Cricket Club; with a personal view by Basil D'Oliveira. Bromley, Christopher Helm, 1989. [v], 288p. illus. stats. bibliog. index.

1432 **Vockins, Michael D.**
■ Worcestershire County Cricket Club: a pictorial history. Severn House in association with Worcestershire C. C. C., 1980. 128p. illus.

1433 **Watson, Frank**
■ Double triumph: Worcestershire's 1988 season: the full story. Studley, Brewin Books, 1989. [viii], 244p. illus. scores, stats.

1434 **Worcestershire County Cricket Club**
■ Year book. Worcester, the Club. illus. (some col. since 1988) scores, stats.
complied by Year Book Sub-Committee. continues 'Padwick I' 2856 to date.

1435 **Worcestershire** County Cricket Club cricket tour to
■ Barbados 1980: souvenir brochure & programme. [Worcester, the Club, 1980]. [32]p. incl. adverts. illus.
11-25 October 1980. pre-tour.

YORKSHIRE

1436 † **Central Yorkshire Cricket League**
□ Official handbook. The League. *annual*. stats.
1987 with title 'Armitage & Norton Central Yorkshire Cricket League'.
1988 to date sponsored by Girobank.
?/1973, 1975/ to date.

1437 † **Cleveland and Teesside Cricket League**
□ Handbook. The League. *annual*.
1985 pub. as special centenary ed. with title '100 not out: the history of the Cleveland & Teesside Cricket League 1885-1985', [compiled by Frank Jewitt and Steve Oakey].
?/1979-83, 85/ to date?

1438 † **Cricket Pennant Alliance**
□ Official handbook. [The Alliance]. *annual*. stats.
based in East Riding; founded 1957.
?/1974, 1978-85/ to date.

1439 **Dales Council Cricket League**
□ Official handbook. [The League]. *annual*. stats.
continues 'Padwick I' 2864 to date

1440 † **East Yorkshire Cricket Cup Competition**
□ Rules and official guide. The Competition, *annual*. stats. *typescript.*
League competition founded in 1924.
?/1967, 1975-86/ to date?

1441 **Girobank North Yorkshire and South Durham Cricket**
□ **League**
[Handbook]. The League. *annual*. stats.
sponsored by Girobank since 1986.
continues 'Padwick I' 2870 to date.

1442 † **Heavy Woollen District Challenge Cup**
□ [Handbook]. [The Challenge Cup Emergency Committee]. *annual*. stats.
Cup competition inaugurated 1883.
?/1973-88/ to date.

1443 † **Howdenshire Evening League**
□ Handbook. The League. *annual*.
?/1964,78,80-82/ to date?

1444 † **Humber-Don Cricket League**
□ Official handbook. The League. *annual*. stats. *typescript.*
Inner League of Yorks Cricket Council.
?/1976-86/ to date.

1445 † **Humberside Cricket Federation**
□ Handbook. [The Federation]. *annual*. *typescript.*
?/1978-82/ to date.

1446 † **Langbaurgh West Rural District Cricket League**
□ [Handbook]. [The League]. *annual*. stats.
League founded in 1938.
?/1979-83/ to date.

1447 † **North Humberside Sunday Cricket League**
□ Handbook. The League. *annual*.
founded 1975.
?/1978-80,83/ to date?

1448 **The Ron Long Sunday Cricket League**
■ Rules. The League. [1984]. [8]p. incl. covers.
West Yorkshire League sponsored by Ron Long, a Keightley bookmaker; later known as Cleckheaton Motors Sunday Cricket League?

1449 † [**Trenholm, Herbert**, *compiler*]
■ North Yorkshire and South Durham Cricket League statistics 1956-68. The League, c.1969. 104p. stats.
supplement to 'Padwick I' 2871.

1450 † **Wensleydale Cricket League**
□ [Rules and fixtures]. The League. *annual*?
?/1979,83/ to date?

1451 **Windmill, Kenneth H.**
■ Only the Ashes are older: 100 years of the Heavy Woollen District Cricket Challenge Cup 1883-1983. [Dewsbury, Heavy Woollen District Cricket Challenge Cup Committee, 1982]. [48]p. illus. scores.

1452 **Woodhouse, Anthony**, *editor*
■ 50 years of cricket in the Central Yorkshire Cricket League 1937-1987. [Leeds, the League, 1987]. 96p. illus.

1453 † **Yorkshire Cricket Association**
□ The Bulletin. The Association. *2 or 3 issues per year.*
all aspects of non first-class cricket in the County.
1978? to date.

1454 Development plan. The Association, 1984. [iv], 21p.
■ diagr.
——rev. ed. 1988.

1455 Yorkshire Cricket Association XI touring Barbados - West Indies, Easter 1984. The Association, [1984]. [20]p. incl. adverts. illus.
pre-tour.

1456 **Yorkshire Cricket League**
■ League handbook. The League, *annual*. stats.
1985-87 Stone's Best Bitter Yorkshire Cricket League.
1988-89 Webster's Yorkshire Cricket League.
continues 'Padwick I' 2883 to date.

1457 † Yorkshire Cricket League (1935-1960) ... annual dinner
■ and trophy presentation ... 21st October 1960. [The League], 1960. [12]p. stats.
summary of the 1960 season.

1458 † **Yorkshire Evening Post**
■ Cricket annual 1926; edited by 'Old Ebor'. Leeds, Yorkshire Conservative Newspaper Co., 1926. 128p. illus. stats.
pre-season; the only issue?

Airedale and Wharfedale

1459 **Airedale and Wharfedale Senior Cricket League**
■ Official handbook. The League, *annual*. stats.
continues 'Padwick I' 2890 to date.

1460 **Sullivan, J. D.**, *editor*
■ Airedale & Wharfedale Senior Cricket League golden jubilee brochure. [The League, 1986]. [75]p. incl. adverts. illus.
limited ed. of 1050 copies of which 50 were produced in a numbered hardback ed.

Barkston Ash

1461 **Barkston Ash and Yorkshire Central Cricket League**
□ Official handbook. The League, *annual*. stats.
continues 'Padwick I' 2892 to date.

Barmby Moor

1462 † **Wood Rees, W. D.**
■ A history of Barmby Moor from pre-historic times. Pocklington, printed by W. & C. Forth, 1911. 109p. frontis. illus.
cricket pp. 84-85.

Barnsley

1463   Barnsley & District Cricket League
☐   Handbook. The League, *annual*. stats.
continues 'Padwick I' 2894 to date.

Bedale

1464   Gillett, Doug, *editor*
■   150 years of cricket at Bedale. The Club, 1985. 40p.
incl. adverts. illus. scores.

Bingley

1465   Twenty wonderful years at Bingley: David Batty
■   testimonial brochure. 48p. incl. covers and adverts.
illus. stats.
*produced for testimonial match, Bingley v Yorkshire XI,
27 May, 1986.*

Blackley

1466 †   Opening of pavilion August 13th, 1978 ...
■   commemorative programme. [Blackley Cricket Club],
1978. [24]p. incl. adverts. illus.
includes a brief history of cricket in the village.

Bradford

1467 †   Allerton Cricket Club
Official handbook the grand bazaar. [Bradford, the
Club], 1904.

1468   Bankfoot Cricket Club
■   Official programme. The Club, 1982. *typescript*.
*13 match programmes for 1982 season each containing
an instalment of the history of Bankfoot C. C.*

1469   Bradford & District Evening Cricket League
☐   Official handbook. The League, *annual*. stats.
continues 'Padwick I' 2897 to date.

1470   Bradford Central Cricket League
☐   Official handbook. The League, *annual*. stats.
with title 'Official guide' to 1977.
continues 'Padwick I' 2898 to date.

1471   Bradford Cricket League
☐   Annual report. The League. scores, stats. *typescript*.
?/1978, 1982-84, 1987/ to date.

1472 Official handbook. The League, *annual*. illus. (from
■   1988), stats.
continues 'Padwick I' 2900 to date.

1473   Bradford Mutual Sunday School Cricket League
☐   Official handbook. The League, *annual*. stats.
continues 'Padwick I' 2902 to date.

1474 † The **conglomerated** chronicles of a country chapel
■   cricket club ... the Wesleyans of Allerton; by one of 'em.
[1906?]. [8]p.
memories of Allerton Wesleyan Cricket Club, 1903-06.

1475 †   Haigh, Austin
Cricket at Lidget Green: some historical reminiscences.
1935. 6p.

1476   Maude, Donald
■   A centenary of Yorkshire cricket at Park Avenue
1881-1981. Bradford, Bradford Cricket Club, 1981.
56p. scores.
Bradford League cricket pp. 9-13.

1477   Pickup, Peter
■   The history of the Bradford Cricket League, 1903 to
1988. Pudsey, Fairhaven Books, [1989]. 129p. illus.
scores, stats.

1478 †   Pitchers, C. W.
The Bradford Mutual Sunday School Cricket League,
1896-1956. Bradford, the League, 1957. 22p.

1479   Thornbury Cricket Club: centenary year 1889-1989.
■   [The Club, 1989]. 28p. incl. covers and adverts. stats.

1480 †   Undercliffe Cricket Club 1875-1975. [Bradford, the
■   Club, 1975]. [32]p. incl. adverts. illus.

Bridlington

1481 †   Bridlington and District Amateur Cricket League
☐   Complete list of rules and fixtures. The League. *annual*.
League founded in 1922.
?/1972,78-82/ to date?

Broad Oak

1482   From little acorns ... a century of cricket at Broad Oak
■   1880-1980. [Broad Oak Cricket and Athletic Club,
1980]. 48p. incl. adverts. illus. stats.

Collingham

1483   Collingham & Linton Cricket Club centenary 1887-1987:
■   women's Test - England v Australia - 21st ... 24th August
1987. 1987. [44]p. illus. (mostly col.)
*includes a history of Collingham & Linton Cricket Club
by Mike Clark.*

Craven

1484   [Coe, Trevor J. F.]
■   A history of the Craven and District Cricket League and
its forerunners 1888-1988. The League, 1988. [v], 164p.
stats.
*comprises vol. 1, 1888-1958, pp. 1-63 - a reprint of
'Padwick I' 2909 - and vol. 2, 1958-1988, pp. 64-164.*

1485   Craven & District Cricket League
■   Official handbook. The League. *annual*. stats.
centenary handbook 1988.
continues 'Padwick I' 2908 to date.

Darfield

1486   Marsden, J. Trevor, *editor*
■   Darfield Cricket Club v Yorkshire C. C.: souvenir
brochure of match to celebrate opening of new pavilion,
22 April 1981. The Club, 1981. 36p. incl. adverts. illus.
includes history of the Club.

1487   Randerson, Ian M.
■   The history of the Darfield Cricket Club. [Darfield, the
Club, 1985]. [iv], 169p. illus. stats.

Dewsbury

1488   The 'A.V. Kitchen Feeds' Dewsbury & District Cricket
☐   **League**
Official handbook. The League. *annual*. stats.
continues 'Padwick I' 2911 to date.

1489   Quaid-E-Azam Sunday Cricket League
☐   Official handbook. The League. *annual*. stats.
established 1980.
?/1986,88/ to date.

1490 Windmill, Kenneth H.
■   Sunset on Savile: the rise and decline of a cricket club.
       [Dewsbury, the Author, 1987]. [ii], 241p. illus. scores,
       stats. *typescript.*
          the story of Dewsbury Cricket Club, 1860-1985.

Doncaster

1491 Doncaster and District Cricket League
□   Official guide. The League. *annual.* stats.
          continues 'Padwick I' 2913 to date?

**1492 † Doncaster and District Cricket League *and* Doncaster
■   & District Umpires Association**
       Joint official guide to ground locations and transport
       services. Doncaster, the League and the Association,
       1959. 40p.
          pub. annually?

**1493 † Doncaster and District Infirmary Evening Cricket
□   League**
       Official guide. The League. *annual.*
          ?/1962 ... 1978-81/ to date?

1494 Scowcroft, Philip L.
■   Cricket in Doncaster and district: an outline history.
       Doncaster, Doncaster Library Service, 1985. [ii]. 53p.
       illus. map, score.

East Riding

1495 East Riding Amateur Cricket League
□   Official handbook. The League. *annual.*
          continues 'Padwick I' 2914 to date.

1496 † East Riding Independent League
□   List of officers, rules and fixtures. The League. *annual.*
          ?/1978-83/ to date?

Elland

1497 † [Gledhill, Derek]
■   Elland Cricket, Athletic & Bowling Club centenary
       brochure 1860-1960. [The Club, 1960]. 56p. incl.
       adverts. illus.

1498 Matchday: official magazine of Elland Cricket Club.
□   *produced for every home game, fortnightly?.* The Club.
       stats.
          special issue 10 August 1986 for Sykes Cup Final.
          ?1986 to date?

Elsecar

1499 [Beachill, Jim]
■   130 years on the Crab Field. [The Author, 1988]. [28]p.
       incl. covers. illus.
          history of Elsecar C. C.

1500 Elsecar Cricket Club: 125 years a Club. Celebratory
■   annual dinner & dance, Friday 11th March 1983. [8]p.
       incl. covers, facsim.
          contains lines composed to celebrate the winning of the
          Wake Challenge Cup by the Elsecar Cricket Club for three
          years in succession - 1881, 1882 and 1883.

Eskdale

1501 † Eskdale Cricket League
□   Rules & fixtures. The League. *annual.*
          ?/1978-81/ to date?

Halifax

1502 Halifax and District Cricket Association
□   Official handbook. The Association. *annual.* stats.
          continues 'Padwick I' 2917 to date.

1503 Halifax Cricket League
□   Official handbook: laws - fixtures - umpires. The
       League. *annual.* stats.
          continues 'Padwick I' 2918 to date.

1504 Illingworth St Mary's Cricket Club
■   Centenary brochure 1884-1984. [Halifax, the Club,
       1984]. 112p. incl. adverts. illus. scores, stats.

1505 King Cross Cricket, Bowling and Athletic Club:
■   centenary year 1882-1982. The Club, [1982]. [20]p. incl.
       adverts. illus.

Harrogate

**1506 Harrogate and District Amateur Evening Cricket
□   League**
       Rules and fixtures. The League. *annual.* stats.
          continues 'Padwick I' 2924 to date.

1507 † Harrogate Cricket Club
■   *'The Taverner'.* Harrogate, the Club. *annual.* map.
          pre-season brochure pub. 1974-77.
          forerunner of 'Padwick I' 2924-1.

Hatfield

1508 † Hatfield Town Cricket Club commemorative brochure.
■   [The Club, 1971]. 28p. incl. adverts. scores, stats.
          cover sub-title: 'one hundred years of cricket: a short
          history of the club'.

Honley

1509 Honley Cricket Club centenary brochure, 1880-1980.
■   [The Club, 1980]. [68]p. incl. adverts. illus, stats.

Horbury Bridge

1510 Centenary year ... of Horbury Bridge Cricket Club,
■   1887-1987. The Club, [1987]. 32p. incl. adverts. scores.
       stats.

Huddersfield

1511 Armitage Bridge Cricket Club 150th anniversary,
■   1939-1989. [Huddersfield, the Club], 1989. 92p. incl.
       adverts. illus.

1512 Hinchliffe, Gordon
■   A history of the Huddersfield Central Cricket League.
       [The League, 1988]. 88p. illus. stats.
          cover title: '75 not out'.

1513 Huddersfield and District Cricket Association
□   Annual handbook. The Association.
          continues 'Padwick I' 2929 to date.

1514 Huddersfield Central Cricket League
□   Annual handbook. The League.
          continues 'Padwick I' 2933 to date.

1515 † Huddersfield cricket festival week - 1949: souvenir
■   brochure. 1949. [24]p. incl. adverts. scores.
          pre-festival; the festival was first held in 1947.

1516 Huddersfield Cricket League
■   Official handbook. The League. *annual.* stats.
          continues 'Padwick I' 2934 to date.

1517 † Scholes Cricket Club
Scholes Cricket Club 1876-1976. Huddersfield, the Club, 1976.

1518 Walton, T.
A history of the Huddersfield and District Cricket Association. [The Association], 1986. 80p. illus. stats.
cover title: 'One hundred partnership'.

Kirkburton

1519 † 1878-1978: cricket at Riley Lane, Kirkburton, 100 years on ... [Kirkburton, Kirkburton Cricket Club, 1978]. 48p. incl. adverts. illus. stats.

Kirkheaton

1520 Stephenson, D. Alan
Kirkheaton Cricket and Bowling Club: 100 years at Bankfield 1883-1983: centenary brochure. [Kirkheaton, the Club, 1983]. [78]p. incl. adverts. illus.

Leeds

1521 30 years on ... New Farnley Cricket Club 1982. [8]p.
brochure to accompany Gala Day and Olde Worlde Cricket Match - includes personal memoirs of the Club.

1522 Alwoodley Cricket Club golden jubilee. [The Club, 1985]. 40p. incl. adverts. illus. stats.

1523 Colton Institute Cricket Club first eleven year book 1985. The Club, 1985. 38p. scores, stats.
limited ed.; the only issue?

1524 † Emsley Challenge Cup contests. Leeds, Leamington Cricket Club, [1882]. 12p. scores.
celebrates Leamington's success in winning the Cup three years running.

1525 Hopwood, W. Arthur *and* **Casperson, Frederic P.**
Meanwood. [Leeds, the Authors?, 1986]. 84p. illus.
history of Meanwood Cricket Club, pp. 42-44.

1526 Jack Gahan Sunday Cricket League
[Handbook]. The League. *annual.*
1982-87

1527 Leeds & District Cricket League
[Handbook]. The League. *annual.* stats.
since 1987 sponsored by Avon Display.
continues 'Padwick I' 2950 to date.

1528 The Sports Bag Evening Cricket League
Official handbook. The League. *annual.* stats.
1987 Gymkhana Sports Evening Cricket League.
1988 Millett (Printers) Evening Cricket League.
1983-88; not pub. 1989.

1529 Whitkirk Cricket Club
[Handbook]. The Club. *annual.*
formed 1892.
?/1985/ to date.

1530 The Yorkshire Copper Works Cricket Club
Members handbook. Leeds, the Club, 1985. 25p. stats.
list of Club records and achievements; the Club's parent company is IMI Yorkshire Imperial Metals Ltd.

Marske-by-the-Sea

1531 Charlton, James Mervyn
'More sand in my shoes'. Kidderminster, the Author, 1983. vi, 112p. illus.
includes reminiscences of Marske Cricket Club.

Menston

1532 Kell, Jack H.
The history of Menston Cricket Club. [The Author? 1980]. [vii], 88p.

Mexborough

1533 Mexborough & District Cricket League
Official handbook. The League. *annual.*
continues 'Padwick I' 2970 to date.

Middlesbrough

1534 Baker, Ray
Iron & willow; a history of Middlesbrough C. C. volume one, 1855 to 1911. The Author, 1989. [iv], 118p. illus. facsims, map, scores.
limited ed. of 300 numbered and signed copies.

1535 Iron and willow: a history of cricket in Middlesbrough 1856-1875 (with notes to 1983). The Author, [1983]. [ii], 145p. map, plans, scores.
ms. limited ed. of 10 numbered and signed copies.

1536 † Middlesbrough & District Mid-week League
Cricket handbook. The League. *annual. typescript.*
?/1979-80/ to date?

Morley

1537 † Crossland, Ken *and* **Jackman, Phil**
Morley Cricket Bowling & Athletic Club: Morley Cricket Club 1975 tour souvenir brochure. [The Club, 1975]. [28]p. incl. adverts.
pub. prior to tour of Worcestershire.

1538 Gledhill, Chris, *compiler, and* **Robson, Reuben,** *editor*
Morley Cricket Bowling & Athletic Club centenary 1889-1989. [The Club, 1989]. [20]p. illus. stats.

Newby Hall

1539 Newby Hall C. C. Select XI v Yorkshire C. C. C. at Newby Hall, Friday September 18th 1987. [16]p. incl. adverts.
includes a short history of Newby Hall Cricket Club.

Nidderdale

1540 Nidderdale & District Amateur Cricket League
Rules and fixtures. The League. *annual.*
continues 'Padwick I' 2974 to date.

Pocklington

1541 † Pocklington & District Cricket League
List of officers, rules and officials. The League. *annual?*
?/1978-82/ to date

Pontefract

1542 Finlux TV Pontefract & District Cricket League
Handbook. The League. *annual.*
continues 'Padwick I' 2976 to date.

Pudsey

1543 Pudsey and District Cricket League
Official handbook. The League. *annual.* stats.
continues 'Padwick I' 2977 to date.

1544 **Pudsey** Congs C. C. v Yorkshire C. C. C. souvenir brochure. Pudsey Congs C.C., 1985. [16]p. incl. covers and adverts. illus. stats.
match played on 2 April 1985 for Phil Carrick's benefit; includes information on history of cricket in Pudsey.

1545 **Pudsey** St. Lawrence Cricket Club ... 100 years of cricket at Tofts Road: centenary brochure. [Pudsey, the Club], 1989. [64]p. incl. adverts. illus.

Saddleworth

1546 **Saddleworth and District Cricket League**
[Handbook]. The League. *annual.* stats.
continues 'Padwick I' 2984 to date.

Scarborough

1547 **Charlton, James Mervyn**
'More sand in my shoes'. Kidderminster, the Author, 1983. vi, 112p. illus.
includes reminiscences of Scarborough Festival.

1548 **Herbert, John S.**
The Scarborough festival: 100 not out. Scarborough, [the Author?], 1986. 64p. incl. adverts. illus. scores, bibliog.
centenary festival booklet.

1549 **Scarborough Cricket Club**
Annual report and statement of accounts. Scarborough, the Club. illus. scores, stats.
continues 'Padwick I 2990 to date.

1550 Boundary talk: weekly programme and scorecard. The Club.
pub. during 1980 season only?

1551 † Rules and regulations of the Scarborough Cricket Club, approved of at a general meeting held at the Savings' Bank, this 11th day of May, 1836. [Scarborough], printed by C. R. Todd, 1836. 2p.

1552 The **Scarborough** cricket festival souvenir programme. Berkhamsted, Dennis Fairey. *annual.* illus. (mostly col.)
1982-87: 'The Asda cricket challenge'.
1988 pub. by Multi-media Services; 1989 pub. by Tesco Stores.
1982 to date.

Sheffield

1553 **Beachill, Jim**
See the conquering hero comes. Conisborough, the Author, 1986. 71p. illus. scores, stats.
the Wake Challenge Cup 1881-1883 - Sheffield area.

1554 **Farnsworth, Keith**
Before and after Bramall Lane: Sheffield United C. C. and Yorkshire cricket in Sheffield. Sheffield, the Author, 1988. [vi], 146p. illus.
club and county cricket.

1555 † **Norton & District Cricket League**
[Handbook]. The League. *annual.*
?/1973,78-83/ to date?

1556 **Sheffield & District Works Sports Association**
Official handbook for cricket. The Association. *annual.*
continues 'Padwick I' 2998 to date.

1557 † **Sheffield Alliance Mid-Week Cricket League**
Jubilee handbook 1928-1978. [Sheffield, the Alliance, 1978]. 61p. incl. adverts. illus.
includes fixtures for 1978 and details of 1977 season.

1558 Rules and fixtures. The League. *annual.*
continues 'Padwick I' 2997 to date.

1559 **Sheffield Collegiate Cricket Club**
Centenary 1981. [Sheffield, the Club, 1981]. [40]p. incl. adverts. illus.

1560 **Sheffield Cricket League**
Official handbook. The League. *annual.*
continues 'Padwick I' 3000 to date.

1561 † **Sime Memorial Cricket League**
Rules and fixtures. The League. *annual.*
League established 1924.
?/1976/ to date?

1562 **Wilson, David**
A century of the Sheffield Collegiate Cricket Club: a short history, 1881-1981. [Sheffield, the Club, 1981]. [ii], 34p. illus.

Skipton

1563 **Hennigan, Terry**
One hundred years of local cricket 1882-1982. [Skipton, Skipton Church Institute Cricket Club, 1982]. 56p. illus.

Slaithwaite

1564 † **Slaithwaite Cricket and Bowling Club**
Centenary, 1873-1973. Huddersfield, the Club, 1973. 92p.

South Riding

1565 **South Riding Cricket League**
Official handbook. The League. *annual.* stats.
continues 'Padwick I' 3006 to date.

Sowerby

1566 † **Sowerby** St. Peter's Cricket Club: county cricket at Sowerby; Yorkshire v Cumberland & Westmorland (under 15) Sunday 24th June 1973. [The Club], 1973. [8]p. incl. covers.
includes brief history of the Club, celebrating its 50th anniversary.

Sprotbrough

1567 **[Johnson, M. K., *compiler*]**
Sprotbrough Cricket Club (1941): centenary year 1886-1986. [The Club, 1986]. 92p. incl. covers and adverts. illus. stats.

Stamford Bridge

1568 † **Foss Evening Cricket League**
List of officers, rules & fixtures. The League. *annual.*
?/1978,80-82/ to date?

Thackley

1569 † **Thackley** Cricket Club centenary brochure. [The Club, 1979]. [48]p. incl. adverts. illus. stats.

Thornhill

1570 **Wood, Herbert**
A history of Thornhill Cricket & Bowling Club. [The Club, 1987]. 24p. illus. map.

Todmorden

1571 **Wild, Ron,** *compiler and editor*
■ Todmorden Cricket Club 1837-1987: 150th anniversary souvenir. [Todmorden], the Club, [1987]. 96p. illus. scores, stats.

Upper Haugh

1572 **Upper Haugh Cricket Club**
■ Centenary 1882-1982. [Upper Haugh, the Club, 1982]. 28p. incl. adverts. illus. scores.

Wakefield

1573 **Wakefield & District Cricket Union**
□ Handbook. The Union. *annual.*
continues 'Padwick I' 3009 to date.

Warmsworth

1574 **Warmsworth C. C. XI ... versus Yorkshire C. C. C. ...**
■ Sunday, 13th September 1987. [The Club], 1987. 32p. incl. covers and adverts. illus.
includes short history of the Club, pp. 5-10.

West Riding

1575 **West Riding Cricket League**
□ [Handbook]. Pontefract, the League. *annual.* stats.
continues 'Padwick I' 3015 to date?

1576 † **The West Riding Sunday Cricket Council**
□ Rules and fixtures. Bradford, the Council. *annual. typescript.*
?/1979-83/ to date?

Wetherby

1577 **Wetherby & District Cricket League**
■ Handbook. The League. *annual.* stats.
continues 'Padwick I' 3017 to date.
1979: 'Brown and White Wetherby ...'
1980-82: 'Tricentrol Wetherby ...'
1983-84: 'Trimoco Wetherby ...'

Yeadon

1578 **Yeadon** Cricket Club [1859-1984]. [Yeadon, the Club,
■ 1984]. [28]p. illus.
brochure to mark 125th anniversary.

York

1579 **Herbert, John S.,** *editor*
■ York Cricket Club 1784-1984: official bi-centennial brochure. [York, the Club, 1984]. 88p. incl. adverts. illus.

1580 † **York and District Saturday Cricket League**
□ Fixtures. The League. *annual.*
now known as the York Vale League.
?/1978-81,84/ to date?

1581 **York and District Senior Cricket League**
□ [Handbook]. The League. *annual.* stats.
continues 'Padwick I' 3020 to date.

YORKSHIRE C. C. C.

1582 **Alton, Fred,** *[compiler]*
■ First and last. Armthorpe, the Author, [1983]. 30p. illus. stats.
'a statistical look at Yorkshiremen who have scored fifties and centuries in Test matches from 1877 to 1982'.

1583 **Association of Cricket Statisticians**
■ Yorkshire cricketers 1863-1985. Haughton Mill (Notts.), the Association, 1986. 43p. + [2]p. of maps. stats.

1584 **Bairstow, David Leslie** *with* **Hodgson, Derek**
■ A Yorkshire diary: year of crisis. Sidgwick & Jackson, 1984. x, 165p. illus.
the 1984 season.

1585 **Boothroyd, Derrick**
■ Half a century of Yorkshire cricket. Keighley, Kennedy Brothers Publishing, 1981. viii, 159p. illus.

1586 † Nowt so queer as folk: a book of reminiscence about Yorkshire and Yorkshiremen. Bradford, Watmoughs, 1976. [xii], 211p.
cricket reminiscences, pp. 181-211.

1587 **Callaghan, John**
■ Yorkshire's pride: 150 years of county cricket Pelham Books, 1984. 240p. illus. scores, stats. index.

1588 **Cardus,** *Sir* **[John Frederick] Neville**
■ The roses matches 1919-1939. Souvenir Press, 1982. 520p. illus. scores.

1589 **Charnock, Jeremy**
■ Tykes review. Bingley, the Author, 1986. scores, stats.
vol. 1, no. 1. June 1986. the only issue?

1590 **Dalby, Ken**
■ The Headingley story vol. 3: white is the rose: a record of county cricket at Headingley 1891-1980. Leeds, the Author, [1981]. [iv], 146p, illus. scores, stats.
vols. 1 and 2 cover rugby.

1591 **East, Harry**
■ Cricket is for fun: a second innings from Yorkshire's golden age. Withy Grove (Manchester), Whitehorn Press, 1981. 81p. illus.

1592 Laughter at the wicket: echoes from the golden age of
■ Yorkshire cricket. Withy Grove (Manchester), Whitehorn Press, 1980. 80p. illus.

1593 **Farnsworth, Keith**
■ Before and after Bramall Lane: Sheffield United C. C. and Yorkshire cricket in Sheffield. Sheffield, the Author, 1988. [vi], 146p. illus.
club and county cricket.

1594 **Hill, Alan**
■ A chain of spin wizards. Keighley, Kennedy Brothers, 1983. x, 147p. illus. scores, index.
Yorkshire slow left arm bowlers from Peate to Wilson.

1595 **Hodgson, Derek**
■ The official history of Yorkshire County Cricket Club. Marlborough (Wilts.), Crowood Press, 1989. x, 336p. illus. stats. bibliog. index.

1596 **Illingworth, Raymond** *with* **Whiting, Steve**
■ The tempestuous years, 1979-83. Sidgwick & Jackson, 1987. 152p. illus. index.

1597 **Maude, Donald**
■ A centenary of Yorkshire cricket at Park Avenue 1881-1981. Bradford, Bradford Cricket Club, 1981. 56p. scores.
county cricket pp. 14-56.

1598 **Mosey, Don**
■ We don't play it for fun: a story of Yorkshire cricket. Methuen, 1988. ix, 207p. illus. index.
——pbk. ed. Sphere, 1989.

1599 **Naylor, Tom**
■ Cricket hotch potch. Keighley, Kennedy Brothers, 1984. xvi, 262p. illus.
principally memories of fifty years of Yorkshire cricket.

1600 † **Pogson, Norman J.,** [*compiler*]
■ The County in Hull. [Hull?, the Author, c.1946]. [12]p. incl. adverts. stats.
complete results and records of all matches played by the Yorkshire C.C.C. in Hull.

1601 **Thornton, David**
■ A century of Headingley: the story of the Leeds Cricket, Football and Athletic Co. Ltd. Leeds, the Author, [1989]. 16p. *strip cartoon format.*
county and Test cricket.

1602 **Trueman, Frederick Sewards** *and* **Mosey, Don**
■ Fred Trueman's Yorkshire. Stanley Paul, 1984. 261p. illus. (some col.)
cricket pp. 117-147.

1603 **Woodhouse, Anthony**
■ The history of Yorkshire County Cricket Club; with a personal view by Sir Leonard Hutton. Bromley, Christopher Helm, 1989. [v], 618p. illus. stats. bibliog. index.

1604 The Yorkshire cricket quiz book. Edinburgh,
■ Mainstream Publishing, 1989. 140p. illus.

1605 **Yorkshire County Cricket Club**
□ Annual report and statement of accounts. Leeds, the Club.
/1986/ to date.
previously incorporated in item 1606.

1606 Annual report. Leeds, the Club. illus. (since 1985),
■ scores, stats.
with title 'Yearbook' since 1985.
1980-88 edited by Joe Lister and Roy D. Wilkinson.
1989 edited by Joe Lister and Derek Hodgson.
continues 'Padwick I' 3051 to date.

1607 Special bulletin. [Leeds, the Club, 1983]. [4]p. illus.
■ *circulated to Yorkshire members prior to the special general meeting on Saturday, 3 December, 1983. Meeting was postponed until 21 January, 1984.*

1608 The white rose: the official quarterly of the Yorkshire
■ County Cricket Club. Leeds, the Club. *pub. Aug, Nov, Feb and May.* illus (some col.) scores, stats.
Aug 1984 to date.
Aug 1985 issue was not published.

1609 The Yorkshire Academy of Cricket. Leeds, the Club
■ Committee, [1989]. [4]p.

1610 **Yorkshire** County Cricket Club, *Yorkshire Post* 1987
■ benefit book. [Benefit Committee, 1987]. 96p. incl. adverts. illus. stats.
in aid of the Indoor School appeal.

1611 **Yorkshire** pride: county cricket souvenir. Leeds,
Yorkshire Evening Post. 24p. col. illus. stats.
special supplement of 'Yorkshire Evening Post', 11 April 1988.

GENTLEMEN v PLAYERS

1612 **Marshall, [Robert] Michael**
■ Gentlemen and players; conversations with cricketers. Grafton Books, 1987. xxii, 362p. illus. scores, stats. bibliog. index.
includes scores of all Gentlemen and Players matches 1947-62.

1613 † **'An Old Stump',** *pseud.*
■ Cricket gossip on cricket and cricketers. no. 1 W.G.Grace; conversation between two old cricketers from North and South. Marylebone Cricket Club for the Author, 1871. [4]p. folded sheet.
pub. on the occasion of the Gentlemen versus Players matches at Lord's beginning 3 July 1871, and at the Oval beginning 6 July 1871. No reference to W.G.Grace except in the title.

LIMITED OVERS CRICKET

1614 **Bose, Mihir**
■ All in a day: great moments in cup cricket. Robin Clark, 1983. vi, 186p. illus. stats. bibliog. index.

1615 **Gatting, Michael William** *with* **Lee, Alan**
■ Limited overs. Queen Anne Press, 1986. 192p. illus. scores, stats. index.

1616 † **Limited Overs Cricket Information Group**
■ A statistical survey of the ... cricket season. [Sheffield], the Group. stats.
1963-1968 [in one vol.], pub. 1981.
1969-1971 [in one vol.], pub. 1982.
1972, pub. 1984.
1980-1984 pub. at end of each season.
continues 'Padwick I' 974-2.

1617 **Marks, Victor James** *and* **Drake, Robin**
■ The ultimate one-day cricket match: your chance to captain England in the first cricket adventure game. Heinemann Kingswood, 1988. 171p. illus.
programmed learning text.

BENSON AND HEDGES CUP

1618 **Limited Overs Cricket Information Group**
■ The Benson and Hedges Cup book of cricket records
1972-1981. [Sheffield], the Group, [1982]. [ii], 48p.
stats.

1619 **Lord's '88.** Derby, *Derby Evening Telegraph*, 1988. 32p.
■ illus. (mostly col.) scores, stats.
*reports by Gerald Mortimer; special issue prior to 1988
final, pub. 25 June 1988.*

GILLETTE CUP

1620 **Ross, Gordon John**
■ The Gillette Cup 1963 to 1980. Queen Anne Press,
1981. 188p. illus. scores, stats.

1621 **Stockwell, John W.,** *compiler*
■ The Gillette Cup book of cricket records 1963-1980.
Hinckley, Limited Overs Cricket Information Group,
[1981]. [ii], 60p. stats.

JOHN PLAYER LEAGUE

1622 **Hatton, Leslie Walter**
■ John Player Special League record book 1969 to 1986.
West Bridgford (Notts.), Association of Cricket
Statisticians, [1987]. 128p. illus. stats.

1623 **Ing, Bryan,** *compiler*
■ John Player League 1976. [Sheffield], Limited Overs
Cricket Information Group, [1981]. [120]p. scores,
stats.

NATWEST TROPHY

1624 **Derbyshire County Cricket Club**
National Westminster Bank Trophy champions 1981.
[Derby, the Club, 1982]. 40p. illus. scores.

1625 **Worcestershire v** Middlesex Natwest Trophy final:
Lord's, Sat. September 3rd 1988. Worcester, *Worcester
Evening News*. [16]p. col. illus. stats.
*special pre-match ed. of 'Worcester Evening News', 27
Aug. 1988.*

WOMEN'S CRICKET

1626 **Hawes, Joan Lillian**
■ Women's Test cricket: the golden triangle 1934-84.
Lewes, Book Guild, 1987. x, 422p. illus. scores, stats.
England v Australia and England v New Zealand.

1627 **McCrone, Kathleen E.**
■ Sport and the physical emancipation of English women
1870-1914. Routledge, 1988. x, 310p. illus. bibliog.
index.
*chapter 5: 'For the sake of the team: hockey, lacrosse and
cricket'; other scattered references.*

1628 **Official** tour brochure: England v India. [Women's
■ Cricket Association, 1986]. [20]p. incl. adverts. illus.
stats.
pre-tour; includes brief history of British women's cricket.

1629 **Sussex Women's Cricket Association**
Golden jubilee 1935-1985. [The Association, 1985].

1630 **Women's Cricket Association**
■ Bulletin. The Association. *irregular. typescript.*
c. monthly until July 1982; final issue July 1983.
continues 'Padwick I' 3108.
continued as 'Cover to cover'.

1631 Cover to cover. The Association. *3 issues per year.* stats.
■ *typescript.*
official bulletin of the Women's Cricket Association.
3 issues pub. 1984.
continued as 'WCA news'.

1632 WCA news. Leeds, the Association. *quarterly.* illus.
□ *vol. 1, no. 1 Spring 1985?* to date.
latterly three issues per year.

1633 Year book. The Association.
■ *continues 'Padwick I' 3103 to date.*

CHARITY TEAMS AND MATCHES

1634 † **Programme** of grand comedy cricket match played at
■ Stamford Bridge Grounds ... between Variety Artists
and London Printers, on Wednesday, August 15th, 1917.
[8]p. incl. covers. illus.
*for the benefit of the Variety Artistes' Benevolent Fund
and Institution and the Printers' Medical Aid and
Sanatoria Association.*

Lord's Taverners

1635 The **long** room: the journal of the Lord's Taverners;
□ edited by David Wynne-Morgan. Hill and Knowlton.
monthly. illus. (mostly col.)
?/Feb. 1989/ to date?

1636 The **Lord's** Taverner; edited by Jack Rayfield. High
□ Ham (Somerset). *quarterly.* illus.
continues 'Padwick I' 3130-1 to date?

1637 The **Lord's** Taverners President's Ball, Grosvenor
■ House, Monday 2nd November 1987. [Lord's Taverners,
1987]. 168p. incl. adverts. illus.
cricket pp. 61, 65, 69 and 73.

CRICKET SOCIETIES

Association of Cricket Statisticians

1638 **Association of Cricket Statisticians**
■ The cricket statistician: the official journal of the Association of Cricket Statisticians. West Bridgford (Notts.), the Association. *quarterly*. illus. scores, stats.
issues 51 to date with sub-title 'the journal ...'
edited by Robert W. Brooke to issue no. 52, winter 1985.
edited by John W. Stockwell, issues 53-61, Spring 1986 - Spring 1988.
edited by Philip Bailey, issue 62, Summer 1988 to date.
continues 'Padwick I' 3136 to date.
——*The cricket statistician* index to contents - no. 1 to 8. compiled by Brian Croudy. The Association, [1975], 3p. *typescript.*
——Index to *The cricket statistician* 1973 to 1981, issues no. 1 to no. 36 inc. compiled by L. T. Newell assisted by L. Hatton. Haughton Mill (Notts.), the Association, [1981]. 24p.
——Index to *The cricket statistician*: issues 1-41 compiled by Andrew Cunningham. The Author, [1983]. [16]p.

1639 † Members' list. The Association.
■ *pub. Nov. 1975, Dec. 1978, Nov. 1986.*

1640 † Rules. The Association.
■ *pub. 1974 and July 1986.*

Chesterfield Cricket Lovers' Society

1641 **Chesterfield Cricket Lovers' Society**
□ Newsletter. Chesterfield, the Society. *irregular.*
continues 'Padwick I' 3137 to date.

Council of Cricket Societies

1642 **Council of Cricket Societies**
□ Newsletter. The Council. *quarterly?*
?/Sep. 1984, Oct. 1988/ to date.

Cricket Memorabilia Society

1643 **Cricket Memorabilia Society**
■ Constitution. The Society, [1987]. 3p.

1644 Cricket Memorabilia Society: the magazine of the CMS;
■ edited by Anthony D. Collis. The Society. *quarterly.* illus.
vol. 1 no. I May-July 1987 to vol. 1 no IV Jan. 1988.
continued with sub-title: 'the magazine for collectors', with varying frequency, /no. 1, June 1888 to date/; *edited by Keith Hayhurst.*
and
'Newsletter', /no. 5, Sep. 88 and no. 6, March 1989/; edited by Keith Hayhurst.

1645 Register of members' collections. The Society.
■ *pub. June 1988 and March 1989.*

The Cricket Society

1646 **The Cricket Society**
■ Barbados tour 1981. [The Society, 1981]. 24p. incl. covers, illus.
pre-tour; March 1981.

1647 Journal. The Society. *biannual.* illus. scores, stats.
■ *to vol. XI, no. 4, edited by J.D.Coldham.*
vol. XII, no. 1 to date, *edited by C.W.Porter.*
continues 'Padwick I' 3145 to date.

1648 Library catalogue, 1982; [compiled by Howard R.
■ Milton]. The Society, 1982. iv, 87p.
——*new ed. 1988, compiled by Howard R. Milton, as print-out from computer database; subsequent copies issued, fully updated, on demand.*
later eds. of 'Padwick I' 3147.

1649 News bulletin; [edited by Stephen de Winton]. The
■ Society. *8 issues per year.* illus.
continues 'Padwick I' 3144 to date.

East Riding Cricket Society

1650 † **East Riding Cricket Society**
□ Programme. *annual.*
1966-67 to date.

Essex Cricket Society

1651 † **Essex Cricket Society**
■ Newsletter. The Society. *irregular.* scores (in various issues).
December 1974 to date.
latterly five issues per year in Feb., April, Aug., Oct. and Dec.

Hampshire Cricket Society

1652 **Hampshire Cricket Society**
Newsletter. The Society. *monthly from September to April.* scores, stats.
edited successively by Phil Bichard, Tony Mitchener and Alan Edwards.
continues 'Padwick I' 3151-1 to date.

Lancashire and Cheshire Cricket Society

1653 **Lancashire and Cheshire Cricket Society**
■ 30th anniversary 1953-83. The Society, 1983. [17]p. incl. adverts & cover, illus.

Limited Overs Cricket Information Group

1654 † **Limited Overs Cricket Information Group**
■ Quarterly journal. The Group. stats.
no. 1, [1977] to no. 38, Dec. 1985.
with title 'Newsletter' to no. 17, Sep. 1980.
issues 1-20 edited by Terry R. Allcock.
issues 21-38 edited by John W. Stockwell.
Group was known as Cricket Statisticians' Limited-Overs Group to May 1978 and eventually amalgamated with the Association of Cricket Statisticians.

Lincolnshire Cricket Lovers' Society

1655 **Lincolnshire Cricket Lovers' Society**
□ [Brochure]. The Society, *annual? typescript.*
entitled 'Yearbook' until 1981-82; 1989-90 issue marks Society's silver jubilee.
continues 'Padwick I' 3153 to date.

Norfolk Cricket Society

1656 **Norfolk Cricket Society**
■ Newsletter. The Society, *biannual*. scores, stats. (in various issues).
no. 1 Autumn/Winter 1986 to date.

Northern Cricket Society

1657 **The Northern Cricket Society**
■ Booklet. Leeds, the Society. *annual*. illus. scores, stats.
1980-81 edited by A. Woodhouse.
1982 edited by A. Snape.
1983-84 edited by P. Snape.
1985 no editor named.
1986-88 edited by K. Harvey.
1989 edited by E. Haywood.
continues 'Padwick I' 3156 to date.

Sheffield Cricket Lovers' Society

1658 **Sheffield Cricket Lovers' Society**
□ Year book. [Sheffield, the Society]. illus. scores, stats.
continues 'Padwick I' 3158 to date?

Sussex Cricket Society

1659 **Sussex Cricket Society**
□ Newsletter. The Society. *monthly*.
July 1982 was 200th issue.
continues 'Padwick I' 3161 to date.

Wombwell Cricket Lovers' Society

1660 **Wombwell Cricket Lovers' Society**
■ 'The twelfth man': Wombwell Cricket Lovers' Society annual magazine. Barnsley, the Society. illus. stats.
1984-89 edited by John Featherstone.
continues 'Padwick I' 3162 to date.

CRICKET IN WALES

GENERAL

1661 **Lloyd, Howard**
Cricedwyr Cymru. Llandysul, Gomer, 1984. 138p. illus. bibliog.
in Welsh.

1662 **Meredith, Allan**
A hard slog: the history of the South Wales Cricket Association. Llandeilo, Towy Press, 1987. 116p. illus. stats.

1663 **South Wales Cricket Association**
□ Official handbook. The Association. *annual*. illus. scores, stats.
continues 'Padwick I' 3164 to date.

1664 † The **Welsh** athlete: a weekly record of football, cricket, lawn tennis, cycling, gymnastics and out-door sports. stats.
?/1891-92/?
1891-92 issues contain reports and averages for a number of Welsh clubs in the 1891 season.

1665 **Welsh Club Cricket Conference**
Rules, fixtures and club directory. The Conference. *annual*.
continues 'Padwick I' 3165-1 to date.

1666 **Welsh Cricket Association**
□ Year book. The Association. illus. scores, stats.
continues 'Padwick I' 3165-2 to date.

1667 † **West Wales Cricket Association**
Official handbook. The Association. *annual*. stats.
?/1961,67/?

1668 **West Wales Cricket Club Conference**
Fixtures and rules. The Conference. *annual*.
?/1988 to date/

ANGLESEY

Holyhead

1669 **Radcliffe, H. Talbot**
■ The power of the game. [Holyhead], the Author, [1988]. 56p. illus. diagrs.
forming and running a village club with special reference to Bodedern C. C. which celebrated its 40th anniversary in 1987.

BRECKNOCKSHIRE

Brecon

1670 † **Brecon Town and Garrison Cricket Club**
Rules and regulations the same as those of the Marylebone Club. [The Club], 1850.
in Brecon Museum according to 'Allen EBC'.

CAERNARVONSHIRE

Bangor

1671 † **Bangor Cricket Club**
Rules. [Bangor, the Club], 1885. 10p.

CARMARTHENSHIRE

Llanelli

1672 † **Llanelli Cricket Club**
100 years of cricket at Stradey Park 1874-1974. [Llanelli, the Club], 1974. 114p. illus.

1673 † **Llanelli Tuesday Cricket League**
Official handbook. Llanelli, [the League]. *annual*.
?/1966/?

Llangennech

1674 **Llangennech** C.C.: 60 years of cricket in the park. [Llangennech, the Club], 1988. 104p. illus. stats.

GLAMORGAN

1675 † **The Morgannwg Cricket League**
Official handbook. Swansea, Walters. *annual*. stats.
1976 to date.

Bridgend

1676 **Bridgend Town Cricket Club**
☐ Handbook. [The Club]. *annual*. stats.
club founded c. 1840.
?/1989/

Briton Ferry

1677 † **James, David H.**
The Briton Ferry Steelworks Cricket Club 1896-1974.
Port Talbot, the Club?, 1974. 99p. illus.

1678 The town: 100 years of Briton Ferry Town and other
■ cricketers. [Briton Ferry, the Club, 1981]. [iv], 161p.
illus.

Cardiff

1679 † **Official** handbook for the Cardiff Cricket Club Bazaar.
1903. 23p. illus.
programme for fund raising jumble sale.

1680 **Parry-Jones, David**
Taff's acre: a history and celebration of Cardiff Arms
Park. Collins Willow, 1984. 198p. illus.
cricket pp. 88-91.

Gowerton

1681 **Gowerton Cricket & Lawn Tennis Club**
Centenary brochure 1880-1980. [Gowerton, the Club,
1980]. 112p. illus.

1682 **Rees, J. Hywel**
■ One hundred years of cricket in Gowerton 1880 to 1980.
[Gowerton, Gowerton Cricket Club], 1980. [xi], 147p.
illus. maps, index.

Maesteg

1683 † **Maesteg Cricket and Tennis Club**
■ The story of the Maesteg Cricket and Tennis Club
1846-1946. [The Club, 1946]. 35p. illus.

Merthyr Tydfil

1684 **Dowlais** Cricket Club centenary brochure 1885-1985.
■ [Dowlais, the Club, 1985]. [32]p. incl. adverts. illus.

1685 † **Penydarren Country XI Cricket Club**
■ Penydarren Country XI 1975. [The Club, 1975]. 28p.
incl. adverts. illus. stats.
marks the fifth year of the club's existence.

Neath

1686 † **Festival** of Britain: sporting events and past records.
Neath, Neath Borough Council, 1951. 64p. incl.
adverts. stats.
cricket in Neath, pp. 27-41.

Southerndown

1687 **Bailey, Michael,** [*editor*]
■ Southerndown Cricket Club centenary season handbook.
[The Club, 1988]. 64p. incl. adverts. illus.

St. Fagans

1688 **St.** Fagans C. C. 1862-1987: 125 not out. The Club,
■ [1987]. 80p. incl. adverts. illus.

GLAMORGAN C. C. C.

1689 **Barrett, Idris**
■ Glamorgan's England cricketers. [Burton-on-Trent, the
Author], 1985. [i], 27p. stats. index. *typescript.*

1690 **Glamorgan County Cricket Club / Clwb Criced**
■ **Morgannwg**
Glamorgan County Cricket Club/Clwb Criced
Morgannwg centenary brochure 1888-1988. [The Club,
1988]. 84p. incl. adverts. illus.

1691 Glamorgan matters. [Cardiff, the Club]. *quarterly?*
stats.
?/Autumn 1986/?

1692 Official programme. [Cardiff, the Club]. *pub. for
Sunday League and tour matches.* col. illus. scores, stats.
edited by Mike Fatkin.
vol. 1, no. 1, 1988 to date.

1693 Yearbook. [Cardiff, the Club]. illus. scores, stats.
■ *since 1987 incorporates Annual Report.*
continues 'Padwick I' 3175 to date.

1694 **Hignell, Andrew Keith**
■ The history of Glamorgan County Cricket Club; with a
personal view by Tony Lewis. Bromley, Christopher
Helm, 1988. [v], 356p. illus. stats. bibliog. index.

1695 **Hignell, Andrew Keith,** [*compiler*]
■ Cricket grounds of Glamorgan. Haughton Mill (Notts.),
Association of Cricket Statisticians, [1985]. 50p. illus.
stats.

1696 Glamorgan cricketers 1887-1987. West Bridgford
■ (Notts.), Association of Cricket Statisticians, 1988. 30p.
map, stats.

MONMOUTHSHIRE

Abergavenny

1697 **Morris, J. W.**
■ Looking back: a history of Abergavenny Cricket Club,
1834-1984. [Abergavenny, the Club], 1984. [v], 106p.
incl. adverts. illus. stats.

Chepstow

1698 **Jacks, Alasdair,** *editor*
■ Chepstow Cricket Club: the first 150 years. [Chepstow,
the Club, 1988]. 64p. incl. adverts. illus.

Machen

1699 † **Machen** Cricket Club centenary year 1878 1978. [The
■ Club], 1978. 44p. incl. covers and adverts. illus.

Newport

1700 † **Newport & District Amateur Cricket League**
Official handbook. The League. *annual.*
?/1931/?

1701 **Newport** Athletic Club 1875-1975. Newport, Starling
■ Press, 1984. 184p. incl. adverts. illus.
'Cricket' by J. F. Burrell and W. E. Davies, pp. 91-101.
updated ed. of 'Padwick I' 3183.

Panteg and Griffithstown

1702 † **Pritchard, A. J.**
Griffithstown. Abergavenny, Browns, 1957. 120p.
Panteg C.C. pp.76-91.

Ponthir

1703 **Mole, Bob**
■ A history of Ponthir Cricket Club Cwmbran, Village
Publishing, 1983. [vi], 58p. incl. adverts illus. scores,
stats. bibliog.

Pontypool

1704 † **Pontypool.** Pontypool, Pontypool Urban District
Council, 1958.
*Pontypool C.C. pp.99-101; pub. to celebrate Festival of
Wales.*

PEMBROKESHIRE

Neyland

1705 **Carne, Bill**
Neyland C.C. 1889-1989. The Club, 1989. 75p.

CRICKET IN SCOTLAND

GENERAL

1706 [**Miller, Richard William Stanley,** *compiler*]
■ Scottish cricketers 1905-1980. Cleethorpes, Association of Cricket Statisticians, [1981]. 31p. map, stats.

1707 † **North of Scotland Cricket Association**
Constitution. The Association, 1964. [28]p.
——*three further rev. eds.*

1708 † Handbook. The Association. *annual.*
Association instituted 1893.
1966? to date.

1709 **Roberts, Paul C. M.,** *editor*
■ The bicentenary of cricket in Scotland: a celebration. [Alloa], Clackmannan C. C. C., 1985. [36]p. incl. adverts. illus. score.

1710 **Scottish County Cricket Board**
■ Handbook. The Board. *annual.* stats.
Board inaugurated 1902.
1989 was first issue.

ANNUALS

1711 **Miller** Homes Scottish cricket guide. Edinburgh,
■ *annual.* illus. scores, stats.
1980-84 published as Aitken & Niven Scottish cricket guide.
1985 published as Bicentenary Scottish cricket guide.
1986 to date continued under present title.
since 1983 edited by Neil Leitch.
continues 'Padwick I' 3200 to date.

PERIODICALS

1712 **Scottish** cricket. Glasgow, Scottish Cricket Union
irregular. illus. stats.
6 issues between April 1985 and December 1986.

1713 The **Scottish** cricketer. Dunfermline, G. T. G. Sports Publications, *irregular.* illus. stats.
7 issues between June 1982 and May 1984.
edited by Harry Pincott.

PRIVATE CLUBS

Capercailzies

1714 The **Capercailzies** Barbados tour 1981. [Edinburgh, the Club, 1981]. 19p. illus.
pre-tour.

1715 The **Capercailzies** Canadian tour 1984. [Edinburgh, the Club, 1984]. [21]p. illus.
pre-tour.

1716 The **Capercailzies** Hong Kong tour 1987. [Edinburgh, the Club, 1987]. [24]p. illus.
pre-tour.

SCHOOLS AND UNIVERSITIES

Edinburgh: Royal High School

1717 † **Barclay, J. B.**
The Tounis Scule: the Royal High School of Edinburgh. Edinburgh, the School, 1974. 152p. illus. stats.
with references to Former Pupils' cricket.

YOUTH CRICKET

1718 **Welcome** to Chesterfield: Scottish youth touring team
■ 1980. Chesterfield & District Youth Cricket Council, [1980]. 28p. illus. scores, stats.
pre-tour; Aug. 1980.

SCOTTISH CLUBS

ABERDEENSHIRE

1719 **Aberdeenshire Cricket Association**
□ Official handbook. The Association *annual.* illus.
continues 'Padwick I' 3227 to date?

1720 † **Aberdeenshire Cricket Club**
■ Commemorative brochure of phase 1 development. [The Club], 1976. 24p. incl. adverts. illus. stats.
renovation of the club pavilion.

1721 **Miller, D. A. C.**
■ Aberdeenshire Cricket Association 1884-1984. [The Association, 1984]. [iv], 181p. incl. adverts. frontis. illus. stats.

1722 **Smith, H. O.** *et al*
■ Aberdeenshire Cricket Club: one hundred and twenty-five years. [Aberdeen, the Club, 1982]. [x], 108p. incl. adverts. illus. scores, stats.
limited ed. of 1500 copies.

1723 **Toft** Cricket Club invitation tour, South Africa, February
■ 1980. [The Club, 1980]. [48]p. incl. adverts. illus.
pre-tour.

Banchory

1724 **Wilkinson, Timothy J. S.**
■ Banchory Cricket Club: a history. Banchory, Advance Publicity, 1987. 112p. incl. adverts. illus. stats.

Ellon

1725   **Ellon** Gordon Cricket Club 125 years 1862-1987. The Club, [1987]. [82]p. incl. adverts. illus. stats.

Huntly

1726   **Scott, Patrick W.**
■   A history of Huntly Cricket Club 1854-1914. [The Author], 1987? [iv], 120p. illus. scores, stats.

Inverurie

1727   **Brownlee, N.,** *editor*
        Inverurie Cricket Club 1931-1981. [Inverurie, the Club] 1982? 92p. illus.

ANGUS

Arbroath

1728   **Sievewright, R. G.**
■   Arbroath United Cricket Club centenary 1887-1987: 100th anniversary of the opening of Lochlands Cricket Ground. [Arbroath, the Club, 1987]. 72p. incl. adverts. illus. scores.

Brechin

1729 † **Gourlay, David**
        A Brechin eleven and a printer's dozen. Brechin, William Hendry, 1956. 156p.
        cricket in chs. 1 and 6 and other scattered references.

AYRSHIRE

Prestwick

1730   **Prestwick** Cricket Club 1955-80 jubilee. [The Club],
■   1980. 82p. incl. adverts. illus. stats.

EAST LOTHIAN

Haddington

1731   **[Bonnington, G. *and* Arrundale, J.]**
■   The 111th anniversary: Haddington Cricket Club, 1877-1988. [The Club, 1988]. 76p. incl. adverts. illus. score.

FIFESHIRE

1732   **Baxter, Alan C.,** *editor*
        Cupar Cricket Club 1884-1984. The Club, 1984. 46p. incl. adverts. illus. stats.

FORFARSHIRE

Dundee

1733 † **Miller, Richard William Stanley,** *compiler*
        Telecoms Cricket Club statistical review 1951-1976. Dundee, the Author, 1976. [18]p. stats.

Strathmore

1734   **Clubsport Strathmore Cricket Union**
□   Handbook. The Union *annual.* stats.
        prior to 1986 published as Strathmore Cricket Union [handbook].
        ?/1985-1989/

LANARKSHIRE

Glasgow

1735 † **Glasgow Academical Club**
        Centenary volume 1866-1966. Blackie, 1966. xii, 97p. illus. stats.
        cricket pp. 23-26, 72-79, 91-92, 95.

Milngavie

1736 † **Milngavie & Bearsden Cricket & Tennis Club**
■   Diamond jubilee, 1904-1964. [Milngavie, the Club, 1964]. [16]p. incl. covers.
        members handbook; other years pub?

Paisley

1737   **Reis, Peter M.**
■   Ferguslie Cricket Club ... one hundred years of cricket 1887-1987. [Paisley, the Club, 1987]. 135p. illus.

Uddingston

1738   **Macfarlane, Bob**
■   Uddingston Cricket Club 1883-1983. [Uddingston, the Club, 1983]. 81p. incl. covers and adverts. illus. scores.

Woodhall

1739   **Thomson, Karen**
■   Woodhall Cricket Club 1887-1987. [The Author?, 1987]. [60]p. illus.

MIDLOTHIAN

Edinburgh

1740   The **Carlton** Cricket Club 125th anniversary commemorative brochure 1863-1988. Edinburgh, the Club, 1988. [20]p. incl. adverts. illus.

1741   **George** Heriots Former Pupils Cricket Club.
■   [Edinburgh, the Club], 1989. 113p. incl. adverts. illus. stats.
        centenary booklet.

1742 † **Mitre** Cricket Club silver jubilee season 1979. The Club, 1979. [20]p. incl. adverts. illus.

1743 † **Watsonian** Cricket Club 1875-1975: 'Myreside cricketing,
■   batting, bowling, wicketing'. Edinburgh, the Club, [1975]. 106, xii p. illus. scores, stats.

1744 † **Watsonian** Cricket Club centenary 1875-1975 brochure. Edinburgh, the Club, 1975. [16]p. incl. adverts. illus. stats.

1745   **Yelland, Phil**
■   The 80th anniversary: London Road Cricket Club, 1909-1989. Edinburgh, the Club, 1989. 64p. illus. scores, stats.

Newtongrange

1746 † **Smith, James A.**
        Newtongrange Lothian cricket records 1879-1962. [The Author?, n.d.]. 128p. stats.

PERTHSHIRE

1747 **McCrea, T. H.**
■ Perth County Cricket Club 1926-76 with backward glimpse, a brief history. Perth, [the Club], 1980. 47p. illus. stats.

1748 **Perth County Cricket Club**
In the middle; edited by C. E. C. Macpherson. Perth, the Club. *fortnightly? during season.*
continues 'Padwick I' 3283-2 to date?

1749 † Memoirs: the history of the Perth County Cricket Club in word and picture. Perth, Perth C. C. C., 1949. 36p. illus.

Perth

1750 † **Sievwright, William**
History of cricket in Perth from 1812 to 1894, with sketches of local players. Perth, 1896. 404p.
partly ms.

Strathearn

1751 † **Strathearn** Cricket Club 1879-1979: centenary weekend
■ ... [Perth, the Club, 1979]. 10p. *typescript.*
includes history of the Club.

WEST LOTHIAN

1752 **West Lothian County Cricket Association**
Handbook. The Association *annual.* illus. stats.
published in 1981 and 1985 only.

CRICKET IN THE CHANNEL ISLANDS

GUERNSEY

1753 **Guernsey Cricket Association**
□ Handbook. The Association. *annual.*
?/1988 to date/

1754 **Guernsey Cricket Council**
□ Report of the season. The Council. *annual.*
pub. in varying formats.
?/1983 to date/

1755 Under 16 county cricket festival August 25th - 29th, 1986.
■ The Council, 1986. [24]p. incl. adverts.
pre-festival; played for the Lazard Bros. (C.I.) Ltd. Trophy.

1756 **Guernsey Island Cricket Club**
□ [Handbook]. The Club. *annual.* stats.
?/1988/ to date.

1757 **Guernsey** under 14 cricket festival. [Guernsey Cricket
□ Council]. *biennial?* illus.
sponsored by Lord's Taverners.
?/1985, 87, 89/

JERSEY

1758 **Jersey Cricket Association**
Fixture book. The Association *annual.*
1982? to date.

1759 **Victoria** College Cricket Club: Sir Garfield Sobers
■ international schoolboy festival Barbados 1989. [Jersey (C.I.), the College, 1989]. [8]p. incl. covers and adverts. illus.
pre-tour; 20th July - 3rd August.

1760 **Youngs, Ronald**
■ Five decades and a future. n.p., [1986]. 32p. illus. stats.
cover sub-title: 'notes on the history of cricket at Victoria College, 1935-1985'.

CRICKET IN IRELAND

GENERAL

1761 ■ **[Liddle, Edward**, *compiler*]
Irish cricketers 1855-1980. Cleethorpes, Association of
Cricket Statisticians, [1980]. 40p. map, stats.

1762 **Match** programme - Ireland in '87. Comber, Aurora
Publications, [1987]. 72p. illus. stats.
programme of all important matches in Ireland.

COUNTY CARLOW

1763 ■ **McMillan, N. D.**
One hundred and fifty years of cricket and sport in
County Carlow: an illustrated social history of conflict
and sport 1823-1981. Dublin, Carlton Publishing, 1983.
60p. illus. stats.

IRISH CRICKET UNION

1764 ■ **Irish Cricket Union**
Yearbook. Dublin, Able Press for the Union. illus.
scores, stats.
from 1986 edited by Francis Xavier Carty.
continues 'Padwick I' 3310 to date.

LEINSTER CRICKET UNION

1765 □ **Leinster Cricket Union**
Handbook. [Dublin], the Union. *annual.* illus.
continues 'Padwick I' 3319-2 to date.

NORTH WEST CRICKET UNION

1766 ■ **Platt, William Henry Walker**, *editor*
North West of Ireland Cricket Union centenary
brochure 1888-1988. The Union, [1988]. 84p. incl.
adverts. illus. stats.

1767 ■ **Platt, William Henry Walker** *and* **Nawn, Rod**, *editors*
Ireland versus Wales; Sandel Lodge, Coleraine, 11th,
12th, 13th June 1986. Coleraine, Coleraine R. F. & C. C.
(Cricket Section), 1986. 52p. incl. adverts. illus.
souvenir brochure; contains history of North West Senior
Cup 1883-1985 and North West Senior League
1894-1985.

NORTHERN CRICKET UNION

1768 ■ **Northern Cricket Union**
100 years of Ulster cricket: centenary brochure
1886-1986. Portadown, In-House Publications [for the]
Union, [1986]. 84p. incl. covers, illus. (one col.)
scores, stats.

1769 ■ Centenary year 1886-1986: fixtures and rules. [The
Union, 1986]. 116p. incl. adverts.
other years pub.?

ANNUALS

1770 □ **Irish** cricket annual. Dublin. illus. scores, stats.
1985 to date?

PERIODICALS

1771 □ **Irish** cricket magazine. Dublin. *irregular.* illus.
edited by Gerard Siggins.
first issue 21 June 1984 - 1988.

1772 ■ The **Ulster** Cricketer. [Belfast], Aurora Promotions and
Publications. *biannual.* illus, scores, stats.
vol. 1, no. 1, May 1985 to date.

IRISH CLUBS

Ballymena

1773 † **Ballymena Cricket Club**
Over 100 years of cricket in Ballymena. Ballymena, the
Club, 1960. 36p. illus.

Dublin University

1774 ■ **Dublin** University Cricket Club 1835-1985. [Dublin, the
Club, 1985]. 28p. incl. covers, illus. stats.

1775 ■ **Milne, M. H. A.** *et al*
A history of the Dublin University Cricket Club. Dublin,
the Club, 1982. [vi], 203p. illus. stats.
cover sub-title: 'a pictorial history'; limited ed. of 350
copies.

Eglington

1776 ■ **Platt, William Henry Walker**
History of Eglington Cricket Club. [The Club, 1981].
72p. incl. adverts. illus. stats.

Holywood

1777 ■ **[McCall, Desmond**, *compiler*]
Holywood 1881-1981. Holywood Cricket Club, 1981.
68p. incl. adverts. illus. scores.

Limerick

1778 ■ **Lynch, Frank**, *editor*
Limerick C. C. 1968-1989: a brief history. Limerick, the
Club, 1989. 64p. incl. adverts. illus. scores, stats.

Lisburn

1779 ■ **Lisburn** Cricket Club 1836-1986. [The Club, 1986]. 92p.
incl. adverts. illus.

Malahide

1780 ■ **Malahide** Cricket Club souvenir brochure 1981.
[Dublin, the Club, 1981]. [72]p. incl. adverts. illus.
stats.

Mount Juliet

1781 ■ **Holohan, Peter**, *editor*
Mount Juliet Cricket Club 1884-1984: centenary
magazine. [The Club, 1984]. 40p. incl. adverts. illus.
(some col.)

Pembroke

1782 **Dempsey, Aidan,** *editor*
☐   Pembroke Cricket Club yearbook. [Dublin], the Club.
    illus. stats.
    /1984/ to date?

Phoenix

1783 **[O'Brien, Conor J.,** *editor*]
■   The Phoenix Club, 1830-1980. [Dublin], the Phoenix
    Club, 1980. 96p. incl. adverts. illus. (some col.) stats.

Strabane

1784 **Doherty, Joe,** *editor*
■   Strabane Cricket Club 1883-1983: centenary brochure.
    Strabane, the Club, 1983. [ii], 62p. illus. stats.

Ulster Grasshoppers

1785 **Ulster** Grasshoppers Cricket Club world tour 1989:
■   commemorative brochure. [Belfast, the Club, 1989].
    48p. incl. covers and adverts. illus.
    pre-tour.

Woodvale

1786 **Godfrey, Dennis,** *editor*
■   Woodvale Cricket Club centenary 1887-1987. [Belfast,
    the Club], 1987. 57p. incl. covers, illus. (some col.)

CRICKET IN AUSTRALIA

GENERAL

1787 **Andrews, Malcolm**
■ The encyclopedia of Australian cricket. Gladesville (N.S.W.), Golden Press, 1980. 159p. illus. stats.

1788 † **The Australasian Cricket Council**
[Constitution and rules]. Adelaide. *annual?*. 8p.
the Council was established in September 1892 and was disbanded in January 1900; latterly known as the Australian Cricket Council.
issues for 1895 and 1898 notified; see also 'Padwick I' 3329.

1789 **Australian Cricket Board**
□ Annual report. Jolimont (Vic.), the Board. illus. (some col.) stats.
in this format, 1983-84 to date.
pub. in different formats, 1907-08 - 1982-83.
known as Australian Board of Control to 1973.

1790 **Australian** cricket superstars. Darlinghurst (N.S.W.),
□ Mason Stewart, 1984. 32p. col. illus.
——*other eds., 1986, 1988 and 1989.*

1791 **Blades, Genevieve C.**
Australian aborigines: cricket and pedestrianism: culture and conflict, 1890-1910. University of Queensland, 1985. viii, 177p.
unpub. thesis.

1792 **Bremner, Ian**
The economics of Australian rules football and cricket (Middle school economics project). Fitzroy (Vic.), VCTA Publishing, 1980. 18p. illus. facsims.

1793 **Cashman, Richard I.**
■ Australian cricket crowds: the attendance cycle; daily figures 1877-1984. (Historical Statistics Monograph, no. 5). Kensington (N.S.W.), History Project Incorporated (University of New South Wales), 1984. ii, 324p. stats. charts, graphs.

1794 'Ave a go, yer mug! Australian cricket crowds from
■ larrikin to ocker. Sydney, Collins, 1984. 192p. illus.

1795 **Cricket** in Australia: ten turbulent years: centenary Test
■ - Bicentenary Test. Birchgrove (N.S.W.), Swan Publishing, 1987. 192p. illus. (mostly col.)

1796 **Crook, Frank**
■ Talking cricket with Frank Crook. Crows Nest (N.S.W.), ABC Enterprises for the Australian Broadcasting Corporation, 1989. 120p. illus.
adapted from a series of interviews on ABC radio.

1797 **Crowley, Brian Mathew**
■ A history of Australian batting, 1850-1986. South Melbourne, Macmillan, 1986. xii, 211p. illus. stats. bibliog. index.

1798 A history of Australian bowling and wicket-keeping,
■ 1850-1986. South Melbourne, Macmillan, 1986. xii, 212p. illus. stats. bibliog. index.

1799 **Crowley, Brian Mathew** *and* **Mullins, Patrick J.,**
■ *compilers and editors*
Cradle days of Australian cricket: an anthology of the writings of 'Felix' (T. P. Horan). South Melbourne, Macmillan Australia, 1989. viii, 182p. illus. index.

1800 **Derriman, Philip**
■ The top 100 & the 1st XI: the top 100 Australian cricketers and the best eleven of all time. [Sydney], the Fairfax Library, 1987. 349p. illus. stats.

1801 **Dobson, David**
■ Records of Australian first class cricket in Australia & overseas 1851-1989. [North Caulfield (Vic.), the Author], 1989. [iv], 146p. stats.
[limited ed. of 1000 signed and numbered copies.]

1802 **Dugan, Michael**
■ Cricketers. (Famous Australians series, no. 12). South Melbourne, Macmillan, 1981. 32p. incl. covers, illus.
for children.

1803 **Egan, Jack**
■ Extra cover: twenty-six interviews with players and people behind the scenes in Australian cricket. Sydney, Pan Books, 1989. 357p. illus.

1804 The story of cricket in Australia. South Melbourne,
■ Macmillan Australia, 1987. 234p. illus. index.

1805 **Francis, Bruce Colin**
■ 'Guilty': Bob Hawke or Kim Hughes? [Sydney, the Author], 1989. xviii, 377p. illus. (some col.) index.
domestic repercussions of Australian 'rebel' tours to South Africa, 1985-87.

1806 **Frewin, Leslie Ronald,** *compiler and editor*
■ The NatWest boundary book: a Lord's Taverners Australia miscellany of cricket. Macmillan, 1988. xii, 348p. illus. (some col.)

1807 **Giffen, George**
■ The golden age of Australian cricket; introduced and edited by Ken Piesse. South Yarra (Vic.), Currey O'Neil, 1982. vi, 137p. illus. facsims. stats.
new ed. of 'Padwick I' 3336.

1808 **Grace, Radcliffe**
The rise and fall of the Australasian Cricket Council, 1892-1900. Canberra, Australian Society for Sports History, 1984. 10p.
paper originally given at A.S.S.H. conference in Melbourne 1983.

1809 **Griffin, Edward,** *pseud.?*
Eight shameful years. Highgate House, 1988. 147p.
administration of Australian cricket, 1979-87.

1810 **James, Alfred B. M.**
■ Averages & results of Australian first-class cricket from 1850/51 to 1914/15. Wahroonga (N.S.W.), the Author, 1985. [vi], 181p. scores, stats.
includes seasonal averages and brief scores.

1811 Averages & results of Australian first-class cricket
■ Volume II: from 1918/19 to 1957/58. Wahroonga (N.S.W.), the Author, 1987. [vi], 205p. scores, stats.
includes scorecards of matches of disputed first-class status.

1812 † **Langlands, W. J.,** *compiler*
Australian cricket record for 1897-8 with full account of the English team; results of all Test matches; particulars of cricket in 1896-7. Melbourne, Stillwell and Co., [1897]. 64p. incl. adverts.

1813 **Lawrence, Geoffrey** and **Rowe, David,** *editors*
Power play: essays in the sociology of Australian sport. Sydney, Hale & Iremonger, 1986. 243p. bibliog. index. *cover sub-title: 'the commercialisation of Australian sport'; includes 'It's just not cricket!' by Geoffrey Lawrence, pp. 151-165, 'The corporate pitch: televised cricket under capitalism' by Geoffrey Lawrence and David Rowe, pp. 166-178, and 'Cricket and bourgeois ideology' by Ian Harriss, pp. 179-195.*

1814 **Mullins, Patrick J.** and **Derriman, Philip,** *compilers*
Bat & pad: writings on Australian cricket 1804-1984. Melbourne; Oxford, Oxford University Press, 1984. viii, 256p. index.

1815 † **Official** souvenir programme of cricket match between the original A. I. F. team and contemporary international XI. Melbourne, C. G. Hartley, 1939. [32]p. incl. adverts. illus. stats.
match played on 15 April 1939 with proceeds in aid of the War Veterans' Homes Trust of Victoria; includes 'How the A.I.F. team originated' by W. A. Oldfield and 'The value of the A.I.F. team to Australian cricket'.

1816 **Piesse, Ken,** *editor*
The A to Z of cricket: interviews with Australia's leading cricketers. Melbourne, Wedneil Publications, 1983. 221p. illus. (some col.)

1817 The great Australian book of cricket stories. South Yarra (Vic.), Currey O'Neil, 1982. xii, 403p. illus. bibliog.
——*pbk. ed. pub. as 'Great Australian cricket stories',* Ringwood (Vic.), Viking O'Neil, 1988.

1818 **Piesse, Ken** and **Ferguson, Ian**
Bradman and the bush: the legend of Australian bush cricket. Melbourne, Newspress, 1986. 138p. illus. map, bibliog.
a 'Cricketer' magazine special.

1819 **Pollard, Jack**
Australian cricket: the game and the players; edited by Ian Moir. Sydney etc., Hodder and Stoughton, 1982. 1162p. illus. (some col.) stats. bibliog.
—— *de luxe leather-bound limited ed. of 452 numbered copies signed by Sir Donald Bradman,* 1982.
—— *rev. and enlarged ed.,* North Ryde (N.S.W.), Angus and Robertson, 1988.

1820 The Bradman years: Australian cricket 1918-1948. North Ryde (N.S.W.), Angus & Robertson, 1988; London, Angus & Robertson, 1989. x, 411p. illus. bibliog. index.

1821 The formative years of Australian cricket: 1803-93. North Ryde (N.S.W.) etc., Angus & Robertson, 1987. viii, 336p. illus. scores, bibliog. index.

1822 The pictorial history of Australian cricket. Boronia (Vic.), Dent, 1983. viii, 344p. illus. (some col.)
——*rev. and enlarged ed.* 1986.
——*3rd. ed.* Hodder & Stoughton, 1989.

1823 The turbulent years of Australian cricket 1893-1917. North Ryde (N.S.W.) etc., Angus & Robertson, 1987. x, 299p. illus. scores, bibliog. index.

1824 **Pollard, Jack,** *compiler*
Six and out. North Sydney, Jack Pollard Publishing, 1980. [x], 499p. illus.
cover sub-title 'the legend of Australian cricket'. enlarged ed. of 'Padwick I' 3348.

1825 **Pollard, Jack,** *editor*
The Primary Club's middle & leg: memorable cricketing moments from the game's cavaliers. South Melbourne, Macmillan Australia, 1988. x, 205p.

1826 **Sparke, Garry**
Australian cricket stars: full colour poster-size pictures of your favourite players in action. Cammeray (N.S.W.), Horwitz Grahame, 1982. [16]p. col. illus.

1827 **Stobo, Richard Montagu**
Australian nationalism and cricket in the 19th century. 1989. v, 88p. bibliog. *typescript.*
unpub. thesis submitted for Bachelor of Arts (Honours) at Sydney University; the author made his debut for New South Wales in 1988-89 season.

1828 **Stoddart, Brian**
Saturday afternoon fever: sport in the Australian culture. North Ryde (N.S.W.), Angus & Robertson, 1986. 232p. bibliog. index.
many cricket references.

1829 **Tatz, Colin**
Aborigines in sport. (ASSH Studies in Sport no. 3). Bedford Park (S.A.), Australian Society for Sports History, 1987. x, 151p. illus. map. index.
'The fast black men' pp. 22-37, and other scattered references to cricket.

1830 **Wat, Charlie**
Australian first class cricket career records. Prahran (Vic.), Cricket Stats Publications. *annual.* stats. index.
1988 limited to 50 signed and numbered copies. 1989 limited to 150 signed and numbered copies.

1831 Register of Australian cricketers. Prahran (Vic.), Cricket Stats. Publications. *annual.* stats.
1986 to date.
each issue limited to 75 signed and numbered copies.

1832 **White, Allen**
Players versus officials: the administration and organisation of Australian cricket, 1878-1913. [Melbourne, Monash University, 1988]. [i], 85p. bibliog.
unpub. thesis submitted in partial fulfilment of ... Bachelor of Arts Degreee (Hons) in History, Monash University; copy in Melbourne Cricket Club Library.

1833 **Whitington, Richard Smallpiece**
An illustrated history of Australian cricket. South Yarra (Vic.), Currey O'Neil, 1982. 176p. illus. (some col.) stats.
——*rev. ed.* Viking O'Neil, 1987, *with updating by John Ross.*
rev. eds. of 'Padwick I' 3352.

1834 **Williams, Ken,** *[compiler]*
Guide to first class cricket matches played in Australia. 2nd ed. Haughton Mill, Association of Cricket Statisticians, 1983. 96p. scores, stats.
rev. and enlarged ed. of 'Padwick I' 3328-2.

ANNUALS

1835 **Allan's** Australian cricket annual; edited by Allan Miller. Busselton (W.A.), the Editor. illus. scores, stats.
1987-88 to date.

1836 **Australian Cricket Board**
■ Cricket almanac. Jolimont (Vic.), the Board, *annual*.
illus. (some col.) scores, stats.
1984-85
1985-86 with title 'Australian cricket incorporating A.C.B. almanac'.
1987
1988 pub. Pymble (N.S.W.), Playbill.
all issues edited by Ian McDonald.

1837 *Australian* cricket summer down under. Darlinghurst
■ (N.S.W.), Mason Stewart Publishing. illus. stats.
1988-89. 1988. [132]p. incl. covers.
1989-90. 1989. [132]p. incl. covers. edited by Bob Guntrip.
pre-season.

1838 **Cricket** in Australia. Glen Waverley (Vic.), Garry
■ Sparke & Associates, *annual*. illus. (some col.) scores,
stats.
1981 - 1986.
nos. 5 and 6 cover title: 'Max Walker's cricket in Australia'.

1839 **Cricket** year. Prahran (Vic.), Peter Isaacson
■ Publications, *annual*. illus. scores, stats.
1980-83; edited by Ken Piesse.
covers previous season.

1840 **Wide** world of sports cricket yearbook. Sydney, Collins.
□ col. illus. scores, stats.
1984 to 1986 compiled by Richie Benaud.
1987 to date edited by Richie Benaud.
1987 and 1988 pub. Methuen Australia.
1989 pub. Hamlyn Australia.

PERIODICALS

1841 **Australian** cricket. Sydney, Mason Stewart Publishing.
□ *monthly during season*. illus. (some col.) scores, stats.
pub. fortnightly during season in broadsheet newspaper format, 23 Oct 1980 to 24 Feb 1984; continued as monthly newspaper throughout the year from Oct 1984 to March/April 1986; continued as monthly magazine during season from Oct 1986 to date.
to 26 Mar 1982 edited by Phil Tresidder.
22 Oct 1982 - 24 Feb 1984 edited by Brad Boxall.
Oct 1984 - March/April 1986 edited by Noel Mengel.
Oct 1986 to date edited by Philip Mason.
continues 'Padwick I' 3380 to date.

1842 **Australian** cricket journal; edited by Chris Harte.
■ Adelaide. *3 issues per year, Sep., Dec., Apr.* illus.
Vol. 1, no. 1, Sep. 1985 - Vol. 5, no. 3, Apr. 1990 (last issue).

1843 The **Australian** cricket lifestyle magazine. Adelaide,
□ S.C. Publications, *monthly*. illus.
4 issues, Vol. 1, no. 1, Sep. 1982 - Vol. 1, no. 4, Dec. 1982; edited by Graeme Goodings.
revived? as 'Cricket lifestyle' Vol. 1, no. 1, October 1983 - vol. 1, no. 7, May 1984 (not pub. April 1984); edited by Peter A. Murray. pub. North Sydney, Neville Watkins & Associates.

1844 **Australian Society for Sports History**
□ Sporting traditions: the journal of the Australian Society
for Sports History. Adelaide, the Society. *biannual*.
vol. 1, no. 1 Nov. 1984 to date.
cricket articles in some issues.

1845 † **Cricket.** Melbourne, Melbourne Press Agency.
□ *fortnightly?* [32]p. incl. adverts. illus. scores.
vol. 1 no. 5 was pub. 16 Jan. 1925.
vol. 1 no. 7 was pub. 13 Feb. 1925.
see also 'Padwick I' 4453-1.

1846 **Cricket** world. Cammeray (N.S.W.), Cricket World Pty.
□ illus. (some col.) scores, stats.
vol. 1, no. 1, Sep. 1984 - vol. 1, no. 3, Dec. 1984. (not pub. Nov. 1984).

1847 **Cricketer;** edited by Ken Piesse. Melbourne,
■ Newspress, *monthly during season, i.e. 7 issues per year,
Oct. to Apr.* illus. scores, stats.
Vol. 7, no. 4, Jan. 1980 to date.
from Vol. 15, no. 2, Nov. 1987 pub. Syme Magazines.
continues 'Padwick' 3384-2.

1848 **Piesse, Ken,** *editor*
■ Cricket glorious cricket: featuring stories from *Cricketer*
magazine, 1973-83. Melbourne, Newspress, [1983].
96p. incl. covers, illus. (one col.)

1849 Cricket's finest decade. Melbourne, Newspress, [1982].
■ 112p. incl. covers, illus. (one col.)
extracts from 'Cricketer' magazine 1973-1982.

PRIVATE CLUBS

Australian Old Collegians

1850 † **Australian Old Collegians' Cricket Association**
1974 world tour programme. The Association, [1974].
[12]p. illus.
pre-tour.

1851 † General prospectus 1962-64. The Association, [1961].
24p.

1852 Silver jubilee world tour 1984 programme. [Sydney, the
■ Association, 1984]. [12]p. illus.
pre-tour.

1853 World tour 1980 programme. [The Association, 1980].
[16]p. incl. covers and adverts. illus.
pre-tour.

Emus

1854 **'Boss',** *pseud.*
The Emu Club 1946-1986. [Tamworth (N.S.W.), the
Club, 1986]. 120p. illus.

1855 † **The Emu Club**
The Emu Club 1954-64. [Tamworth (N.S.W.), the Club,
1964]. 16p. illus.

1856 † The Emu Club statistical record 1949-1971. [Tamworth
(N.S.W.), the Club, 1971]. 36p. illus. stats.

1857 The Emu Club statistical record 1949-50 to 1981-82.
■ [Tamworth (N.S.W.)], the Club, [1982]. 48p. illus.
stats.
includes brief historical survey of the club.

I Zingari Australia

1858 **Eldershaw, John M.**
■ I Zingari in Australia 1888-1988. North Sydney, Allen &
Unwin, 1989. viii, 199p. stats. index.

1859 **I Zingari Australia**
□ Annual report. Sydney, the Club. stats.
continues 'Padwick I' 3402 to date.

Old Cranbrookians

1860 † **Old Cranbrookians' Cricket Club**
Tour of England, July 1975. [The Club], 1975. [14]p.
pre-tour.

1861 † Tour of England, 1975. [The Club], 1975. 26p. illus. scores, stats.
post tour.

SCHOOL AND YOUTH CRICKET

1862 **A.C.T. Cricket Association,** *Junior Committee*
Barclays junior cricket handbook. Curtin (A.C.T.), the Committee. *annual.*
?/1985-86, 1986-87/
continued? with title 'Canterbury junior cricket handbook' to date?

1863 **Australian** Wool Corporation under 17 cricket championship, Launceston, 11th-22nd January 1988: in conjunction with Australian Cricket Board, Tasmanian Cricket Council & Tasmanian Youth and Schools Cricket Association. Launceston, Foot & Playsted, [1988]. 31p. incl. adverts. illus. stats.
post tournament?

1864 **Barclays** under 19 Championship. various. *annual.*
☐ *1984 held at Melbourne with pre-tournament brochure, [28]p. and post tournament brochure, 33p. + scores. 1985 held at Hobart with pre-tournament brochure, 28p. and post tournament typescript brochure, 29p. + scores. brochures for other years pub.?*

1865 The **combined** public schools of Western Australia
■ England tour 1985. [Perth, 1985]. [32]p. incl. covers & adverts. illus.
pre-tour.

1866 The **combined** public schools of Western Australia
■ England tour 1987. [Perth, 1987]. [34]p. incl. covers & adverts. illus.
pre-tour.

1867 **Fellows-Smith, G. R.**
The history of the Victorian Junior Cricket Association. Bundoora (Vic.), Preston Institute of Technology, 1980.
unpub. thesis.

1868 † **Hobart and Suburban Junior Cricket Association**
Annual report and balance sheet 1899-1900. Hobart, Tasmanian News, 1900. 1p.
the only one published?

1869 **Innisfail Junior Cricket Association**
Caught and bowled: official publication of the Innisfail Junior Cricket Association. Innisfail (Qld.), the Association. scores.
9 issues in 1983 noted.

1870 **McDonald, Ian,** *editor*
Australian Cricket Board junior cricket policy. Jolimont (Vic.), Australian Cricket Board, 1984. 14p.

1871 † **New South Wales Junior Cricket Union**
Junior cricket weekly: the official organ of the New South Wales Junior Cricket Union. Sydney, the Union. illus. stats.
vol. 1, no. 4 was pub. 3 Oct. 1934; It was previously incorporated in 'New South Wales Junior Cricket Union amateur sports weekly'? (Vol. 1, no. 1, Sep. 1928).

1872 † **Parramatta District Junior Cricket Association**
Diamond jubilee 1919-1979: a sixty year summary. Parramatta, the Association, [1979]. 76p. illus. scores, stats.

1873 **Queensland Junior Cricket Association.** *Brisbane Division*
Annual report. Brisbane, the Association. illus. stats.
from 1987-88 name changed to Brisbane Junior Cricket Association Inc.
continues 'Padwick I' 3515-1 to date?

1874 † **Queensland Junior Cricket Union**
☐ Constitution and general information and fixture book. The Union. illus. stats.
?/1968-69/?

1875 General information and year book. The Union.
?/1980-81/?

1876 † **Queensland State Schools Association**
☐ Annual report and financial statement. The Association. illus. stats.
?/1969-70/?

1877 **South Australian Cricket Association**
■ Australian Cricket Board U16 cricket championships. [Adelaide, the Association, 1981]. 20p. incl. adverts. map, stats.
pre-tournament (26 Dec 1981 to 2 Jan 1982); brochures pub. for other years?

1878 † **Suburban Junior Cricket Association of Southern Tasmania**
Fixtures, 1913-14: all matches played on the Lindisfarne Recreation Ground for the Davies Shield. Hobart, the Association, 1913. 4p.

1879 **The Sutherland Shire Junior Cricket Association**
■ Silver jubilee. the Association, 1982. [106]p. incl. covers and adverts. illus. stats.
includes report and financial statement 1981-82.

1880 † **Tasmanian Schoolboys Cricket Association**
Eighth annual Australian schoolboys cricket championships: Hobart, 12-19 January 1977. Hobart, [the Association], [1977]. [30]p. incl. adverts. stats.
pre-tournament.

1881 **Victorian Schools Cricket Association**
☐ Victorian schools cricket handbook. [Melbourne], the Association. *annual?*
1988-89 ed. sponsored by Lord's Taverners Australia (Victorian branch).
/1988-89/ to date?

1882 **Wyman, Grant A.** *and* **Vincent, Russell G.,** *compilers*
■ A plan for junior cricket development in South Australia. Adelaide, South Australian Cricket Association, [1988]. 28p. tables, diagrs.
includes notes on Kanga cricket, Average cricket and Progressive cricket.

Assumption College

1883 **Carroll, Ray**
Hat trick: football and cricket at Assumption 1978-80. Kilmore (Vic.), the Author, 1980. 59p. illus.

Brisbane Grammar School

1884 † **Francis, R. P.,** *editor*
Records of the Brisbane Grammar School. Brisbane, Pole, Outridge & Co, 1891. 135p.
cricket pp. 13-57.

Carey Baptist Grammar School

1885 **Carey Baptist Grammar Junior School**
■ Cricket tour to England and Scotland 1987. [Melbourne, the School], 1987. 32p. illus.
pre-tour; June-July 1987.

King's School, Parramatta

1886 † The **King's** School cricket tour - Malaysia 1972. [1972] 26p. scores.
post tour.

St Peter's College, Adelaide

1887 **Curtis, John William** *et al*
■ St Peter's College England cricket tour 1981. Adelaide, Lutheran Publishing House, 1981. 72p. incl. adverts. illus.
includes 'C. E. 'Nip' Pellew and the cricket of his time' pp. 50-61.
pre-tour.

1888 St Peter's College, Adelaide, tour to Sri Lanka 1984.
■ Adelaide, LPH, 1984. 32p. illus.
pre-tour.

Wesley College

1889 **Trend, P. T.,** *editor*
■ Wesley College, South Perth, Western Australia, cricket tour to England 1985. [The College, 1985]. [16]p. illus.
pre-tour.

UNIVERSITY CRICKET

1890 **Australian Universities Sports Association**
■ Cricket tour of England, May-June 1982. [The Association, 1982]. 24p. incl. adverts. illus.
pre-tour.

Adelaide University

1891 **[Howe, Gregory,** *editor***]**
■ Adelaide University Cricket Club: 75 years, 1908-83. [Adelaide], the Club, [1983]. 39p. facsims. stats.

Australian National University

1892 **Australian National University Cricket Club**
Year book. [Canberra, the Club]. illus. scores, stats.
continues 'Padwick I' 3407-2 to date?

Sydney University

1893 **Sydney University Cricket Club**
Annual report. Sydney, the Club. illus. stats.
continues 'Padwick I' 3407-4 to date.
special issue 1985 to mark 120th anniversary.

1894 A souvenir of the anniversary celebration. [Sydney, the Club, 1985]. 4p.
120th anniversary of what is believed to be the oldest existing and continuous club in Australia.

Tasmania University

1895 † **Tasmania University Cricket Club**
Annual report. [Hobart, the Club].
/1978-79 to 1983-84/ to date?

University of New South Wales

1896 **Ingleson, John,** *editor*
A decade in grade cricket. [Kensington (N.S.W.)], University of New South Wales Cricket Club, 1983. iii, 33p. illus. stats.

1897 **University** of N.S.W. Cricket Club U.K. and Ireland tour
■ 1988: commemorative booklet. [Sydney, the Club, 1988]. 32p. illus.
pre-tour.

INTERSTATE AND SHEFFIELD SHIELD CRICKET

1898 **Harte, Christopher John ('Chris')**
■ The history of the Sheffield Shield. Sydney etc., George Allen & Unwin, 1987. ix, 365p. illus. scores, stats. bibliog.
contains summary scores of every Shield game to 1985-86 and records of every player.

1899 **King, John**
■ New South Wales versus Queensland 1892/3 to 1986/7. Perth, the Author, 1987. 58p. stats.
cover sub-title: 'a statistical survey'. [limited ed. of 60 copies].

1900 New South Wales versus Victoria 1855/6 to 1988/9.
■ Subiaco (W.A.), the Author, 1989. [i], 76p. stats.
cover sub-title: 'a statistical survey'. [limited ed. of 70 copies].

1901 New South Wales versus Western Australia 1906-7 to
■ 1983-4. Perth, the Author, 1984. 31p. stats.
cover sub-title: 'a statistical survey'. [limited ed. of 100 copies].

1902 Queensland versus South Australia 1898/9 to 1987/8.
■ Subiaco (W.A.), the Author, 1988. 46p. stats.
cover sub-title: 'a statistical survey'. [limited ed. of 70 copies].

1903 Queensland versus Victoria 1902-3 to 1985-6. Perth, the
■ Author, 1986. 44p. stats.
cover sub-title: 'a statistical survey'. [limited ed. of 50 copies].

1904 Queensland versus Western Australia 1947-8 to 1981-2.
■ South Perth, the Author, 1982. 23p. stats.
cover sub-title: 'a statistical survey'. [limited ed. of 100 copies].

1905 South Australia versus Western Australia 1892-3 to
■ 1984-5. Perth, the Author, 1985. 36p. stats.
cover sub-title: 'a statistical survey'. [limited ed. of 50 copies].

1906 Victoria versus Western Australia 1892-3 to 1982-3.
■ South Perth, the Author, 1983. 32p. stats.
cover sub-title: 'a statistical survey'. [limited ed. of 100 copies].

1907 **[Mullins, [John] Ross]**
■ New South Wales v South Australia: 100 years of cricket ... 1890-1990 centenary souvenir. [Sydney, New South Wales Cricket Association, 1989]. [16]p. incl. covers illus. scores, stats.

1908 † **Oakley, Julian,** *editor*
■ 200th Sheffield Shield souvenir. Canberra, Australian Cricket Society (Canberra Branch), [1974]. [12]p. incl. covers, illus. scores.
Victoria v New South Wales; includes description of first Sheffield Shield match (Dec. 1892) and 200th match overall (Dec. 1974).

1909 **Wat, Charlie**
■ A statistical survey of the Australian states in first class cricket. Prahran (Vic.), Cricket Stats Publications.
annual. stats.
records since 1850-51.
1988-89 limited to 75 signed and numbered copies.
1989-90 limited to 150 signed and numbered copies.

CRICKET STATE BY STATE

AUSTRALIAN CAPITAL TERRITORY

1910 **Australian Capital Territory Cricket Association**
☐ Year book ... incorporating annual report. The Association. illus. scores, stats. *typescript.*
continues 'Padwick I' 3434 to date.

1911 **Barrow, Graeme** *et al*
Northies, the first 25 years, 1963-64 to 1987-88; written compiled and edited by Graeme Barrow, John Eichholzer and Steve Glaznieks. [Kaleen (A.C.T.), J. Eichholzer, 1989]. 112p. illus.
Northern Suburbs District C. C.

1912 **Capital** cricket: magazine of the A.C.T. Cricket Association. Manuka (A.C.T.), the Association. *3 issues per season.* illus.
vol. 1, no. 1 1983 to date.

1913 † **Federal Capital Territory Cricket Association**
Year book; together with constitution, by-laws, competition rules and fixtures. Canberra, Federal Capital Press.
incorporates annual report.
predecessor of 'Padwick I' 3434.
1922-23? ... 1929-30 ...?

1914 **Foskett, Alan**
Cricket in the ACT 1922-1969: some information and highlights. [Campbell (A.C.T.), Alan Foskett Consultancy Service, 1989]. 57p.

Weston Creek

1915 **Samara-Wickrama, Percy,** *editor and compiler*
■ Reports, photos, stories, statistics of the Weston Creek Cricket Club tour of England, August 1985. Holder (A.C.T.), the Club, 1985. 48p. illus. scores.
cover title: 'Reflections: Weston Creek Cricket Club tour of England, August 1985'; post tour.

1916 Weston Creek Cricket Club tour of England 1985: tour
■ program. Holder (A.C.T.), the Club, [1985]. 33p. incl. inside cover, illus. map.
pre-tour.

1917 Weston Creek Cricket Club tour of England 1988: the
■ tour brochure. Weston Creek (A.C.T.), the Club, 1988. 40p. illus. stats.
pre-tour.

1918 **Samara-Wickrama, Percy** and **Mackenzie, Ewan,** *editors*
■ Reflections: a souvenir of the Club's second tour of England. Weston Creek (A.C.T.), the Club, [1988]. [ii], 54p. illus. scores, stats.
tour of July 1988; post tour.

1919 **Weston Creek Cricket Club**
☐ Cover point: Weston Creek Cricket Club magazine. Weston Creek (A.C.T.), the Club, *monthly during season.* illus. maps, stats.
continues 'Padwick I' 3436-2 to date?

1920 Year book; compiled and edited by Percy
☐ Samara-Wickrama. Weston Creek (A.C.T.), the Club. illus. scores, stats.
continues 'Padwick I' 3436-3 to date.

NEW SOUTH WALES

1921 **Association of Cricket Statisticians**
■ New South Wales cricketers 1855-1981. Haughton Mill (Notts.), the Association, 1981. 64p. maps, stats.

1922 **Derriman, Philip**
■ True to the blue: a history of the New South Wales Cricket Association. [Mosman (N.S.W.)], Richard Smart Publishing, 1985. x, 245p. illus. stats. index.

1923 **Ellem, Lewis**
Ellem tree: a story of a North Coast family. [Grafton (N.S.W.), the Author, 1983]. 68p. illus. maps.
a New South Wales cricketing family.

1924 **Far North Coast Cricket Council**
Rules & by-laws, 1981. The Council, 1981. 24p. map.
rev. ed.

1925 **Greenwood, Michael J.**
■ The Grinsted Cup: a cricket tradition. Dubbo (N.S.W.), [the Author], 1985. 116p. incl. covers, illus. scores, stats.
history of the Western New South Wales cricket competition.

1926 † **New South Wales Churches' Cricket Union**
The Church Cricketer. Parramatta, Australia Post, *monthly during season?*
?1946 to date?

1927 **New South Wales Cricket Association**
Annual report and balance sheet. Sydney, the Association. scores.
continues 'Padwick I' 3443 to 1983-84 season; since 1984-85 incorporated in Yearbook.

1928 † Memorandum and articles of association of New South Wales Cricket Association. Sydney, 1929. 20p.
certificate of incorporation as limited company 31 March 1922.

1929 N.S.W.C.A. media guide; edited by Ross Mullins. Sydney, the Association, *annual.* stats, scores.
1987-88 to date.

1930 Sheffield Shield cricket. Sydney, the Association, *annual.*
'a digest of information ... relating to the participation of New South Wales in the Sheffield Shield competition'.
1981-82 the only issue?

1931 Yearbook. Sydney, the Association. illus. (some col.)
☐ scores, stats.
continues 'Padwick I' 3445 to date;
since 1984-1985 has incorporated annual report.

Casino

1932 **Hendley, John V.**
■ Casino: a cricket history, 1861-1986. [Casino (N.S.W.), Ron Howard, 1987]. 128p. illus. stats.

Deniliquin

1933 **O'Connell, Max,** *editor*
■ Deniliquin and District Cricket Association 1988 reunion souvenir booklet. [Deniliquin, the Association, 1988]. 112p. illus. scores, stats.
cover sub-title: 'brief history of Deniliquin and District Cricket Association'.

Glen Innes

1934 **Duncan, B.**
Glenn Innes District Cricket Association. Glen Innes (N.S.W.), E.P.S. Print for the Association and Northern Tablelands Cricket Council, [1983]. 72p. incl. adverts. scores, stats.

Newcastle

1935 **Piggford, George** *[and]* **Hay, John**
■ Runs, wickets and reminiscence: the NDCA's first 100 years. [Newcastle, the Association], 1989. 96p. illus. scores, stats.

Nowra

1936 **Clark, Alan**
One hundred and one not out!: Nowra Cricket Club centenary. [Nowra (N.S.W.), the Club], 1982? [50]p. illus.

Sydney

1937 † **City Houses Cricket Association**
Annual report and financial statement. Sydney, the Association.
16th report 1937-38; to date?

1938 † Rules. [Sydney], the Association, 1935. 22p.

1939 † **Cricketers Club of New South Wales**
Memorandum and articles of association of the Cricketers Club of New South Wales. Sydney, the Club, 1939. 20p.
certificate of incorporation, 14 November 1939.

1940 † **Cumberland** Argus cricketers' guide: season 1888-89. Parramatta (N.S.W.), Cumberland Argus, [1888]. 40p. incl. adverts.
includes report on 1887-88 season and fixtures for season 1888 for Central Cumberland Cricket Association.

1941 **Derriman, Philip**
■ The grand old ground: a history of the Sydney Cricket Ground. North Ryde (N.S.W.); North Melbourne (Vic.), Cassell, 1981. [x], 150p. illus. bibliog. index.

1942 **Eglington, John**
The Sydney Cricket Ground. [Sydney, University of New South Wales School of Architecture, 1988]. vii, 211 leaves, illus. plans.

1943 **Ingleson, John,** *editor*
A decade in grade cricket. [Kensington (N.S.W.)], University of New South Wales Cricket Club, 1983. iii, 33p. illus. stats.

1944 **James, Alfred B. M.**
■ Hornsby-Kuring-gai Cricket Association: golden jubilee history: 1926/27 - 1985/86. Wahroonga (N.S.W.), the Association, [1986]. 63p. map. stats.

1945 † **Moore Park Cricket Association**
Annual report and financial statement. Sydney, the Association.
1898? to date?

1946 **Pace, John**
A history to commemorate eighty years of social cricket in Sydney promoted by the City and Suburban Cricket Association, 1903-1983. The Association?, 1985. 20p. map.

1947 **Polkinghorne, Richard Thomas**
The history of development at the Sydney Cricket Ground. Sydney, University of New South Wales School of Architecture, 1987. v, 71 leaves, illus. map. plans.

1948 † **Scott, James W.**
■ Early cricket in Sydney with brief biographies of some of the old-time players. Sydney, [the Author, 1935]. 2 vols. scores, stats.
ms. in New South Wales Cricket Association Library.

1949 **Sharp, Martin P.**
'A degenerate race': cricket and rugby crowds in Sydney 1890-1912. Canberra, Australian Society for Sports History, 1987. 16p.

1950 Sporting spectacles: cricket and football in Sydney 1890-1912. Canberra, 1986. 461p. illus. bibliog.
published for private circulation.

1951 St George District Cricket Club 1911-1986: 75 years of cricket achievement. Kingsgrove (N.S.W.), the Club, [1986]. 95p. illus. stats.

1952 **Sydney Cricket & Sports Ground Trust**
■ A new tradition in the making. [Sydney, the Trust, 1985]. [10]p. folded brochure, illus. (some col.)
the re-development of the Sydney Cricket and Sports Ground complex.

1953 **Sydney Cricket Association**
Competition rules and playing conditions. The Association. *annual?*
?/1986-87/?

1954 **Winning, Clifford**
■ Cricket Balmainia: official history, Balmain District Cricket Club, 1897-1980. Rozelle (N.S.W.), Standard Publishing House, 1981. 284p. illus. scores, stats.
limited ed. of 600 signed and numbered copies.

1955 **Wood, John**
Sydney Cricket Association competition programmes, rules and playing conditions. Sydney, [New South Wales Cricket Association], 1988. 108p. scores, stats.
records and statistics of all Grade clubs.

1956 † **[Yaralla Cricket Club]**
History of Yaralla Cricket Club. [The Club, 1952]. 7p.

1957 † **Yaralla Cricket Club**
Record of office bearers and cricket statistics, 1891-1964/5. [Concord (N.S.W.), the Club, 1965]. 8p. stats.

NORTHERN TERRITORY

1958 **Northern Territory Cricket Association**
Proposed development, Abala Road, Marrara, N.T. The Association, 1984. illus. plans.

QUEENSLAND

1959 **Armstrong, Tom**
The effect of transport development on the history of cricket in Queensland 1846-1896. n.d.
conference paper; listed in Mullins.

1960 **Howell, Maxwell L.** *and* **McKay, James,** *editors*
Socio-historical perspectives; volume 9 of the Proceedings of the VIIth Commonwealth and International Conference on Sport, Physical Education, Recreation and Dance (Conference'82).
includes 'Sport, aborigines and racism: a case study of cricket and the Deebing Creek Aboriginal Reserve (1892-1916)' by Genevieve Blades.

1961 † **Mullins, Patrick J.**
■ Cricket tours to the tropics 1894-1977. The Author, 1977. [v], 64 leaves, illus. map. stats. *typescript.*
record of tours to North Queensland.
six copies privately circulated, one of which is now in Melbourne Cricket Club Library.

1962 **Queensland Churches Cricket Association**
□ Annual report. The Association. stats.
formerly Queensland Church Cricket Union?
continues 'Padwick I' 3509-1 to date?

1963 **Queensland Country Cricket Association**
□ Annual report. The Association. stats.
continues 'Padwick I' 3509-3 to date?

1964 **Queensland Cricket Association**
■ Annual report and financial statement. Brisbane, the Association. illus. (some col. since 1989-90) scores, stats.
continues 'Padwick I' 3510 to date.

1965 Official cricket handbook. Brisbane, the Association.
□ *annual.*
continues 'Padwick I' 3513 to date?

1966 **Queensland** cricket news. Wynnum (Qld.). *monthly*
□ *during season.* illus. (some col.) scores. stats.
Sept. 1988 to date.
edited by Ray Mason.

1967 **Sturgess, Ian**
Queensland cricket directory 1989-1990. Brisbane, Queensland Cricket Association, 1989. 60p. incl. adverts. illus. scores, stats.
who's who of cricket throughout Queensland.

1968 **Torrens, Warwick W.,** *editor*
■ Queensland cricket and cricketers, 1862-1981. [Indooroopilly (Qld.), the Author, 1981]. 209p. stats.

1969 **Young, Ken**
Chinchilla cricket digest. Chinchilla Newspapers, 1985. 52p. illus. stats.
the story of Western Downs zone cricket.

1970 Runs, wickets and records. Chinchilla Newspapers, 1983. 48p. illus. stats. index.
facts and figures of Western Downs zone cricket and Brisbane Country Week.

Brisbane

1971 **Ansty, Cec**
History of Toombul District C.C. [The Author], 1982. 24p.

1972 † The **Brisbane** Cricket Ground 1975. [Brisbane, Queensland Cricket Association?, 1975]. [8]p. col. illus.
in celebration of the building of the Sir Leslie Wilson Stand.

1973 **Brisbane Cricket Ground Trust**
□ Members handbook. 2nd ed. [Brisbane, the Trust, 1985]. 9p.
——*1st ed. pub.* 1982.

1974 † **Official** photo souvenir of Brisbane cricketers 1st grade
■ and leading officials of the Q. C. A. season 1912-13 ... Queensland v New South Wales, 'Gabba Ground, 22nd, 23rd, 25th and 26th November. Brisbane, Queensland Cricket Association, 1912. [8]p. incl. covers, illus.
individual and team portraits.

1975 † **Queensland Cricketers' Club**
Annual report of the committee. [Brisbane, the Club].
1959-60 to date.

1976 † Constitution and regulations, February 1975. Brisbane,
■ the Club. 30p.

1977 Cricklet; edited by Noel Gorman. Brisbane, the Club.
□ *monthly?* illus. (some col.)
Aug. 1984 was 25th anniversary ed.
continues 'Padwick I' 3514-2 to date.

1978 News. Brisbane, the Club. *monthly?* illus.
□ *?/Feb. 88, July 88/ to date?*

1979 **Spence, Robert**
Western Suburbs District Cricket Club. Toowong (Qld.), the Club, 1988. 56p. scores, stats. index.
history of the Club incorporating 1987-88 annual report and financial statements.

Cairns

1980 † **McDonald, Hugh** *et al*
■ Easter cricket carnival at Cairns: New South Wales eleven's visit to far North: souvenir programme. Cairns, Cairns Cricket Association, 1954. 43p. incl. adverts. illus.
Jack Chegwyn's NSW XI; includes scores of 1952 visit.

1981 † J. Chegwyn's touring eleven v Cairns. Cairns, Cairns Cricket Association, [1952]. 44p. incl. adverts. illus.

Canaga

1982 **Young, Ken**
Canaga Cricket Club: twenty years on top. Chinchilla Newspapers, 1984. 20p. illus. stats.

Chinchilla

1983 **Young, Ken**
■ Chinchilla and District Cricket Association silver anniversary, 1965-1990, souvenir book. Brigalow (Qld.), Chinchilla & District Cricket Association, 1989. 212p. incl. adverts. illus. stats.
cover title.

1984 Chinchilla champions. Chinchilla Newspapers, 1987. 24p. illus. stats.

1985 Concrete to turf: Chinchilla's cricket history 1965-85. [The Author], 1986. 84p. illus. stats.

Maryborough

1986 **[Steele, Sam]**
■ Hit for a century: one hundred hard-hitting years: Maryborough District Cricket Association 1887-1987. [Maryborough (Qld.), the Association, 1988]. 56p. illus.

Townsville

1987 † **Smallwood, H. E.**
Official souvenir of the visit of a N.S.W. eleven Easter
1931. Townsville (Qld.), Townsville Cricket
Association, [1931]. 96p. incl. adverts. illus.

SOUTH AUSTRALIA

1988 **Country Carnival Cricket Association**
[Programme]. Adelaide, *Adelaide Advertiser. annual.*
continues 'Padwick I' 3520 to date.

1989 † **Cricket Union of South Australia**
☐ Rules, constitution and general information book.
[Adelaide], Arcadia Publishing Co. for the Union.
annual. illus.
1932-33/1966-67/ to date.

1990 **Daly, John A.**
■ Elysian fields: sport, class and community in colonial
South Australia 1836-1890. Adelaide, the Author, 1982.
[viii], 229p. illus. facsims. maps, bibliog. index.
cricket pp. 38-42, 65-70 and other references.

1991 **Forster, Clive**
The changing geography of country cricket in South
Australia 1836-1914. [Adelaide, Flinders University of
South Australia], 1985. 25p. facsims, maps, diag.

1992 **[Harte, Christopher John ('Chris')]**
■ A corporate strategy for the South Australian Cricket
Association. The Association, [1983]. xii, 167 leaves +
12 leaves of appendices. bibliog.

1993 **Harte, Christopher John ('Chris')**
Edwin Smith: the grand old man of early South
Australian football and cricket. North Adelaide, Sports
Marketing, 1989. 28p.
limited ed. of 50 copies.
*Smith founded Norwood District Cricket Club (later East
Torrens C.C.)*

1994 Harry McKay: the cause of the last class clash in South
Australian cricket. North Adelaide, Sports Marketing,
1989. 32p.
limited ed. of 50 copies.

1995 John Creswell: cricket administrator supreme. North
Adelaide, Sports Marketing, 1989. 64p.
limited ed. of 50 copies.
Creswell was SACA secretary from 1883-1909.

1996 South Australian Cricket Association: domestic one day
cricket records 1969-89. Adelaide, the Association,
1989. 106p. scores, stats.
*a complete statistical record of South Australia in
one-day domestic limited overs competitions.*

1997 South Australian Cricket Association: players statistics
and records guide. Adelaide, the Association, *annual.*
illus. scores, stats.
/1986-87 to date/

1998 South Australian Cricket Association: Sheffield Shield
records 1892-1989. Adelaide, the Association, 1989.
56p. scores, stats.
*a complete statistical record of South Australia in the
Sheffield Shield competition.*

1999 W.H. Jeanes: the man who made modern South
Australian cricket. North Adelaide, Sports Marketing,
1989. 24p.
limited ed. of 50 copies.
Bill Jeanes was SACA secretary from 1926-55.

2000 Yorke Sparks: founder of the Adelaide Oval. North
Adelaide, Sports Marketing, 1989. 24p.
limited ed. of 50 copies.
*——reissued limited ed. of 100 unnumbered copies for
the Glenelg Council; Sparks was Mayor of Glenelg and
founder of the Glenelg Oval.*

2001 **Harvey, Brian M.**
The Cricket Union of South Australia. Brighton (S.A.),
Arcadia Publishing, [1984]. 64p. incl. adverts. scores.

2002 † **McInnes, Stephen**
Cricket and South Australian society. University of
Adelaide, 1970.
unpub. thesis; listed in Mullins.

2003 **Millbank, Susan Irene**
■ South Australian Cricket Association, cricket and South
Australia: 1871-1914. Adelaide, Flinders University of
South Australia, 1981. x, 82p. bibliog.
*unpub. thesis for B.A. (Hons) degree; copy in Melbourne
Cricket Club Library.*

2004 **Page, Roger, [*compiler*]**
■ South Australian cricketers 1877-1984. Haughton Mill
(Notts.), Association of Cricket Statisticians, 1984. 63p.
maps, stats.

2005 **South Australian Cricket Association**
☐ Annual report ... and statement of accounts ... Adelaide,
the Association. illus. (some col.) scores, stats.
continues 'Padwick I' 3526 to date.

2006 Official handbook. Adelaide, the Association, *annual.*
☐ maps.
continues 'Padwick I' 3527.
1894-95 to date.

2007 The SACA member. Adelaide, the Association, *3
issues per season.*
No. 1, Oct. 1985, to date; edited by Chris Harte.

Adelaide

2008 **Adelaide & Suburban Cricket Association**
☐ Yearbook. Adelaide, the Association.
continues 'Padwick I' 3530-1 to date.

2009 **Adelaide Turf Cricket Association**
Yearbook. Adelaide, the Association.
/1931-32 to date/

2010 **Allrounder;** edited by George Gandy. Adelaide Cricket
Club, *monthly during season?*
vol. 1, no. 1, Sep. 1981 to c.1984.

2011 **Doherty, M. J. ('Jack')**
■ The Talbot-Smith fielding trophy. Adelaide, the
Author, 1984. [v], 14p. + 3p. of ports. stats.
*history of the prize awarded for fielding in 'A' Grade
District Competition played under the auspices of the
South Australian Cricket Association.*

2012 **Gum, Dennis W.** *and* **Stanley, Michael,** *compilers*
From saltbush to turf: 100 years of Grange Cricket Club.
[Henley Beach (S.A.)], the Club, 1985. 222p. illus.
facsims. maps. scores, stats.

2013 **Harte, Christopher John ('Chris')**
South Australian Cricket Association: records of district
cricket up to 1988/89. Adelaide, the Association, 1989.
160p. scores, stats.
a statistical record of Adelaide District cricket.

2014 Marlow, Alfred T.
Adelaide Turf Cricket Association: the first 50 years.
Adelaide, the Association, 1982. 54p. scores, stats.
includes 50th annual report.

Coromandel Valley

2015 Mableson, Roger *and* Griffin, C.
Coromandel Cricket Club: 125 years, 1862 to 1987.
Coromandel Valley (S.A.), the Club, 1987. 35p. illus.
facsims. stats.

Kimba

2016 Kelly's first fifty: a history of the Katinga-Kelly Cricket
Club 1934 to 1984. Kimba (S.A), the Club, 1984. 40p.

Port Pirie

2017 † King, Bert
'From the fifties to the seventies': the story of cricket in
Port Pirie. Port Pirie (S.A.), North Cricket Club for
Port Pirie Cricket Association, 1976. 44p. incl. adverts.
illus.

Snowtown

2018 Snowtown Cricket Club 1881-1981. Snowtown (S.A.),
the Club, 1981. 32p. illus.

TASMANIA

2019 Association of Cricket Statisticians
Tasmanian cricketers 1850-1982. Haughton Mill
(Notts.), the Association, [1982]. 40p. maps, stats.

2020 † Australia and New Zealand Railways Institutes
Cricket carnival: Hobart, 1975: souvenir programme.
Hobart, [1975?]. [24]p.
pre-tournament.

2021 Chapple, Stewart G.
50 years of cricket in Tasmania's north-east.
Launceston, [the Author], 1985. 93p. illus.

2022 † Country Cricket Council
Rules for Country Week. Franklin (Tas.), Huon and
Derwent Times, 1927. 4p.

2023 † The **Cricketers'** bazaar gazette. Hobart, Mercury Steam
Press. *monthly.*
no. 1, 14th Aug 1880 to no. 6, 7th Feb 1881.

2024 † Cygnet Municipal Cricket Association
Constitution and rules. Franklin (Tas.), Huon News,
1948. 12p.

2025 † Huon Cricket Association
Constitution and rules. Franklin (Tas.), Huon News.
12p.
various years 1959?, 1973, 1983 to date?

2026 † [Sheehy, Thomas]
Retrospect of cricket. Hobart, Southern Tasmania
Cricket Association, 1870. 24p.
*amended reprint of an article in the 'Mercury' 26 May
1870.*

2027 Smith, Richard Mark
Prominent Tasmanian cricketers: from Marshall to
Boon. Launceston, Foot & Playsted, 1985. xii, 297p.
illus. stats.

2028 Tasmanian Cricket Association
Annual report and financial statements. Hobart, the
Association. illus. stats.
continues 'Padwick I' 3584 to date.

2029 Tasmanian cricket yearbook. Hobart, Tasmanian
Sporting Publications. illus. scores, stats.
1980-81 to 1985-86; edited by Tony Hassett.
1986-87; compiled by Ric Finlay.
1987-88; compiled by Ric Finlay and Ray Webster.
1988-89; compiled by Ric Finlay.
1989-90 with title 'Cricket Tasmania' pub. by Sportsnews
Tasmania, *edited by Ric Finlay.*
continues 'Padwick I' 3585-1 to date.

Devonport

2030 † Devonport Cricket Club
Annual report. Devonport, the Club. stats.
?/1958-59, 1963-64/ to date?

2031 † North Western Tasmanian Cricket Association
Annual report and financial statements. Devonport, the
Association. *annual.* stats.
1952?/1984-86/ to date.

Hobart

2032 Mitchell, Brian
The history of the Kingborough District Cricket Club.
Hobart, [the Club, 1982]. [iii], 67p. illus. stats.

2033 Kingborough District Cricket Club first grade statistics
1931-32 to 1982-83. Hobart, [the Club, 1983]. [28]p.
stats.

2034 † West Hobart District Cricket Club
Rules and by-laws: season 1910-11. Hobart, the Club,
[1910]. 4p.

Launceston

2035 Gunn, D. V.
As time goes by: a record of the first fifty years of the
Old Launcestonians Football Club from 1931 to 1980
together with a record of the Old Launcestonians
Cricket Club from 1947 to 1980; compiled by E. J.
Coulter and D. V. Gunn, written by D. V. Gunn.
Launceston, the Club, 1981. 277p. illus. stats.

2036 † Launceston Cricket Club
Annual report and financial statement. Launceston, the
Club. 4p.
?/1843-44, 1969-70 ... 1980-81/ to date?

2037 † Rules of the Launceston Cricket Club: season 1876 and
1877. Launceston, J. Stephenson, 1876. 8p.

2038 Northern Tasmanian Cricket Association
Annual report and balance sheet. Launceston, the
Association. illus. scores, stats.
continues 'Padwick I' 3581 to 1989.
1985-86 was centenary issue.

2039 [Williams, Ron J.]
South Launceston Cricket Club: a history 1907-1982.
[Launceston, the Club, 1982?]. 40p. illus. stats.

2040 Williams, Ron J., *compiler and editor*
The history of the Launceston Cricket Club, 1841-1987.
[Launceston, the Club, 1987]. x, 158p. incl. adverts.
illus. scores, stats.

2041 **Williams, Ron J.,** *compiler and editor, and* **Smith,**
■ **Richard Mark**
To celebrate a century of Northern Tasmanian cricket:
the story of the Northern Tasmanian Cricket
Association. [Launceston, the Association, 1986]. xii,
143p. illus. scores, stats.

VICTORIA

2042 † **Mullen, Clarence Cecil**
■ Victorian cricket to 1964-65. [1965]. 129p. *typescript.*
copy in Melbourne Cricket Club Library.

2043 **Victorian Cricket Association**
■ Annual report. Jolimont (Vic.), the Association. illus.
scores, stats.
*since 1979-80, issued in two parts with separate statistical
report.*
continues 'Padwick I' 3537 to date.

2044 † Memorandum and articles of association. Melbourne,
[1926]. 24p.
certificate of incorporation, 3 September 1926.

2045 Official handbook. Jolimont (Vic.), Magenta Press for
□ the Association, *annual.* illus. facsims. diagrs. maps,
scores, stats.
?/1981-82/ to date.
from 1987-88; edited by Peter W. Binns.

2046 Victorian cricket: the official magazine of the Victorian
■ Cricket Association. Jolimont (Vic.), the Association,
bimonthly during the season; Oct., Dec., Feb. illus. stats.
first issue, vol. 1, no. 1, Oct. 1985 to date.

Donald

2047 **Kirk, L. B.**
Country for heroes: Rich Avon Soldiers' Settlement and
Rich Avon Cricket Club. Donald (Vic.), History and
Natural History Group of the M.L.A. Society, 1984.
28p. illus. bibliog. index.

Euroa

2048 † **Halsall, C. W.**
■ A history of sport in Euroa and district. Euroa, Euroa
Shire Council, 1979. 151p. illus.
includes '120 years of cricket in Euroa District' pp. 61-95.

Geelong

2049 **Barnes, David**
■ The history of the Newtown & Chilwell Cricket Club.
Geelong, the Club, 1988. v.p. illus. facsims. scores,
stats.

2050 **Geelong Churches Cricket Association**
□ Cricket guide. [Geelong, the Association]. *annual.*
?/1989-90.

2051 **O'Dowd, Kevin**
■ Geelong's blazing century. [Geelong, *Geelong
Advertiser*], 1989. xiii, 322p. illus. scores, stats. index.
limited ed. of 1000 copies.

2052 International cricket in Geelong. Geelong, Geelong
■ Cricket Association, 1987. 42p. facsims. scores.
*issued for the 125th anniversary of touring teams playing
in Geelong.*

Gippsland

2053 **History** of the Nerrena Cricket Club 1935-36 to 1985-86.
[The Club], 1986. 34p.

Hamilton

2054 **Maloney, Bruce J.**
St. Andrew's Cricket Club, Hamilton, 1943/44 to 1984/85.
Hamilton (Vic.), the Club, 1985. 40p. illus. scores,
stats.

Kellalac

2055 **A summarized** history of the Kellalac Cricket Club and
■ club records at beginning of 1987/88 season. [the Club,
1988]. 16p. illlus. stats. *typescript.*

Maryborough

2056 **Sinclair, Ron**
■ A history of cricket in Maryborough and district.
Maryborough (Vic.), M. K. M. Cricket Club, 1989. [xi],
273p.

Melbourne

2057 **Boicos, A.**
Footscray Cricket Club 1933-88. Melbourne, the Club,
1988. 60p.? scores, stats.

2058 **Braham, S. J.**
Coburg Cricket Club golden years. North Melbourne,
Magazine Art, [1988]. 68p. incl. adverts. illus. scores,
stats.

2059 † **Chalmers, Robert W.**
■ A history of Essendon & Broadmeadows Churches
Cricket Association [1903-1978]. [Melbourne the
Author, 1978]. [i], 97p. stats. *typescript.*

2060 † **Congregational Churches Cricket Association**
□ [Rules and fixtures]. Richmond (Vic.), the Association.
annual.
?/1910-11/?

2061 **Cranfield, Louis Radnor**
■ Cricket by the riverside. The Club, [1980]. 34p. incl.
covers and adverts. illus. scores.
to commemorate 125 years of cricket at Warrandyte.

2062 † **Cranfield, Louis Radnor,** *compiler, and* **Hudson, Harry**
■ The Warrandyte story 1855-1955; illustrated by Harry
Hudson. [Melbourne], Warrandyte Cricket Club, 1955.
64p. stats.

2063 † **Essendon** Cricket Club: centenary 1872-1972.
■ [Essendon, the Club, 1972]. [20]p. stats.

2064 **Mathews, Douglas C.,** *editor*
■ From the well of cricket: the history of the Camberwell
Cricket Club 1864-1989. [The Club], 1989. [iv], 153p.
illus. stats. index.

2065 **Melbourne** Cricket Ground: environment effects
statement and report on proposed floodlighting.
Melbourne, A. T. Cocks & Partners, 1983. v.p., illus.
maps.
——*supplementary report* 1983.

2066 **Mentone Cricket Club**
■ History of the Mentone Cricket Club. the Club, 1983.
176p. illus. scores, stats. *typescript.*
*includes annual report and financial statement for
1982-83 season.*

2067 † **Metropolitan Cricket League**
□ Rules and fixture book. [Melbourne], the League.
annual.
?/1969-70/ to date?

2068 **Quinn, Brian,** *editor*
■ Mentone Cricket Club 1888-1988: centenary book. [Melbourne, the Club, 1988]. 132p. illus. stats.

2069 **Scholefield, Ian Lindsay**
□ From khakis to whites: diamond jubilee of Burwood District Cricket Club, 1928-1987. The Author, 1988. 176p. illus. stats.
cover sub-title: 'story and statistical record of Burwood District Cricket Club, 1928-1987'.
——*rev. ed.* 1989.

2070 **St Kilda Cricket Table Tennis Club**
50th anniversary: formed 1933. St Kilda (Vic.), the Club, 1983. 28p.

2071 **Stremski, Richard**
■ Kill for Collingwood. North Sydney, Allen & Unwin, 1986. x, 340p. illus. (some col.) bibliog. index.
the story of Collingwood Football Club; includes 'War against cricket: the battle for Victoria Park', pp. 99-111, and other cricket references.

2072 **Tsilimanis, Vic**
■ Ivanhoe Cricket Club 1906/07 to 1986/87: the first eighty years. [Melbourne, the Author, 1987]. [53] leaves, stats. *typescript.*
unpub. statistical account; copy in Melbourne Cricket Club Library.

2073 **Tyson, Frank Holmes**
■ The history of the Richmond Cricket Club. East Melbourne, the Club in association with Hudson Publishing, 1987. ix, 259p. illus. stats. index.

2074 † **Warehousemen's Cricket Club**
□ Annual report. Melbourne, the Club.
annual report and balance sheet; Club founded 1863?. ?/1870-71/?

Melbourne C. C.

2075 **Bouwmann, Richard**
■ Glorious innings: treasures from the Melbourne Cricket Club collection. Hawthorn (Vic.), Hutchinson Australia, 1987. xi, 131p. illus. (some col.) bibliog. index.

2076 **Dunstan, Keith**
■ The paddock that grew: the story of the Melbourne Cricket Club. Surry Hills (N.S.W.), Hutchinson of Australia, 1988. xi, 404p. illus. scores, stats. index.
3rd ed. of 'Padwick I' 3550; pub. for 150th anniversary of the Club.

2077 **Gray, William I.,** *compiler*
■ Melbourne Cricket Club year book: notable events in the club's histroy: achievements by sporting teams and members. Melbourne, the Club, 1980. [138]p.

2078 **Melbourne Cricket Club**
■ Annual report. Melbourne, the Club. col. illus. stats.
continues 'Padwick I' 3552 to date.

2079 MCC News. Melbourne, the Club, *3 issues per year.* col.
□ illus.
continues 'Padwick I' 3555 to date.

2080 † Rules. Melbourne, the Club.
■ *November 1861.*
13 September 1881.
18 June 1969 with title 'Rules and by-laws'.
October 1984.
additional eds. of 'Padwick I' 3554.

2081 † **[Melbourne Cricket Club]**
■ Souvenir of the Melbourne Cricket Club 1838 to 1934. The Club, 1934. 8p. illus.

2082 † **Melbourne Cricket Club: XXIX Club**
□ Annual report. Melbourne, the Club. illus. stats.
social cricket club for M.C.C. members 'past their prime'. 1956-57/1959-60 ... 1987-88/ to date.

2083 **Moffatt, Heather**
■ Aspects of the organisation of the Melbourne Cricket Club at the MCG. [Melbourne], Chisholm Institute of Technology, 1984. [iv], iv, 41 leaves.
thesis submitted for graduate diploma in secretarial studies; copy in Melbourne Cricket Club Library.

2084 † **Perryman, Charles Henry**
■ Sydney, Brisbane, Newcastle and Ipswich with Melbourne Cricket Club - Easter 1896. 19p.
ms. diary of tour 31 March to 24 April 1896; in Melbourne Cricket Club Museum.

Mirboo

2085 **Snell, Bernice**
Mirboo North Cricket Club 1887-1987. Mirboo, the Club, 1987? 56 leaves, illus.

Moe

2086 A **history** of the Moe Cricket Club Incorporated
■ 1881-1989. [The Club, 1989]. [60]p. illus. facsims. scores, stats. *typescript.*

Pomborneit

2087 **O'Neill, Kenneth W.**
■ Hundreds and hat-tricks: the history of Pomborneit Cricket Club. Terang (Vic.), the Club, 1986. 80p. illus. facsims. scores.

Sale

2088 **Hollands, Alan** *and* **Wrigglesworth, Neil**
Bundalaguah Cricket Club 1921-1986. Sale (Vic.), [the Club?], 1986. 87p. illus.

Yarragon

2089 **Chaproniere, Cyril**
100 not out 1881-1981: a brief history of the first one hundred years of the Yarragon Cricket Club. Yarragon (Vic.), the Club, 1981. 31p. illus.

Yea District

2090 **Dignam, Thomas G.,** *editor*
■ Yea and District Cricket Association 1928-1988: a brief history. Alexander (Vic.), the Association, 1988. 40p. incl. covers.

WESTERN AUSTRALIA

2091 **Arlow, W. R.** *and* **Firkin, R. J.**
West Australian Suburban Turf Cricket Association. Perth, the Association, 1988. 72p. incl. adverts. scores, stats.
statistical history of the Association, 1896 to date.

2092 **Cricket** West: WA's own Cricket Magazine. Morley,
■ Sportscene. *irregular.* illus. diagr.
No. 1, Jan. 1982, no. 2, 1982-83; others pub?

2093 **Reynolds, William P.,** [*compiler*]
■ Western Australian cricketers 1892-1983. Haughton Mill (Notts.), Association of Cricket Statisticians, 1983. 39p. maps, stats.

2094 **Western Australia Cricket Association**
□ WACA chatter. Perth, the Association. *monthly?* illus. (some col.)
June? 1986 to date.

2095 The Western cricketer ... year book of the Western
□ Australia Cricket Association. Perth, the Association. illus. (some col.) scores, stats.
continues 'Padwick I' 3579 to date.

2096 **Western Australian (sic) Cricket Association**
■ Sheffield Shield guide 1982/83 season. [Perth, the Association, 1982]. 48p. illus. stats.
the only issue?

Fremantle

2097 **Smith, Gilbert R.**
Fremantle District Cricket Club centenary book: 100 years of cricket in Fremantle. O'Connor (W.A.), the Club, 1987. 24p. illus. scores, stats.

Lake Grace

2098 **Walker, Andrew**
Lake Grace Cricket Club. [The Author], 1988.

Perth

2099 **McAullay, N.**
Bayswater & Morley Districts Cricket Club. Bayswater (W.A.), the Club, 1988. 16p. illus. scores, stats.

2100 † **McMullan, Enid**
History & records of the Midland-Guildford Cricket Club. Revised ed. Perth, the Club, 1988. 124p. illus. scores, stats.
——*first ed.* 1970.

2101 **Scott, P. R.**
Report on the application of an evapotranspiration equation to the WACA dome. South Perth, Dept. of Agriculture Division of Resource Management, 1989. xvii, 4p. illus.

2102 **Smith, Alan J.,** *and others*
Mt. Lawley District Cricket Club. Dianella (W.A.), Metro Press, 1987. 52p. scores, stats. index.

2103 † **Subiaco District Cricket Club**
■ Official opening ... November 7th, 1965, Rosalie Park Pavilion: souvenir brochure. [Subiaco, the Club, 1965]. [32]p. incl. adverts. illus.
includes brief history of the Club.

2104 **Wilson, Colin S.**
Perth Mercantile Cricket Association. Cloverdale (W.A.), the Association, 1988. 68p. scores, stats.

Wanneroo

2105 **McLaren, Noel**
Wanneroo Districts Cricket Club. Greenwood (W.A.), the Club, 1988. 84p. illus. scores, stats.

WOMEN'S CRICKET

2106 † **Australian Women's Cricket Council**
□ Australian women's cricket: the magazine of the Australian Women's Cricket Council; edited by Dot Debnam. The Council. *quarterly?* illus.
/*vol. 1, no. 1, March 1938/?*

2107 Between overs: official magazine of the Australian
□ Women's Cricket Council. Chadstone Centre (Vic.), the Council. *monthly during season?* illus. scores, stats.
Oct. 1984 was first issue.

2108 **Boyle, Sallie-Ann**
■ Women's cricket in Australia: a resource guide. Royal Melbourne Institute of Technology, 1989. [i], 22 leaves. bibliog. *typescript.*
required element for Bachelor of Social Science in Library and Information Services; copy in Melbourne Cricket Club Library.

2109 **Butcher, Betty**
■ The sport of grace: women's cricket in Victoria: the beginning. Melbourne, Sports Federation of Victoria, 1984. [ix], 34p. illus. scores.

2110 **Frost, Lenore,** *compiler*
Donex Ladies Cricket Club record book 1945-46 to 1984-85. [Essendon (Vic.), the Author], 1986. 55p. illus. stats.

2111 † **McDonnell, Agnes E.** *and* **Ruddell, Mabel E.**
■ Women's cricket then and now. [1954]. 30 leaves. *typescript.*
Agnes McDonnell was the first secretary of the Pioneer Victorian Ladies' Cricket Association founded in 1930; copy in Melbourne Cricket Club Library.

2112 **Papasergio, Clare** *and* **Moy, Janice**
■ The history of women's cricket in Western Australia 1930-1980. [Perth, Western Australian Women's Cricket Association], 1981. [iv], 18 + 25p. illus. stats.

2113 **Powell, Jill**
Development plan 1984-1987. Wembley (W.A.), Western Australian Women's Cricket Association, 1984. 22p.

2114 **Short, Pauline**
Married v maiden: the development of Australian women's cricket 1874-1934. 1981.
conference paper; listed in Mullins.

2115 **Victorian Women's Cricket Association**
□ From the boundary: [newsletter of the V.W.C.A.}, [Melbourne], the Association. *bimonthly?*
3 issues pub. in 1988-89 season.

2116 **Webber, Horace**
■ The beginnings of ladies' cricket. c.1986. 15 leaves. *typescript.*
principally in Victoria; copy in Melbourne Cricket Club Library.

CHARITY TEAMS

Lord's Taverners Australia

2117 **Lord's Taverners Australia**
□ The Taverner. Sydney, the Club. *biannual?* illus. (some col.)
/*Dec. 1985 ... Dec. 1987/* to date?

The Primary Club of Australia

2118 † **The Primary Club of Australia**
☐   Annual report. Sydney, the Club. illus.
      1974-75/1982-83, 83-4, 85-6/ to date.

2119 † Newsletter. Sydney, the Club. *quarterly?*
☐   *1975?/no 14, June 1979; no 31. Oct. 1986/ to date?*

2120   Record of achievement since 1974. Cammeray (N.S.W),
■   the Club, 1981. [20]p. illus.

AUSTRALIAN CRICKET SOCIETY

Adelaide Branch

2121   **Cathedral** end: the journal of the Australian Cricket
☐   Society, Adelaide Branch. Adelaide, the Society,
       varying frequency. illus, stats. *typescript.*
       since vol. 2, no. 1, Aug. 1981, edited by Chris Harte.
       continues 'Padwick I' 3586-4 to date.

Hobart Branch

2122   **Break** o' Day: the newsletter of the Australian Cricket
       Society, Hobart Branch. Hobart, the Society, *irregular.*
       No. 1, Aug. 1988 entitled 'Australian Cricket Society
       Hobart Branch Newsletter'.
       branch founded 21st March 1988.

Melbourne Branch

2123   **Pavilion.** Melbourne, the Society, *annual.* illus. stats.
■   *continues 'Padwick I' 3588 to date.*

2124   **'Scoresheet':** the official newsletter of the Melbourne
☐   Branch of the A.C.S. Melbourne, the Society, *quarterly.*
       continues 'Padwick I' 3589 to date.

Sydney Branch

2125   **Cardwell, Ronald L.,** *editor*
■   Australian Cricket Society USA Caribbean tour 1981
       souvenir tour brochure. The Society, [1981]. 24p. illus.
       pre-tour.

2126   **Hill** chatter: official journal of the Australian Cricket
☐   Society (Sydney Branch). Sydney, the Society. *irregular.*
       typescript.
       continues 'Padwick I' 3590-1 to 1986.

CRICKET IN SOUTH AFRICA AND ZIMBABWE

(* indicates items on non-white cricket)

GENERAL

2127　**Archer, Robert** *and* **Bouillon, Antoine**
The South African game: sport and racism. Zed Press, 1982. [xvi], 352p. bibliog. index.
—— *originally pub. in France as 'Sport et apartheid',*
Albatros, 1981.
cricket pp. 79-97, 259-262, and many other references.

2128　**[Bassano, Brian Stanley]**
SA cricket news: centenary edition, 1889-1989.
Northlands (Transvaal), South African Cricket Union. 60p. incl. covers and adverts. illus.
special ed. pub. March 1989; series by series listing of South African Test cricket and discussion of current issues in South African cricket.

2129　**Crowley, Brian Mathew**
Cricket's exiles: the saga of South African cricket. Angus & Robertson, 1984. 160p. illus. (some col.) stats. bibliog. index.
——*first pub. in South Africa by* Don Nelson Publishers, 1983.
includes ch. on the history of non-white cricket.

2130　**Een** van S.A. krieket. Pretoria, 1989. 12p. illus. stats.
in Afrikaans; 'Rapport' cricket centenary celebrations supplement.

2131　**Giants** of South African cricket. Cape Town, Don Nelson, 1987. 216p. illus.
updated and enlarged ed. of 'Padwick I' 3597.

2132　**[Heesom, H. Denys A.** *compiler, and* **Bailey, Philip Jonathan,** *editor*]
A guide to important cricket matches played in South Africa. Haughton Mill (Notts.), Association of Cricket Statisticians, [1981]. 38p. scores, stats.
includes full scores of eight first class matches, details of which had previously been difficult to obtain.

2133　**Ramsamy, Sam**
Apartheid, the real hurdle: sport in South Africa and the international boycott. International Defence and Aid Fund for Southern Africa, 1982?

2134 †　**S.A.** Coloured Cricket Association souvenir brochure
*　Durban 1954. Durban, Natal Coloured Cricket Board, 1954. 32p. incl. adverts. illus.

2135　**South African Cricket Union**
□　Financial report for the year ended ... Johannesburg, the Union. stats.
continues 'Padwick I' 3604? to date.

2136　**South** African Cricket Union: commemorative centenary supplement, 1889-1989. Port Elizabeth, 1989. xx, illus.
a 'Weekend Post' supplement.

2137　**Sports Council**
Sport in South Africa: report of the Sports Council's fact-finding delegation. The Council, 1980. [ii], 184p.
cricket pp. 71-77.

ANNUALS

2138　**Benson** & Hedges South African cricket yearbook 1984; edited by Colin Bryden. Greenside, Robin Binckes Promotions, 1984. 104p. illus. (mostly col.) scores, stats.
review of 1983-84 season; the only issue.

2139　**Protea** cricket annual of South Africa. Cape Town, Protea Assurance. illus. (some col. since 1984), scores, stats.
1980-81, edited by Michael Owen-Smith and Peter Sichel.
1982, edited by Eric Litchfield and Peter Sichel.
1983-84, edited by Ted Partridge and Peter Sichel.
1985-88, edited by Ted Partridge, Frank Heydenrych and Peter Sichel.
1989, edited by Ted Partridge and Frank Heydenrych.
continues 'Padwick I' 3611-1.

PERIODICALS

2140　**Kardwi** cricketer. Cape Town, Kardwi Cricket Club.
□ *　irregular? illus.*
'devoted to non-racial cricket'.
?/vol. 1, no. 2, c.Dec. 1983/ to date?

2141　**South** African cricketer. Cape Town, *monthly during*
□　*season? illus. (some col.) scores, stats.*
vol. 1, no. 1, 1983 to vol. 3, no. 7, April 1986; edited by Richard Whittingdale.

PRIVATE CLUBS

Kingsmead Mynahs

2142　**Kingsmead Mynahs Club**
Mynahs tour, England 1987. Durban the Club, [1987]. [20]p. illus.
pre-tour?

Wilfred Isaacs XI

2143　**Festival** of cricket, Grahamstown, 9-11 September 1988. [Grahamstown], 1988. [4]p. illus.
Wilf Isaacs XI vs Eastern Province Cricket Union, St Andrew's College, Pirates Cricket Club.

Zingari

2144　**Zingari Cricket Club**
Tour of England 1983. [Pietermaritzburg (Natal), the Club, 1983]. 16p. incl. covers & adverts.
pre-tour.

SCHOOL AND UNIVERSITY CRICKET

2145　**Cape** primary schools cricket week. *annual.* illus.
?/1982, 87, 88/ to date?
1982 ed. includes brief history of the week.

2146　**Clifton** cricket tour of England. [1988]. [4]p. illus.
post tour.

2147 **OK** under-twelve cricket festival, Woodridge ... souvenir brochure. [Woodridge College]. *annual* illus. *1987 with title 'Safren under 12 cricket festival'. /1987 to date/*

2148 † **Perm** primary schools cricket week / Perm Laerskole - □ kricketweek. East London, *annual.* stats. *pub. since inauguration of tournament in 1968 to date; sponsored by Perm since 1972; pre-tournament.*

2149 † **South African Universities Cricket Association** SAU cricket tournament. Various, the Association, *annual.* illus. stats. *pub. pre-tournament every year under different titles. continues 'Padwick I' 3624 to date?*

Dale College

2150 † **Cricket** at Dale College: a brief history and tribute to Percy Davis. King William's Town, the College, 1975. 28p. illus. stats.

Dale Junior School

2151 **Dale Junior School** Dale junior 1986 cricket festival ... 21-25 September 1986. King William's Town, 1986. 10p. illus. *pre-festival.*

Kingswood College

2152 † **Kingswood College** Cricket tour: British Isles 1978. Grahamstown, the College, [1978]. 31p. *pre-tour.*

2153 Cricket tour: England and Channel Islands April/May 1981. Grahamstown, the College, [1981]. 30p. illus. stats. *pre-tour.*

Maritzburg College

2154 **Maritzburg College** Michaelmas invitation cricket week. [Pietermaritzburg], 1989. [8]p.

Union High School

2155 **Union High School** Graaff-Reinet United Kingdom cricket tour 1988: commemorative booklet. [Graaff-Reinet], 1988. 16p. illus. *pre-tour.*

Woodridge College

2156 **Woodridge College** Woodridge College England tour 1982. The College, [1982]. [12]p. illus. stats. *post tour.*

OLD SCHOOL CLUBS

2157 **Old Andrean Club** Old Andrean Club centenary cricket festival 12-14 September 1986. Grahamstown, 1986. [20]p. incl. adverts. *matches involving Wilf Isaac's XI, Eastern Province XI, Old Andrean XI and St Andrew's College 1st XI.*

2158 **Old** Johannian Cricket Club: 1980 cricket tour Great ■ Britain and Holland. [The Club, 1980]. 35p. incl. adverts. illus. *pre-tour.*

TOURNAMENTS

Benoni

2159 **Actonville Spurs Cricket Club** Under 16 junior cricket tournament, 21st and 22nd December, 1985, souvenir brochure. Benoni, the Club, 1985. 36p. illus. *pre-tournament.*

Howa Bowl

2160 **Natal Cricket Board** * Howa Bowl inter-provincial ... 14, 15, 16 March 1981: souvenir brochure. Pietermaritzburg, 1981. 16p. illus. *other years pub.? continues 'Padwick I' 3633?*

Nuffield Cricket Week

2161 **Nuffield** Cricket Week. Various, Nuffield Week □ Standing Committee. *annual.* stats. *pre-tournament; the tournament is held every December, each year at a different location; the 47th week was held in December 1989. continues 'Padwick I' 3628-1 to date.*

Permkleen

2162 **Permkleen** club championship, Wanderers 8-9-10 October '87. [Johannesburg, 1987]. 14p. illus. *brochure for inaugural competition.*

South African Country Districts Festival

2163 † **South African Country Cricket Association** Festival week [official souvenir brochure]. Various, *annual.* *7th Festival,* Welkom and Virginia, 1960. 16p. *21st Festival,* Queenstown, 1974. 18p. *25th Festival,* Kimberley, 1978. 32p. *31st Festival,* Welkom Virginia, 1984. 48p. *32nd Festival,* Boland, 1985. 24p. *33rd Festival,* Vaal Triangle, 1986. 28p. *34th Festival,* Kimberley, 1987. 24p. *35th Festival,* Pietermaritzburg, 1988. 24p. *presumably other souvenir brochures pub. additional to and continues 'Padwick I' 3631.*

South African Cricket Board of Control: Dadabhai Trophy

2164 † **South African Cricket Board of Control** * Rules of Dadabhai Bros. Trophy competition, October 1972. Athlone, 1972. [8]p.

South African Cricket Board of Control: Under 16

2165 **South African Cricket Board of Control** * Under 16 tournament [souvenir brochure]. [The Board]. *annual.* illus. *1985 at Johannesburg. 1987 at Port Elizabeth. other years pub.?*

South African Cricket Board of Control: Under 21

2166 **South African Cricket Board** * First Under 21 Tournament organised by Natal Cricket Board: 7 to 10 January 1985: souvenir brochure. [Durban, the Board, 1985]. 20p. illus. *pre-tournament?*

Vagrants Festival Week

2167   **Vagrants** festival week, East London, 12-16 September 1989. East London, 1989. [36]p. illus.
pre-festival.

BOLAND

2168   **Boland** cricket news. Paarl, Boland Cricket Union. 16p. illus.
vol. 1, no. 1, 1984/85 to date?

BORDER

East London

2169 †   A **short** history of the Buffalo Football Club 1811-1977
■   and the Buffalo Cricket Club 1878-1977. East London, the Club, [1978]. 64p. illus. stats.
'Trials, tribulations and triumphs: history of the Buffalo Cricket Club, East London' compiled by Ian King, pp. 36-53.

King William's Town

2170   **Looking** back: KWT Pirates Club 1888-1988. King William's Town, the Club, 1988. 80p. illus.

2171 †   **Gardner, Les,** *editor*
100 not out: the story of the Albert Cricket Club and Albert Rugby Football Club, King William's Town, South Africa. [1978] xvi, 144p. incl. adverts. illus. stats.

Stutterheim

2172 †   **Stutterheim Cricket Club**
Double cricket tournament. Stutterheim, the Club. *annual.* illus.
?/1977-80/?

EASTERN PROVINCE

2173   **Eastern Province Cricket Union**
E.P. cricket yearbook 1984. Port Elizabeth, the Union, 1984. 36p. illus. stats.
the only issue.

Standard Cricket Club

2174   **Standard.** S.C.C. 1864-1989: 125th anniversary. Cradock, [the Club], 1989. 64p. illus. stats.

Uitenhage Cricket Club

2175   **Uitenhage** Cricket Club: 125th anniversary, 1862-1987. Uitenhage, the Club, 1987. [92]p. incl. adverts. illus.

NATAL

2176   **Bradshaw, Tony,** *compiler*
■   Natal, Currie Cup champions 1980-81. 1981. 22p. illus. (some col.) stats.
cover title: 'Computer Sciences present Natal the 1980-81 Currie Cup champions'.

2177   **Natal Cricket Association**
☐   The outside edge: the official newsletter of the Natal Cricket Association. The Association, *monthly.* illus. stats.
bimonthly from 1985-86 season.
vol. 1, no. 1. Nov. 1984 to date?

2178   **Natal Cricket Board**
■ *   25th anniversary souvenir brochure: 1961-62 - 1985-86. [Durban, the Board, 1986]. 72p. incl. adverts. illus. scores, stats.
includes summarised scores of every game played under the auspices of the Board during the period.

2179 †   **Basil's XI** versus Tiny's XI ... Feb. 4-5: souvenir brochure
*   1967. Durban, [1967]. [16]p. illus.
Basil D'Oliveira's XI vs. Tiny Abed's XI.

2180 †   **Northern Districts Cricket Union**
*   Golden jubilee anniversary. Northern Districts Cricket Union 1925-26 / 1975-76. [Ladysmith, the Union, 1976]. 36p. illus.

2181 †   **Seedat, D. M.**
*   Natal team's managerial report: re South African inter-provincial cricket tournament, Cape Town, January 1968. Ladysmith, Natal Cricket Board, 1968. 12p. stats.

Durban

2182   **Durban and District Cricket Union**
☐   Annual report and financial statements. Durban, the Union. *typescript.*
inaugurated 1920; ?/1982/ to date?

Stanger

2183   **Stanger and District Cricket Union**
*   40 anniversary jubilee brochure 1986. Stanger, the Union, [1986]. 12p. illus.

Umzinto

2184 †   **Barker, Denis**
Umzinto cricket: the first 100 years. Durban, Interprint, [1979]. xiv, 210p. illus. scores, stats.

NORTHERN TRANSVAAL

2185   **Northern Transvaal Cricket Union**
Annual report 1988-89 incorporating a review of the period 1980-1989. [Pretoria, the Union, 1989]. 62p.
includes financial statements.

2186   Programme. [Pretoria, the Union]. *annual.* illus.
/1987-88 to date/

ORANGE FREE STATE

2187   **Orange Free State Cricket Union**
Springbok Park, Bloemfontein, official opening, 20 September 1989. Bloemfontein, the Union, 1989. 24p. illus.
super challenge Benson & Hedges champions, OFS vs Diners Club Rest of S.A.

TRANSVAAL

2188   **Transvaal Cricket Club**
☐   Coverdrive: official newsletter of the Transvaal Cricket Club. Northlands (Transvaal), the Club, *irregular.* illus. stats.
1982 to date.

2189   **Transvaal Cricket Council**
☐   Official yearbook. Johannesburg, the Council.
fixture list, rules and by-laws for provincial and league cricket.
?/1987-88/ to date.

2190   Transvaal cricket '81/2. Johannesburg, the Council, 1981. 22p. illus. stats.

Johannesburg

2191 † **Wanderers Club**
■   Ninetieth anniversary 1888-1978. Johannesburg, the Club, 1978. 84p. illus.
Sept. 1978 issue of the Wanderers Club magazine; contains much cricket.
——*rev. and updated in Sept. 1988 issue with title 'Centenary 1888-1988'.*
special issues of 'Padwick I' 3655.

2192   **Wanderers Cricket Club**
■   England tour 1982. [Johannesburg, the Club, 1982]. 68p. mostly adverts. illus.
pre-tour.

WESTERN PROVINCE

2193   The **Googly**; edited by Trevor Quelch. Claremont
■   (W.P.), Peter Kirsten Publications, *monthly during season.* illus. scores, stats.
Sept 1989 to date.
sanctioned by the W.P. Cricket Union.

2194   **Western Province Cricket Club**
□   Annual report and statement of accounts. Cape Town, the Club. illus. stats.
continues 'Padwick I' 3658-1 to date.

WOMEN'S CRICKET

2195 † **South African and Rhodesian Women's Cricket**
■   **Association**
Inter-provincial tournament 1972, Pietermaritzburg. [Bloemfontein], the Association, [1972]. 16p. illus. stats.
pre-tournament.

CRICKET SOCIETY OF SOUTH AFRICA

2196   **Cricket Society of South Africa**
□   Cricket of the veld: the journal of the Cricket Society of South Africa. Sandton (Transvaal), the Society, *monthly?* illus. stats. *typescript.*
inaugural issue, Autumn 1985 - vol. 2 no. III, Nov. 1985? edited by Anthony Collis.

2197   Newsletter. Sandton (Transvaal), the Society, *monthly.*
vol. 1, no. 1, Sept 1984 to date.

CRICKET IN ZIMBABWE (FORMERLY RHODESIA)

2198   **Byrom, Glen**
Rhodesian sports profiles 1907-1979; illustrated by Henk Van Rooyen. Bulawayo, Books of Zimbabwe, 1980. 255p. illus.
9 cricketers featured.
limited ed. of 250 copies.

2199   **Cricket** in Zimbabwe: the case for test status. Zisa, n.d.

2200   **Mashonaland Country Districts Winter Cricket**
□   **Association**
Cricket annual. Harare, the Association. illus. scores, stats.
continues 'Padwick I' 3660 to date?

2201   **Winch, Jonty**
■   Cricket's rich heritage: a history of Rhodesian and Zimbabwean cricket, 1890-1982. Bulawayo, Books of Zimbabwe, 1983. [xii], 232p. illus. scores, stats.

2202   **Zimbabwe** Cricketer: the official journal of the
□   Zimbabwe Cricket Union; edited by Mike Rogan. Harare, Pangolin Press. *biannual.* illus. stats..
vol. 1 no. 1 Nov. 82 to date.

Women's Cricket

2203 † **South African and Rhodesian Women's Cricket**
■   **Association**
Inter-provincial tournament 1972, Pietermaritzburg. [Bloemfontein], the Association, [1972]. 16p. illus. stats.
pre-tournament.

CRICKET IN THE WEST INDIES

GENERAL

2204 Association of Cricket Statisticians, *compiler*
A guide to first class cricket matches played in the West Indies. Haughton Mill (Notts.), the Association, [1984]. 64p. scores, stats.
contains collections of scorecards for matches, full details of which are not generally available.

2205 † Beckford, George W.
Beckford's cricket manual. Kingston, the Author, [1973]. 80p. incl. adverts. illus. stats.
issued prior to 1973 Australian visit; see also 'Padwick I' 3678.

2206 Birbalsingh, Frank *and* **Shiwcharan, Clem**
Indo-Westindian cricket. Hansib, 1988. 135p. illus.
one of a series of books pub. to mark the 150th anniversary of the arrival of Indians in the Caribbean.

2207 Cumberbatch, Colin, *editor*
Leeward Islands cricket review. [St John's (Antigua), the Editor, 1985]. 44p. illus. scores, stats.
review of West Indian cricket and cricketers from 1983 to 1985.

2208 Goodwin, Clayton
Caribbean cricketers: from the pioneers to Packer. Harrap, 1980. xii, 260p. illus. map. stats. index.

2209
West Indians at the wicket. Macmillan Caribbean, 1986. viii, 200p. illus. map. glossary, index.

2210 † Greaves, George C.
At the crossroads: a survey of big cricket in the West Indies 1924-1936. [Bridgetown], 1937? 54p. incl. adverts.

2211 James, Cyril Lionel Robert
Beyond a boundary. New York, Pantheon Books, 1983. xviii, 255p.
US ed. of 'Padwick I' 3672-1.
——*pbk. ed.* London, Stanley Paul, 1986, *with a foreword by Mike Brearley.*

2212 Mangan, James Anthony, *editor*
Pleasure, profit, proselytism: British culture and sport at home and abroad 1700-1914. Frank Cass, 1988. xiii, 284p. illus. index.
includes 'Cricket and colonialism in the English-speaking Caribbean to 1914: towards a cultural analysis' by Brian Stoddart pp. 231-257.

2213 Manley, Michael Norman
A history of West Indies cricket. Andre Deutsch, 1988. xvi, 575p. illus. map, scores, stats. index.
——*pbk. ed.* Pan, 1989 *with 4p. amendment.*

2214 † Sowdon, N. *and* **McMillan, L.**
A complete history of the West Indies in the cricket field ... 1886 to 1960. n.d. [73] leaves, stats. *typescript.*
copy in Melbourne Cricket Club Library.

ANNUALS

2215
Benson & Hedges West Indies cricket annual; edited by Tony Cozier. Worthing (Barbados) and Hersham (Surrey), Caribbean Communications. illus. (some col.) scores, stats.
1983 ed. with title 'West Indies cricket annual'.
continues 'Padwick I' 3682 to date.

INTER-COLONIAL

2216 † Intercolonial cricket souvenir pamphlet 1929. Port of Spain, *The Sporting Chronicle,* [1929]. 28p. incl. adverts. illus. stats.

SHELL SHIELD

2217 Bell, Carl, *compiler*
A complete statistical history of Shell Shield cricket, 1966-1987. Kingston, Management Research & Computing Services, 1988. [iv], iv, 265p. scores, stats.
includes full scorecards of every Shell Shield game.

RED STRIPE CUP

2218
Red Stripe Cup 1989 annual. [Kingston, n.p. 1989]. 40p. illus. map. stats.
pre-tournament.

BARBADOS

Barbados Wanderers

2219 † Barbados Wanderers tour of England and South Wales 1979. [The Club], 1979. [20]p. illus.
pre-tour.

2220
The **Barbados** Wanderers tour of England, South Wales and Holland, 1985. [The Club], 1985. [24]p. illus.
pre-tour; June-July 1985.

Ricks Cavaliers

2221 Ricks Cavaliers Cricket Club
Tour of England and Geneva 1980. [Bridgetown, the Club, 1980]. [80]p. incl. adverts. illus.
pre-tour; May-June 1980.

2222
Tour of England and Geneva 1982. [Bridgetown, the Club, 1982]. 128p. incl. adverts. illus.
pre-tour; May-June 1982.

Sunjet Cavaliers

2223 Desmond Haynes Cavaliers U.K. tour '84: official souvenir programme. [1984]. 28p. incl. covers and adverts. illus.
pre-tour; August 1984.

CAYMAN ISLANDS

2224 Cayman Islands Village Greenies Cricket Club
England and Canada tours 1988. [The Club, 1988]. [8]p. illus.
pre-tour.

JAMAICA

2225 **Becca, Lascell**
The Melbourne annual. Kingston, Melbourne Cricket Club, 1982. 40p. incl. adverts. illus.
the only issue?

2226 † The **Owen** Davies' memorial magazine: edited by Julius Dixon. Kingston, St. Mary Cricket Association, [1979]. 36p. incl. adverts. illus. stats.
first ed. of cricket annual; others pub.?

ST LUCIA

2227 **Justin, Augustus**
Welcome to Mindoo Phillip Park. St Lucia, Lithographic Press, 1984. illus. scores.
souvenir brochure commemorating Australia's visit to St Lucia in April 1984; includes brief history of the Mindoo Phillip Park.

TRINIDAD

2228 † **Khan, Karim B.,** *compiler and editor*
■ Trinidad & Tobago Cricket Council: 50 years of cricket 1926-76, Beaumont Cup; statistics by Mervyn Wong. The Author, 1976. 25p. incl. inside back cover, illus. diagr. scores, stats.
full scores 1926 and 1927; potted scores from 1964.

2229 **Trinidad & Tobago Cricket Board**
■ Silver jubilee issue 1956-1981. [Port of Spain, the Board, 1981]. 270p. illus. scores, stats.
on cover: 'Annual'; other years pub?

WINDWARD ISLANDS

2230 † **Cork** Cup tournament played in Saint Vincent, June and
■ July, 1938: souvenir. [1938]. [14]p.
contains blank scoresheets and names of players from Dominica, Grenada, St. Lucia and St. Vincent.

2231 † **Dominica Amateur Sports Association**
Cricket souvenir: official score card goodwill series played at the Botanic Gardens, Roseau, Dominica ... St. Lucia vs St. Vincent ... Grenada vs Dominica ... finals. Roseau (Dominica), the Association, [1964]. 24p. incl. adverts. scores.
post series?; May 1964.

CRICKET IN NEW ZEALAND

GENERAL

2232   **Brittenden, Richard Trevor ('Dick')**
■   Big names in New Zealand cricket: fifty profiles.
Auckland, MOA Publications, 1983. 343p. illus. (some
col.)
    *includes some material derived from 'Padwick I' 3742
and 5522-3.*

2233 † **Church Missionary Society**
    *ms archives of the Society housed in the University of
Birmingham library include in the papers of the New
Zealand Mission, the diary of Henry Williams, later
Archdeacon of Waimate. Included in the entry for
Thursday 20 December 1832 is the following: 'Distributed
prizes to the girls. All fatigued; turned the boys out to play
cricket by way of a finish and to prepare them for
operations in the morning. Very expert - good bowlers'.
CN 093/200. p. 24.
This is the first reference to cricket being played in New
Zealand, pace 'Padwick I' 3744.*

2234   **[Croudy, Brian Albert Charles,** *compiler***]**
■   A guide to first class matches played in New Zealand
1863 to 1980. Haughton Mill (Notts.), Association of
Cricket Statisticians, [1981]. 120p. maps, scores.
    *contains full scores of first class matches played in New
Zealand 1936 to 1946 together with scorecards of other
matches not easily accessible; also contains checklist of
every first class match played in New Zealand.*

2235   **Hadlee,** *Sir* **Richard John** *et al*
■   The New Zealand cricketers' who's who. Christchurch,
Whitcoulls, 1985. 120p. illus.
    ---- *pbk. ed.* 1987.

2236   **Palenski, Ron,** *editor*
■   Bat and pad: an anthology of writings on New Zealand
cricket. Glenfield (Auckland), Benton Ross, 1987. [x],
166p.

ANNUALS

2237   The **DB** cricket annual; edited by Donald O. Neely.
■   Auckland, MOA Publications. illus. (some col.) scores,
stats.
    *1986 entitled 'New Zealand cricket annual'
1987 to date entitled 'Radio New Zealand cricket annual'
continues 'Padwick I' 3754 to date.*

2238   **New** Zealand domestic cricket 1988-89; edited by Bruce
■   Mountain. Tauranga (N.Z.), Action Publications for
Major Cricket Associations, 1988. 112p. incl. adverts.
illus. (some col.) stats.
    continued as 'Shell New Zealand cricket guide 1989-90'.

2239   **Rothmans** New Zealand first class cricket; compiled and
■   edited by Francis Payne. Auckland West, Cricket
Publications. illus. scores, stats.
    *1979-80. 1980. 100p.
1980-81. 1981. 100p.
continues 'Padwick I' 3757-1.*

2240   The **Shell** cricket almanack of New Zealand. Auckland,
■   MOA Publications in association with Shell, *annual*.
illus. scores, stats.
    *1980-82 edited by Arthur H. Carman and pub. by
Sporting Publications, Linden, Tawa;
1983 to date, edited by Francis Payne and Ian Smith.
continues 'Padwick I' 3753.*

PERIODICALS

2241   **Howzat!** DB New Zealand cricket news. Auckland,
Dominion Breweries. *irregular.*
    /vol. 1, no. 1 Dec 1987 - vol. 1, no. 4, Feb 1988/

2242   **New** Zealand cricket. Parnell (Auckland), RPL
☐   Sporting Publications. *varying frequency.* illus. (some
col.) scores, stats.
    *edited successively by Don Cameron, Richard Becht and
Don Cameron.
with title 'Cricket Player' to 1984.
with title 'New Zealand cricket player' from Sep./Oct.
1984.
with title 'New Zealand cricket' from Oct 1986.
continues 'Padwick I' 3758-1 to date.*

AUCKLAND

2243   **Auckland Cricket Association**
■   100 not out: a centennial history of the Auckland Cricket
Association. Auckland, the Association, 1983. 216p.
illus. (some col.) scores, stats.

2244   Annual report and balance sheet. The Association.
☐   scores, stats.
    continues 'Padwick I' 3769-1 to date?

2245 † **Auckland** cricketers' trip to the South in 1873-4.
    *described as the 'first known cricket publication in New
Zealand' in Bowen's 'Cricket: a history of its growth and
development throughout the world' (see 'Padwick I' 62).*

CANTERBURY

2246 † **Ashburton County Cricket Association**
■   Constitution and by-laws. [The Association], 1968. 20p.
    originally printed 1956.

2247   **Brittenden, Richard Trevor ('Dick')**
■   A cricket century: the first 100 years of the Lancaster
Park Cricket Club Inc. [Christchurch, the Club], 1981.
122p. illus. stats.
    cover sub-title '1881-1981'.

2248   **Murdoch, Peter Wallace**
Seventy five years of Sumner cricket, 1906-1981.
Christchurch, Sumner Cricket Club, 1981. 36p. illus.

2249   **Ogilvie, Ken**
100 years of cricket in Temuka, 1884-1984. Temuka,
Temuka C.C., 1984. 24p. illus.
    *a booklet for the Centennial weekend of the Temuka
C.C., 30 Nov. - 2 Dec. 1984.*

2250   The **umpires** pavilion. Canterbury, Canterbury Cricket
■   Umpires Association, 1989. [4]p. folded sheet, illus.
    *brochure publicising appeal for the restoration of 'the
oldest cricket pavilion in the Southern Hemisphere'.*

CENTRAL DISTRICTS

2251 **Jellyman, Arthur Henry**
The Wairau story: the Wairau Cricket Club 1884-1984: 100 years in Marlborough cricket. Blenheim (N.Z.), [the Club], 1985. 56p. illus.

NORTHERN DISTRICTS

2252 † **Brook, Kip** *and* **Frew, Garry**
50 not out: fifty years of Northland cricket. Whangarei, Northern Advocate, 1977. 138p. illus. scores, stats.

2253 **Midlands Cricket Association (Inc.)**
□ Official handbook. [The Association], *annual*. 64p. stats.
?/1982-3,83-4/ to date.

2254 **Power, Terry,** *compiler*
■ Innings established: Northern Districts cricket, 1956/7-1981/2. Hamilton, [Northern Districts Cricket Association], 1982. 48p. illus. map, scores, stats.

OTAGO

2255 **125** not out: the story of the Oamaru Cricket Club, 1864-1989. [Oamaru], the Club, 1989. 16p. illus.

2256 **Duff, Herbert**
80 years of cricket at Edievale Edievale (Otago), the Author, 1986. [64]p. illus. map.

SOUTHLAND

2257 **McConnell, Lynn**
100 summers at the Rec.: the centennial history of the Mataura Cricket Club. Invercargill (N.Z.), the Club, 1986. 30p. illus.

WELLINGTON

2258 **Bouzaid, Tony**
Taxes Cricket Club, Wellington, 50th Jubilee 1932-33 to 1982-83. Wellington, the Club, 1985. 100p. illus. stats.

2259 **Cater, Stewart Bruce**
One hundred years of village cricket, Johnsonville Cricket Club: the first hundred years of the Johnsonville C. C. Wellington, the Club, [1985]. 98p. illus.

2260 **Hackett, John**
Hutt District Cricket Club, 75th Jubilee, 1984-85. Lower Hutt (Wellington), the Club, 1985. 56p. illus.

2261 **Heather, Bruce,** *compiler*
■ Onslow Cricket Club 1930-1980. [The Club, 1980]. 70p. illus. stats.

2262 **Neely, Donald Owen**
A pictorial history of the Basin Reserve. Wellington, Wellington Cricket Association, 1980. [13]p. illus.
produced to celebrate the opening of the Vance Stand.

2263 The re-opening of the Basin Reserve, 29 November 1980.
■ Wellington, Wellington City Council, 1980. [16]p. incl. covers, illus.

2264 **Stribling, John**
■ One hundred years: Karori Cricket Club 1880-1980. Wellington, the Club, 1980. 142p. illus. stats. bibliog.

2265 **Stumps:** official newspaper of the Kilbirnie Cricket Club. Wellington, Johnman Press, *quarterly*. illus. stats. *1989* to date.
edited by Barry Borman.

2266 **Turner, John H.**
Century at the Basin Reserve. Wellington, Midland St. Pats C. C., 1983. 127p. illus. stats.
history of the Midland St. Pats C. C.

2267 **Wellington Cricket Association**
□ Handbook. The Association, *annual*. stats. index.
continues 'Padwick I' 3796 to date?

2268 † Report of the special committee on Wellington cricket.
■ Wellington, the Association, 1976. 16p.

CRICKET IN INDIA

GENERAL

2269 **Association of Cricket Statisticians**
■ A guide to first-class cricket matches played in India. Haughton Mill (Notts.), the Association, [1986]. 208p. maps, scores, stats. bibliog.
contains complete list of first-class matches and full scores of first-class matches for which the scores are difficult to obtain.

2270 **Balan, Raja**
All the beautiful boys. Calcutta, etc., Rupa, 1989? 245p. illus.

2271 **Bose, Mihir**
■ A maidan view: the magic of Indian cricket. George Allen & Unwin, 1986. xii, 179p. illus. index.

2272 **Cashman, Richard I.**
■ Patrons, players and the crowd: the phenomenon of Indian cricket. New Delhi, Orient Longman, 1980. [viii], 194p.
includes appendix on social background of all Indian Test players.

2273 **Nandy, Ashis**
■ The tao of cricket: on games of destiny and the destiny of games. New Delhi, Penguin Books, 1989. 150p. index.
the cultural psychology of cricket with special reference to Indian cricket.

2274 **Sriraman, S. and Chandgadkar, M. V.,** *editors*
■ Board of Control for Cricket in India 1929-1979: golden jubilee commemoration volume. Bombay, the Board, [1980]. 304p. incl. adverts. illus. scores, stats.

ANNUALS

2275 **Board of Control for Cricket in India**
■ Cricontrol statistical annual. New Delhi, the Board. illus. scores, stats.
continues 'Padwick I' 3850-1 to date.
from 1984-85, edited by Sudhir Vaidya.

2276 **Indian** cricket; compiled by S. Thyagarajan. Madras,
■ Kasturi, *annual.* illus. (some col. from 1985), scores, stats. index.
continues 'Padwick I' 3855 to date.

2277 † **Services** sports annual. New Delhi, Services Sports
□ Control Board. illus. scores.
includes details of services cricket championships.
?/1951-52 - 54-55/?

2278 **Sportsweek** annual. Bombay, Inquilab Publications.
continues 'Padwick I' 3864 to 1986.

PERIODICALS

2279 **Aashtpailu.** Bombay, Pioneer Book Company.
fortnightly. illus. scores, stats.
in Marathi - 'All-rounder'; edited by Ajit Wadekar; 1986 to date?

2280 **Chauka.** New Delhi, Madhu Muskau Publications.
fortnightly. illus. scores, stats.
in Hindi - 'Boundary'; edited by Deepak Kapoor.
vol. 1, no. 1, 15-31 July 1987 to date?

2281 **Cri-champs.** Bombay, Marcus Couto. *three issues per year.* illus. scores, stats.
vol. 1, no. 1, May to Aug 1983; the only issue? edited by Marcus D. Couto.

2282 † **Cricket** samrat. New Delhi, Cricket Samrat Publishers.
monthly. illus. scores, stats.
in Hindi - 'Cricket emperor'; edited by Anand Dewan.
vol. 1, no. 1, Nov 1978 to date; to June 1987 entitled 'Khel samrat'.

2283 **Ekach** Shatkaar. Bombay, Shatkar Prakashan.
fortnightly. illus. scores, stats.
in Marathi - 'Sixer'; edited by Sandip Patil.
1983 to date.
Gujerati ed. pub. since 1987.

2284 **Ekmar** chaukar. Pune, Vardha Publications. *fortnightly.* illus. scores, stats.
in Marathi - 'Solitary boundary'; edited by Dilip Devdhar.
1986 to date?

2285 **Indian** cricket scene. Bombay, Jayashree Publications.
quarterly. illus. scores, stats.
vol. 1, no. 1, Jan-March 1981; only one more issue pub.?

2286 **Indian** cricketer. Calcutta, Aajkaal Publishers.
monthly. illus. scores, stats.
edited by Sunil Gavaskar.
/vol. 1, no. 1, April 1983 - vol. 2, no. 8, Dec. 1984/

2287 **Khel** halchul. Indore, Nai Duniya Publications. *weekly.* illus. scores, stats.
several cricket specials pub. every year.
in Hindi - 'Sports activity'.
/vol. 1, no. 1, 2 Oct. 1983 to date.

2288 † **Krirangan.** Pune, Chandersen Ghorpade. *fortnightly.* illus. scores, stats.
in Marathi - 'Sports field'; large proportion of cricket.
1970? to date?

2289 † **Oriental** sporting magazine. Calcutta. *quarterly.*
vol. II, no. IV, Oct. to Dec. 1867 contains cricket pp. 57-73.

2290 † **Sportstar.** Madras, S. Rangarajan for Kasturi and Sons.
□ *weekly.* illus. scores, stats.
large proportion of cricket; edited by G. Kasturi.
vol. 1, no. 1, 15 July 1978 to date.

2291 **Sportsweek.** Bombay, Khalid Ansari for Inquilab
□ Publications. illus.
latterly with title 'Sportsweek & Lifestyle'.
continues 'Padwick I' 3870-1 to issue no 1054, 15-21 Jan., 1989.

2292 **Sportsweek** cricket quarterly. Bombay, Inquilab
□ Publications. illus. scores, stats.
continues 'Padwick I' 3870-2 to vol. 11, no. 3, July-Sept 1984.
subsequently appeared monthly with title 'Sportsweek's WOC', vol. 13, no. 1, Sept 1985 - vol. 14, no. 9, Nov. 1987.

2293 † **Sportsworld.** Calcutta. *weekly.* illus. scores, stats.
predominantly cricket; ed. by Mansur Ali Khan Pataudi.
vol. 1, no. 1, 18 Oct. 1978 to date.

PARSI CRICKET

2294 **Meher-Homji, Kersi,** *compiler*
■ Parsee cricket centenary 1886-1986. St. Ives (N.S.W.), the Author, 1986. 32p. illus. facsims. stats.
limited ed. of 130 copies; inspired by a play (produced by the Australian Zoroastrian Association) on the Parsee tour to England 1886.

2295 **Raiji, Vasant**
■ India's Hambledon men. Bombay, Tyeby Press, 1986. 156p. illus. scores, stats. bibliog.

RANJI TROPHY

2296 **Board of Control for Cricket in India**
■ Forty-five years of Ranji Trophy; edited by P. N. Sundaresan. Bombay, the Board, 1980. 2 vols. xii, 1776p. illus. scores, stats.
vol. I (1934-1959)
vol. II (1960-1979)
scores of all Ranji Trophy games to the end of the 1978-79 season.

2297 **Mathur, Lalit Narain**
■ Dramatic moments in Ranji Trophy. Udaipur, the Author, 1987. [xiv], 184p. incl. adverts. illus. stats.

2298 **Raiji, Vasant**
■ The romance of Ranji Trophy: 50 golden years. Bombay, Tyeby Press, 1984. [x], 65p. illus. scores, stats.

2299 **Sundaresan, P. N.**
■ Ranji Trophy: golden years 1934-35 to 1983-84. Bombay, Board of Control for Cricket in India, [1984]. [x], 369. illus. stats.

OTHER TOURNAMENTS

2300 **All-India Sheesh Mahal cricket tournament, Lucknow**
Sheesh Mahal sports magazine. Lucknow, [the Tournament Committee]. *annual.* illus.
continues 'Padwick I' 3892 to date?.

2301 **Central Civil Services Sports Board**
XXI All India civil services cricket tournament 1985-86. New Delhi, the Board, 1986. [52]p. incl. adverts. illus. stats.
pre-tournament.

2302 **Chandigarh Cricket Association**
Deodhar Trophy cricket tournament - 1981. Chandigarh, the Association, 1981. [86]p. mostly adverts.
pre-tournament.

2303 **Gwalior Division Cricket Association**
All-India Scindia Invitation Cup cricket tournament souvenir. Gwalior, the Association, 1986. 54p. incl. adverts. illus. stats.

2304 **Hyderabad Cricket Association**
Moin-ud-Dowlah Gold Cup golden jubilee. Hyderabad, the Association, 1980. [110]p. incl. adverts. illus.

2305 **Sahara** Trophy '88. Lucknow, Sahara India, 1988. [74]p. incl. adverts.
'first All-India invitation cricket tournament'.

ANDHRA PRADESH

2306 † **Hyderabad Blues Cricket Club**
■ Tour of West Indies, USA, Canada, UK: souvenir 1975. The Club, [1975]. [292]p. mostly adverts. illus. stats.

2307 **Rao, S. Venunadha**
■ Who is who [in] Andhra cricket. Guntur (A.P.), Andhra Cricket Association?, 1984. [x], xxxiv, 376p. illus. stats.

BENGAL

2308 **Dutt, B. N.,** *editor*
Cricket Association of Bengal golden jubilee 1930-1980: official souvenir. Calcutta, Cricket Association of Bengal, 1980. [160]p. incl. adverts. illus. stats.

MAHARASHTRA

2309 **Bombay Cricket Association**
■ Bombay Cricket Association golden jubilee commemoration volume 1930-80. Bombay, the Association, [1980]. [130]p. incl. adverts. illus. stats.

2310 **Pandit, Bal J.,** *editor*
Maharashtra Cricket Association golden jubilee souvenir (1934 to 1984). Pune, the Association, 1985. [44]p. incl. adverts. illus. stats.
in English and Marathi.

2311 **Raiji, Vasant** *and* **Dossa, Anandji**
■ CCI & the Brabourne Stadium: 1937-1987. Bombay, The Cricket Club of India, 1987. 114p. illus. stats.

TAMIL NADU

2312 **Ramaswami, N. S.,** *editor*
■ Tamil Nadu Cricket Association golden jubilee commemoration volume, 1930-1980. Madras, the Association, 1980. viii, 280p. incl. adverts. illus. stats.

VIDARBHA

2313 **Tapaswi, Prakash**
■ Golden jubilee of the Vidarbha Ranji cricket 1934-35 to 1984-85. Nagpur, Vidarbha Cricket Players' Association, 1985. [vii], 25p. stats.

INDIAN CRICKET SOCIETIES

2314 **Association of Cricket Statisticians and Scorers of India**
■ ACSSI yearbook. Bombay, Marine Sports. illus. scores, stats.
1987-88 edited by Anandji Dossa.
1988-89 edited and compiled by Anandji Dossa, Sudhir Vaidya and Mohandas Menon.

2315 Anka: the official newsletter of the Association of
■ Cricket Statisticians and Scorers of India; edited by Vasant Naik. Bombay, ACSSI. *quarterly.* illus. scores, stats.
first issue entitled 'Newsletter: the Association of Cricket Statisticians and Scorers of India'.
from vol. 3, no. 1, Jul-Sept 1989, with sub-title: 'the official journal of...'
vol. 1, no. 1, Jul-Spet 1987 to date.

2316 Annual report. Bombay, the Association.
■ *includes accounts; first? pub. for financial year July 1988 to June 1989.*

CRICKET IN PAKISTAN

GENERAL

2317 **Anwar Noman** *and* **Javaid Sadiq,** *compilers and editors*
■ Pakistan cricket diary 1984. Karachi, National Development Finance Corporation, [1983]. 48p. illus. stats.
other years pub?

2318 **Association of Cricket Statisticians,** *compiler*
■ A guide to first-class cricket matches played in Pakistan. West Bridgford (Notts.), the Association, 1989. 52p. map.
also contains many corrections to pub. first-class scores.

2319 † **Bhatti, Mukhtar**
Twenty years of sports in Pakistan. Lahore, Bhatti Publications, 1969. 394p. illus.
cricket pp. 67-245.

2320 † **Canser, G. A.**
My cricket 1888-1941. Karachi, [the Author], 1941. 80p. illus.

2321 **Kureishi, Omer,** *chief editor*
Cricket fever. Karachi, *Cricketer Pakistan,* [1982]. [196]p. incl. covers and adverts. col. illus.
examines in depth the state of the game.

ANNUALS

2322 **Pakistan** book of cricket; edited by Qamar Ahmed.
■ Karachi, Sportsman Publications. *annual.* illus. (some col.) scores, stats.
pub. 1980-81, 1982-83, 1983-84, 1985-86, 1988. 1988-89 ed. with title 'Pakistan cricket yearbook'. continues 'Padwick I' 3959-1.

PERIODICALS

2323 **Cricket** herald; edited by A. Aziz Rehmatullah. Karachi,
□ A. Aziz Rehmatullah. *monthly.* illus. (some col.) scores, stats.
1986 to date.

2324 **The Cricketer** (Pakistan); chief editor Hanif
□ Mohammed; editor Gul Hameed Bhatti. Karachi, U. Chughtai. *monthly.* illus. (some col.) scores, stats.
continues 'Padwick I' 3961 to date. formerly edited by Riaz Ahmed Mansuri.

2325 **The Cricketer** (Pakistan) quarterly facts and figures;
■ edited by Gul Hameed Bhatti. [Karachi, U. Chughtai]. illus. stats.
vol. 1, no. 1, Spring 1986 to vol. 2, no. 3, Autumn 1987.

2326 **Cricketstar;** edited by Gul Hameed Bhatti. Lahore,
□ Syed Abbas Kazim. *monthly.* illus. (some col.) scores, stats.
vol. 1, no. 1 June 1985 to date.

2327 **Sportsman:** the national sports monthly. Lahore, Agha
□ Mohammad Akbar. *monthly.* illus. (some col.) scores, stats.
vol. 1 no. 1 Jan 1989 to date. mainly cricket.

2328 **World** of Pakistan cricket. Karachi, Munir Hussain.
□ *monthly.* illus. (some col.) scores, stats.
continues 'Padwick I' 3962-1 to date.

PUNJAB

2329 **Rawalpindi Club**
■ The Rawalpindi Club centenary 1885-1985: celebrations 9 Nov - 1 Dec. [Rawalpindi, the Club, 1985]. [viii], 30p. incl. adverts. illus.
includes article on Rawalpindi Club cricket team, pp. 13-14.

2330 **Rawalpindi** Club cricket team tour of England 1986.
■ [Rawalpindi, the Club, 1986]. [36]p. incl. adverts.
pre-tour.

2331 **Rawalpindi Division Cricket Association**
■ England & Netherlands tour 1987. [Rawalpindi, the Association, 1987. [34]p. incl. adverts. illus. (some col.)
pre-tour.

SIND

2332 † **Nazimabad Sports Club**
■ Cricket tour UAE 1979. [Karachi, the Club, 1979]. [32]p. incl. adverts. illus.
pre-tour.

2333 † **Programme** for the Sind Cricket Tournament and Lord Tennyson's XI visit, October 2nd - November 2nd 1937. Karachi, *Daily Gazette Press,* 1937. 34p.
includes a who's who of past and present Sind cricketers.

CRICKET IN SRI LANKA

GENERAL

2334 **Association of Cricket Statisticians,** *compiler*
■ A guide to first-class cricket matches played in Sri Lanka. West Bridgford (Notts.), the Association, [1987]. 32p. scores, stats.
contains collection of scorecards for matches, full details of which are not generally available.

2335 **Board of Control for Cricket in Sri Lanka**
☐ Annual report. Colombo, the Board. illus. (some col.) scores.
continues 'Padwick I' 3978 to date?

2336 **Cooray, Evans** *and* **Fernando, S. J. Anthony,** *editors*
■ The Kettarama cricket stadium and sports complex: opening ... 2nd February 1986. Colombo, Colombo Municipal Press, [1986]. [16]p. col. illus. map.

2337 **Galle** cricket stadium. Colombo, Board of Control for
■ Cricket in Sri Lanka / Sri Lanka Cricket Foundation, 1984. [8]p. illus.

2338 **Herat, Gwen**
Turf heroes ... [Wennapuwa, Sahana Printers], 1987. 122p. illus.

2339 The **Khettarama** (sic.) Cricket Stadium and sports
■ complex: a stadium of international standard. Colombo, Hermes International, 1986. [16]p. incl. covers, col. illus. score.
souvenir brochure to commemorate opening of stadium on 2 Feb. 1986 and report of inaugural match, Sri Lanka XI v England XI.

2340 **New** Asgiriya Stadium ceremonial opening ... 5th
■ February 1982. Kandy, Trinity College, 1982. [28]p. illus.

2341 **Sri Lanka Cricket Foundation**
■ A souvenir to commemorate the opening of the indoor cricket nets .. on 7th February 1984. Colombo, the Foundation, 1984. [ii], 9p. illus. (some col.)

2342 **Wettimuny, Sunil Ramsay de Silva**
■ Cricket: the noble art. Colombo, Lake House, 1985. [x], 186p. illus. (some col.)

ANNUALS

2343 **John** Player cricket annual '86; edited by Harold de
■ Andrado. [Colombo], Sri Lanka Cricket Foundation in association with Ceylon Tobacco Company, 1986. 56p. incl. covers, illus. (mostly col.) scores.
the only issue?

TOURNAMENTS

2344 † **Hapugalle, S. Dennis N.,** *compiler and editor*
Official souvenir ... Robert Senanayake Trophy: 1966 inaugural award: Ceylon Schools vs Mercantile Services. Colombo, Board of Control for Cricket in Ceylon, [1966]. 18p. illus.

SCHOOLS AND COLLEGES
Royal College v St Thomas' College

2345 **Perera, S. S.**
■ History of Royal College. Colombo, Royal College Union, 1986. xxii, 607p. illus.
Royal v St Thomas cricket match pp. 375-403, and other cricket references.

2346 **Seneviratne, Indrani**
Battle of the blues 1980-1981. Colombo, Felix Printers, 1981. scores, stats.

St Joseph's v St Peter's

2347 The **saga** of 50 years of Josephian-Peterite cricket. 1984. [156]p. illus. scores, stats.

CLUBS
Colombo

2348 † **Nondescripts Cricket Club**
■ Rules. Colombo, the Club, 1911. 6p.
Club founded 19 March 1888.

Dimbula

2349 **Dimbula Athletic & Cricket Club**
'125th anniversary ball' at Radella, 7th November 1981.

2350 **Cricket** tour of the Maldives, 30 April to 7 May 1984.
■ [Dimbula, the Club, 1984]. 4p. folded sheet, illus.
pre-tour; in connection with the Maldives cricket silver jubilee celebrations.

Galle

2351 **Daily** News trophy winners, 1980: Galle Cricket Club.
■ [Galle, the Club, 1980]. [50]p. incl. adverts. + 4p. supplement.
includes some background information on Galle C. C.

Talduwa

2352 **De Jacolyn, Neil** *and* **De Alwis, Theo,** *compilers*
■ The centenary souvenir of the Kelani Valley Club, 1884-1984. [Talduwa, the Club, 1984]. [64]p. illus.

CRICKET IN THE REST OF THE WORLD

(including international tours)

CRICKET IN EUROPE

DENMARK

2353 **Dansk Cricket Forbund**
□   Cricket: saernummer af 'Cricket' udgivet af Dansk
      Cricket Forbund. The Forbund. *annual.* diagrs. stats.
      continues 'Padwick I' 4195-1 to date.

2354 Cricket: udgivet af Dansk Cricket Forbund. The
□   Forbund. *fortnightly during season?* illus. stats.
      continues 'Padwick I' 4195 to date.

2355 **Dansk XL Cricket Club 1963-88.** Viborg, the Club,
      1988. 32p. illus. stats.

2356 **Provis, Thomas A. J.,** *editor*
      Akademisk Boldklub: 100 år med bolden. Copenhagen,
      the Club, 1989. 110p. illus.
      includes cricket section by Peter S. Hargreaves.

FINLAND

2357 **Helsinki** cricketer. Helsinki, Helsinki Cricket Club.
□   *irregular.* illus.
      some text in English.
      no. 1 June 1981; no. 2 June 1984.

FRANCE

2358 † **[Garrison Cricket Club]**
■   [Rules]. Valenciennes, 1816. 4p.
        Club formed for English officers in France during
        Napoleonic War. Rules drawn up 4 Aug. 1816. Rule 4
        requires that 'The game will be played upon the Plain of
        Mons'.

GERMANY

2359 **Coldham, James Desmond**
■   German cricket: a brief history. The Author, 1983. [ii],
      24p. bibliog.
      limited ed. of 125 signed and numbered copies.

2360 **Die Welt des crickets;** edited by Brian Fell. Hanau,
□   Deutscher Cricket Bund. *irregular.* illus. stats. *typescript.*
      Aug. 1988 to date.
      some text in English.

GIBRALTAR

2361 **Finlayson, Thomas J.,** *editor*
      Gibraltar: the ICC World Cup, England 1986: souvenir
      brochure. Gibraltar, Gibraltar Cricket Association,
      1986. 52p. illus.
      pre-tournament.
      includes articles on the history of cricket in Gibraltar.

2362 **Gibraltar Cricket Association**
□   Handbook. Gibraltar, the Association. *annual.* illus.
      scores, stats.
      written and compiled by T. J. Finlayson.
      pub. in 1981, 1983, 1984 and 1985.

GREECE

2363 **Forte, John Knox**
■   Play's the thing: a medley of Corfu and cricket. Darf,
      1988. xvi, 126p. illus. facsims.

2364 **Tennant, Ivo,** *editor*
■   Corfu and cricket: a booklet ... to commemorate the
      150th anniversary of the first cricket match between
      Greek teams in 1835. Anglo-Corfiot Cricket
      Association, 1985. 48p. illus. (mostly col.)

ITALY

2365 **Associazione Italiana Cricket**
□   Annuario del cricket Italiano. Rome, [The Association].
      illus. (some col.) scores, stats.
      Association founded March 1981.
      1985 ed. contains full scores of Italy's tour of England.
      /1981 to date/.

THE NETHERLANDS

2366 **Cricket:** officiële mededelingen van de Koninklijke
□   Nederlandse Cricket Bond. Den Haag, the Bond.
      weekly during season. illus. scores, stats.
      continues 'Padwick I' 4213 to date.

2367 † **De Flamingo's Cricket Club**
■   Cricket touring club De Flamingo's 1932. The Club,
        [1932]. [16]p.
        fixture list, list of members etc., with a historical summary
        1921-31. later ed. of 'Padwick I 4223; other years pub?

2368 **Excelsior 20 Sportclub**
■   Excelsior cricket tournament for B juniors, 31.7.1989 [to
      4.8.1989. Schiedam, the Club, 1989. [8]p. incl covers.
      pre-tournament; includes brief history of the club in
      English.

2369 † **Hermes Cricket and Football Club**
■   Hermes - D.V.S. 1884-1959. Schiedam, the Club, 1959.
        [54]p. illus. stats.

2370 † **Hickey, Thomas James Owen**
        Cricket in the Netherlands. [1963]. [12]p. incl. covers.
        reprinted from 'Progress: the Unilever Quarterly', vol. 49,
        no. 278, Autumn 1963.

2371 **Ingelse, D. L.**
'Vyftig plus vyf': een cricket leven. Eindhoven, [the Author], 1983. 71p. illus. index.
the author's cricketing life in the Netherlands, 1928-83, covering 50 years of league cricket and 5 years of friendly cricket.
limited ed. of 120 copies.

2372 † **Ingelse, D. L. and Vervelde, K. K.**
Still Going Strong Cricket Club 1969-1979. Den Haag, the Club, 1979. 64p. illus. stats. index.
jubilee book for the Club's 50th anniversary.
updates 'Padwick I' 4242.

2373 † **Kampong Sports Club**
Kampong 1902-1952. Utrecht, the Club, 1952. 119p. illus.
includes much cricket.

2374 **Koch, J. E.**
Cricket in oude ansichten. Zaltcommel, Europese Bibliotheck, 1983. 53p. mostly illus.
development of the game in Holland 1876-1942.

2375 **Nederlandsche Cricket Bond, Koninklijke**
Een eeuw georganisaerd cricket in Nederland, 1883-1983. Den Haag, the Bond, 1983. 123p. illus. scores, stats.

2376 Jaarboekje. Den Haag, the Bond. *annual.*
continues 'Padwick I' 4219 to date.

2377 **Nederlandsche Dames Cricket Bond**
50 jaar damescricket in Nederland. Den Haag, the Bond, 1984. 64p. illus. scores, stats.

2378 † V.U.C. 40 cricket jaren 1928-1968. Den Haag, the Club, 1968. 24p. illus.
special issue of VUC Nieuws, no. 774, June 1968.

SPAIN

2379 **De Morales, Nicolás Díaz-Saavedra**
Approximación a la historia del British Club (Club Inglés) de Las Palmas. Las Palmas de Gran Canaria, El Museo Canario, 1988. 140p. col. frontis. + detachable appendix of illus.
'el Club de Cricket' pp. 21-22 and other cricket references.

2380 **Madrid** cricket annual / Anuario de la A. C. M. Madrid, Madrid Cricket Club, 1989. 56p. illus. (mostly col.) scores, stats.
first issue; all content pub. in English and Spanish.

2381 **Malaga Cricket Association**
Tyndall Bank cricket festival. [The Association, 1989]. 16p.
the fourth Costa del Sol cricket festival; includes a brief history of cricket in Spain.

CRICKET IN AMERICA

2382 **Clynes, Chris J.,** *compiler*
A guide to first class and other important cricket matches in North and South America. West Bridgford (Notts.), Association of Cricket Statisticians, [1987]. 32p. score, stats.

2383 † **North American Society for Sport History**
The journal of sport history: the journal of the North American Society for Sport History. The Society. *three issues per year.* illus.
cricket in some issues.
/vol. 1, no. 1 spring 1974 ... winter 1984/ to date?

ARGENTINA

2384 **Associacion Argentina de Cricket**
Annual report. Buenos Aires, the Association. scores, stats.
until 1982 known as Argentina Cricket Association.
1980-81 and 1981-82 pub. in one issue.
continues 'Padwick I' 4253 to date?

2385 † **Brazil Cricket Association**
Argentine cricket tour 1927-28. Rio de Janeiro, the Association, [1928]. 32p. illus. scores, stats.
post tour.

2386 **St.** Alban's College 1st international cricket tour: Australia - Fiji - New Zealand, 1988. [Buenos Aires, the College, 1988]. [114]p. incl. adverts. illus. maps.
text in Spanish and English.

BERMUDA

2387 † **Bermuda Cricket Association**
Bermuda cricket tour of Europe 1960. Hamilton (Bermuda), the Association, [1960]. 4p. incl covers. illus.
pre-tour; 2 Aug. - 11 Sep.

2388 The **Shell** cricket annual, Bermuda; edited by Thomas C. Aitchison. St. George's, Shell Company of Bermuda. illus. (some col.) scores, stats.
1980 to date.
1980-87 with title 'Bermuda cricket annual' Hamilton, Bermuda Cricket Publications.

CANADA

2389 The **Canadian** cricketer: the official magazine of the Canadian Cricket Association. Vanvier (Ontario), Canadian Cricket Association. *3 issues per year?* illus. scores, stats. *typescript.*
continues 'Padwick I' 4120 to date?

2390 † **Howell, Nancy and Howell, Maxwell L.**
Sports and games in Canadian life: 1700 to the present. Toronto, Macmillan of Canada, 1969. xii, 378p. illus. bibliog. index.
many references to cricket.

Alberta

2391 † The **Calgary** cricketer: an occasional publication of the Calgary & District Cricket League. [Calgary, the League]. *irregular.*
May 1977 issue was vol. 2 no. 1.
edited by Horace R. Gopeesingh.

2392 † **Strathcona Cricket Club**
Cricket tour to the West Indies: July 18 to August 8, 1968. Edmonton, the Club, [1968]. 8p. illus.
pre-tour.

British Columbia

2393 **100** years of cricket in Vancouver: British Columbia, Canada, 1889 to 1988. Vancouver, British Columbia Mainland Cricket League, 1988. 88p. incl. adverts. illus. stats.

2394 **British Columbia Cricket Association**
Victoria international six-a-side cricket festival, June 21st - 29th 1986, Victoria, B.C., Canada. [Victoria (B.C.), the Association], 1986. [30]p. incl. adverts. illus.

2395 **British Columbia Mainland Cricket League**
Schedule. Vancouver, the League. *annual*. stats.
continues 'Padwick I' 4136 to date?

2396 † **Vancouver Island Vagabonds Cricket Club**
'1978 England tour'. [The Club, 1978]. 20p. incl. adverts. illus.
pre-tour; 'dedicated to Captain Cook bi-centennial 1778-1978'.

2397 **Victoria** international six-a-side cricket festival, September 2nd - 11th, 1988. [The Festival Committee, 1988]. [40]p. incl. adverts. illus.

2398 **Victoria** international six-a-side cricket festival, Victoria v Canada, July 22-28 1989. Victoria (B.C.). 42p. illus. stats.

Nova Scotia

2399 The **Nova** Scotia cricketer: the official magazine of the Nova Scotia Cricket Association; edited by Deepal R. Peiris. Halifax (N.S.), *bimonthly*. illus. scores, stats. *typescript.*
vol. 1, no. 6 was Nov.-Dec. 1984 issue; pub. to date?

Ontario

2400 **Toronto Cricket, Skating and Curling Club**
The bulletin. Toronto, the Club. *monthly*. illus.
?/1988 to date/

2401 † Cricket tour: England and France, July 1966. Toronto, the Club, [1966]. [16]p. illus.
pre-tour.

Wandering Clubs

2402 **Canada / U.K. '40' Cricket Club**
[Annual]. Toronto, the Club. illus.
1975-76?/1983-84/ to date?

UNITED STATES OF AMERICA

2403 **American** cricketer magazine; edited by Peter A. Murray. New York, Lesley Lowe. illus. scores, stats.
vol. 1 no. 1 Sep./Oct. 1984 the only issue.

2404 **Kirsch, George B.**
The creation of American team sports: baseball and cricket, 1838-72. (Sport and Society series). Urbana (Ill.) and Chicago, University of Illinois Press, 1989. xiv, 278p. illus. bibliog. index.

California

2405 **Northern California Cricket Association**
Fixtures. The Association. *annual*. illus.
1980 ed. contains factsheet on cricket in the U.S.A. continues 'Padwick I' 4058-1 to date.

2406 † **Southern California Cricketers Chapter of British Social and Athletic Club**
The Cricketer. The Club. *irregular*.
1965 to date.

Illinois

2407 † **Winnetka Cricket Club**
Dinner dance of the Winnetka Cricket Club held at Ferris Inn, Morton Grove, Ill. on ... December 3, 1938. [Winnetka (Ill.), the Club, 1938]. [4]p. illus.
in celebration of their double achievement in winning the K. A. Auty 'Century of Progress' Trophy; for similar publications, see 'Padwick I' 4066-2 and 4066-3.

New Jersey

2408 **New Jersey Cricket Association**
New Jersey cricket annual. The Association, 1982. illus.
only issue.

New York

2409 **Adelman, Melvin Leonard**
A sporting time: New York City and the rise of modern athletics 1820-70. Urbana (Ill.), University of Illinois Press, 1986. [x], 388p. illus.
ch. 5 : 'The failure of cricket as an American sport' pp. 97-119, and other references.

2410 **[Huggins, Felix]**
100 years at Walker Park: cricket festival, July 1st-4th 1988. [Staten Island Cricket Club]. [36]p. mostly adverts. illus.
includes short history of the ground; Staten Island C.C. was founded in 1872.

Pennsylvania

2411 **Mangan, James Anthony**, *editor*
Pleasure, profit, proselytism: British culture and sport at home and abroad 1700-1914. Frank Cass, 1988. xiii, 284p. illus. index.
includes 'Latter-day cultural imperialists: the British influence on the establishment of cricket in Philadelphia, 1842-1872' by J. Thomas Jable, pp. 175-192.

2412 † **Merion Cricket Club**
Annual report. Haverford (Penn.), the Club.
1988 was 123rd annual report.
1856?/1988-1989/

2413 † Club book of Merion C.C. 2nd ed. Philadelphia, the Club, 1953. 70p. illus.
includes history, list of members and rules.

CRICKET IN ASIA

2414 **Cricketer** Asia. Hong Kong, A. Mohamed. *monthly.*
☐ illus. (some col.) scores, stats.
vol. 1, no. 1, May? 1983 to date?

CRICKET IN THE MIDDLE EAST

ISRAEL

2415 **Israel** national cricket team World Cup tour of England
■ 1986. [Israel Cricket Association and Israel Cricket
Supporters Association, 1986]. [16]p. mostly adverts.
illus.
contains brief history of cricket in Israel by G. Davis.

KUWAIT

2416 **Rangers Cricket Club (Kuwait)**
Rangers Invitation XI cricketers India tour, 1982.
Kuwait, the Club, 1982. [36]p. incl. adverts. illus.
*the Club participated in the Sheesh Mahal cricket
tournament in Lucknow; pre-tour.*

2417 **Select** Kuwait Wanderers cricket tour 1980: Sidmouth
■ international cricket week, England. [Kuwait, the Club,
1980]. [32]p. incl. adverts. illus.
pre-tour.

UNITED ARAB EMIRATES

2418 **Emirates Gentlemen's Cricket Club**
■ Tour of England & Holland, July 1988. [Sharjah
(U.A.E.), the Club, 1988]. [40]p. incl. adverts. illus.
pre-tour; July 1988 - the Club was founded in Oct. 1987.

2419 **Emirates** India cricket team's tour of India. Dubai,
Indian Sports Club, 1989. [94]p. incl. adverts. illus.
pre-tour souvenir.

CRICKET IN THE FAR EAST

HONG KONG

2420 **Grubb, Malcolm,** *editor*
■ Hong Kong to the ICC world Cup England 1982:
souvenir brochure. Hong Kong, [Hong Kong Cricket
Association, 1982]. 72p. incl. adverts. illus. scores,
map.
post tournament.

2421 **Hall, Peter A.**
■ Kowloon Cricket Club: a history. Hong Kong, the Club,
1980. ix, 102p. illus. (one col.)

2422 **Hong Kong Cricket Association**
Handbook. Hong Kong, the Association. *annual.* stats.
?/1984-85/ to date?

2423 **Hong Kong Cricket Club**
☐ Annual report & accounts. Hong Kong, the Club. stats.
continues 'Padwick I' 4306 to date.

2424 The pinkun. Hong Kong, the Club. *monthly.* illus.
☐ *continues 'Padwick I' 4308* to date.

2425 The Witherers in Corfu, 21st July - 5th August, 1985.
■ Hong Kong, the Club. 1985. 24p. incl. covers and
adverts. illus.
*the Witherers team, part of the H.K.C.C. was formed in
1970; pre-tour.*

2426 † The **Hong** Kong cricket tour of Australia 1979. [1979].
72p. incl. adverts. illus.
pre-tour.

2427 † **Hongkong Cricket League**
Interport souvenir programme: Bangkok v Hong Kong,
Malaya v Hong Kong, December 4th - 14th 1959. Hong
Kong, the League, [1959]. 52p. incl. adverts. illus.
stats.

2428 **Robinson, Spencer,** *editor*
■ A history of the Hong Kong Cricket Club 1851-1989.
Centurion Books, 1989. 120p. illus. (one col.)

INDONESIA

2429 † **British** Cricket Club, Djakarta, Java: notes on the
history of the club, 1844-1954. [Djakarta, the Club,
1954], 12p. illus.

MALAYSIA

2430 **Malaysian Cricket Association**
■ Under-23 North Zone and final (10th-16th April 1982)
and Under 20 Dunlop Trophy (18th-22nd April 1982) at
Pulau Pinang. The Association, 1982. [32]p. incl.
adverts.
organised by Penang Cricket Association.

2431 **Royal** Selangor Club tour of England 1989. [Kuala
■ Lumpur, the Club], 1989. [64]p. incl. adverts. illus.
pre-tour.

2432 **Selangor Club**
☐ Annual report and accounts. Kuala Lumpur, the Club.
?/1982/ to date.

SINGAPORE

2433 **Sharp, Ilsa**
■ The Singapore Cricket Club 1852-1985. Singapore, Singapore Cricket Club, 1985. 200p. illus. (some col.) bibliog.

2434 **Singapore Cricket Association**
■ Singapore Cricket Association ICC Trophy, June/July 1982. [Singapore, the Association, 1982]. [96]p. incl. adverts. illus. (some col.) scores.
pre-tournament.

2435 † Tour of New South Wales, 4th Oct - 18th Nov 1973. The
■ Association, [1973]. [92]p. incl. adverts. illus.
pre-tour.

2436 **Singapore Cricket Club**
□ Annual report. Singapore, the Club. illus. (some col. since 1985).
continues 'Padwick I' 4318 to date.

2437 Cricket tour Australia 1981. [Singapore, the Club,
■ 1981]. 44p. illus. map.

2438 † Newsletter. Singapore, the Club. *monthly.* illus. (some
□ col.)
May 1979 to date.
since June 1986 with title 'The SCC magazine'.

CRICKET IN EAST AFRICA

KENYA

2439 **Club** Cricket. Nairobi, County Enterprises. *bimonthly.*
□ illus.
/no. 1, Nov. 1980 - no. 4 Apr-May 1981/?

2440 **Kenya Cricket Association**
Zimbabwe Tour 80-81. [Nairobi], the Association, 1980.

2441 **Kenya Kongonis Cricket Club**
□ Annual report. Nairobi, the Club. illus. stats.
continues 'Padwick I' 4271 to date.

CRICKET IN WEST AFRICA

NIGERIA

2442 † **The Nigerian Cricket Association**
Nigeria v Ghana, Lagos: 20th, 21st, & 23rd March 1964 score-card and handbook. Nigeria, the Association, 1964. 19p. scores, stats.

CRICKET IN THE PACIFIC

FIJI

2443 † **Bibliography** of Fiji, Tonga and Rotuma. Canberra, Australian National University, 1969.
contains a bibliography of Fijian cricket by Philip A. Snow.

2444 **Fiji Cricket Association**
■ Souvenir programme: ICC Trophy Competition, Birmingham, U.K., June-July 1986. [the Association, 1986]. 80p. incl. adverts. illus. diagrs.
pre-tournament; includes brief history of Fiji cricket; edited by Harry Ranchhod.

NEW CALEDONIA

2445 **Fédération Francaise de Cricket Nouvelle-Calédonie**
Reglements de jeu du cricket traditionel. [Nouméa, the Federation], 1984. 28p. illus. diagrs.

PAPUA NEW GUINEA

2446 **Papua** New Guinea: I.C.C. mini World Cup tour 1982.
■ 4p. folded card, illus.
includes brief history of cricket in Papua New Guinea.

CRICKET IN OTHER COUNTRIES

MAURITIUS

2447 † **Mauritius Cricket Club**
■ Rules and regulations of the Mauritius Cricket Club
1864. Printed by E. Dupuy & P. Dubois for the Club,
[1864]. 33 + [v]p.

INTERNATIONAL CRICKET

2448 Arnold, Peter *and* **Wynne-Thomas, Peter**
■ The illustrated history of the Test match. Sidgwick &
Jackson, 1988. 256p. illus. (some col.) stats.

2449 Atkinson, Graeme *et al*
■ The Nissan-Datsun book of Test cricket lists.
Canterbury (Vic.), Five Mile Press, 1982. xv, 335p.
illus. stats.

2450 Aziz Rehmatullah, A.
■ An eye on Test cricket decade. Karachi, Farhad A. Aziz,
[1985]. 224p. incl. adverts. illus.
*includes reviews and potted scores of 267 Test matches
played from the West Indies visit to India 1974-75 to
Pakistan tour to NZ in 1984-85.*

2451 Aziz Rehmatullah, A., *compiler and editor*
■ Who's who in Test cricket. Karachi, Mohammad Moin,
1984. 368p. incl. adverts. ports. stats.

2452 Blofeld, Henry Calthorpe
■ My dear old thing: talking cricket. Stanley Paul, 1988.
[iv], 156p. illus. stats. index.
international cricket 1984-88.

2453 One test after another: life in international cricket.
■ Stanley Paul, 1985. 172p. illus.
international cricket October 1983 to March 1985.

2454 Crowley, Brian Mathew
■ A cavalcade of international cricketers: more than 1500
Test cricketers. Sidgwick & Jackson, 1988. vii, 872p.
illus. stats. bibliog. index.

2455 Deloitte Haskins & Sells
■ Career profiles and comparisons. August 1988. 4p.
folded sheet. illus.
*includes 8p. insert 'Algorithm technical discussion'
[update] and 4p. insert 'World rating - Test batsmen;
world rating - Test bowlers; Gatting's decline'.*

2456 Deloittes ratings performance review of Test batsmen
■ and Test bowlers over 1987/88 winter series. May 1988.
4p. folded sheet.
*includes 4p. insert 'Algorithm technical discussion' and
3p. insert 'Preview of England v West Indies Test series
using Deloittes ratings 1984 & 1988'.*

2457 England v Australia. May 1989. 4p. folded sheet. illus.
■ *includes 4p. insert 'Deloitte ratings: a layman's guide' and
6p. insert 'Algorithm technical discussion' [update].*

2458 Eagar, Patrick *[and]* **Wright, Graeme**
■ Test decade 1972/1982. Kingswood (Surrey), World's
Work, 1982. 224p. illus. (some col.) index.

2459 Emery, David, *editor*
■ Who's who in international cricket. (Who's Who in Sport
series). Queen Anne Press, 1984. 192p. illus.

2460 Frindall, William Howard ('Bill'), *compiler and editor*
■ The Wisden book of Test cricket 1877-1984. Queen
Anne Press, 1985. 1104p. scores, stats.
*rev. and updated ed. of 'Padwick I' 4337-3;
contains full scores of 994 Test matches.*

2461 Giller, Norman
■ The world's greatest cricket matches. Octopus Books,
1989. 160p. illus. scores.
*short accounts of 44 Tests played since 1945, all but 12
involving England.*

2462 Graveney, Thomas William *with* **Giller, Norman**
□ The ten greatest Test teams. Sidgwick & Jackson, 1988.
176p. illus.
——*pbk. ed.* 1989.

2463 Martin-Jenkins, Christopher Dennis Alexander
■ The complete who's who of Test cricketers; research by
James Coldham. Orbis, 1980. 424p. illus. stats.
——*rev. updated ed.* Orbis 1983.
——*rev. updated ed.* Queen Anne Press, 1987.

2464 Mason, Percy
■ Cricketing stars. Melbourne, Mason Publishers, 1987.
ix, 194p. illus. stats.
*cover sub-title: '1743 Test cricketers who represented their
countries from 1877 to the present day'; examines Test
records in relation to astrology and numerology.*

2465 Meher-Homji, Kersi
■ 1000 Tests; edited by Peter A. Murray. St. Leonards
(N.S.W.), Straton Publications, 1984. 80p. illus.
(mostly col.) scores.

2466 Morparia, Ravindra *and* **Zarapar, Shashikant**
■ Vishvana test cricketaro. [1987]. 698p. incl. adverts.
illus. stats.
*in Gujarati?; statistics of all Test cricketers; updated to 20
October 1986.*

2467 Patherya, Mudar *and* **Pataudi, Mansur Ali Khan,** *editor*
■ Cricket - Wills book of excellence. Calcutta, Orient
Longman, 1987. 208p. illus. (some col.) stats. index.

2468 South Australian souvenir Test cricket book 1983-84.
■ Barry John & Associates, [1983]. 44p. incl. adverts.
illus.

2469 Walmsley, Keith Spencer
■ 'Mosts without' in Test cricket. [Reading], The Author,
[1982]. 46p. stats.
3 amendment sheets issued to Sep. 1983.
——*rev. and expanded ed.* Reading, the Author, 1986.
[ix], 375p.
7 supplements issued to June 1989.

2470 Wat, Charlie
■ The Test year. Prahran (Vic.), Cricket Stats.
Publications. *annual.* scores, stats.
1986 to date.

2471 Willis, Robert George Dylan ('Bob') *with* **Murphy,**
■ **Patrick**
The cricket revolution: Test cricket in the 1970s.
Sidgwick & Jackson, 1981. [vi], 194p. illus. index.

2472 † *Wireless weekly* portrait album of international cricketers.
Sydney, Sun Newspapers, 1936?. [48]p.
*paste-in scrapbook for illustrations from the publication
'Wireless weekly' - Australian and English cricketers.*

2473 World cricket, 1982. Lahore, Vision Publications, 1983.
■ 166p. illus. scores, stats.

LIMITED OVERS INTERNATIONAL CRICKET

2474 **Frindall, William Howard ('Bill')** *and* **Isaacs, Victor H,**
 compilers
 The Wisden book of one-day international cricket
 1971-1985. John Wisden, 1985. [i], 372p. scores, stats.
 index.

2475 **Isaacs, Victor H**
 International limited-overs cricket records.
 Southampton, Limited Overs Cricket Information
 Group, 1984. [ii], 77p. stats.

2476 **Lemmon, David Hector**
 The book of one-day internationals. Stanley Paul, 1983.
 328p. illus. scores.
 scores of all matches 1971-82.

2477 Great one-day cricket matches. Pelham Books, 1982.
 151p. illus. scores.
 ——*pbk. ed.* Unwin, 1984.

2478 One-day cricket with full coverage of the four World
 Cups. Marks and Spencer, 1988. 190p. illus. (mostly
 col.) scores, stats. index.

2479 **Menon, Mohandas K.,** *compiler*
 The Reliance book of one-day international cricket
 records. Bombay, Keep Busy Books, 1987. 188p. illus.
 stats.

2480 **Morparia, Ravindra** *and* **Zarapar, Shashikant**
 Who's who in one day international (sic). Bombay,
 Sports Publications, 1987. 184p. incl. adverts. illus.

WORLD CUPS

2481 **Khurana, Renu**
 Almanac one-day cricket. New Delhi, Reliance Sports
 Publications, 1987. 152p. illus. (some col.) scores,
 stats.
 limited over tournaments 1975 to 1987.

2482 **Puri, Narottam**
 World Cup cricket. New Delhi, Konark Publishers,
 1987. xii, 168p. scores, stats.
 history of first three tournaments.

2483 **Saeed Mustafa Ali**
 World Cup cricket: from Lord's 1975 to Calcutta 1987.
 Lucknow, the Author, 1988. [viii], 193p. scores, stats.

2484 **Syed Khalid Mahmood,** *editor*
 Focus on World Cup 1975-87. Karachi, Vintage
 International, 1987. 60p. incl. covers and adverts. illus.
 stats.

I. C. C. Trophy

2485 I.C.C. Trophy competitions 1979, 1982, 1986. West
 Bridgford (Notts.), Association of Cricket Statisticians,
 [1989]. [ii], 113p. illus. scores, stats.
 *contains full scorecards of every match played in the
 competitions.*

1982 I. C. C. Trophy

2486 The I.C.C. Trophy 1982. [International Cricket
 Conference, 1982]. 64p. incl. adverts. illus. map.
 pre-tournament.

1983 Prudential World Cup

2487 **Eagar, Patrick** *[and]* **Ross, Alan**
 Kiwis and Indians: Test, World Cup and Championship
 cricket in England, 1983. Collins, 1983. 128p. illus.
 scores.

2488 **Hodgson, Derek**
 Cricket World Cup '83. George Allen & Unwin, 1983.
 48p. illus. (some col.) scores.
 post tournament.

2489 **Prudential** cricket World Cup. Bordon (Hants.),
 Speciality Leisure, [1983]. 20p. illus. stats.
 pre-tournament.

2490 **Prudential** Cup, June 9-25 1983: official souvenir. Test
 & County Cricket Board, 1983. 40p. incl. covers &
 adverts. illus. (some col.)
 pre-tournament.

2491 **Qamar Ahmed** *and* **Murray, Peter Allan,** *editors*
 World Cup cricket 1983. Sydney, Wide World of Sport
 Publications, [1983]. 128p. col. illus. stats.

2492 **Sirajul Islam Bukhari, S.,** *editor*
 World Cup cricket special '83: Pakistan. [Karachi, n.p.,
 1983]. 80p. incl. covers and adverts. illus. (some col.)
 scores, stats.
 pre-tournament.

1986 I. C. C. Trophy

2493 The I.C.C. Trophy 1986. [International Cricket
 Conference, 1986]. [44]p. illus.
 pre-tournament.

1987 Reliance World Cup

2494 **Ansari, Khalid A. H.,** *editor*
 Sportsweek's book of the Reliance Cup. Bombay,
 Mid-Day Publications, [1988]. [iii], 75p. illus. (some
 col). scores, stats.
 post tournament.

2495 **Australia's** World Cup champions. Pymble (N.S.W.),
 Playbill, [1987]. 36p. incl. covers, col. illus. score, stats.
 post tournament; Australia's participation only.

2496 **Berry, Scyld**
 A cricket odyssey: England on tour 1987-88; photographs
 by Graham Morris. Pavilion Books, 1988. [x], 214p.
 illus. map. scores, stats.
 World Cup, pp. 8-83.

2497 **Bindra, I. S.**
 Reliance Cup 87: convenor's report. New Delhi,
 Reliance Cup Organising Committee, [1988]. 51p. col.
 illus. scores.
 post tournament.

2498 **Board of Control for Cricket in Pakistan**
 World Cup cricket 1987. Stroudgate Publications for the
 Board, 1987. [56]p. incl. adverts. col. illus. stats.
 pre-tournament.

2499 **Cricket:** special report, November 4, 1987. Dubai?,
■ 1987. 16p. incl. covers, illus. scores.
  a 'Khaleej Times' special, pub. before semi-finals;
  includes selected group scores.

2500 **Dovey.** Bombay, Hiralal. *monthly.* illus.
  pub. prior to 1987 World Cup, May - Oct? 1987, *to*
  promote the mascot of the tournament.

2501 **Ghosh, Shankar**
  World Cup cricket. 1987?
  in Hindi.

2502 **ICC World Cup Management Committee**
  Reliance Cup 1987 playing conditions. New Delhi, the
  Committee, 1987. 16p.

2503 **Johnson, Martin** *and* **Blofeld, Henry Calthorpe**
■ *The Independent* World Cup cricket '87; photography by
  Michael Steele. Kingswood Press, 1987. 144p. illus.
  scores, stats.
  post tournament.

2504 **Lawrence, Ben,** *compiler and editor*
■ Ben Lawrence's World Cup 1987 guide. Karachi, the
  Author, [1987]. 120p. illus. (mostly col.) stats.
  pre-tournament.

2505 **Mudra Communications**
■ The world of one-day cricket: the official book. Bombay,
  Hiralal Printing Works, 1987. 104p. incl. adverts. illus.
  (mostly col.) stats.
  cover title: 'Reliance Cup '87: the world of one-day
  cricket'; pre-tournament.

2506 **Reliance** Cup; photography Raghu Rai, Bhawan Singh,
■ Mahendra Sinh, J.S. Chawla. Bombay, Mudra
  Communications, 1988. 151p. col. illus. scores.
  cover title: 'Reliance Cup: reliving the triumph'; post
  tournament.

2507 **Reliance** Cup 1987. [Karachi, 1987]. [52]p. illus.
■ scores, stats.
  pre-tournament.

2508 **Reliance Cup Organising Committee**
  Handbook: guidelines for staging centres. New Delhi,
  the Committee, 1987. 36p.

2509 **Salve, N. K. P.**
■ The story of the Reliance Cup. New Delhi, Vikas, 1987.
  xi, 261p. illus.
  how India & Pakistan came to host the fourth World Cup.

2510 **World** cricket extravaganza Pakistan - October /
■ November 1987: the official book. Karachi, Elite
  Publishers, 1987. 74p. col. illus. stats.
  pre-tournament.

OTHER TOURNAMENTS

1984 South-East Asian ICC Associate Members Tournament

2511 **Bangladesh Cricket Control Board**
■ South-east Asian associate members tournament,
  January 13-21 1984. [The Board, 1984]. [68]p. incl.
  adverts. illus.
  Bangladesh, Hong Kong, Singapore, Bangladesh Tigers;
  pre-tournament.

1985 Benson and Hedges World Championship of Cricket

2512 **Benson** and Hedges World Championship of cricket
■ official players' handbook: the greatest show on turf.
  Pymble (N.S.W.), Playbill, [1985]. 68p. incl. covers.
  col. illus.
  Feb. - Mar. 1985; pre-tournament.

2513 **Gavaskar, Sunil Manohar**
■ One-day wonders. Calcutta etc., Rupa, 1985. 137p.
  illus. (some col.)

2514 The **greatest** show on turf: official souvenir of Australia's
■ first world championship of cricket. Sydney, PBL
  Marketing, 1985. 82p. illus. (some col.) scores.
  post tournament.

2515 **Murray, Peter Allan**
■ The World Championship of cricket, Australia 1985.
  [The Author, 1985]. 144p. col. illus. scores, stats.
  post tournament.

2516 The **National** Nine World Championship guide 1985.
■ Sydney, PBL Marketing, 1984. 80p. illus. (some col.)
  stats.
  pre-tournament.

2517 **Victorian Cricket Association**
  World Championship of cricket: February 17 - March 10,
  1985. Jolimont (Vic.), the Association, 1985. 29p. col.
  illus.

1985 Silk Cut Challenge

2518 **Silk Cut Challenge**
■ Official programme & scorecard: Arundel, September
  20-21, 1985. [16]p. illus. (mostly col.) stats.
  all-rounders challenge; pre-tournament.

1986 Austral-Asia Cup

2519 **Cricketers' Benefit Fund Series**
■ Austral-Asia Cup: international one day cricket at the
  Sharjah Cricket Stadium on April 10, 11, 13, 15 and 18.
  Sharjah (U.A.E.), the Fund, [1986]. [194]p. incl.
  adverts. illus. (some col.) stats.
  Australia, India, New Zealand, Pakistan, Sri Lanka;
  pre-tournament.

1986 John Player Asia Cup

2520 **Board of Control for Cricket in Sri Lanka**
■ John Player Asia Cup '86. [Colombo, the Board, 1986].
  [20]p. incl. adverts. col. illus.
  Bangladesh, Pakistan, Sri Lanka - March/April 1986;
  pre-tournament.

1986-87 Benson and Hedges Challenge

2521 **Benson** and Hedges Challenge official players'
■ handbook: Australia, England, Pakistan, West Indies.
  Pymble (N.S.W.), Playbill, [1986]. 68p. incl. covers.
  col. illus.
  the Perth Challenge, Dec. 1986 - Jan. 1987;
  pre-tournament.

2522 **Benson** and Hedges Challenge: Perth 1987. Pymble
■ (N.S.W.), Playbill, 1987 [i.e. 1986]. 40p. incl. covers,
  col. illus.
  pre-tournament.

1987 Sharjah Cup

2523 ■ **Sharjah** cricket '87. Dubai?, 1987. 24p. incl. covers. illus. stats.
Pakistan, India, England, Australia.
a 'Khaleej Times' special report; pre-tournament.

1988 McDonald's Bicentennial Youth World Cup

2524 ■ **Harte, Christopher John ('Chris'),** *editor*
Riverland-Sunraysia-Adelaide 1988: souvenir programme, February 28th - March 13th, 1988. Melbourne, Australian Cricket Board, 1988. 91p. illus.
pre-tournament.

1988 Wills Asia Cup

2525 ■ **Bangladesh Cricket Control Board**
Wills Asia Cup 1988 official souvenir. [The Board, 1988]. [52]p. incl. adverts. illus. stats.
India, Pakistan, Sri Lanka, Bangladesh; pre-tournament.

Benson and Hedges World Series Cup

2526 ■ **Benaud, Richard ('Richie')**
World Series Cup cricket. Sydney, Lansdowne Press, 1981. 127p. illus. (some col.) scores, stats.
review of 1980-81 Cup.

2527 ■ **Benaud, Richard ('Richie'),** [*compiler*]
World Series Cup cricket, 1981-82 season. Dee Why West (N.S.W.), Lansdowne Press, 1982. 128p. col. illus. scores, stats.
post tournament; includes McDonald's Cup.

2528 ■ **Benson** and Hedges World Series Cup: official one day cricket book. Pymble (N.S.W.), Playbill. *annual.* col. illus. stats.
1980-81 to 1988-89 seasons.
1989-90 with title 'Benson and Hedges official one-day World Series guide' pub. by Federal Publishing Company.
pre-tournament.

2529 ■ **Furness, Diane,** *editor*
One-day cricket. Dee Why West (N.S.W.), Summit Books, 1980. 111p. illus. (some col.) scores, stats.
review of Benson and Hedges World Series Cup and McDonald's Cup, 1979-80.

2530 ■ **The hottest** summer: World Series Cup cricket, 1982-83 season. Sydney, Lansdowne Press, 1983. 128p. col. illus. scores, stats.
post tournament; includes Prudential World Cup 1983 and McDonald's Cup review.

2531 □ **National** Nine tour guide. Sydney, PBL Marketing. *annual.* illus. (some col.) stats.
each year's issue contains preview of the Benson and Hedges World Series Cup.
1982-83 season to date.

Golden Oldies

2532 ■ **The Auckland** Golden Oldies: a souvenir record of the inaugural 1984 International Golden Oldies cricket festival, February 18 - February 26, 1984. Auckland, International Golden Oldies Cricket, [1984]. 48p. illus. (some col.) scores.
post tournament.

2533 ■ **The Brighton** Golden Oldies experience: a souvenir of the 1986 International Golden Oldies cricket festival, August 16-24, 1986. Auckland, International Golden Oldies Cricket, [1986]. 32p. incl. covers. illus. (some col.)
post tournament.

Prudential Trophy

2534 † **Jenkinson, Derek**
The Prudential Trophy: a statistical survey. The Author, 1977. 8p. incl. covers, stats.
limited ed. of 150 signed and numbered copies.

OTHER TOURNAMENTS (WOMEN)

1986 Satzenbrau ... Women's Cricket Tournament

2535 ■ **Satzenbrau** international quadrangular women's cricket tournament ... Dublin 17th, 18th, 19th July 1986. [Dublin, Irish Women's Cricket Union], 1986. 28p. incl. adverts. illus. stats.
pre-tournament; featuring Denmark, England (selection), Holland, Ireland.

1988 Shell Bicentennial World Cup

2536 **Shell** bicentennial World Cup. [Australian Women's Cricket Council], 1988. 38p. incl. adverts. illus.
pre-tournament.

INTERNATIONAL CRICKET - ENGLAND

GENERAL

2537 **Alton, Fred,** [*compiler*]
■ First and last. Armthorpe, the Author, [1983]. 30p.
illus. stats.
'a statistical look at Yorkshiremen who have scored fifties and centuries in Test matches from 1877 to 1982'.

2538 **Baxter, Peter,** *editor*
■ From Brisbane to Karachi with the Test Match Special team. Queen Anne Press, 1988. 159p. illus. scores.
England's Test matches, November 1986 to December 1987, and 1987 World Cup.

2539 Test Match Special. Queen Anne Press, 1981. 159p.
■ illus. scores.
includes England's Test matches in 1980.
——*pbk. ed.* Unwin, 1982.

2540 Test Match Special 2. Queen Anne Press, 1983. 175p.
■ illus. scores.
includes England's Test tours 1981-82, 1982-83 and 1983 World Cup.
——*pbk. ed.* Unwin, 1985.

2541 Test Match Special 3. Queen Anne Press, 1985. 160p.
■ illus. scores.
includes England's Test matches in 1984.

2542 **Chimes, Ian**
■ Refuge Assurance review of Test cricket 1981. Ilkley, Educational Design, [1981]. 128p. illus. scores, stats.
England in Test cricket, 1981.

2543 **Dyson, Paul E.**
■ The counties and Test cricket 1877-1988. Easingwold, the Author, 1989. [v], 30p. stats.
counties' representation in England's Test teams, match by match.

2544 **Frindall, William Howard ('Bill')**
■ 10 Tests for England: scorebook and journal for 1988. Columbus Books, 1989. 256p. illus. scores, stats.
England's Test matches, January to August 1988.

2545 England Test cricketers: the complete record from 1877.
■ Willow Books, 1989. viii, 518p. illus. stats. index.
sponsored by the Carphone Group.

2546 **Gibson, Alan**
■ The cricket captains of England: a survey. Pavilion Books, 1989. xi, 242p. illus. index.
reprinted ed. of 'Padwick I' 767-1 with additional chapter 'Ten more years' written in 1988.

2547 **Lee, Alan** *and* **Barraclough, John,** *editor*
■ The official England cricket team annual. Grandreams. illus. (some col.)
pub. 1980 and 1981 only.

2548 **Ronayne, Michael Peter,** *compiler*
■ Test cricket: selecting the English team 1946-1988. Norwich, the Author, 1989. [32]p. incl. covers.
includes match-by-match, the names of the 12th man, injured players, reserves, withdrawals and players called on stand-by into the pre-Test squad.
limited ed. of 60 signed and numbered copies.

2549 **Wynne-Thomas, Peter**
■ England on tour: a record of all England cricket tours overseas, with accounts, results and statistics. Hamlyn, 1982. 192p. illus. (some col.) scores, stats. index.
——*rev. and enlarged ed. with title* 'The complete history of cricket tours at home and abroad', Hamlyn, 1989, *updated to tour of Australia and New Zealand 1987-88 and including new section on all tours to England from the Australian Aboriginal tour of 1868 to the second Aboriginal tour of 1988.*

ENGLAND v AUSTRALIA

2550 **Arnold, Peter** *and* **Wynne-Thomas, Peter,** *compilers*
■ An Ashes anthology: England v Australia. Bromley, Christopher Helm, 1989. x, 246p. illus. stats. index.

2551 **Australian Broadcasting Corporation**
■ Bradman to Border: a history of Australia-England Test matches from 1946. Sydney, ABC Enterprises for the Corporation, 1986. 224p. illus. scores.
updated ed. of 'Padwick I' 4357-1.

2552 **[Baxter, Peter** *and* **Hayter, Reginald James]**
■ The Ashes: highlights since 1948. BBC Books, 1989. 192p. illus. scores, index.
includes excerpts from archive radio commentary.

2553 **Bromby, Robin,** *editor*
■ A century of Ashes: an anthology. Sydney, Resolution Press, 1982. 334p. illus. scores, index.

2554 † **'C.J.'**
■ 'The Ashes of remembrance': the Test match-itis Club: a cricketer's dream. Melbourne, Barker & Co., [1924]. [8]p.
satirical story containing puns on the names of Ashes protagonists.

2555 **Cardus,** *Sir* **[John Frederick] Neville**
■ Cardus on the Ashes; edited by Margaret Hughes. Souvenir Press, 1989. vii, 279p.
anthology from daily journalism and books.

2556 † **Centenary** of England - Australia cricket 1861-1961.
■ [Qantas, 1961]. [8]p. folded sheet. illus. stats.
souvenir of factual information to accompany Qantas exhibition; see also 'Padwick I' 4379.

2557 **Cotter, Gerry**
■ The Ashes captains. Marlborough (Wilts.), Crowood Press, 1989. 320p. illus. (some col.) stats. bibliog. index.

2558 **Frith, David Edward John**
□ England versus Australia: a pictorial history of the Test matches since 1877. Sydney, Australian Broadcasting Commission in association with Richard Smart Publishing, 1980. 320p. illus. facsims. scores.
rev. 2nd ed. of 'Padwick I' 4370-3.
——*3rd ed.* Lutterworth Press in association with Richard Smart Publishing, 1981. 320p.
——*4th ed.* Australian Broadcasting Commission in association with Richard Smart Publishing. 1982. 328p.
——*5th ed.* Willow Books, 1984. 336p.
——*6th ed.* Queen Anne Press, 1989. 352p.

2559   **Frith, David Edward John,** *editor*
■   England v Australia: Test match records 1877-1985. Willow Books, 1986. 256p. illus. stats.

2560 †   **[Henderson, L. J.]**
■   200 not out: a record of Anglo-Australian Test cricket matches. [Sydney, the Author, c.1967]. [11] leaves. *typescript.*
    outline notes for comprehensive statistical work that was never published.

2561   **Ibbotson, Doug** *and* **Dellor, Ralph**
■   A hundred years of the Ashes; edited by David Frith. Aylesbury, Rothmans Publications, 1982. 228p. illus. index.

2562   **Illingworth, Raymond** *and* **Gregory, Kenneth**
■   The Ashes: a centenary. Collins, 1982. 272p. illus. index.

2563   **Mahony, Peter**
■   Sundry extras: England v Australia. Hambledon Press, 1984. x, 206p. illus. index.

2564   **The National Times**
■   Cricket: 100 years of change. Sydney, John Fairfax & Sons, [1982]. 32p. incl. covers. illus. (some col.)
    special issue of colour magazine to mark 100 years of battles for the Ashes.

2565   **Rippon, Anton**
■   Classic moments of the Ashes. Ashbourne, Moorland Publishing, 1982. 160p. illus. scores.

2566 †   **Scott, James W.**
■   Cricket matches played by English teams in Australasia and Australian teams on tour. Sydney, 1938. 703p. scores, stats. index.
    ms. in New South Wales Cricket Association Library.

2567   **Tyson, Frank Holmes**
■   The century-makers: the men behind the Ashes 1877-1977. Sidgwick & Jackson, 1980. 267p. illus. (some col.) index.

ENGLISH TOURS TO AUSTRALIA

2568   **Jenkins, Lloyd**
■   England versus Victoria, Eastern Oval, Ballarat, Tuesday, 19th February, 1985. Ballarat (Vic.), [1985]. 44p. incl. adverts. illus. stats.
    a history of English touring sides in Ballarat.

2569   **Piesse, Ken** *and* **Main, Jim**
■   Duel for glory: England tours to Australia, 1862-1982. Melbourne, Wednail Publications, 1982. 170p. illus. (some col.) stats. bibliog.

2570   **Torrens, Warwick W.,** *editor*
■   A cricket centenary: England in Queensland. [Brisbane], the Author, [1982]. 94p. scores, stats.
    includes scores of all games played by English teams in Queensland, 1883-1979.

1878-79 Test Tour (Lord Harris)

2571 †   **Royle, Vernon Peter Fanshawe Archer**
■   [Diary of tour to Australia with Lord Harris's team].
    copy of ms in Lancashire C. C. C. Library at Old Trafford.

1882-83 Test Tour (Hon. Ivo Bligh)

2572   **Willis, Ronald**
■   Cricket's biggest mystery: the Ashes. Guildford, Lutterworth Press, 1983. 159p. illus. facsims. scores, bibliog.
    ——*first pub.* Adelaide, Rigby, 1982.
    an analysis of the origin of the Ashes.

1884-85 Test Tour (A. Shrewsbury)

2573   **Shaw, Alfred** *and* **Shrewsbury, Arthur**
■   Cricket: Shaw and Shrewsbury's team in Australia 1884-5: the voyage out - description of matches, description of the players, the voyage home, batting and bowling averages etc. [Ewell], J.W.McKenzie, 1985. [vii], 181p. frontis. scores, stats.
    facsimile reprint of 'Padwick I' 4409 with a new introduction by John Arlott; limited ed. of 200 numbered copies.

1897-98 Test Tour (A. E. Stoddart)

2574   **Ranjitsinhji, Kumar Shri,**
■   **H.H.Maharaja Jam Saheb of Nawanagar**
    With Stoddart's team in Australia. Constable, 1985. 288p. illus. stats.
    reprint of 'Padwick I' 4423 with a new introduction by Alan Ross.

1902-03 Lord Hawke's Team

2575 †   **Lord** Hawke's eleven against an eleven of South Australia on the Unley Oval: souvenir. Adelaide, Scrymgour & Sons, 1903. 32p. illus.

2576 †   **Official** souvenir of Lord Hawke's English cricket team in New South Wales: season 1902-1903. Sydney, N.S.W. Bookstall, [1902]. [12]p. illus. stats.
    pre-tour?

1903-04 Test Tour (P. F. Warner)

2577   **Cardwell, Ronald L.**
■   The M.C.C. tour to Australia 1903-1904. [Sydney], Cricket Publishing Company, 1988. 56p. illus. scores, stats.
    limited ed. of 287 signed and numbered copies.

2578 †   **Foster, Reginald Erskine**
■   Australia 1903-04. [168] leaves.
    tour diary; ms in M.C.C. Library at Lord's.

2579 †   **Relf, Albert Edward**
    [Diary].
    tour diary, 25 Sep. 1903 - 2 Jan. 1904; ceases after Relf had been dropped from Test team.
    ms. in Sussex C.C.C. Library at Hove.

1911-12 Test Tour (J. W. H. T. Douglas)

2580 †   **England** - Australia: official cricket souvenir. [Sydney, 1911]. [48]p. incl. adverts. illus. stats.
    issued by authority of the Board of Control; pre-tour.

1924-25 Test Tour (A. E. R. Gilligan)

2581 †   **Mailey, Arthur Alfred**
    Cricket sketches. Sydney, printed by W.C.Penfold, 1924. [24]p. illus.
    issued prior to M.C.C. tour of Australia, 1924-25.

2582 †   **S.A.** Cricketer souvenir: third Test, Adelaide, Jan 16th 1925. [Adelaide, 1925]. 48p. incl. covers and adverts. illus. stats.

1928-29 Test Tour (A. P. F. Chapman)

2583 † **Campbell, Reginald Harry**, *editor*
The Jack Ryder book: a souvenir of the 1928-9 Tests.
[Melbourne, Farrow Falcon Press, 1929]. 26p. illus.
scores, stats.

2584 † **'Heck' and 'Walnut'**, *pseuds.*
Cricket comicalities: souvenir of the English cricketers
Australian tour 1928-1929. Melbourne, National Press,
[1928]. [30]p. illus.
pre-tour.

2585 † **International** programme and score card. [4]p.
■ *produced for*
*(i) Tasmanian XI v English XI at Launceston with score
of third Test.*
*(ii) Australian XI v England XI at Brisbane with score of
England v Queensland.*

2586 † **M.C.C.** Australian tour 1928-29: R.M.S. 'Ormonde'. R.
■ M. S. Ormonde, 1929. [8]p. illus.
printed on board ship; includes results of all matches.

2587 † **M.C.C.** Australian tour, 1928-29: itinerary, fixtures,
travelling schedule ... 1928. [8]p.
pre-tour.

1932-33 Test Tour (D. R. Jardine)

2588 **Bass, Marco** *et al*
Bodyline: a study guide. North Melbourne, Australian
Children's Television Foundation, 1984. 28p. illus.

2589 **Derriman, Philip**
■ Bodyline. Grafton, 1986. 204p. scores, stats.
*cover sub-title: 'the cricket war between England and
Australia'.*
——*first pub.* Melbourne, Fontana, 1984, *as tie-in with
TV drama series of the same name.*

2590 Bodyline. Sydney, Collins, 1984. 160p. illus. diagrs.
■ scores, stats. bibliog.
*text originally appeared as series of articles in 'Sydney
Morning Herald', December 1982; many illustrations
taken from 'Sydney Morning Herald' archives.*

2591 **Docker, Edward Wybergh**
■ Bradman and the bodyline. Angus & Robertson, 1983.
[v], 165p. illus. bibliog. index.
pbk. ed. of 'Padwick I' 4472-1.

2592 † **Empire** cricket: season 1932-33. Melbourne, A. E.
■ Spring, [1933]. 32p. illus. stats.
post tour.

2593 **Fingleton, John Henry Webb ('Jack')**
■ Cricket crisis: bodyline and other lines. Pavilion Books,
1984. xx, 313p. illus. index.
*reprinted ed. of 'Padwick I' 4473 with a new introduction
by Michael Parkinson.*

2594 † The **'Gripu'** gallery cricket souvenir of the English team
touring Australia 1932-1933. Chatswood (N.S.W.),
G.W.Hall, [1932]. 48p. illus.
pre-tour.

2595 **Jardine, Douglas Robert**
In quest of the Ashes. Orbis, 1984. 292p. illus. scores,
stats.
*reprinted ed. of 'Padwick I' 4477 with a new foreword by
John Arlott.*

2596 **Larwood, Harold** *with* **Perkins, Kevin**
■ The Larwood story. Sydney, Bonapara, 1982. 234p.
illus. index.
——*U.K. ed.* Harmondsworth, Penguin Books, 1985.
rev. ed. of 'Padwick I' 4480.

2597 **Le Quesne, [A.] Laurence**
■ The bodyline controversy. Secker & Warburg, 1983. xiv,
242p. illus. index.
——*pbk. ed.* Unwin, 1985.

2598 **Mason, Ronald Charles**
■ Ashes in the mouth: the story of the bodyline tour
1932-33. Hambledon Press, 1982. x, 238p. illus. scores,
stats. index.
——*pbk. ed.* Penguin, 1984.

2599 **Sissons, Ric** *and* **Stoddart, Brian**
■ Cricket and Empire: the 1932-33 bodyline tour of
Australia. George Allen & Unwin, 1984. vii, 150p.
illus. bibliog. index.

2600 **Stoddart, Brian**
■ Cricket's imperial crisis of 1932-33. Canberra,
Australian Cricket Society, [1983]. 38p. illus. scores,
stats.
limited ed. of 200 numbered copies.
——*originally appeared in 'Sport in history',* Brisbane,
University of Queensland Press, 1979.

2601 † **[Wilmot, R. W. E.]**, *compiler*
■ The *Argus* and *The Australasian* cricket guide 1932-33.
Melbourne, [1932]. 16p. incl. covers.
additional ed. of 'Padwick I' 3356.

1936-37 Test Tour (G. O. Allen)

2602 **Cardus, Sir [John Frederick] Neville**
■ Australian summer: England's tour of Australia 1936-37.
Souvenir Press, 1987. 205p. scores.
reprinted ed. of 'Padwick I' 4491.

2603 † **Sunday** Sun souvenir Test cricket supplement. Sydney,
Sunday Sun & Guardian, 1936. 16p. incl. adverts. illus.
supplement pub. 29 November 1936.

1946-47 Test Tour (W. R. Hammond)

2604 **Fingleton, John Henry Webb ('Jack')**
■ Cricket crisis: bodyline and other lines. Pavilion Books,
1984. xx, 313p. illus. index.
*reprinted ed. of 'Padwick I' 4473 with a new introduction
by Michael Parkinson; contains an additional chapter on
1946-47 England tour of Australia.*

1954-55 Test Tour (L. Hutton)

2605 **Ross, Alan**
■ Australia 55: a journal. Constable, 1985. 271p. illus.
scores, stats. index.
*reprinted ed. of 'Padwick I' 4548 with a new introduction
by the author.*

1970-71 Test Tour (R. Illingworth)

2606 † **Western Australia Cricket Association**
Australia v England 1969-70 tour [i.e. 1970-71 tour]:
application for a Perth Test match. The Association,
1968. 10p. illus.

1976-77 Centenary Test (A. W. Greig)

2607 **Wilson, Lorraine**
The centenary cricket Test 1977; illustrated by Alex Stitt.
Melbourne, Nelson, 1984. 28p. illus.
for children.

1978-79 Test Tour (J. M. Brearley)

2608 **Boycott, Geoffrey**
■ Put to the test - England in Australia 1978-79. Sphere, 1980. 219p. illus. scores, stats.
pbk. ed. of 'Padwick I' 4615-41.

2609 **Yallop, Graham Neil**
■ Lambs to the slaughter. New English Library, 1980. 174p. illus. scores, stats.
pbk. ed. of 'Padwick I' 4615-56.

1979-80 Test Tour (J. M. Brearley)

2610 † The **Cornhill** Insurance tour digest: England's Test cricketers in Australia 1979-80. 1979. 40p. illus. stats.
pre-tour.

2611 **Frindall, William Howard ('Bill')**
■ Frindall's score book volume VI: Australia v West Indies and England 1979-80. Queen Anne Press, 1980. 120p. illus. scores, stats.

2612 **Martin-Jenkins, Christopher Dennis Alexander**
■ Cricket contest 1979-80: the post-Packer Tests. Queen Anne Press, 1980. [ix], 181p. illus. scores, stats.

2613 **Partington, Jennifer,** *editor*
■ Test cricket. Dee Why West (N.S.W.), Summit Books, 1980. 112p. illus. (some col.) scores, stats.
on cover: 'Australia vs England and The West Indies'; post tour.

2614 **Tyson, Frank Holmes**
■ War or peace. Ashburton (Vic.), Garry Sparke and Associates, 1980. 159p. illus. scores, stats.

2615 **Underwood, Derek Leslie**
■ Deadly down under; photographs by Eric Piper. Arthur Barker, 1980. 143p. illus. scores, stats.

1982-83 Test Tour (R. G. D. Willis)

2616 The **battle** for the Ashes. Ashburton (Vic.), Garry
■ Sparke & Associates, 1983. 80p. illus. (mostly col.) scores, stats.

2617 **Benaud, Richard ('Richie')**
■ The Ashes 1982-83: Australia v England. Sydney, Lansdowne, 1983. 128p. col. illus. scores, stats.

2618 **Benson** and Hedges Test series official book 1982/83: the
■ Ashes centenary, Australia, England. Pymble (N.S.W.), Playbill, [1982]. 68p. incl. covers, illus. (mostly col.) stats.
pre-tour.

2619 **Berry, Scyld**
■ Train to Julia Creek: a journey to the heart of Australia. Hodder and Stoughton, 1985. 208p. illus. maps.
includes an account of the Melbourne Test.

2620 **Botham, Ian Terence** *and* **Jarrett, Ian**
■ Botham down under: the 1982/3 England-Australia Test series. Collins, 1983. 111p. illus. scores.

2621 **Boxall, Brad,** *editor*
■ *Australian cricket* tour guide. Sydney, Murray Publishers, 1982. 116p. incl. covers, illus. diagrs. stats.
pre-tour.

2622 **Carey, Michael**
▨ The Ashes: Chappell's revenge; Bill Frindall statistics and scorecards. Daily Telegraph, 1983. 175p. illus. scores, stats.

2623 **[Chappell, Ian Michael]**
■ The Ashes centenary series. Melbourne, Taurus Publishing Company, 1983. 96p. illus. (mostly col.) scores, stats.
cover title: '1882-1982: the Ashes centenary series'.

2624 **Eagar, Patrick** *[and]* **Ross, Alan**
■ Summer of speed: the fight for the Ashes in Australia 1982/3. Collins, 1983. 128p. illus. scores.

2625 **Harte, Christopher John ('Chris')**
■ The fight for the Ashes 1982-83. Adelaide, the Author, 1983. [vi], 253p. illus. scores, stats. index. *typescript. limited ed. of 400 signed and numbered copies.*

2626 **McGilvray, Alan David,** *editor*
■ England in Australia 1982-83. Sydney, Australian Broadcasting Commission, 1982. 112p. illus. (some col.) stats.
pre-tour.

2627 **Marlar, Robin Geoffrey**
■ Decision against England: the centenary Ashes 1982-83. Methuen, 1983. x, 214p. illus. scores, stats.
includes Australian Cricket Board's players' code of behaviour.

2628 **National** Nine tour guide: the hottest cricket in 100
■ summers: Australia, England, New Zealand. Sydney, PBL Marketing, 1982. 80p. illus. (some col.) stats.
pre-tour.

2629 **Piesse, Ken,** *editor*
■ 100 summers: an Ashes centenary special. Melbourne, Newspress, [1982]. 72p. incl. covers. illus. stats.
'Cricketer' magazine special; pre-tour.

2630 **Willis, Robert George Dylan ('Bob')** *in conjunction with*
■ **Lee, Alan**
The captain's diary: England in Australia and New Zealand 1982-83; photographs by Adrian Murrell. Willow Books, 1983. 187p. illus. scores, stats.

1986-87 Test Tour (M. W. Gatting)

2631 **Ashes** ablaze. Melbourne, Newspress, 1986. 68p. illus.
■ stats.
a 'Cricketer' tour guide; pre-tour.

2632 **Benson** and Hedges Test series official book 1986-87:
■ the clashes for the Ashes, Australia vs England. Pymble (N.S.W.), Playbill, 1986. 64p. incl. covers, illus. (mostly col.) stats.
cover title; pre-tour.

2633 The **clashes** for the Ashes: 1986-87 media guide. [P.B.L. Marketing, 1986]. 96p. illus. stats.
pre-tour.

2634 **Edmonds, Frances**
■ Cricket XXXX cricket. Kingswood Press, 1987. [xiv], 187p. illus.
——*pbk. ed.* Pan, 1988.

2635 **Gatting, Michael William ('Mike')**
■ Triumph in Australia: Mike Gatting's 1986-87 cricket diary. Queen Anne Press, 1987. 192p. illus. (some col.) scores, stats.

2636 **Martin-Jenkins, Christopher Dennis Alexander**
■ Grand slam: England in Australia 1986/87. (A *Cricketer* special); photographs by Adrian Murrell, statistics by Richard Lockwood. Simon & Schuster, 1987. 111p. illus. (some col.) scores, stats.

2637 **National** Nine tour guide 1986-87: Australia v England v
■ West Indies. Sydney, PBL Marketing, 1986. 80p. illus.
(some col.) stats.
pre-tour.

2638 **Roebuck, Peter Michael**
■ Ashes to ashes: the 1986-87 Test series. Kingswood
Press, 1987. x, 209p. illus. scores, stats.

2639 **Tasker, Norman,** *compiler and editor*
■ England tour of Australia 1986-87. Sydney, ABC
Enterprises for the Australian Broadcasting
Corporation, 1986. 112p. illus. (some col.) diagr. stats.
pre-tour.

2640 **West, Peter**
■ Clean sweep. W.H.Allen, 1987. [x], 178p. illus. scores.

2641 **West, Peter** *and* **Wimbush, Wendy**
■ The battle for the Ashes '87: *The Daily Telegraph* story of
the 1986-87 Australia v England Test series. The Daily
Telegraph, 1987. 144p. illus. scores, stats.
edited by Norman Barrett.

1987-88 Bicentennial Test (M. W. Gatting)

2642 **Benson** and Hedges Bicentennial Test and one-day
■ international. Pymble (N.S.W.), Playbill, [1987]. 68p.
incl. covers, illus. (some col.) stats.
pre-match.

2643 **Mengel, Noel,** *editor*
■ *Australian cricket* 1987-88 guide. Darlinghurst (N.S.W.),
Mason Stewart Publishing, [1987]. 132p. incl. covers,
illus. (some col.) scores, stats.

2644 **The Primary Club of Australia**
■ The captain's dinner, 28 January 1988. [Sydney, the
Club, 1987]. [32]p. illus.
text by Jack Pollard; limited ed.

ENGLISH TOURS TO SOUTH AFRICA

1888-89 Test Tour (C. Aubrey Smith)

2645 The **cricketing** record of Major Warton's tour 1888-9: a
■ detailed account of the first English tour to South Africa.
Ewell, J. W. McKenzie, 1987. [viii], [viii], 219p. illus.
scores.
*facsimile reprint of 'Padwick I' 4619 in a limited ed. of
200 numbered copies with a new introduction by David
Rayvern Allen.*

1948-49 Test Tour (F. G. Mann)

2646 † **Day, Cedric** *and* **Mason, Michael**
The story of Test cricket: South Africa v England.
Windsor, [1948]. 16p. illus.
pre-tour.

1956-57 Test Tour (P. B. H. May)

2647 **Ross, Alan**
■ Cape summer and the Australians in England.
Constable, 1986. 255p. illus. scores, stats.
*reprinted ed. of 'Padwick I' 4656 with a new introduction
by the author.*

2648 † **Safmarine**
The M.C.C. team in South Africa 1956-57. [Cape Town],
1956. folder.
pre-tour.

1965-66 MCC Schoolboys to South Africa

2649 † **M.C.C.** Schoolboys XI official tour of South Africa
1965/1966: souvenir programme. [Johannesburg, 1965].
24p. illus.
pre-tour.

1982 SAB England Tour (G. A. Gooch)

2650 **Binckes, Robin,** *editor*
■ The 1982 SAB English team tour of South Africa
souvenier (sic) brochure. [South African Cricket Union,
1982]. [8]p. incl. covers, illus. stats.
pre-tour.

ENGLISH TOURS TO THE WEST INDIES

2651 **Lockwood, Richard David,** *compiler*
■ West Indies v England at Bridgetown, Barbados.
[Birmingham], the Author, 1986. 8p. stats.

1935 Test Tour (R. E. S. Wyatt)

2652 † The **M.C.C.** in British Guiana 1935. Georgetown, *Daily
Chronicle*, 1935. 102p. incl. adverts. illus. scores, stats.
reprinted from 'The Daily Chronicle'.

1948 Test Tour (G. O. Allen)

2653 † A **record** of the M.C.C. tour to the West Indies in 1948.
■ Port-of-Spain, Shell Leasehold Distributing Co. and
Petroleum Marketing Co. (West Indies), [1948]. [24]p.
illus. diagrs. scores, stats.
post tour.

1960 Test Tour (P. B. H. May)

2654 **Peebles, Ian Alexander Ross**
■ Bowler's turn: a further ramble round the realm of
cricket. Pavilion Books, 1987. [viii], 195p. illus. scores,
stats.
*reprinted ed. of 'Padwick I' 4708 with a new introduction
by Frank Keating.*

2655 **Ross, Alan**
■ Through the Caribbean: England in the West Indies,
1960. Pavilion Books, 1986. vi, 296p. illus. scores, stats.
*reprinted ed. of 'Padwick I' 4709 with a new introduction
by the author.*

1974 Test Tour (M. H. Denness)

2656 † **Dabdoub, Robert S.,** *editor*
West Indies vs England in Jamaica: official souvenir
programme. Kingston, Jamaica Cricket Association,
[1974]. 68p. incl. adverts. illus. scores, stats.
pre-tour.

1980 England Young Cricketers to West Indies

2657 † **Agatha** Christie under-19 Test series: England tour of
■ West Indies 1980. National Cricket Association, [1979].
[12]p. incl. covers. illus.
pre-tour; 1 Jan. - 13 Feb.

1981 Test Tour (I. T. Botham)

2658 **Boycott, Geoffrey**
■ In the fast lane: West Indies tour 1981. Arthur Barker,
1981. 224p. illus. scores, stats.
includes text of Gleneagles Accord.
——*pbk. ed.* Sphere, 1982.

2659 Cozier, Tony, *editor*
■ Benson & Hedges Test series 1981: West Indies vs England [official souvenir programme]. Weybridge (Surrey), Goodyear Gibbs Caribbean, [1981]. 48p. illus. (some col.) stats.
pre-tour.

2660 Fray, Robert Neville
Profile in cricket 1981. Kingston, the Author, 1981. 43p. incl. adverts. illus.
pre-tour.

2661 Gomes, J. M. Cajetan
■ After a remarkable recovery. Lewes, Book Guild, 1982. xii, 154p.
memories of 1981 Test series pp. 108-136.

2662 Keating, Francis ('Frank')
■ Another bloody day in paradise! Andre Deutsch, 1981. [viii], 177p. illus. map, scores, stats.

2663 Murrell, Irene
■ A tour in the game: being a comment on the West Indies tour by the M.C.C. Lewes, Book Guild, 1986. 31, viii p. illus.

2664 Smith, Peter, *editor*
■ England v West Indies 1981: the official England team tour book. Pelham Books, 1981. 192p. illus. scores, stats.

1986 Test Tour (D. I. Gower)

2665 Cozier, Tony, *editor*
■ Cable and Wireless Test series 1986: West Indies vs England. Christ Church (Barbados); Walton-on-Thames (Surrey), Caribbean Communications, [1986]. 32p. illus. (some col.) stats.
pre-tour.

2666 Edmonds, Frances
■ Another bloody tour: England in the West Indies 1986. Kingswood Press, 1986. [xi], 162p. illus.
——*pbk. ed.* Fontana, 1987.

2667 Mathias, Richard Watson
Great moments in Test matches: England - West Indies. Kingston, the Author, 1986. 32p. incl. adverts. illus. stats.
pre-tour.

ENGLISH TOURS TO NEW ZEALAND

1922-23 M.C.C. Tour (A. C. MacLaren)

2668 Kynaston, David
■ Archie's last stand; M.C.C. in New Zealand 1922-23: being an account of Mr A. C. MacLaren's tour and his last stand. Queen Anne Press, 1984. 176p. illus. map, scores, stats.

1932-33 Test Tour (D. R. Jardine)

2669 † M.C.C. tour of New Zealand 1933. Christchurch, New
■ Zealand Cricket Council, [1933]. [32]p. illus.
pre-tour.

1983-84 Test Tour (R. G. D. Willis)

2670 Rothmans series: England in New Zealand 1984: official
■ tour souvenir programme. Auckland, TVNZ Enterprises, [1983]. 54p. illus. (some col.) stats.
pre-tour.

2671 Willis, Robert George Dylan ('Bob') *and* **Lee, Alan**
■ The captain's diary: England in Fiji, New Zealand and Pakistan 1983-84; photographs by Adrian Murrell. Willow Books, 1984. 160p. illus. scores, stats.

1987-88 Test Tour (M. W. Gatting)

2672 Berry, Scyld
■ A cricket odyssey: England on tour 1987-88; photographs by Graham Morris. Pavilion Books, 1988. [x], 214p. illus. map. scores, stats.
tour of New Zealand, pp. 173-203.

2673 New Zealand Cricket Council
■ Rothmans series: England in New Zealand '88. Auckland, Harvard Sports Marketing, [1988]. 40p. col. illus. stats.
pre-tour.

1988-89 Intended Test Tour

2674 England tour to New Zealand: the official New Zealand Cricket Council cricket guide. [Christchurch, the Council], 1988. [8]p. illus. stats.
the tour was scheduled for Feb.-Mar. 1989, but did not take place.

ENGLAND v INDIA

2675 Parashar, Naresh, *editor*
Cric India's cricket statistics: India vs. England 1932 to 1982. Ganaur Mandi, Cric India, 1981. 144p. incl. adverts. illus. stats.

ENGLISH TOURS TO INDIA

1937-38 Lord Tennyson's Team

2676 † Programme for the Sind Cricket Tournament and Lord Tennyson's XI visit, October 2nd - November 2nd 1937. Karachi, *Daily Gazette Press*, 1937. 34p.

1979-80 Jubilee Test (J. M. Brearley)

2677 Underwood, Derek Leslie
■ Deadly down under; photographs by Eric Piper. Arthur Barker, 1980. 143p. illus. scores, stats.
includes a chapter on the Indian Jubilee Test.

1981-82 Test Tour (K. W. R. Fletcher)

2678 Berry, Scyld
■ Cricket wallah: with England in India 1981-82; with photographs by Adrian Murrell. Hodder and Stoughton, 1982. 192p. illus. map. scores, stats. index.

2679 Bhupathy, D. R., *editor*
England tour of India, 1981-82. Madras, Bhupathy, 1981. [126]p. incl. adverts. illus. stats.
pre-tour.

2680 Desai, Mrunal *and* **Joshi, Suhas,** *editors*
■ India v/s England: bumper cricket souvenir. Bombay, the Authors, [1981]. 60p. incl. adverts. illus. stats.
pre-tour.

2681 Haridass, C. K.
■ England in India 1981-82. Madras, C. K. Haridass, 1981. 200p. incl. adverts. illus. scores, stats.
pre-tour.

2682 The Hindu
■ England tour of India 1981-82. [Madras, Nagaraj & Co., 1981]. 100p. incl. covers and adverts. illus. stats.
pre-tour.

1984-85 Test Tour (D. I. Gower)

2683 **Cowdrey, Christopher Stuart** *and* **Smith, Jonathan B.**
■ Good enough? Pelham Books, 1986. 187p. illus. scores.
includes personal account of 1984-85 tour to India.

2684 **Marks, Victor James**
■ Marks out of XI: England's winter tour of India and
Australia 1984-85. George Allen & Unwin, 1985. [viii],
157p. illus. scores, stats.

ENGLISH TOURS TO PAKISTAN

1983-84 Test Tour (R. G. D. Willis)

2685 **Agfa** cricket album: Pakistan vs England.
■ *Akhbar-e-Watan Monthly*, [1983]. [28]p. col. illus.

2686 **Willis, Robert George Dylan ('Bob')** *and* **Lee, Alan**
■ The captain's diary: England in Fiji, New Zealand and
Pakistan 1983-84; photographs by Adrian Murrell.
Willow Books, 1984. 160p. illus. scores, stats.

1987-88 Test Tour (M. W. Gatting)

2687 **Berry, Scyld**
■ A cricket odyssey: England on tour 1987-88; photographs
by Graham Morris. Pavilion Books, 1988. [x], 214p.
illus. map. scores, stats.
tour of Pakistan, pp. 84-162.

ENGLISH TOURS TO SRI LANKA

1911-12 M.C.C. Tour (P. F. Warner)

2688 † **Amicus Illustrated Weekly**
[Special cricket issue], vol. XIV, no. 151, Oct. 26, 1911.
Colombo. 38p. illus.
*contains two articles by 'Ubique' - 'The English cricketers
in Colombo: chats with some of the players' and 'How
the M.C.C. defeated All-Ceylon'; see also 'Padwick I'
4876.*

1982 Test Tour (K. W. R. Fletcher)

2689 **Board of Control for Cricket in Sri Lanka**
■ Official tour programme of England team to Sri Lanka,
6th to 23rd February 1982. Colombo, the Board, 1982.
[8]p. folded sheet.

2690 **Perera, S. S.,** *editor*
■ Official souvenir of the first Test match, England v Sri
Lanka 17, 18, 20, 21, 22 February ... commemorating 100
years of cricket with England / MCC 1882-1982 and the
visit of the 27th MCC / English team to Sri Lanka.
Grant, Kenyon & Eckhardt (Lanka), [1982]. [72]p.
illus. (some col.) stats.
*pre-match; includes review of previous MCC visits to Sri
Lanka.*

2691 **Wijeya** Test match souvenir 1982: the first Test match,
■ England vs Sri Lanka. Wijeya, 1982. [8]p. col. illus.
pre-match; most of the text in Singhalese.

OTHER ENGLISH TOURS

1859 Tour to Canada and the United States

2692 **Lillywhite, Frederick William**
■ The English cricketers' trip to Canada and the United
States in 1859. Kingswood (Surrey), World's Work,
1980. [xxvi], viii, 68p. frontis. illus. map, scores.
*facsimile reprint of 'Padwick I' 4893 with a new
introduction by Robin Marlar and profiles of the players.*

1959 Surrey C. C. C. to Rhodesia

2693 † The **Surrey** visit. [Salisbury], Anne Buckley for the
■ Mashonaland Cricket Association, [1959]. 24p. incl.
adverts. illus.
*issued prior to Rhodesia v Surrey match at Salisbury,
October 1959.*

1965 Worcestershire C. C. C. World Tour

2694 † **Worcestershire** County Cricket Club visit to Hong Kong
■ 1965. Hong Kong, Hongkong Cricket League, 1965.
50p. incl. adverts. illus.

1983-84 Tour to Fiji

2695 **Fiji Cricket Association**
■ Souvenir programme: English cricket tour 31 December
1983 - 4 January 1984. [The Association, 1983]. 60p.
incl. adverts. illus. diagr.
pre-tour; edited by Harry Ranchhod.

1985 English Counties XI to Zimbabwe

2696 **English** counties XI: Zimbabwe tour: 1985. 40p. illus.
■ *pre-tour.*

1989 Tour to The Netherlands

2697 **Nederland** v England: official brochure of matches
■ played in Amsterdam on 16 and 17 August 1989.
Amsterdam, 1989. 20p. illus.

ENGLISH WOMEN'S TOURS

1934-35 Tour to Australia and New Zealand

2698 † **England** v New Zealand, Lancaster Park, Saturday, Feb
■ 16th and Monday, Feb 18th, 1935. Christchurch, New
Zealand Women's Cricket Council, 1935. [12]p. illus.
*the first Test match between England and New Zealand.
programme also seen for match v Otago.*

2699 † **England** v West Australia 1934: official programme and
■ souvenir, W.A.C.A. Ground, Saturday, Nov. 24 and
Monday, Nov. 26. Perth, W. A. Women's Cricket
Association, 1934. 16p. illus. diagr.
*'World's first women's international cricket match'.
programmes also seen for subsequent matches v Victoria,
New South Wales, in Queensland and v Australia (2nd
and 3rd Tests).*

1984-85 Tour to Australia

2700 **Australia** England jubilee Test series and one day
■ internationals souvenir programme. Australian
Women's Cricket Council, 1984. [16]p. illus.

INTERNATIONAL CRICKET - AUSTRALIA

GENERAL

2701 † **Australian Board of Control for International Cricket Matches**
Constitution, rules and by-laws. Sydney, the Board, [1914]. 24p.
——*another ed. with title* 'Constitution and rules', [1950].
these are additional eds. of 'Padwick I' 4958.

2702 **Brayshaw, Ian John**
■ Warriors in baggy green caps. Milson's Point (N.S.W.), Currawong Press, 1982. 173p. illus. stats.
sub-title on cover: 'The great Ian Chappell era and its survivors'.

2703 **Chizmeysa, John**
■ Cricket classics. North Ryde (N.S.W.), Cassell Australia, 1981. [208]p. illus.
sub-title on cover: '100 great Test matches from a century of cricket'; Australian Test matches only.

2704 **Cricket**: a pictorial history of Australian Test players.
■ [Ashburton (Vic.)], Garry Sparke & Associates, [1982]. 64p. illus. (some col.) stats.

2705 **Dundas, Ross** *and* **Pollard, Jack**
■ The complete book of Australian Test cricket records 1877-1987: includes international one day records. ABC Enterprises for the Australian Broadcasting Corporation, 1987. xvii, 393p. illus. stats.

2706 **Harte, Christopher John ('Chris')**
Adelaide's century of cricket. Adelaide, Wakefield Press, 1984. 200p. illus.
limited ed. of 200 copies; pub. to celebrate Adelaide's century of Test cricket.

2707 **McGilvray, Alan David** *with* **Tasker, Norman**
■ Alan McGilvray's backpage of cricket. (Backpage series). Paddington (N.S.W.), Lester-Townsend Publishing, 1989. [168]p. facsims.
sub-title on cover: '60 golden seasons' [1925-1987].

2708 **Robinson, Raymond John**
■ On top down under: Australia's cricket captains. North Ryde (N.S.W.), Cassell Australia, 1981. 285p. illus. bibliog. index.
pbk. ed. of 'Padwick I' 7245-1, updated to include Greg Chappell, Graham Yallop and Kim Hughes.

2709 **Ronayne, Michael Peter,** *compiler*
■ Test cricket tours: Australia. (Test cricket tours: no 3). [Norwich, the Author], 1987. 120p. illus. stats.
to March 1985.

2710 **Wat, Charlie**
■ The Australians' Test record. Prahran (Vic.), Cricket Stats Publications. *annual.* stats.
1988 to date.
1989 with title 'The Australians' playing record in Tests'.
each issue limited to 75 signed and numbered copies.

2711 **Whimpress, Bernard** *and* **Hart, Nigel**
■ Adelaide Oval Test cricket 1884-1984. Adelaide, Wakefield Press and South Australian Cricket Association, 1984. x, 262p. illus. scores, bibliog. index.
——*special ed. limited to 299 numbered copies, 1984; 299 is the highest individual score made at the Adelaide Oval in a Test match.*

2712 **Whitington, Richard Smallpiece**
■ Australians abroad: Australia's overseas test tours. Canterbury (Vic.), Five Mile Press, 1983. xii, 476p. illus. scores, stats.

2713 The Datsun book of Australian Test cricket 1877-1981.
■ Canterbury (Vic.), Five Mile Press, 1981. x, 413p. illus. scores, stats.
updated ed. of 'Padwick I' 4960-4.

LIMITED OVERS

2714 **Wat, Charlie**
■ The Australian cricketers' LOI records. Prahran (Vic.), Cricket Stats Publications. *annual.* stats.
1988 to date.
each issue limited to 75 signed and numbered copies.

AUSTRALIAN TOURS TO ENGLAND

2715 **Lockwood, Richard David**
■ The Australians at Edgbaston: a history. [Birmingham], the Author, 1985. [30]p. scores, stats.

2716 **Porter, Clive Willoughby**
■ The white horse and the kangaroo: Kent v the Australians 1882-1977. Rainham (Kent), Meresborough Books, 1981. 128p. illus. scores, stats.

2717 † **Rodgerson, R.**
Australian cricketers 1878-1938 seen through English eyes. The Author, 1943? [ii], 21p. stats. *typescript.*
statistical list of Australian cricketers' performances on tour in England.

2718 **Slater, Richard W.**
■ The Australians at Trent Bridge 1878-1980. Newark, the Author, [1981]. 84p. illus. scores, stats.

1868 Australian Aboriginals Tour (C. Lawrence)

2719 **Mulvaney, [Derek] John** *and* **Harcourt, Rex**
■ Cricket walkabout: the Australian Aboriginal cricketers on tour 1867-68. Macmillan in association with The Department of Aboriginal Affairs, 1988. xv, 204p. illus. facsims. scores. stats. index.
revised ed. of 'Padwick I' 4967.

1878 Australian XI Tour (D. W. Gregory)

2720 **[Reynolds, P. E.]**
■ The Australian cricketers' tour through Australia, New Zealand and Great Britain in 1878. [Ewell], J. W. McKenzie, 1980. [x], [ii], 94p. frontis. illus.
facsimile reprint of 'Padwick I' 4968 with a new introduction and frontispiece.
limited ed. of 150 numbered copies.

1882 Test Tour (W. L. Murdoch)

2721 **Pardon, Charles Frederick**
■ The Australians in England: a complete record of the cricket tour of 1882. [Ewell], J.W.McKenzie, 1982. [xi], viii, 192p. scores, stats.
facsimile reprint of 'Padwick I' 4974 with a new introduction by Geoffrey Moorhouse; limited ed. of 120 numbered copies.

2722 The **third** Australian team in England: a complete
■ record of all the matches with portrait and biography of each member. [Ewell], J.W.McKenzie, 1989. [vi], vi, 131p. frontis. illus. scores, stats.
facsimile reprint of 'Padwick I' 4975 with a new introduction by John Arlott.

1884 Test Tour (W. L. Murdoch)

2723 **Pardon, Charles Frederick**
■ The Australians in England: a complete record of the cricket tour of 1884. [Ewell], J.W.McKenzie, 1984. [x], viii, 184p. scores, stats.
facsimile reprint of 'Padwick I' 4977 with a new introduction by Geoffrey Moorhouse; limited ed. of 150 numbered copies.

1902 Test Tour (J. Darling)

2724 **Brown, Lionel H.**
■ Victor Trumper and the 1902 Australians. Secker & Warburg, 1981. xv, 208p. illus. scores, stats. bibliog. index.

1919 A.I.F. Australian XI (H. L. Collins)

2725 **Cardwell, Ronald L.**
■ The A.I.F. cricket team. [Balgowlah Heights (N.S.W.)], the Author, 1980. 80p. illus. stats. scores.
limited ed. of 200 signed and numbered copies.

1930 Test Tour (W. M. Woodfull)

2726 **Bradman's** first tour. Adelaide etc., Rigby, 1981. 159p.
■ illus. scores, stats.
compiled from newspaper cuttings from the scrapbooks of George Garnsey.

2727 † **Souvenir** of the visit of the Australian team and friends
■ to Jodrell Hall. Allied Newspapers, 1930. [3]p. + [29] plates.
photographic record of the visit.

1934 Test Tour (W. M. Woodfull)

2728 † **In** quest of the Ashes 1934: the Don Bradman souvenir
■ booklet and scoring record. [Sydney], 1934. [24]p. illus. stats.
pre-tour.

1938 Test Tour (D. G. Bradman)

2729 † **Programme** of Test matches between England and
■ Australia, season 1938. Essendon (Vic.), Essendon Speed Coursing Club, 1938. 20p. incl. covers, illus.
pre-tour.

1948 Test Tour (D. G. Bradman)

2730 **Arlott, [Leslie Thomas] John**
■ Two summers at the Tests: England v South Africa 1947; England v Australia 1948. Pavilion Books, 1986. viii, 320p. illus. scores, stats.
composite ed. of 'Gone to the cricket' ('Padwick I' 5355) and 'Gone to the Test match' ('Padwick I' 5078) with a new introduction by the author.

2731 **Fingleton, John Henry Webb ('Jack')**
■ Brightly fades the Don. Pavilion Books, 1985. 261p. illus. scores, index.
reprinted ed. of 'Padwick I' 5091-1 with a new introduction by Michael Parkinson.

1953 Test Tour (A. L. Hassett)

2732 **Fingleton, John Henry Webb ('Jack')**
■ The Ashes crown the year: a coronation cricket diary. Pavilion Books, 1986. vii, 320p. illus. scores, stats.
reprinted ed. of 'Padwick I' 5121 with a new introduction by Michael Parkinson.

2733 **Ross, Gordon John,** *editor*
■ 'Thirty years on': the story of the famous England teams of 1953 - then, and now. NatWest Bank, 1983. [28]p. illus. (some col.) scores.
celebrates reunion dinner, 27 June 1983.
pub. as supplement to 'Cricketer International' vol. 64, no. 12, December 1983.

1956 Test Tour (I. W. Johnson)

2734 **Ross, Alan**
■ Cape summer and the Australians in England. Constable, 1986. 255p. illus. scores, stats.
reprinted ed. of 'Padwick I' 5151 with a new introduction by the author.

1968 Test Tour (W. M. Lawry)

2735 † **Australia** 1968 test tour. Hammersmith, Starkey,
■ [1968]. [8]p. illus.
pre-tour.

1980 Centenary Test (G. S. Chappell)

2736 **Gill, Tony,** *editor*
■ Cornhill Centenary Test 1980: the story of the Cornhill Centenary Test match between England and Australia at Lord's 1980. Prism for Garuda Indonesian Airways, [1980]. 36p. illus. diagr. scores.

2737 **Roe, R. J.,** *editor*
■ Cornhill Insurance centenary Test official souvenir. Test & County Cricket Board, 1980. 64p. illus. (some col.) facsims. stats.
pre-match.

1981 Test Tour (K. J. Hughes)

2738 **Barrett, Norman,** *editor*
■ 'I was there': 20 great sporting memories from the writers of *The Daily Telegraph* and *The Sunday Telegraph*. Telegraph Publications, 1985. 158p. illus. score.
includes 'Comeback of the century' by Michael Melford, pp. 112-119 [England v Australia, Headingley 1981].

2739 **Botham, Ian Terence**
■ The incredible Tests 1981. Pelham Books, 1981. 160p. illus. diagr. scores, stats.
——*pbk. ed.* Sphere, 1983.

2740 Brearley, John Michael ('Mike')
Phoenix from the Ashes: the story of the England -
Australia series 1981. Hodder and Stoughton, 1982.
160p. illus. (some col.) diagrs. scores, index.
——*pbk. ed.* Unwin, 1982.

2741 Eagar, Patrick [and] Ross, Alan
A summer to remember: England v Australia. Collins,
1981. 128p. illus. scores.

2742 McGilvray, Alan David, *editor*
Australian tour of England 1981. Sydney, Australian
Broadcasting Commission, 1981. 112p. illus. (some
col.) diagr. stats.
pre-tour.

2743 Melford, Michael Austin
Botham rekindles the Ashes: *The Daily Telegraph* story
of the '81 Test series. The Daily Telegraph, 1981. 153p.
illus. scores.
——*2nd. ed.* 1981.

2744 Symes, Patrick & Thompson, Roger
1981 Australians' tour official souvenir brochure.
Taniard, [1981]. 40p. incl. adverts. illus. (some col.)
stats.
pre-tour.

1985 Test Tour (A. R. Border)

2745 Australian Broadcasting Corporation
Australian tour of United Kingdom 1985. Sydney, ABC
Enterprises for the Corporation, 1985. 113p. illus.
(some col.) map, diagr. stats.

2746 Carey, Michael *et al*
The battle for the Ashes: *The Daily Telegraph* story of
the 1985 England v Australia Test series. Daily
Telegraph, 1985. 224p. illus. scores, charts, stats.

2747 Eagar, Patrick [and] Ross, Alan
An Australian summer: the recovery of the Ashes 1985.
Tadworth (Surrey), Kingswood Press, 1985. 125p. illus.
scores.

2748 Engel, Matthew
Ashes '85; with photographs by Graham Morris. Pelham
Books, 1985. viii, 216p. scores, stats. illus.

2749 National Nine Ashes viewers guide: Australian cricket
tour of England 1985. Sydney, PBL Marketing, 1985.
80p. illus. (some col.) stats.
pre-tour.

1988 Aboriginal Tour (J. Maguire)

2750 Background to the Aboriginal cricket tour of England,
12 May - 25 June 1988. Official Tour Co-ordinators
Interaction Associates, 1988. [16] leaves.
pre-tour.

2751 Qantas Aboriginal cricket tour of England 1988.
[Aboriginal Cricket Association, 1988]. 36p. illus.
(some col.)
pre-tour.

1989 Test Tour (A. R. Border)

2752 Alexander, Brian, *editor*
The Ashes '89: your viewing guide to England versus
Australia. Redwood Publishing for BBC Magazines,
1989. 100p. incl. covers and adverts. illus. (mostly col.)
stats.
pre-series; BBC Sportsyear series: June-August 1989.

2753 Ashes '89: Australia v England. Pymble (N.S.W.);
London, Playbill, [1989]. 56p. incl covers, illus.
(mostly col.) stats.
an official Australian Cricket Board publication; pre-tour.

2754 The *Australian cricket* armchair guide to the Ashes.
Darlinghurst (N.S.W.), Mason Stewart Publishing,
[1989]. 68p. incl covers, illus. (some col.) ground
plans, stats.
pre-tour.

2755 *Australian* cricket: Australia's Ashes triumph.
Darlinghurst (N.S.W.), Mason Stewart Publishing,
[1989]. 48p. illus. (some col.) scores, stats.
post tour souvenir issue.

2756 Barrett, Norman, *editor*
Battle for the Ashes '89: *The Daily Telegraph* story of the
1989 England v Australia Test series. Pan Books, 1989.
176p. illus. scores, stats.

2757 Border, Allan Robert
Ashes glory: Allan Border's own story. Byron Bay
(N.S.W.), Swan Publishing, 1989. 159p. illus. (mostly
col.) scores, stats.

2758 The clash for the Ashes; edited by Chuck Smeeton.
Surry Hills (N.S.W.), Century Magazines, [1989]. 36p.
incl. covers, col. illus.
pre-tour.

2759 Derriman, Philip, *compiler*
Ashes from Ashes: how the 1989 Australians recaptured
cricket's greatest prize; photography by Patrick Eagar.
Crows Nest (N.S.W.), ABC Enterprises for the
Australian Broadcasting Corporation, 1989. 128p. illus.
scores, stats.

2760 Eagar, Patrick *and* **Ross, Alan**
Tour of tours: Border's victorious Australians of 1989.
Hodder and Stoughton, 1989. 128p. illus. (some col.)
scores, stats.

2761 Huxley, John, *editor*
Border's heroes: Australia's Ashes triumph of 1989.
Sydney, Lester-Townsend Publishing, 1989. 176p. illus.
(mostly col.) scores, stats.

2762 Lemmon, David Hector, *editor*
Official 1989 tour guide. Test & County Cricket Board,
1989. 64p. illus. (mostly col.) stats.
incorporating 'Cricket '89'; pre-tour.

2763 Maxwell, Jim, *editor*
Australian tour of England, 1989. Sydney, ABC
Enterprises for the Australian Broadcasting
Corporation, 1989. 112p. illus. (some col.) map.
pre-tour.

2764 Nicholson, Rod
Border's heroes: return of the Ashes. Scoresby (Vic.),
Magenta Press, 1989. 152p. illus. scores, stats.

2765 Robson, Andy
Battle for the Ashes: the 1989 Australian tour of
England. Dennis Oneshots, 1989. 52p. incl. covers, col.
illus.
pre-Tests but pub. after start of the tour.

2766 Selvey, Michael Walter William
The Ashes surrendered: the *Guardian* book of the 1989
Ashes series. Queen Anne Press, 1989. 125p. illus.
scores, stats.

2767 The victors: poster-size action pictures of the conquering
Aussie XI of '89. Dubbo (N.S.W.), Macquarie
Publications, 1989. 12p. col. illus.

AUSTRALIAN TOURS TO SOUTH AFRICA

1935-36 Test Tour (V. Y. Richardson)

2768 † **Mailey, Arthur Alfred**
■ Cricket sketches: South African tour 1935-36. Cape Town, Vacuum Oil Co., 1936. [32]p. incl. adverts. illus.
post tour.

1957-58 Test Tour (I. D. Craig)

2769 † **S.A. Marine Corporation Ltd.**
Australian cricket tour of South Africa 1957-58. [Cape Town], 1957. folder.
pre-tour.

1969-70 Test Tour (W. M. Lawry)

2770 † **Australië** in Suid-Afrika 1970. Johannesburg, Springbok Sport, [1970]. [24]p. illus. stats.
pre-tour; in Afrikaans.

1985-86 and 1986-87 Tours (K. J. Hughes)

2771 **Bryden, Colin,** *editor*
■ Aussies in South Africa: S.A. tour 1985-7: official tour brochure. Johannesburg, South African Cricket Union, [1985]. 72p. illus. (some col.) scores, stats.
some material in Afrikaans.
——*reissued 1986, before second tour.*

2772 **Francis, Bruce Colin**
■ 'Guilty': Bob Hawke or Kim Hughes? [Sydney, the Author], 1989. xviii, 377p. illus. (some col.) index.

2773 **Harte, Christopher John ('Chris')**
■ Cricket safari: a pictorial view of the Australian team in South Africa 1985-87. North Adelaide, Sports Marketing, 1987. [32]p. illus. stats.

2774 Seven Tests. North Adelaide, Sports Marketing, 1988.
■ [38]p. incl. covers, illus. scores.
cover sub-title: 'an album of the 'Tests' between South Africa and the Australians 1985-87'.
limited ed. of 200 signed and numbered copies.

2775 Two tours and Pollock: the Australians in South Africa
■ 1985-87. Adelaide; London, Sports Marketing, 1988. 320p. illus. scores, stats.
limited ed. of 1000 signed and numbered copies.

2776 **Harte, Christopher John ('Chris')** *and* **Hadfield,**
■ **Warwick**
Cricket rebels. Sydney, QB Books, 1985. 174p. illus. bibliog.
the planning behind the first tour; includes text of the Australian Cricket Board's player contract.

AUSTRALIA v WEST INDIES

2777 **Piesse, Ken** *and* **Main, Jim**
■ Calypso summers. Melbourne, Wedneil Publications, 1981. 210p. illus. (some col.) scores, stats.
cover sub-title: 'a history of Australia - West Indies Test cricket'.

AUSTRALIAN TOURS TO THE WEST INDIES

1984 Test Tour (K. J. Hughes)

2778 **Benson** and Hedges Test series: West Indies v Australia. Kingston, Communication Consultants, 1984. 44p. incl. adverts. illus.
pre-tour.

2779 **Justin, Augustus**
Welcome to Mindoo Phillip Park. St Lucia, Lithographic Press, 1984. illus. scores.
souvenir brochure commemorating Australia's visit to St Lucia in April 1984.

2780 **Mathias, Richard Watson**
Great moments in Test matches: Australia - West Indies. Kingston, the Author, [1984]. 32p. incl. adverts. illus.
pre-tour.

2781 **Nation, Fitzroy,** *editor*
Know your cricketers. Kingston, Atlantic Productions, [1984]. 40p. incl. adverts. illus.
pre-tour.

AUSTRALIAN TOURS TO NEW ZEALAND

1877-78 Australian XI Tour (D. W. Gregory)

2782 **[Reynolds, P. E.]**
■ The Australian cricketers' tour through Australia, New Zealand and Great Britain in 1878. [Ewell], J. W. McKenzie, 1980. [x], [ii], 94p. frontis. illus.
facsimile reprint of 'Padwick I' 5255 with a new introduction and frontispiece.
limited ed. of 150 numbered copies.

1884 Tasmanian Team Tour

2783 † **'One of the team',** *pseud.* **[Davies, John George?]**
Trip of the Tasmanian cricketing team to New Zealand, 1884. Hobart, the Mercury, 1884. 35p. scores, stats.
post tour.

1905 Australian XI Tour

2784 † **Australia** v Auckland, Feb 10, 11, & 13, 1905. [Auckland, Auckland Cricket Association, 1905]. 20p. incl. adverts. illus.

1920-21 Australian XI Tour (V. S. Ransford)

2785 † **Australia** v Ashburton, Ashburton Domain ... March 23
■ & 24, 1921: official scoring card. [Christchurch], H. E. Lawrence, [1921]. [8]p. incl. adverts. illus. diagrs.

1981-82 Test Tour (G. S. Chappell)

2786 **Brittenden, Richard Trevor ('Dick')** *and* **Cameron,**
■ **Donald John**
Test series '82: the Australian cricket tour of New Zealand. Wellington etc., Reed, 1982. [vi], 152p. illus. scores, stats.

2787 **New Zealand Cricket Council**
■ Rothmans series: Australia in New Zealand, February - March 1982. The Council, [1982]. 64p. col. illus. stats.
pre-tour.

1985-86 Test Tour (A. R. Border)

2788 **New Zealand Cricket Council**
The official New Zealand Cricket Council cricket guide: a full preview of the season's events including the Rothmans series Australia in New Zealand. [Auckland], Harvard Sports Marketing, 1985? 56p. col. illus. stats.

AUSTRALIAN TOURS TO PAKISTAN

1988-89 Test Tour (A. R. Border)

2789 **Wat, Charlie**
■ The 1988 Australian touring team. Prahran (Vic.), Cricket Stats Publications, 1988. [80]p. stats.
limited ed. of 50 signed and numbered copies; pre-tour.

AUSTRALIAN TOURS TO SRI LANKA

1981 Tour (K. J. Hughes)

2790 **Board of Control for Cricket in Sri Lanka**
■ Australian cricket tour of Sri Lanka 1981. [Colombo, the Board, 1981]. [32]p. incl. adverts. illus. stats.
pre-tour.

1982-83 Test Tour (G. S. Chappell)

2791 **Board of Control for Cricket in Sri Lanka**
■ Australian cricket tour of Sri Lanka 1983: official souvenir ... [Colombo, the Board, 1983]. 44p. incl. adverts. illus. stats.
pre-tour.

OTHER AUSTRALIAN TOURS

1952 Jack Chegwyn's Australian XI Tour to Hong Kong

2792 † **Hongkong Cricket League**
Souvenir programme in honour of the visit of Jack Chegwyn's Australian XI. The League, 1952. 28p. incl. adverts. illus.
pre-tour; 8-18 Oct. 1952.

1978 Bermuda Tour

2793 † **Bermuda Cricket Board of Control**
■ Australians here! Bermuda tour - May 1978. Bermuda, the Board, 1978. [12]p. incl. covers, illus. score.
pre-tour.

1983 Young Australia to Zimbabwe

2794 **Zimbabwe Cricket Union**
■ Zimbabwe vs Young Australia. [Harare], the Union, [1983]. 24p. incl. adverts. illus.
pre-tour brochure for two one-day matches, one 3-day match and one 4-day match, March/April 1983.

1985 Young Australia to Zimbabwe

2795 **Zimbabwe Cricket Union**
■ Zimbabwe vs. Young Australia. Harare, the Union, 1985. 36p. incl. adverts. illus.
pre-tour brochure for three one-day matches and two 3-day matches, Sep./Oct. 1985.

1986 New South Wales to Zimbabwe

2796 **Zimbabwe Cricket Union**
Zimbabwe vs. New South Wales. Harare, the Union, 1986. 44p. incl. adverts. illus.
pre-tour brochure for four one-day matches and two 3-day matches, March/April 1986.

1987 New South Wales to Zimbabwe

2797 **Zimbabwe Cricket Union**
Zimbabwe vs. New South Wales at Harare Sports Club. Harare, the Union, 1987. 46p. incl. adverts. illus.
pre-tour brochure for three one-day matches and two 3-day matches, Sep. 1987.

WORLD SERIES CRICKET

2798 † **All** England law reports 1978, vol. 3. Butterworths,
■ 1978. [x], 1248p.
pp. 449-512 contain the High Court judgement in the case of Greig v Insole concerning the banning of players contracted to World Series cricket.

2799 **Barrett, Norman,** *editor*
■ 'I was there': 20 great sporting memories from the writers of *The Daily Telegraph* and *The Sunday Telegraph*. Telegraph Publications, 1985. 158p. illus. score.
includes 'The Packer revolution' by Tony Lewis pp.85-90.

2800 **Bonney, Bill**
Packer and televised cricket. (Media papers no. 2). Broadway (N.S.W.), New South Wales Institute of Technology, 1980. 27p. bibliog.

2801 **Burrowes, Sydney Ignatius,** *editor*
Neal & Massy World Series Cricket 1979 Caribbean tour: WSC Australians vs WSC West Indians February - April 1979. Kingston, World Series Cricket Caribbean, 1979. 68p. incl. adverts. illus. stats.
pre-tour.

AUSTRALIAN WOMEN'S TOURS

1976 Tour to the West Indies

2802 † **Caribbean Women's Cricket Federation**
Inaugural Test series: West Indies vs Australia, May 1-17, 1976. Kingston, the Federation, [1976]. 40p. incl. adverts. illus.
pre-tour.

1987 Tour to England

2803 **Lawrence, Bridgette** *and* **Salmon, Carol,** *editors*
■ Women's cricket 50th jubilee Test tour: England v Australia - 1987 tour brochure. Women's Cricket Association, 1987. 28p. incl. covers, illus. stats.
pre-tour; celebrates 50th anniversary of first Australian tour to England.

2804 **Middlesex Women's Cricket Association**
■ Middlesex W.C.A.: Australia. [The Association, 1987]. [8]p. illus.
'Middlesex W.C.A. welcomes the Australian touring team 1987'.

INTERNATIONAL CRICKET - SOUTH AFRICA and ZIMBABWE

GENERAL

2805 **Bradshaw, Tony,** *compiler*
■ S.A. cricket goes international. Durban, Masprint, 1983. 32p. illus. (some col.) scores, stats.

2806 A **century** of South Africa in Test & international
■ cricket: 1889-1989, a tribute in words and pictures. Johannesburg, Jonathan Ball Publishers, 1989. [vi], 90p. illus. (some col.) stats.

2807 **Eriksen, Ronnie**
■ A view from the dressing room: the memoirs of a cricket manager. Knysna (Cape Province), Amorique, 1989. xii, 220p. illus. (some col.)
includes accounts of visits by touring sides between 1973 and 1986.

2808 **Greyvenstein, Chris,** *compiler*
Great Springbok cricket Tests: 100 years of headlines, a cricket centenary scrapbook. Cape Town, Don Nelson, 1989. 71p. illus.
facsimile reproductions of newspaper reports.

2809 **Ronayne, Michael Peter,** *compiler*
■ Test cricket tours: South Africa. (Test cricket tours: no. 4). [Norwich, the Author], 1987. 48p. illus. maps. stats.
includes information on cancelled tours to England 1970 and to Australia and New Zealand 1971-72.

2810 **Van Vuuren, Jan,** *editor*
■ Centenary of South Africa's greatest Springbok cricketers 1889-1989. Johannesburg, Goods Galore in association with the South African Cricket Players' Association, 1989. 94p. col. illus. stats.

SOUTH AFRICAN TOURS TO ENGLAND

1924 Test Tour (H. W. Taylor)

2811 † **South African Cricket Association**
South African cricket team 1924 list of matches. [Johannesburg, 1924]. [4]p. folder.
pocket folder issued to team members.

1935 Test Tour (H. F. Wade)

2812 † **Visit** of the Springbok cricket Test team to England 1935. Cape Town?, Union Castle Line, 1935. [16]p. illus.
pre-tour.

1947 Test Tour (A. Melville)

2813 **Arlott, [Leslie Thomas] John**
■ Two summers at the Tests: England v South Africa 1947; England v Australia 1948. Pavilion Books, 1986. viii, 320p. illus. scores, stats.
composite ed. of 'Gone to the cricket' ('Padwick I' 5355) and 'Gone to the Test match' ('Padwick I' 5078) with a new introduction by the author.

OTHER SOUTH AFRICAN TOURS

1967 South African Schools to England

2814 † **South** African Schools overseas cricket tour, England, July 1967. South African Schoolboys' Cricket Overseas Tour Fund Committee, 1967. 8p. illus.

1971 South African Country Cricket Association to Argentina

2815 † **Argentine Cricket Association**
South African Country Cricket Association tour December 1971. [Buenos Aires, the Association, 1971]. [24]p. incl. adverts. illus.
pre-tour.

ZIMBABWE TOURS

1983 Tour to Sri Lanka

2816 **Board of Control for Cricket in Sri Lanka**
Zimbabwe cricket tour of Sri Lanka 1983. [Colombo, the Board, 1983].
pre-tour.

1985 Mashonaland Country Districts Tour to New Zealand

2817 **Mashonaland Country Districts Winter Cricket Association**
Tour to New Zealand 13th March - 12th April, 1985. The Association, 1985.
pre-tour; brochure containing reports and scorecards also notified.

INTERNATIONAL CRICKET - WEST INDIES

GENERAL

2818 † **50** golden years of West Indies Test cricket. [Bridgetown], Magpub Limited, [1978]. 391p. incl. adverts. illus. scores, stats.

2819 **Dalrymple, Henderson**
50 great West Indian Test cricketers. Hansib, 1983. xxii, 281p. illus. stats.

2820 **Foster, William Alred Amos**
A stage for victory ... drama at Sabina. Kingston, Zodiac Worldwide International Co., 1985. 36p. illus.

2821 † **Inniss, Erlyn**
West Indies Test cricket and its social implications. (Caribbean Studies project). University of the West Indies, 1978. [v], 29p. *typescript.*

2822 **Jones, Brunell**
Cricket pepper pot. [Port of Spain?, the Author, 1980]. [i], 108p. incl. adverts. illus. scores.
includes West Indies tour to India, 1978-79; West Indies v Australia WSC Supertests 1979; Prudential World Cup 1979; Australia v West Indies and England 1979-80; West Indies in New Zealand 1980.

2823 **Lawrence, Bridgette**
Diamond jubilee of Westindian Test cricket, 1928-1988. Hansib, 1988. 80p. illus.

2824 **Lawrence, Bridgette** with **Scarlett, Reg O.**
100 great Westindian Test cricketers from Challenor to Richards. Hansib, 1988. 231p. illus. stats.

2825 **Mathias, Richard Watson**
Great moments for West Indies Test players. Kingston, the Author, 1985. 40p. incl. adverts. illus.

2826 **Ronayne, Michael Peter,** *compiler*
Test cricket tours: West Indies. (Test cricket tours: no. 5). [Wymondham (Norfolk), the Author], 1984. 96p. illus. maps. stats.
to Feb. 1984.

WEST INDIES TOURS TO ENGLAND

2827 **Lockwood, Richard David**
The West Indians at Edgbaston: a statistical review. [Birmingham], the Author, [1984]. [18]p. scores, stats.

1963 Test Tour (F. M. Worrell)

2828 **Ross, Alan**
West Indies at Lord's; drawings by Lawrence Toynbee. Constable, 1986. 104p. illus. diagrs. scores, stats.
new ed. of 'Padwick I' 5435.

1980 Test Tour (C. H. Lloyd)

2829 **Hayter, Reginald James,** *editor*
The official West Indies tour brochure England, 1980. Ashurst (Kent), *The Cricketer International*; London, *Sportsworld*, 1980. 48p. illus. (some col.) stats.
sponsored by Red Stripe Marketing Company; pre-tour.

2830 **Test** match pictorial: England's historic battles with the West Indies. Mirror Group Newspapers, 1980. [48]p. col. illus. scores, stats.
pre-tour.

1982 Young West Indies to England

2831 **Agatha** Christie under 19 Test series: England v West Indies 1982. [National Cricket Association], 1982. [15]p. illus.
pre-tour.

1984 Test Tour (C. H. Lloyd)

2832 **Beaumont, William Blackledge ('Bill')**
Bill Beaumont's sporting year: looking in on the best of British sport. Stanley Paul, 1984. 160p. illus.
includes 1984 Lord's Test match pp. 96-107.

2833 **Cozier, Tony,** *compiler*
West Indies cricket tour of United Kingdom 1984. Maidstone, South Eastern Newspapers [for] *Jamaican Weekly Gleaner*, 1984. 40p. incl. covers and adverts. illus (some col.) stats.
pre-tour.

1988 Test Tour (I. V. A. Richards)

2834 **Alexander, Brian,** *editor*
England v West Indies. Esher, Alexander Publishing, 1988. 50p. incl. adverts. illus. (mostly col.) stats.
'Sports year 88' special souvenir guide; pre-tour.

2835 **Blumberg, Michael,** *editor*
West Indies cricket tour of England 1988 official tour souvenir. *Cricket World* for West Indies Cricket Board of Control, [1988]. 48p. illus. (some col.) scores, stats.
pre-tour.

2836 **Eagar, Patrick** *and* **Ross, Alan**
West Indian summer: the Test series of 1988. Hodder and Stoughton, 1988. 112p. illus. (some col.) scores.

2837 **Lemmon, David Hector,** *editor*
Official 1988 tour guide. Test & County Cricket Board, 1988. 70p. illus. (mostly col.) stats.
sponsored by Red Stripe; incorporating 'Cricket '88'; pre-tour.

WEST INDIES TOURS TO AUSTRALIA

1979-80 Test Tour (C. H. Lloyd)

2838 **Frindall, William Howard ('Bill')**
Frindall's score book volume VI: Australia v West Indies and England 1979-80. Queen Anne Press, 1980. 120p. illus. scores, stats.

2839 **Martin-Jenkins, Christopher Dennis Alexander**
Cricket contest 1979-80: the post-Packer Tests. Queen Anne Press, 1980. [ix], 181p. illus. scores, stats.

2840 **Partington, Jennifer,** *editor*
Test cricket. Dee Why West (N.S.W.), Summit Books, 1980. 112p. illus. (some col.) scores, stats.
on cover: 'Australia vs England and the West Indies'; post tour.

2841   Tyson, Frank Holmes
■   War or peace. Ashburton (Vic.), Garry Sparke and
         Associates, 1980. 159p. illus. scores, stats.

1981-82 Test Tour (C. H. Lloyd)

2842   Alkins, Albert
         West Indies down under. Port of Spain, Imprint
         Caribbean, 1982? 72p. illus.
         post tour?

2843   Benaud, Richard ('Richie')
■   Test cricket. Sydney, Lansdowne Press, 1982. 128p.
         col. illus. scores, stats.
         post tour.

2844   Benson and Hedges Test series official book 1981-82:
■   Australia, Pakistan, West Indies. Pymble (N.S.W.),
         Playbill, 1981. 52p. illus. (some col.)
         pre-tour.

2845   McGilvray, Alan David, *editor*
■   Pakistan, West Indies in Australia 1981-82. Sydney,
         Australian Broadcasting Commission, 1981. 104p. illus.
         (some col.) diagr. stats.
         pre-tour.

2846   National Nine television tour guide 1981-82. Waterloo
■   (N.S.W.), Murray, 1981. 112p. incl. covers. illus.
         (some col.) diagr. stats.
         pre-tour.

2847   Piesse, Ken, *editor*
■   Cricket fantastic. Melbourne, *Cricketer*, [1981]. 72p.
         illus. (one col.) stats.
         cover sub-title: 'A 1981-82 tour guide featuring Australia,
         West Indies & Pakistan'; pre-tour.

1984-85 Test Tour (C. H. Lloyd)

2848   Australia cricket pictorial magazine. Surry Hills
■   (N.S.W.), Wayward Publishing Company, 1984. [16]p.
         fold-out, col. illus. stats.
         pre-tour.

2849   Benson and Hedges Test series official book 1984-85:
■   Australia v West Indies. Pymble (N.S.W.), Playbill,
         1984. 62p. illus. (some col.)
         pre-tour.

2850   Boxall, Brad, *editor*
■   TNT Roadfast tour guide. Waterloo (N.S.W.), Federal
         Publishing, [1984]. 116p. incl. covers illus. (some col.)
         stats.
         pre-tour.

2851   Cadigan, Neil, *editor*
         Australian cricket tour guide. Waterloo (N.S.W.),
         Federal Publishing, 1984. 98p. illus. (some col.)

2852   Cozier, Tony *and* **Jameson, Neil**
■   Supercat's summer: the inside story of how the Windies
         decimated Australian cricket ... and how we spun back.
         Melbourne, ACCA Sporting Publications, 1985. 103p.
         illus. (some col.) scores, stats.

2853   McGilvray, Alan David, *compiler and editor*
■   West Indies tour of Australia 1984-85. Sydney, ABC
         Enterprises for Australian Broadcasting Corporation,
         1984. 104p. illus. (some col.) diagr. scores, stats.

2854   Mengel, Noel, *editor*
■   West Indies down under: world champs' Australian tour
         1984-85. Waterloo (N.S.W.), Federal Publishing
         Company, [1984]. 52p. incl. covers, illus. (some col.)
         stats.
         pre-tour.

2855   National Nine tour guide: showdown for the crown,
■   1984-85: Australia, West Indies, Sri Lanka. Sydney,
         PBL Marketing, 1984. 80p. illus. (some col.) stats.
         pre-tour.

2856   Piesse, Ken, *editor*
■   Calypso crusaders: West Indies in Australia, 1984-85.
         Melbourne, Newspress, [1984]. 72p. incl. covers, illus.
         (some col.) stats.
         'Cricketer' magazine guide; pre-tour.

2857   Test of the best: Benson and Hedges test series -
■   Australia v West Indies 1984-85 official pictorial review.
         Sydney, PBL Marketing, 1985. 84p. incl. covers, col.
         illus. scores.
         post tour.

2858   West Indies cricket pictorial magazine. Surry Hills
■   (N.S.W.), Wayward Publishing Company, 1984. [16]p.
         fold-out, col. illus. stats.
         pre-tour.

1988-89 Test Tour (I. V. A. Richards)

2859   Australian *cricket* summer down under 1988-89.
■   Darlinghurst (N.S.W.), Mason Stewart Publishing,
         [1988]. 132p. illus. diagr. stats.
         pre-tour.

2860   Benson and Hedges official Test book: Australia v West
■   Indies 1988-89. Pymble (N.S.W.), Playbill, [1988]. 68p.
         incl. covers. illus. (mostly col.) stats.
         pre-tour.

2861   Maxwell, Jim, *editor*
■   ABC cricket book. Sydney, Australian Broadcasting
         Corporation, 1988. 112p. illus. (some col.) stats.
         on cover: 'West Indies in Australia 1988-89'; pre-tour.

2862   National Nine tour guide 1988-89: Australia, West
■   Indies, Pakistan. Pymble (N.S.W.), Playbill, [1988].
         80p. illus. (some col.) stats.
         pre-tour.

2863   Piesse, Ken, *editor*
■   Supermen of cricket: the 1988-89 *Cricketer* tour guide.
         Melbourne, Syme Magazines, [1988]. 76p. incl. covers,
         illus. (some col.) stats.
         pre-tour.

2864   Wat, Charlie
■   The 1988-89 West Indian cricketers. Prahran (Vic.),
         Cricket Stats Publications, 1988. [116]p. stats.
         Test and limited over statistical records of 1988-89 West
         Indian tourists.
         limited ed. of 75 signed and numbered copies.

2865   The West Indies in Australia 1988-89: an alternate guide.
■   Prahran (Vic.), Cricket Stats Publications, 1988. [ii],
         54p. stats.
         limited ed. of 75 signed and numbered copies.

WEST INDIES TOURS TO SOUTH AFRICA

1983 and 1983-84 Tours (L. G. Rowe)

2866   Crowley, Brian Mathew
■   Calypso cavaliers: West Indian cricketers in South
         Africa; the story of the 1983 tour. Cape Town,
         Ibbotson, 1983. 64p. illus. (some col.) scores, stats.

2867 **Crowley, Brian Mathew,** *compiler and editor*
■ Calypso whirlwind: the second West Indies XI tour of
South Africa 1983/84. Cape Town, Ibbotson, [1984].
48p. illus. (mostly col.) scores, stats.
post tour.

2868 Greet the Windies 1983/84: official South African
■ Cricket Union brochure. Cape Town, Ibbotson, 1983.
80p. incl. adverts. col. illus. scores, stats.
pre-tour.

2869 **Souvenir** brochure West Indies XI tour of South Africa
■ '83. [South African Cricket Union, 1983]. [12]p. incl.
covers and adverts. illus. stats.
pre-tour.

WEST INDIES TOURS TO NEW ZEALAND

1986-87 Test Tour (I. V. A. Richards)

2870 **New Zealand Cricket Council**
The official New Zealand Cricket Council cricket guide:
a full preview of the season's events: Rothmans series,
West Indies in New Zealand. [Auckland], Harvard
Sports Marketing for the Council, 1986. 48p. illus.
(mostly col.) stats.

WEST INDIES TOURS TO INDIA

1948-49 Test Tour (J. D. C. Goddard)

2871 † **Board of Control for Cricket in India**
Official souvenir of West Indies cricket team 1948-49.
[New Delhi], the Board, 1948. 66p. incl. adverts. illus.
scores, stats.
pre-tour.

1983-84 Test Tour (C. H. Lloyd)

2872 **Gavaskar, Sunil Manohar**
■ Runs 'n ruins. Calcutta etc., Rupa, 1984. 161p. illus.
post tour.

2873 **Gavaskar, Sunil Manohar,** *editor*
India vs West Indies 1983-84. Calcutta, Aajkaal
Publishers, 1983. 72p. incl. covers and adverts. illus.
stats.
pre-series; 'Indian Cricketer' souvenir.

2874 **Haridass, C. K.**
■ West Indies in India 1983: silver jubilee number.
Madras, the Author, 1983. 276p. incl. adverts. illus.
diagr. stats.
pre-tour.

WEST INDIES v PAKISTAN

2875 **Syed Khalid Mahmood**
■ The Caribbean challenge: a history of Pakistan -
W.Indies matches. Karachi, Liliana International, 1989.
100p. incl. covers & adverts. illus. stats.

OTHER WEST INDIES TOURS

1974 Barbados to Bermuda

2876 † **Shell** Shield champions from Barbados: June 7th to June
20th. Hamilton (Bermuda), Southampton Rangers
Sports Club, [1974]. 28p. incl. adverts. illus. stats.

1989 to Canada

2877 The **United** Way cricket match: the West Indies v the
Rest of the World at the Skydome, Toronto, Canada,
November 5th 1989. Ontario, Sun Controlled Ventures
Ltd., [1989]. 36p. illus. stats.
*the first cricket match played under cover in an indoor
stadium.*

INTERNATIONAL CRICKET - NEW ZEALAND

GENERAL

2878 **Devlin, Peter**
■ Victorious 80's. Auckland, MOA Publications, 1987. 227p. illus. (some col.) stats.

2879 **Hutchins, Graham**
■ The Howarth years: ten New Zealand cricket victories 1980-1985. Dunedin, John McIndoe, 1985. 142p. illus. scores.

2880 **Neely, Donald Owen** *and* **King, Richard P.**
■ Men in white: the history of New Zealand international cricket 1894-1985; statistics by Francis Payne. Auckland, MOA Publications, 1986. 656p. illus. (some col.) scores, stats. bibliog.
——de luxe limited ed. of 1200 numbered copies, 1986.

2881 **Ronayne, Michael Peter,** *compiler*
■ Test cricket tours: New Zealand. (Test cricket tours: no. 8). [Wymondham (Norfolk), the Author], 1984. 60p. maps, stats.
to February 1984.

2882 **Taylor, Mark**
■ White knights: 100 centuries of New Zealand Test cricket. Taita (Wellington), Imprint Books, 1987. 294p. illus. scores, stats.
description of the first 100 centuries scored for New Zealand in Test cricket, 1930-87.

NEW ZEALAND TOURS TO ENGLAND

1927 Tour (T. C. Lowry)

2883 † **New Zealand Cricket Limited**
■ Report and balance sheet of English tour 1927. Christchurch, N. Z. Cricket Ltd., 1928. [4]p. folded sheet.

1983 Test Tour (G. P. Howarth)

2884 **Eagar, Patrick** *[and]* **Ross, Alan**
■ Kiwis and Indians: Test, World Cup and Championship cricket in England, 1983. Collins, 1983. 128p. illus. scores.

1986 Test Tour (J. V. Coney)

2885 **Crowe, Dave**
■ The Crowe report: inside story of the English tour 1986. Auckland, South Sea Visuals, [1986]. 92p. illus. (some col.) scores, stats.

2886 **Eagar, Patrick** *[and]* **Ross, Alan**
■ Summer of suspense: 1986 Cornhill Test series: England v India and New Zealand. Haywards Heath, Partridge Press, 1986. 95p. illus. (some col.) scores.

2887 **Lemmon, David Hector,** *editor*
■ Official 1986 tour guide. Test & County Cricket Board, 1986. 48p. illus. (mostly col.) stats.
incorporating 'Cricket '86'; pre-tour.

1987 New Zealand Young Cricketers to England

2888 **British** Telecom Phonecard under 19 series: England v
■ New Zealand 1989. [Test and County Cricket Board], 1989. [16]p. illus.
pre-tour; 27 July - 11 Sep.

NEW ZEALAND TOURS TO AUSTRALIA

1980-81 Test Tour (G. P. Howarth)

2889 **Australian Cricket Board**
■ Official Test cricket book: the summer of 1980/81. [Jolimont (Vic.), the Board, 1980]. [52]p. illus. (mostly col.)
pre-tour.

2890 **Benaud, Richard ('Richie')**
■ Test cricket. Sydney, Lansdowne Press, 1981. 128p. illus. (some col.) scores, stats.
review of 1980-81 series and Sheffield Shield.

2891 **McGilvray, Alan David,** *editor*
■ New Zealand & India in Australia 1980-81. Sydney, Australian Broadcasting Commission, 1980. 88p. illus. (some col.) diagr. stats.
pre-tour.

2892 **National** Nine television tour guide 1980-81.
■ Rushcutters Bay (N.S.W.), Modern Magazines, [1980]. 112p. incl. covers, illus. (some col.) stats.
pre-tour.

1985-86 Test Tour (J. V. Coney)

2893 **Australia** v India/New Zealand. Surry Hills (N.S.W.),
■ Wayward Publishing Company, 1985. [16]p. fold-out. col. illus. stats.
cover title: 'Australia cricket pictorial magazine'; pre-tour.

2894 **Australian Broadcasting Corporation**
■ New Zealand and India tour of Australia 1985-86. Sydney, ABC Enterprises for the Corporation, 1985. 96p. illus. (some col.) stats.
pre-tour.

2895 **Benson** and Hedges Test series official book 1985-86:
■ double trouble. Pymble (N.S.W.), Playbill, 1985. 62p. illus. (some col.) stats.
pre-tour.

2896 **Double** trouble: 1985-86 media guide. Pymble (N.S.W.),
■ Playbill, [1985]. 82p. illus. stats.

2897 **Mengel, Noel,** *editor*
■ Summer down under 1985-86. Waterloo (N.S.W.), Federal Publishing, [1985]. 132p. incl. covers, illus. (some col.) stats.
pre-tour.

2898 **National** Nine tour guide 1985-86: double trouble:
■ Australia v India v New Zealand. Sydney, PBL Marketing, 1985. 80p. illus. (some col.)
pre-tour.

2899 Piesse, Ken, *editor*
■ The big test: *Cricketer* magazine 1985-86 tour guide. Melbourne, Newspress, [1985]. 72p. incl. covers, illus. (one col.) stats.
pre-tour.

1987-88 Test Tour (J. J. Crowe)

2900 Benson and Hedges Test & World Series Cup: Australia
■ v New Zealand v Sri Lanka: official book 1987-88. Pymble (N.S.W.), Playbill, [1987]. 68p. incl. covers, col. illus. stats.
pre-tour.

2901 Mengel, Noel, *editor*
■ *Australian cricket* 1987-88 guide. Darlinghurst (N.S.W.), Mason Stewart Publishing, [1987]. 132p. incl. covers. illus. (some col.) scores, stats.

2902 National Nine tour guide 1987-88: Australia v New
■ Zealand v Sri Lanka. Pymble (N.S.W.), Playbill, [1987]. 78p. illus. (mostly col.) stats.
pre-tour.

2903 Piesse, Ken, *editor*
■ Kangas & Kiwis. Melbourne, Newspress, 1987. 72p. incl. covers, illus. (some col.) stats.
a 'Cricketer' magazine special.

1989-90 Test Tour (J. G. Wright)

2904 Boxall, Brad, *editor*
■ Benson and Hedges official Test souvenir program 1989/90. Alexandria (N.S.W.), Federal Publishing Company, 1989. 84p. incl. covers & adverts. col. illus.
pre-tour.

2905 National Nine tour guide 1989/90. Alexandria (N.S.W.),
■ Federal Publishing Company, [1989]. 100p. incl. covers & adverts. illus. (some col.) stats.
pre-tour.

2906 Maxwell, Jim, *editor*
■ ABC cricket book: Pakistan, Sri Lanka and New Zealand in Australia 1989-90. Crows Nest (N.S.W.), Australian Broadcasting Corporation, 1989. 112p. illus. (some col.) diagr. stats.
pre-tour.

2907 Piesse, Ken, *editor*
■ The best v the rest. Melbourne, Syme Magazines, [1989]. 76p. incl. covers. illus. stats.
'Cricketer' guide; pre-tour.

2908 Wat, Charlie
■ The 1989-90 New Zealanders' Test records. Prahran (Vic.), Cricket Stats Publications, 1989. 50p. stats.
Test records of 1989-90 New Zealand tourists.
limited ed. of 50 signed and numbered copies.

NEW ZEALAND v INDIA

2909 Bala, Vijayan
Test cricket records: India vs New Zealand and Sri Lanka. New Delhi, Konark, 1988. xii, 99p. illus. scores, stats.
issued prior to New Zealand tour to India, Nov.-Dec. 1988.

2910 Lutra, Vikas
India & New Zealand in Test cricket. 1988?
in Hindi.

NEW ZEALAND TOURS TO INDIA

1988 Test Tour (J. G. Wright)

2911 New Zealand cricket team tour of India, 1988. Wellington, New Zealand Ministry of Foreign Affairs' Overseas Publicity Section, 1988. 9p. illus.

2912 Vijayakar, Pradeep, *editor*
■ New Zealand in India 1988. Bombay, Theodore Braganza for the Marine Sports Publishing Division, [1988]. 80p. illus. (some col.) stats.
pre-tour.

OTHER NEW ZEALAND TOURS

1924 Tour to Fiji

2913 † New Zealand cricketers' tour in Fiji official programme Easter 1924. Suva, Patipi Press, [1924]. [24]p.

NEW ZEALAND WOMEN'S TOURS

1984 Tour to England

2914 Women's Cricket Association
■ St George Assurance international women's cricket 1984. [The Association, 1984]. [24]p. incl. adverts. illus. stats.
pre-tour.

INTERNATIONAL CRICKET - INDIA

GENERAL

2915 Mathur, Lalit Narain
■ Compendium of Indian Test cricket. Udaipur, [the Author, 1989]. xv, 368p. illus. stats.

2916 Portraits of Indian Test cricketers. [with 2 page foreword
■ insert by P. M. Rungta]. Delhi, Himanshu Publications, 1985. viii, 261p. illus. scores, stats. index.

2917 Mukherjee, Sujit
■ Playing for India. Sangam Books, 1988. [xi], 267p. illus. index.
expanded and updated ed. of 'Padwick I' 5594.

2918 Ramchand, Partab
■ Great feats of Indian cricket. Calcutta etc., Rupa, 1984. vii, 215p. illus. scores.

2919 Ronayne, Michael Peter, *compiler*
■ Test cricket tours: India. (Test cricket tours: no. 6). [Wymondham (Norfolk), the Author], 1984. 76p. maps. stats.
to May 1983.

2920 Sundaresan, P. N.
■ Navle to Kirmani: story of Indian stumpers. Madras, Free India Publications, 1985. viii, 86p. incl. adverts. illus.

2921 Not so unofficial. Madras, Free India Publishing House,
■ 1980. 122p. illus. scores.
covers all unofficial Tests played by India.

2922 Sundaresan, P. N., *editor*
■ India in Test cricket 1932-1980: golden jubilee edition. Bombay, Board of Control for Cricket in India, 1980. [viii], 203p. illus. scores, stats.

2923 Vaidya, Sudhir
■ Know your cricketers. Calcutta etc., Rupa, 1981. viii, 105p. illus. stats.
statistical record of all Indian Test players.

LIMITED OVERS

2924 Ansari, Khalid A. H., *editor*
■ Champions of one-day cricket. (Wills 'Tribute to Excellence' series). Hyderabad (India), Orient Longman, 1985. 72p. illus. (some col.) stats.

INDIAN TOURS TO ENGLAND

1982 Test Tour (S. M. Gavaskar)

2925 Eagar, Patrick *[and]* **Ross, Alan**
■ Summer of the all-rounder: Test and championship cricket in England 1982. Collins, 1982. 128p. illus. scores.

2926 Grant, Graeme, *editor*
■ The official tour brochure, England 1982. Keith Prowse & Co., 1982. 68p. incl. covers and adverts. illus. (some col.) stats.
pre-tour.

1986 Test Tour (R. N. Kapil Dev)

2927 Eagar, Patrick *[and]* **Ross, Alan**
■ Summer of suspense: 1986 Cornhill Test series: England v India and New Zealand. Haywards Heath, Partridge Press, 1986. 95p. illus. (some col.) scores.

2928 Lemmon, David Hector, *editor*
■ Official 1986 tour guide. Test & County Cricket Board, 1986. 48p. illus. (mostly col.) stats.
incorporating 'Cricket '86'; pre-tour.

INDIAN TOURS TO AUSTRALIA

1968-69 Indian Schoolboys to Australia

2929 † **Australian** tour by All-India schoolboys' cricket team 1968-1969. [Australian Schoolboys' Cricket Club, 1968]. 12p. incl. adverts.
pre-tour.

1980-81 Test Tour (S. M. Gavaskar)

2930 Amarnath, Nanik Bhardwaj ('Lala')
■ Indo-Aussie '81. New Delhi, the Author for M/S Starlet Publications, [1980]. 86p. illus. scores, stats.
pre-tour.

2931 Australian Cricket Board
■ Official Test cricket book: the summer of 1980/81. [Jolimont (Vic.), the Board, 1980]. [52]p. illus. (mostly col.)
pre-tour.

2932 Benaud, Richard ('Richie')
■ Test cricket. Sydney, Lansdowne Press, 1981. 128p. illus. (some col.) scores, stats.
review of 1980-81 series and Sheffield Shield.

2933 McGilvray, Alan David, *editor*
■ New Zealand & India in Australia 1980-81. Sydney, Australian Broadcasting Commission, 1980. 88p. illus. (some col.) diagr. stats.
pre-tour.

2934 National Nine television tour guide 1980-81.
■ Rushcutters Bay (N.S.W.), Modern Magazines, [1980]. 112p. incl. covers. illus. (some col.) stats.
pre-tour.

1985-86 Test Tour (R. N. Kapil Dev)

2935 Amarnath, Nanik Bhardwaj ('Lala')
■ India in Australia 1985-86. New Delhi, the Author for Lala's Enterprises / Starlet Publications, [1985]. [50]p. incl. adverts. illus. stats.
pre-tour.

2936 Australia v India/New Zealand. Surry Hills (N.S.W.),
■ Wayward Publishing Company, 1985. [16]p. fold-out, col. illus. stats.
cover title: 'Australia cricket pictorial magazine'; pre-tour.

2937 Australian Broadcasting Corporation
■ New Zealand and India tour of Australia 1985-86. Sydney, ABC Enterprises for the Corporation, 1985. 96p. illus. (some col.) stats.
pre-tour.

2938 **Benson** and Hedges Test series official book 1985-86:
■ double trouble. Pymble (N.S.W.), Playbill, 1985. 62p.
illus. (some col.) stats.
pre-tour.

2939 **Double** trouble: 1985-86 media guide. Pymble (N.S.W.),
■ Playbill, [1985]. 82p. illus. stats.

2940 **Mengel, Noel,** *editor*
■ Summer down under 1985-86. Waterloo (N.S.W.),
Federal Publishing, [1985]. 132p. incl. covers, illus.
(some col.) stats.
pre-tour.

2941 **National** Nine tour guide 1985-86: double trouble:
■ Australia v India v New Zealand. Sydney, PBL
Marketing, 1985. 80p. illus. (some col.)
pre-tour.

2942 **Pervez Qaiser, S.**
■ India's tour of Australia 1985-86. Delhi, Al-Faisel
Publications, 1985. 32p. illus. stats.
pre-tour.

2943 **Piesse, Ken,** *editor*
■ The big test: *Cricketer* magazine 1985-86 tour guide.
Melbourne, Newspress, [1985]. 72p. incl. covers, illus.
(one col.) stats.
pre-tour.

INDIAN TOURS TO THE WEST INDIES

1971 Test Tour (A. L. Wadekar)

2944 † **Board of Control for Cricket in India**
India team's tour of West Indies 1971. [Bombay], the
Board, 1971. 17p. illus.
pre-tour.

1976 Test Tour (B. S. Bedi)

2945 † **Gray, Hubert,** *editor*
West Indies vs India in Jamaica: official souvenir
programme. Kingston, Jamaica Cricket Association,
1976. 68p. incl. adverts. illus. scores, stats.
pre-tour.

1983 Test Tour (R. N. Kapil Dev)

2946 **Benson** and Hedges Test series, February - April 1983:
■ West Indies vs India ... Kingston, Communications
Consultants, [1983]. 44p. incl. adverts. illus. stats.
*brochure for India visit to Jamaica to play Jamaica and
the West Indies, February 1983.*

2947 **Cozier, Tony,** *editor*
■ Benson & Hedges Test series 1983: West Indies vs India:
official souvenir programme. Christ Church (Barbados);
Walton-on-Thames (Surrey), Caribbean
Communications, [1983]. 32p. illus. (some col.) stats.
pre-tour.

1989 Test Tour (D. B. Vengsarkar)

2948 **Gibbes, Michael,** *editor*
Cable and Wireless Test series 1989: West Indies vs
India. San Fernando (Trinidad), Cable and Wireless
Ltd., [1989]. 32p. illus. stats.
pre-tour.

2949 **Kumar, Rajesh** *and* **Gordon, Everard**
India in the West Indies 1989. Port of Spain, Coripress,
1989. illus. stats.
pre-tour.

2950 **Nation, Fitzroy,** *editor*
The Indian challenge. Kingston, J. P. Publications,
1989. 48p. incl. adverts. illus. scores, stats.
pre-tour?

INDIAN TOURS TO PAKISTAN

1982-83 Test Tour (S. M. Gavaskar)

2951 **Munir Hussain,** *editor*
■ Wills Series cricket: Pakistan vs India tour guide 1982-83.
[Karachi], Pasban Co-operative Finance Corporation,
1982. 46p. col. illus. diagr. stats.

2952 **Pakistan** vs India autograph book: cricket series -
■ 1982'83. [1982]. [40]p. col. illus.

2953 **Qamar Ahmed**
■ Testing time. Karachi, Liberty Book Stall, 1983. [iv],
40p. illus. scores, stats.
post series.

INDIA v SRI LANKA

2954 **Bala, Vijayan**
Test cricket records: India vs New Zealand and Sri
Lanka. New Delhi, Konark, 1988. xii, 99p. illus.
scores, stats.

INDIAN TOURS TO SRI LANKA

1985-86 Test Tour (Kapil Dev)

2955 **Board of Control for Cricket in Sri Lanka**
■ India - Sri Lanka cricket tour, Aug - Sept 1985: official
souvenir ... [Colombo, the Board, 1985]. [40]p. incl.
adverts. illus. stats.
pre-tour.

1985-86 Test Tour (R. N. Kapil Dev)

2956 **Seneviratne, Sarath**
Cricatoon portraits in ink to mark a historic tour.
Colombo, ANCL, [1985]. 20p. incl. covers, illus.

OTHER INDIAN TOURS

1981 India to Fiji

2957 **Fiji Cricket Association**
■ India cricket tour, March 21-27, 1981. [The Association,
1981]. 60p. illus.
pre-tour.

1984 Young India to Zimbabwe

2958 **Zimbabwe Cricket Union**
Zimbabwe vs. Young India: Harare Sports Club.
Harare, the Union, 1984. 32p. incl. adverts. illus.
*pre-tour brochure for 2 one day matches, 1 three day
match and 1 four day match, March 1984.*

INDIAN WOMEN'S TOURS

1986 Tour to England

2959 **Official** tour brochure: England v India. [Women's
■ Cricket Association, 1986]. [20]p. incl. adverts. illus.
stats.
pre-tour; includes brief history of Indian women's cricket.

INTERNATIONAL CRICKET - PAKISTAN

GENERAL

2960 **Abid Ali Kazi** and **Masood Hamid**, *compilers and editors*
■ The Pakistan book of Test cricket, 1952-53 to 1982.
Karachi, Abid Ali Kazi, 1982. [ix], 193p. scores, stats.

2961 **Aziz Rehmatullah, A.**, *compiler and editor*
■ 35 years of Pakistan Test cricket. Karachi, Mohammed
Moin Aziz, [1987]. 224p. incl. adverts. illus. scores,
stats.
*includes full scorecards of all Pakistan Tests to 31 Aug.
1987.*
rev. and updated ed. of 'Padwick I' 5661-2.

2962 **Aziz Rehmatullah, A.**, *editor*
■ Pakistan Test cricketers. Karachi, the Author, 1982?
96p. illus. stats.

2963 **Pakistan** cricket year book: a book of cricket records.
■ Karachi, Sports Publications. illus. (some col.) scores,
stats.
1980-81 ed. xiv, 521p. [1981] - *contains all Test
matches played by Pakistan.*
1982 ed. 186p. [1983] - *covers 1982-83 Pakistan season.*

2964 **Rashid Aziz** and **Afia Salam**, *editors*
■ Pakistan Test cricket. Karachi, Sportsworld
Publications. illus. scores, stats.
1982-83 and 1983-84 eds. pub.

2965 **Ronayne, Michael Peter**, *compiler*
■ Test cricket tours: Pakistan. (Test cricket tours: no. 7).
Wymondham (Norfolk), the Author, 1984. 68p. maps.
stats.
to Feb. 1984.

LIMITED OVERS

2966 **Ahsan A. Qureshi**, *editor*
■ The book of Pakistan's one-day internationals 1972-73 to
1986-87; statistics by Syed Rizwan Akhter. Karachi, the
Editor, [1987]. 288p. incl. adverts. illus. scores, stats.

2967 **Arshad Hasan Zaidi**, *editor*
■ Pakistan one-day international (sic). Karachi, n.p.,
1984. 79p. illus. scores, stats.

2968 **Bader, Nauman**, *compiler and editor*
■ Pakistan book of one-day internationals. Lahore,
Pakistan International Publishers, 1987. 177p. incl.
adverts. illus. scores, stats.
*cover title: 'Wills Pakistan book of one-day internationals
1973-87'.*

2969 **Wat, Charlie**
■ The Pakistan cricketers LOI. Prahran (Vic.), Cricket
Stats Publications, 1988. 52p. stats.
*international limited over career records of 1988-89
Pakistan tourists who played in Benson and Hedges series.
limited ed. of 75 signed and numbered copies.*

PAKISTAN TOURS TO ENGLAND

1971 Test Tour (Intikhab Alam)

2970 † **Husain, Sultan F.**
The fourth trip: a match-by-match tour record of the
1971 Pakistan cricket team in England. Lahore,
Sportimes, 1971. 168p. illus. scores, stats.

1982 Test Tour (Imran Khan)

2971 **Eagar, Patrick** *[and]* **Ross, Alan**
■ Summer of the all-rounder: Test and championship
cricket in England 1982. Collins, 1982. 128p. illus.
scores.

2972 **Grant, Graeme**, *editor*
■ The official tour brochure, England 1982. Keith Prowse
& Co., 1982. 68p. incl. covers and adverts. illus. (some
col.) stats.
pre-tour.

2973 **Shahzad Humayun** and **Masood Hasan**
■ Pakistan vs England 1982. Lahore, Cricket Writers'
Association, [1982]. [72]p. illus. (some col.) stats.

1987 Test Tour (Imran Khan)

2974 **Khadim Hussain Baloch**
■ Imran's summer of fulfilment: an account of the 1987
Pakistan cricket tour of England. [Dedham], the
Author, [1987]. [xi], 166p. illus. scores, stats.

2975 **Lemmon, David Hector**, *editor*
■ Official 1987 tour guide. Test & County Cricket Board,
1987. 48p. illus. (mostly col.) stats.
incorporating 'Cricket '87'; pre-tour.

2976 **Official** tour souvenir: Pakistan cricket tour of England,
■ 1987. Stroudgate Publications, 1987. [56]p. illus.
(some col.)
pre-tour.

PAKISTAN TOURS TO AUSTRALIA

1978-79 Test Tour (Mushtaq Mohammad)

2977 **Yallop, Graham Neil**
■ Lambs to the slaughter. New English Library, 1980.
174p. illus. scores, stats.
pbk. ed. of 'Padwick I' 5694-9.

1981-82 Test Tour (Javed Miandad)

2978 **Benaud, Richard ('Richie')**
■ Test cricket. Sydney, Lansdowne Press, 1982. 128p.
col. illus. scores, stats.
post tour.

2979 **Benson** and Hedges Test series official book 1981-82:
■ Australia, Pakistan, West Indies. Pymble (N.S.W.),
Playbill, 1981. 52p. illus. (some col.)
pre-tour.

2980 **McGilvray, Alan David,** *editor*
■ Pakistan, West Indies in Australia 1981-82. Sydney, Australian Broadcasting Commission, 1981. 104p. illus. (some col.) diagr. stats.
pre-tour.

2981 **National** Nine television tour guide 1981-82. Waterloo (N.S.W.), Murray, 1981. 112p. incl. covers. illus. (some col.) diagr. stats.
■ *pre-tour.*

2982 **Piesse, Ken,** *editor*
■ Cricket fantastic. Melbourne, *Cricketer*, [1981]. 72p. illus. (one col.) stats.
cover sub-title: 'a 1981-82 tour guide featuring Australia, West Indies & Pakistan'; pre-tour.

1983-84 Test Tour (Imran Khan)

2983 **Benson** and Hedges Test series official book 1983/84: Australia versus Pakistan: thunder down under. Pymble (N.S.W.), Playbill, [1983]. 64p. incl. covers, col. illus. stats.
■ *pre-tour.*

2984 **McGilvray, Alan David,** *editor*
Pakistan in Australia, 1983-84: ABC cricket book. Sydney, Australian Broadcasting Corporation, 1983. 88p. illus. (some col.) stats.
pre-tour.

2985 **National** Nine tour guide: thunder down under: Australia, Pakistan, West Indies. Sydney, PBL Marketing, 1983. 80p. illus. (some col.)
■

2986 **Piesse, Ken,** *editor*
■ Kings of cricket. Melbourne, *Cricketer*, [1983]. 72p. incl. covers, illus. diagrs. stats.
1983-84 tour guide featuring Australia, Pakistan and the West Indies; pre-tour.

2987 **Thunder** down under pictorial review. Sydney, PBL
■ Marketing, [1984]. 82p. col. illus. scores, stats.
cover sub-title: 'the Tests'; post tour.

1989-90 Test Tour (Imran Khan)

2988 **Boxall, Brad,** *editor*
■ Benson and Hedges official Test souvenir program 1989/90. Alexandria (N.S.W.), Federal Publishing Company, 1989. 84p. incl. covers & adverts. col. illus.
pre-tour.

2989 National Nine tour guide 1989/90. Alexandria (N.S.W.),
■ Federal Publishing Company, [1989]. 100p. incl. covers & adverts. illus. (some col.) stats.
pre-tour.

2990 **Maxwell, Jim,** *editor*
■ ABC cricket book: Pakistan, Sri Lanka and New Zealand in Australia 1989-90. Crows Nest (N.S.W.), Australian Broadcasting Corporation, 1989. 112p. illus. (some col.) diagr. stats.
pre-tour.

2991 **Piesse, Ken,** *editor*
■ The best v the rest. Melbourne, Syme Magazines, [1989]. 76p. incl. covers, illus. stats.
'Cricketer' guide; pre-tour.

2992 **Wat, Charlie**
■ The 1989-90 Pakistan cricketers in Australia. Prahran (Vic.), Cricket Stats Publications, 1989. [112]p. stats.
Test and international limited over records of 1989-90 Pakistani tourists.
limited ed. of 75 signed and numbered copies.

2993 Pakistan & Sri Lanka in Australia 1989-90: an alternate
■ guide. Prahran (Vic.), Cricket Stats Publications, 1989. 42p. stats.
limited ed. of 75 signed and numbered copies.

PAKISTAN TOURS TO NEW ZEALAND

1984-85 Test Tour (Javed Miandad)

2994 **Pakistan** in New Zealand 1985: Rothmans series.
■ Auckland, Harvard Sports Marketing, 1985. 56p. col. illus. stats.
pre-tour.

PAKISTAN TOURS TO THE WEST INDIES

1977 Test Tour (Mushtaq Mohammed)

2995 † **Gray, Hubert,** *editor*
West Indies vs Pakistan in Jamaica: official souvenir programme. Kingston, Jamaica Cricket Association, [1977]. 48p. incl. adverts. illus. stats.
pre-tour.

PAKISTAN TOURS TO INDIA

1952-53 Test Tour (A. H. Kardar)

2996 † *National Sports* India-Pakistan special. New Delhi,
■ Services Press, 1952. illus.
issue of 15 Oct. 1952, vol. 2 no. 10 largely concerned with forthcoming India-Pakistan series.

2997 † *Players' Magazine* souvenir of the Pakistan cricket tour
■ of India 1952-53. Calcutta, H. K. Dey for Players Association, Calcutta, 1952. [72]p. incl. covers and adverts. illus. scores, stats.
cricket number of 'Players' Magazine', vol. II, no. V, Dec. 1952.

1960-61 Test Tour (Fazal Mahmood)

2998 † **Cricket** souvenir: Pakistan vs India 1960-61. Bombay,
■ Maya Publications, [1960]. [32]p. incl. adverts. illus. stats.
pre-tour.

1979-80 Test Tour (Asif Iqbal)

2999 **Talati, Sudhir**
■ Glorious battle. Ahmedabad, Hemal Publication, 1980. 128p. illus. scores, stats.

1986-87 Test Tour (Imran Khan)

3000 **Amarnath, Nanik Bhardwaj ('Lala')**
India-Pakistan series 1987. Delhi, Starlet Publications, 1987. [68]p. incl. adverts. illus. stats.
pre-tour.

3001 **Bashir Khan**
Over to Bashir Khan: Pakistan in India, 1987: an eyewitness account of Pakistan 1987 cricket tour of India. Karachi, the Author, 1989. 230p. illus. scores, stats.

3002 **Bhupathy, D. R.,** *editor*
Pakistan tour of India 1987: souvenir. Madras, Bhupathy, 1987. [88]p. incl. adverts. illus. stats.
pre-tour.

3003 *Nai Duniya* cricket special. Indore, Nai Duniya. 1987. 8p. incl. adverts.
Hindi daily newspaper issue of 17 Jan. 1987.

PAKISTAN TOURS TO SRI LANKA

1985-86 Test Tour (Imran Khan)

3004 **Board of Control for Cricket in Sri Lanka**
■ Sri Lanka - Pakistan cricket tour, February - March 1986:
official souvenir ... [Colombo, the Board, 1986]. [44]p.
incl. adverts. illus. stats.
pre-tour.

INTERNATIONAL CRICKET - SRI LANKA

GENERAL

3005   Board of Control for Cricket in Sri Lanka
■   A reunion of Sri Lanka cricket internationals ... 4
November 1980. [Colombo, the Board, 1980]. 16p.

SRI LANKAN TOURS TO ENGLAND

1981 Tour (B. Warnapura)

3006   Sri Lanka U.K. tour 1981: grand cricket ball, 4th July
■   1981 ... Steering Committee U.K. for the Board of
Control for Cricket in Sri Lanka, 1981. [40]p. incl
adverts. illus. stats.
pre-tour.

SRI LANKAN TOURS TO AUSTRALIA

1987-88 Test Tour (R. S. Madugalle)

3007   **Benson** and Hedges Test & World Series Cup: Australia
■   v New Zealand v Sri Lanka: official book 1987-88.
Pymble (N.S.W.), Playbill, [1987]. 68p. incl. covers,
col. illus. stats.
pre-tour.

3008   **Mengel, Noel,** *editor*
■   *Australian cricket* 1987-88 guide. Darlinghurst (N.S.W.),
Mason Stewart Publishing, [1987]. 132p. incl. covers,
illus. (some col.) scores, stats.

3009   **National** Nine tour guide 1987-88: Australia v New
■   Zealand v Sri Lanka. Pymble (N.S.W.), Playbill, [1987].
78p. illus. (mostly col.) stats.
pre-tour.

1989-90 Test Tour (A. Ranatunga)

3010   **Australia** v Sri Lanka, Bellerive Oval, December 16-20
■   1989: commemorating the first Test cricket match to be
played in Tasmania. Hobart, Corporate
Communications (Tas.) for the Clarence City Council,
1989. [4]p. illus.

3011   **Boxall, Brad,** *editor*
■   Benson and Hedges official Test souvenir program
1989/90. Alexandria (N.S.W.), Federal Publishing
Company, 1989. 84p. incl. covers & adverts. col. illus.
pre-tour.

3012   National Nine tour guide 1989/90. Alexandria (N.S.W.),
■   Federal Publishing Company, [1989]. 100p. incl. covers
& adverts. illus. (some col.) stats.
pre-tour.

3013   **Maxwell, Jim,** *editor*
■   ABC cricket book: Pakistan, Sri Lanka and New Zealand
in Australia 1989-90. Crows Nest (N.S.W.), Australian
Broadcasting Corporation, 1989. 112p. illus. (some
col.) diagr. stats.
pre-tour.

3014   **Piesse, Ken,** *editor*
■   The best v the rest. Melbourne, Syme Magazines,
[1989]. 76p. incl. covers. illus. stats.
'Cricketer' guide; pre-tour.

3015   **Wat, Charlie**
■   The 1989-90 Sri Lankan touring team in Australia.
Prahran (Vic.), Cricket Stats Publications, 1989. 66p.
stats.
*Test and international limited over records of 1989-90 Sri
Lankan tourists.*
limited ed. of [75] signed and numbered copies.

3016   Pakistan & Sri Lanka in Australia 1989-90: an alternate
■   guide. Prahran (Vic.), Cricket Stats Publications, 1989.
42p. stats.
limited ed. of 75 signed and numbered copies.

SRI LANKAN TOURS TO SOUTH AFRICA

1982-83 Arosa Sri Lanka Tour (B. Warnapura)

3017   **Bassano, Brian Stanley,** *editor*
Cricket in South Africa: welcome Arosa Sri Lankans.
Port Elizabeth, S.A. Sporting Publications, [1982]. 20p.
col. illus.
pre-tour.

SRI LANKAN TOURS TO INDIA

1982-83 Test Tour (B. Warnapura)

3018   **Bhupathy, D. R.**
■   Sri Lanka tour of India 1982. [Madras], Bhupathy,
[1982]. [96]p. incl. adverts. illus. stats.
pre-tour.

INTERNATIONAL TEAMS

1962 Tour to Singapore

3019 † **Singapore Cricket Association**
Souvenir programme to commemorate the visit of the Commonwealth XI, 12th, 13th, 14th October 1962. The Association, [1962]. 52p. incl. adverts. illus. stats.
pre-tour.

1964 Tour to Far East

3020 † **E.W.** Swanton's Commonwealth XI visit to Hong Kong. Hong Kong, Hongkong Cricket League, 1964. 67p. incl. adverts. illus.

3021 † **E.W.** Swanton's Commonwealth XI visit to Malaysia 1964. Kuala Lumpur, Malayan Cricket Association, 1964. 72p. incl. adverts. illus.

1980 Tour to Kuwait

3022 **Kazi, M. K.,** *editor*
■ Younis Ahmed International XI cricket tour 1980 Kuwait souvenir. [Kuwait, 1980]. [48]p. incl. adverts. illus.
pre-tour.

1985 Tour to Cayman Islands

3023 **Fred** Trueman's International XI Cayman Islands cricket
■ tour November 1985: souvenir brochure. [8]p. incl. adverts. illus.
pre-tour.

CRICKET IN LITERATURE

ANTHOLOGIES

3024 Adams, Roger, *compiler*
Famous writers on cricket; with photographs by Patrick Eagar and Adrian Murrell. Partridge Press, 1988. 107p. illus.

3025 Allen, David Rayvern
Cricket's silver lining, 1864-1914: the 50 years from the birth of Wisden to the beginning of the Great War. Willlow Books, 1987. xi, 436p. illus. index.

3026 Arlott, [Leslie Thomas] John, *editor*
My favourite cricket stories. Peerage, 1986. 145p. illus. facsims.
new ed. of 'Padwick I' 5830-1.

3027 Ball, Peter *and* **Hopps, David**
The book of cricket quotations. Stanley Paul, 1986. 256p. illus. index.

3028 Berry, Scyld, *editor and compiler*
The Observer on cricket: an anthology of the best cricket writing. Unwin Hyman, 1987. xxi, 221p. illus. index.
——*pbk. ed.* Unwin, 1988.

3029 Bright-Holmes, John, *editor*
The joy of cricket. Secker & Warburg, 1984. xi, 276p. illus. (some col.)
——*pbk. ed.* Unwin, 1985.
——*reissued,* Peerage Books, 1986.

3030 Lord's & commons: cricket in novels and stories. Andre Deutsch, 1988. xi, 352p.
includes revised updated checklist of 'cricket in fiction' compiled by Gerald Brodribb (see also 'Padwick I' 0006).

3031 Byrne, John, *editor*
Modern sports writers: a collection of prose. Batsford Educational, 1982. 173p. indices.
cricket pp. 9-44.

3032 Cooper, Leo *and* **Synge, Allen,** *compilers*
Beyond the far pavilions. Pavilion Books, 1986. x, 158p.
——*pbk. ed.* Arrow, 1987.

3033 Davie, Michael *and* **Davie, Simon,** *editors*
The Faber book of cricket. Faber and Faber, 1987. xxxii, 366p. index.

3034 Dexter, Edward Ralph *and* **Lemmon, David Hector**
A walk to the wicket. George Allen & Unwin, 1984. 221p. illus.

3035 Egan, Jack, *editor*
World cricket digest. Woollahra (N.S.W.), C. P. Publishing. *quarterly.* illus. scores, stats.
/vol. 2, no. 1, Nov. 1982; no. 2, March 1983; no. 3, June 1983/
new series of 'Padwick I' 5881-1.

3036 World Cup cricket 1983. Woollahra (N.S.W.), Jack Egan and David Moeller, 1983. 116p. incl. covers. illus.
'a "World Cricket Digest" publication'.

3037 Engel, Matthew, *editor*
The Guardian book of cricket. Pavilion Books, 1986. 320p. index.
——*pbk. ed.* Penguin, 1986.

3038 † Forget me not: a Christmas and New Year's present for MDCCCXXIX; edited by Frederick Schoberl. R. Ackermann, [1828].
annual anthology.
this ed. contains 'Lost and won', a cricket story by Mary Russell Mitford, pp. 217-228.

3039 Frewin, Leslie Ronald, *editor*
The boundary book: a Lord's Taverners' miscellany of cricket: second innings. Pelham Books, 1986. 384p. illus.
sequel to 'Padwick I' 5847.

3040 Green, Benny, *editor*
Benny Green's cricket archive. Pavilion Books, 1985. xiv, 257p.
rev. ed. of 'Padwick I' 5848-1.

3041 Gregory, Kenneth, *compiler*
In celebration of cricket. Pavilion Books, 1987. xiii, 336p. illus. bibliog. index.
reprinted ed. of 'Padwick I' 5848-2.

3042 Gregory, Kenneth, *[editor]*
From Grace to Botham: fifty master cricketers from 'The Times'. Times Books, 1989. 353p. illus. diagrs. scores, index.
reports from 'The Times' celebrating outstanding individual performances.

3043 Lee, Christopher
Nicely nurdled, sir! Elm Tree Books, 1986. viii, 103p. illus. bibliog.
cover sub-title: 'two centuries in prose and poetry'.
——*new enlarged ed.* Bantam Press, 1988.

3044 Lemmon, David Hector, *editor*
The Wisden book of cricket quotations. Queen Anne Press, 1982. 224p. illus. indices.

3045 Liddle, Barry, *compiler*
Dictionary of sports quotations. Routledge & Kegan Paul, 1987. [224]p. index.
some cricket.

3046 Looker, Samuel Joseph, *compiler*
Cricket anthology. Tunbridge Wells (Kent), Spellmount, 1988. xxix, 225p.
new ed. of 'Padwick I' 5851.

3047 Meyer, Michael, *editor*
Summer days: writers on cricket. Eyre Methuen, 1981. 255p.
——*pbk. ed.* Oxford University Press, 1983.

3048 P. J. M., *pseud. [i.e.* **Mills, Penny J.]** *editor*
Cricket capers. Michael Joseph, 1985. 48p. illus. (mostly col.)

3049 Peskett, Roy, *compiler*
The best of cricket: an anthology of stories, reports and quotes. Hamlyn, 1982. 239p. scores.

3050 Ross, Alan, *editor*
The Penguin cricketer's companion. Penguin Books, 1981. xix, 582p. index.
pbk. ed. of 2nd. ed. of 'Padwick I' 5867.

3051 Synge, Allen *and* **Cooper, Leo,** *compilers*
■ Tales from far pavilions. Pavilion Books, 1984. x, 161p.
——*pbk. ed.* Arrow, 1985.

3052 Williams, Marcus, *editor*
■ Double century: 200 years of cricket in *The Times*. Willow Books, 1985. xi, 621p. illus. scores, index.
——*new ed. comprising first half of book with title 'Double century: cricket in The Times, vol. 1, 1785-1934,* Pavilion Books, 1989.

ADULT FICTION

3053 Alington, Adrian Richard
■ The amazing Test match crime. Hogarth Press, 1984. [vii], 248p.
reprinted ed. of 'Padwick I' 5925 with a new introduction by Brian Johnston.

3054 † Andom, R.
We three and Troddles: a tale of London life. Tylston & Edwards, [1894]. [viii], 242p. illus.
ch. xvii: 'Our cricket club'.

3055 Bingham, Stella
■ Charters & Caldicott. British Broadcasting Corporation, 1985. 180p.
much cricket; based on the BBC TV serial by Keith Waterhouse.

3056 Carr, James Joseph Lloyd
■ A season in Sinji. Penguin Books, 1985. 192p.
new ed. of 'Padwick I' 5931.

3057 Castle, Dennis
Run out the Raj. Constable, 1986. 283p.
new ed. of 'Padwick I' 5982-1.

3058 Caudwell, Sarah
□ The shortest way to Hades. Century, 1984. 207p.
——*pbk. ed.* Penguin, 1986.

3059 Couch, Anthony
■ Memoirs of a twelfth man: the recollections of J. A. P. Withers of Stripford Rural Cricket Club. Ramsbury (Wilts.), Crowood Press, 1984. [x], 140p.
——*pbk. ed.* Unwin, 1985.

3060 Crampsey, Robert Anthony
■ The run-out. Glasgow, Richard Drew Publishing, 1985. 224p.

3061 † de Selincourt, Hugh
■ The cricket match. Oxford, Oxford University Press, 1979. xiv, 194p.
new ed. of 'Padwick I' 5932 with an introduction by Benny Green.

3062 Digance, Richard
■ Run out in the country. Macmillan, 1983. [vi], 203p.

3063 † Gillett, Leslie
■ The apprentice: a novel. Victor Gollancz, 1978. 238p.
much incidental cricket.

3064 † Hamilton, Bruce
■ Pro. Pocket Books (G.B.) Ltd., 1950. 246p.
pbk. ed. of 'Padwick I' 5936.

3065 Hardcastle, Michael
■ The gigantic hit. Pelham Books, 1982. [vi], 122p.

3066 Hardwick, Mollie
■ Willowwood. Eyre Methuen, 1980. 317p.
——*pbk. ed.* 1981.

3067 † Harker, Lizzie Allen
Concerning Paul and Fiametta. Edward Arnold, 1906. xii, 252p.
ch. xx: 'Fiametta's test cricket match'.
——*another ed.* John Murray, 1923.

3068 † Herriot, James
Vet in harness; drawings by Larry. Michael Joseph, 1974. 253p. illus.
cricket, pp. 163-77.
——*pbk. ed.* Pan, 1975.

3069 Hone, Joseph
■ The valley of the fox. Secker & Warburg, 1982. [vii], 309p.
includes account of cricket match in the Cotswolds, pp. 267-271.
——*pbk. ed.* Hamlyn, 1984.

3070 Jenkins, Alan C.
■ A village year. Exeter, Webb & Bower, 1981. 160p. illus. (some col.) bibliog. index.
evocation of village life featuring fictional cricket match pp. 98-104.

3071 Marqusee, Mike
■ Slow turn. Michael Joseph, [1986]. 219p.
——*pbk. ed.* Sphere, 1988.

3072 † Marshall, Bruce
George Brown's schooldays. Constable, 1946. viii, 224p.
cricket pp. 115-119, 124-128 and other references.

3073 Meynell, Lawrence
■ Hooky and the prancing horse. Macmillan, 1980. 223p.

3074 † Miller, Ian
School tie. Newnes, 1935. 311p.
cricket pp. 83-94.

3075 Miller, Ian
■ Wet wickets and dusty balls: a diary of a cricketing year. Hamish Hamilton, 1986. [vi], 186p.

3076 † Mitton, Geraldine Edith
The gifts of enemies. A. & C. Black, 1900. vi, 368p.
much incidental cricket.

3077 Norman, Barry Leslie
■ Sticky wicket. Hodder and Stoughton, 1984. 208p.
——*pbk. ed.* Coronet, 1985.

3078 Parker, John
■ First wicket down. W. H. Allen, 1987. 223p.

3079 † Test time at Tillingfold. Weidenfeld and Nicolson, 1979.
■ 176p.
——*pbk. ed.* 1987.

3080 Tillingfold's tour. W. H. Allen, 1986. 189p.
■

3081 Petri, David
■ Horton's Test. Heathfield, Rotabook Publishing, [1983]. vii, 248p.

3082 † Richards, W. E.
Mother Hubbard. John Gifford, 1945. 292p.
cricket pp. 91-96 and other references.

3083 Richardson, Robert
■ Bellringer Street. Victor Gollancz, 1988. 183p.
murder mystery with much incidental cricket.

3084 **Rushton, William George**
■ W.G. Grace's last case or the war of the worlds - part two. Methuen, 1984. 288p. illus.
——*pbk. ed.* 1985.

3085 **Shaw, Stanley**
■ Sherlock Holmes at the 1902 fifth Test; illustrations by John Lawrence. W. H. Allen, 1985. 160p. score.
——*pbk. ed.* Star, 1986.

3086 **Smith, A. C. H.**
■ Extra cover. Weidenfeld & Nicolson, 1981. [viii], 152p.

3087 † **Swinnerton, Frank Arthur**
English maiden: parable of a happy life. Hutchinson, [1946]. 336p.
ch. vii: 'The cricket match'.

3088 **Synge, Allen**
■ Bowler, batsman, spy. Weidenfeld & Nicolson, 1985. viii, 176p.

3089 Hunters of the lost Ashes. Weidenfeld & Nicolson,
■ 1987. [vi], 178p.

3090 The voyage of the *Colin Cowdrey*. Weidenfeld &
■ Nicolson, 1989. 192p.

3091 **Wheeler, Paul**
■ Bodyline: the novel. Faber and Faber, 1983. 211p.
——*pbk. ed.* 1984.

3092 **Williams, Peter Stanley**
■ The Pantybont challenge. Bognor Regis, New Horizon, 1984. 141p.

3093 † **Young, Francis Brett**
Mr Lucton's freedom. Heinemann, 1940. viii, 456p.
cricket pp. 330-340.

3094 † My brother Jonathan. Heinemann, 1928. 595p.
cricket pp. 20-23 and 130-140.

SHORT STORIES

3095 **Archer, Jeffrey Howard**
■ A quiver full of arrows. Hodder and Stoughton, 1980. 190p.
includes 'The century' pp. 101-110.

3096 **Bainbridge, Beryl**
■ Mum and Mr Armitage: selected stories. Duckworth, 1985. 144p.
includes 'The longstop', pp. 41-49.

3097 † **Countryside** tales from *Blackwood*. William Blackwood & Sons, 1946. [viii], 610p.
contains: 'An innings apiece' by Edward Shaw.

3098 **de Selincourt, Hugh**
▣ The game of the season. Oxford, Oxford University Press, 1982. xiii, 121p.
new ed. of 'Padwick I' 6108 with an introduction by John Arlott.

3099 † **Gee, Herbert Leslie**
Five hundred tales to tell again. Epworth Press, 1955. viii, 278p.
contains four cricket stories.

3100 † **'Grainger, Dan'l',** *pseud. [i.e. Gass, David J.]*
Down-along talks. (Somerset Folk series, no. 6). Folk Press, 1922. iv, 82p.
'The cricket club', pp. 53-61.

3101 **Harris, Herbert,** *editor*
■ John Creasey's crime collection 1981: an anthology by members of the Crime Writers' Association. Victor Gollancz, 1981. 189p.
includes 'Caught and bowled, Mrs Craggs' by H.R.F. Keating, pp. 83-94.

3102 † **'Hodger, Barney',** *pseud.*
Down whoäme. (Somerset Folk series, no. 15). Folk Press, 1924. 115p.
includes 'The village v the manor'.

3103 **Hornung, Ernest William**
■ The complete short stories of Raffles - the amateur cracksman. Souvenir Press, 1984. 475p.
'Gentlemen and players' pp. 76-93.
'The return match' pp. 139-153.

3104 † **Maerens**
Beardwell, and other tales. 1869. vi, 160p.
contains 'Mr Bungray's cricket bat'.

3105 † **Percival, Alfred**
Somerset neighbours. Mills and Boon, 1921. 251p.
includes 'The keeper's catch'.

3106 † **Read, John**
Cluster-o'-vive: stories and studies of old-world Wessex. (Somerset Folk series, no. 11). Folk Press, 1923. vii, 207p.
contains 'King willow, pp. 71-82.
——*story subsequently appeared in 'Farmer's joy',* Nelson, 1949.

3107 † **Symons, Julian Gustave**
Murder! murder. Collins, 1961. 190p.
includes 'Test match murder'.

CHILDREN'S FICTION

3108 † **Adams, Henry Cadwallader**
The Indian boy. Routledge, Warne & Routledge, 1865. 153p.
cricket in chs. 2 and 3.

3109 † The **adventures** of Cousin Bruin. Henry Potter & Co., 1891. 74p.
'Cousin Bruin plays at cricket', pp. 39-45.

3110 † **Ashton, Deryck**
■ Change for Chalwood. Victory Press, 1960. 120p.
ch. 4: 'The cricket match'.

3111 † **Avery, [Charles] Harold**
An armchair adventurer. Simpkin, Marshall & Co., 1903. vii, 176p.
short stories; 'A cricket match' pp. 76-88.

3112 † **Bateman, Robert** *and* **Marrat, Nicholas**
■ A book of boy's stories. Hamlyn, 1964. 360p. illus.
includes 'Match with a catch', pp. 309-321.

3113 **Bond, Ruskin**
■ Cricket for the crocodile; illustrated by Barbara Walker. Julia MacRae Books, 1986. 48p. illus.

3114 † **Bowled** out. (Nelson Lee Library, no. 210). 1919. 24p.

3115 † **'A Boy',** *pseud.*
■ Fifteen: diary of the teens. Fortune Press, [1938]. 300p.
scattered cricket references.

3116 † Twelve: a diary of the preteens. Fortune Press, [1948].
■ 204p.
scattered cricket references.

3117 † **Brazil, Angela**
The girls of St Cyprian's. Blackie & Son, [1914]. 288p.
St Cyprian's versus Templeton in ch. VIII.

3118 † **Brooks, Edwy Searles**
All his own fault. (Nelson Lee Library, no. 103). 1923.
44p.

3119 † Fenton's cricket sensation! (Nelson Lee Library, no.
516). 1925. 40p.

3120 † The monster library of complete stories. Amalgamated
Press, 1925-27.
issued in 19 parts; part 9, 'The boy from the 'Bush''.

3121 † Playing for the first. (Nelson Lee Library, no. 518). 1925.
40p.

3122 † A schoolgirl's word of honour. (Nelson Lee Library, no.
474). 1924. 28p.

3123 † St Frank's Test match! (Nelson Lee Library, no. 517).
1925. 40p.

3124 † The three substitutes. (Nelson Lee LIbrary, no. 520).
1925. 40p.

3125 † **Brown, Roy**
■ Cover drive. Abelard-Schuman, 1979. 86p.

3126 † **Bruce, Dorita Fairlie**
Dimsie moves up. Oxford University Press, 1921. 254p.
cricket in chs. v, xvii and xxvi.

3127 † The new house captain. Oxford University Press, 1928.
288p.
ch. xiv: 'An inter-house match'.

3128 † That boarding school girl. Oxford University Press,
1925. 160p.
cricket in chs. vi, xxvii and xxviii.

3129 † **Buckeridge, Anthony**
■ Jenning's little hut. Collins, 1954. 255p.
ch. 2: 'Last wicket stand', ch. 15: 'Mr Wilkins hits a six'.

3130 † Rex Milligan reporting. Lutterworth Press, 1961. 191p.
cricket in chs. 3, 4, 13 and 14.

3131 † Take Jennings for instance. Collins, 1958. 256p.
■ *cricket in chs. 8 and 9.*

3132 † **Buckley, Horace Henry Clement**
What sort of chap? illustrated by Gordon Browne and R.
Wheelwright. Wells, Gardner & Co., 1913. x, 230p.
illus.
ch. xii: 'The cricket match'.

3133 † **Butcher, James Williams**
The making of Treherne. C. H. Kelly, 1911. xiii, 264p.
ch. xvi: 'Cricket in Wales'.

3134 **Cadogan, Mary Rose,** *compiler*
■ Chin up chest out Jemima! Haslemere, Bonnington
Books, 1989. 192p. illus.
*celebration of the schoolgirl's story containing 'Fiona the
funk (or the girl who wouldn't)' pp. 150-153, and other
incidental cricket.*

3135 **Childs, Rob**
■ Sandford in to bat. Blackie, 1985. 110p.

3136 † **Clarke, B. A.**
Minnows and tritons. Ward Lock & Co., 1903. 293p.
illus.
*contains two stories with cricket, 'An attack of the blues'
and 'Minnows and tritons'.*

3137 † **Cleaver, Hylton Reginald**
The term of thrills. Frederick Warne & Co., 1931. 288p.
cricket in chs. ix, xvi and xxiii.

3138 **Coren, Alan**
■ Arthur v. the rest; illustrated by John Astrop. Robson
Books, 1981. 64p. illus.
——*pbk. ed.* Puffin, 1983.

3139 † **Cule, William Edward**
The captain's fags: a story of school life. Sunday School
Union, [1901]. 176p. illus.
cricket in ch. xiii.

3140 **Cunliffe, John Arthur**
■ Postman Pat plays for Greendale; pictures by Joan
Hickson. (A Postman Pat easy reader). Andre Deutsch /
Hippo Books, 1986. [32]p. col. illus.

3141 † The **demon** cricketer. (Nelson Lee Library, no. 314).
1921. 32p.

3142 **Drake, Tony**
Playing it right. Puffin, 1981. 123p.
pbk. ed. of 'Padwick I' 6202-1.

3143 † **Drummond, V. H.**
■ Tidgie's innings. Faber, 1947. [64]p. col. illus.

3144 † The **duffer** of St Frank's. (Nelson Lee Library, no. 209).
■ 1919. 24p. illus.

3145 † **Eady, K. M.**
■ Two Barchester boys: a tale of adventure in the Malay
States; with illustrations by Wal Paget. S. W. Partridge
& Co., [1905]. 330p. illus.
cricket in ch. iii.

3146 **English, David**
■ Bunbury tales; pictures by Jan Brychta. Arthur Barker,
1986. 30p. illus. (some col.)

3147 The Bunburys bun noel; pictures by Jan Brychta.
■ Fontana, 1989. [32]p. col. illus.

3148 The Bunburys down under; pictures by Jan Brychta.
Arthur Barker, 1987. 28p. col. illus.

3149 The Bunburys play ball; pictures by Jan Brychta. Collins,
■ 1989. [32]p. col. illus.

3150 The Bunburys: a winter's tail; pictures by Jan Brychta.
■ Arthur Barker, [1988]. 30p. illus. (some col.)

3151 The Bunburys: Rajbun's story; pictures by Jan Brychta.
■ Collins, 1989. [32]p. col. illus.

3152 Bunnybados; pictures by Jan Brychta. Arthur Barker,
■ 1986. 30p. illus. (some col.)

3153 Excalibat; pictures by Jan Brychta. Arthur Barker, 1987.
30p. col. illus.

3154 The tail of two kitties; pictures by Jan Brychta. Collins,
■ 1989. [32]p. col. illus.

3155 † **Farrar, Frederic William**
The three homes. Cassell, 1911. 389p. frontis. (col.) illus.
——*originally pub. with sub-title: 'a tale for fathers and sons' under the pseudonym F. T. L. Hope 1873.*
——*reprinted with additional preface 1896.*
some cricket content.

3156 † **Forster, William J.**
Frank Heaton's dilemma: and other stories. Robert Culley, [1899]. 128p.
ch. 1: 'A big score!'.

3157 † **Frith, Henry**
The captains of cadets: a story of the rule of Britannia; illustrated by D. Knowles. Griffin, Farran & Co., [1889]. 223p. illus.
cricket in chs. i and ii.

3158 † **Girvin, Brenda**
Little heroine: the story of a last medal. S. W. Partridge & Co., [1912]. 169p. illus.
ch. xiv: 'A game of cricket'.

3159 † The **golden** image. (Nelson Lee Library, no. 313). 1921. 32p.

3160 † **Goodyear, Robert Arthur Hanson**
The captain of Glendale. S. W. Partridge & Co., 1935. 256p.
cricket in chs. vii, viii, xv and xvi.

3161 † The **Greenway** heathens. Nisbet & Co., [1922]. 287p.
cricket in chs. xx and xxiv.

3162 † The new boy at Baxtergate. A. & C. Black, 1926. vi, 250p.
cricket in chs. vii, xvii, xviii and xxi.

3163 † **Gordon, [James] Geoffrey**
Caught out! (The Boys Friend Library, no. 471). n.d. 64p.

3164 **Greenhalgh, Angela**
■ Kee-wee plays cricket. (Kiwi-tales series); illustrations by Raymond Wilson. The Author, 1983. [32]p. incl. covers, col. illus.

3165 † **Hadath, [John Edward] Gunby**
The outlaws of St Martyn's; or, the school on the downs. S. W. Partridge & Co., [1915]. 384p.
cricket in chs. xxii and xxvi.

3166 † The shepherd's guide; with drawings by John Drever. C. & J. Temple, 1949. 236p. illus.
ch. vi: 'The match of the season'.

3167 † **Hammond, Walter Reginald**
Captain of Claverhouse. (The Boys Friend Library, no. 293). 1931. 64p.

3168 **Hardcastle, Michael**
■ Caught out; illustrated by Trevor Parkin. Methuen, 1983. 112p. illus.
——*pbk. ed.* Magnet, 1985.

3169 † **Haydon, Arthur Lincoln**
Shandy of the shell: a school story. Warne, 1931. vii, 88p.
ch. 1: 'At Lord's'.

3170 † Stand fast, Wymondham! Warne, [1928]. 280p.
cricket in chs. vii and xiii.

3171 † **Home, Andrew**
■ Out of bounds: a series of school stories; with illustrations by Harold Copping. W. & R. Chambers, [1901]. [viii], 348p. illus.
'Well caught' pp. 129-142.

3172 **Hunt, Nan**
When Ollie spat on the ball; illustrated by Mark David. Sydney, Collins, 1985. 29p. col. illus.

3173 **Ireson, Barbara,** *editor*
■ In a class of their own: school stories. Faber, 1985. 148p.
includes 'Seymour's century' by Jan Mark pp. 49-58.
——*pbk. ed.* Puffin, 1987.

3174 † **Irvine, Amy Mary**
The girl who was expelled. S. W. Partridge & Co., [1920]. 315p.
ch. xxix: 'The bowler'; ch. xxxvi: 'A great match'.

3175 † **Judd, Alfred**
Forrester's fag. Blackie & Son, [1926]. 208p.
cricket in chs. ix and xii.

3176 † Poddy's progress. Collins, [1928]. 318p. col frontis.
■ *part 3, ch vi: 'Cricket and a crisis'.*

3177 † **Leighton, Robert**
The cleverest chap in the school; illustrated by P. A. Staynes. Jarrold & Sons, [1910]. 274p. illus.
ch. vi: 'Tony Mumford's substitute'.

3178 † **Lind, Anton**
Riot at Altonbury. Sampson Low, [1937]. 252p.
cricket in four chs.

3179 † **Lisle, Margaret**
One glorious term. Sampson Low, [1939]. v, 250p.
cricket in chs. x, xi, xx and xxi.

3180 † **MacIlwaine, Herbert C.**
■ The white stone; illustrated by G. D. Rowlandson. Wells, Gardner, Darton & Co., 1906. viii, 408p. illus.
cricket in ch. xvi.

3181 † **Macleod, Kathleen Millar**
Grafton days: stories of Scots schoolboys. Pickering & Inglis, [1932]. 128p. illus.
ch. iv: 'Willie Gordon - the slacker'.

3182 † The **match** of destiny. (Nelson Lee Library, no. 316). 1921. 32p.

3183 † **Merry** Merrilees: a great cricket story. (Adventure Vest
■ Pocket Library, no. 3). n.d. 52p. incl. covers. frontis.

3184 † **Moore, Dorothea**
Tam of Tiffany's: a school story. S. W. Partridge & Co., [1918]. 384p.
cricket in chs. xv, xviii and xxvi.

3185 † **Mossop, Irene**
Barbara black-sheep. Warne, [1932]. vi, 90p.
cricket pp. 39-61.

3186 † The fifth at Cliff House. Warne, [1934]. 256p.
cricket in chs. xii and xv.

3187 † **Mowbray, John,** *pseud.* [*i.e.* **Vahey, John George Haslette**]
Feversham's brother. Cassell, 1929. 215p.
cricket in ch. xi.

3188 † **Norling, Winifred**
The daring of Daryl. Ward Lock & Co., 1948. 224p.
cricket in ch. 7.

3189 † **Oldmeadow, Katherine Louise**
The fortunes of Jacky. The Childrens Press, n.d. 188p.
ch. 9: 'Village cricket'.

3190 **Owen, Gareth**
■ The final test; illustrated by Paul Wright. Victor
Gollancz, 1985. 139p. illus.

3191 † **Parker, Mary Louise**
Fifth form quins. Sampson Low, [1938]. vi, 242p.
ch. xix: 'Cricket'.

3192 † 'Miss Spitfire' at school. Sampson Low, 1931. vi, 218p.
cricket in chs. v and vi.

3193 **Parkinson, Michael**
■ The Woofits play cricket. Collins Colour Cubs, 1980.
[48]p. col. illus.
based on the ITV television series 'The Woofits'.

3194 † **Phillips, John Sydney**
Malay adventure; illustrated by Stanislaus Brien.
Nelson, 1937. viii, 231p. illus.
ch. ii: 'The cricket match'.
——*pbk. ed.* Penguin, 1955.

3195 **Phipson, Joan**
■ The grannie season; illustrated by Sally Holmes. Hamish
Hamilton, 1985. 94p. illus.

3196 † **Plunket, Irene Arthur Lifford**
Sally Cocksure: a school story. Humphrey Milford,
1925. 160p.
cricket in chs. 3, 9 and 10.

3197 † **Poole, Michael,** *pseud. [i.e. Poole, Reginald Heber]*
Barnston's big year. Blackie, [1931]. 256p.
cricket in chs. iii, iv and vii.

3198 † **Protheroe, Ernest**
The redemption of the duffer. Robert Culley, [1909].
336p. illus.
ch. xxvi: 'No butter-fingers'.

3199 † **Pyke, Lilian Maxwell**
Max the sport. Ward Locke & Co., 1916. 250p
cricket in chs. iii, v and xvii.

3200 † **Randolph, Richard**
Brother pros. (The Boys Friend Library, no. 717). 1924.
64p.

3201 † **Rhoades, Walter C.**
□ The last lap: a school story. Humphrey Milford, 1923.
288p. col. frontis.
——*another ed.* Oxford University Press, 1930.
cricket in chs. iv and x.

3202 † **Richards, Frank,** *pseud. [i.e. Hamilton, Charles Harold
St. John]*
Lord Billy Bunter. Cassell, 1956. 224p.
ch. 5: 'The St Jim's match'.

3203 † Trouble for Tom Merry. Spring Books, n.d. 280p.
cricket pp. 52-132.

3204 † **Roberts, John L.**
The glory of Greystone. Thomas Nelson & Sons, [1935].
295p.
ch. xv: 'The Highcliffe match'.

3205 † **Rutley, Cecil Bernard**
The box of St Bidolph's. Blackie & Sons, [1929]. 95p.
ch v: 'The Wellchester match'.

3206 **Sackett, Peter**
■ First team at cricket; illustrated by Mike Francis.
Dragon Books, 1986. 95p. illus. diagrs.

3207 † **Sewell, J. S. N.**
Gray's school days: a school story. Sheldon Press,
[1935]. 158p.
cricket in ch. 22.

3208 † **Simmonds, Ralph**
For school and country: a story for boys. Cassell, 1911.
iv, 312p. illus.
cricket pp. 85-128.

3209 † **Six-hit** Samson's Chinese puzzle. (Dixon Hawke Library,
no. 330). [1932]. 132p.

3210 † **Strang, Herbert,** *pseud. [i.e. Ely, George Herbert and
L'Estrange, C. J.]*
The adventures of Harry Rochester. Blackie, 1906. ix,
418p.
cricket in ch. 1.

3211 † **Talbot, Ethel**
The girls of the Rookery School. Thomas Nelson &
Sons, [1925]. 299p.
cricket in chs. xi, xx and xxvii.

3212 † Just the girl for St Jude's. Cassell, 1927. 185p.
cricket in chs. i and ii and other references.

3213 † The **Test** match triumph. (Nelson Lee Library, no. 319).
1921. 32p.

3214 † **Titmarsh, M. A.**
Doctor Bird and his young friends. Chapman and Hall,
1849. [iv], 49p. illus.
plate opposite p. 29 concerns cricket.

3215 † The **troubles** of Harry Careless, or going too far. A.
■ Park, 1830. [8]p. col. illus.
some cricket content.

3216 † **Unsworth, Madge**
Wilminster High School and Wilminster Old Girls.
Salvationist Publishing & Supplier, 1929. viii, 179p.
ch vi: 'A last-wicket stand'.

3217 † **Wain, Louis**
A little book of pussy-cats. Sands & Co., n.d. 94p. illus.
'The club match', pp. 79-81; 'Well stopped, sir!', pp. 83-85.

3218 † **White, Heather,** *pseud. [i.e. Foster, Jess Mary Marden]*
■ The new broom at Priors Rigg. F. Warne & Co., [1938].
256p. col. frontis. illus.
cricket in ch. vii.

3219 † **Wynne, May,** *pseud. [i.e. Knowles, Mabel Winifred]*
The girl who played the game. Ward Lock & Co., 1924.
255p.
ch. x: 'The Manor cricket match'.

3220 † Peggy's first term Ward Lock & Co., 1922. 256p.
ch. ix: 'The cricket match'.

3221 † Who was Wendy? Newnes, [1932]. 255p.
ch. vii: 'The cricket match'.

POETRY

3222 † **Carnie, William**
Waifs of rhyme. Aberdeen, 1890. viii, 81p.
*expanded ed. of 'Padwick I' 6430 including extra cricket
poem 'A cricket lay'.*

3223 **Christie, Donald, D.**
A bumpy wicket: the Horace cricket sagas. Poole, the Author, 1987. 15p.

3224 **Cloves, Jeff**
Line & length. Hitchin, The Dodman Press, [1984]. 12p. illus.
seven cricket poems.
limited ed. of 100 copies.

3225 † **Craig, Albert**
A few of my personal experiences on our famous cricket centres. Printed by T. Hughes, 1902? [16]p.

3226 † [Verses]. The Author. bs.
the following verses are additional to those recorded in 'Padwick I' 6444.

Brockwell: a sound cricketer and true friend.

Lockwood in form: secures a century against Leicester, July 4th 1900.

Lord Hawke and his noble band: a nobleman in every true sense.

M.C.C. v Australia, at Lord's, June 11th 1896: Pougher, the illustrious Leicestershire bowler and batsman, creates a new record in first-class cricket by securing five Australian wickets without a single run being scored.

One of our noble veterans.

Oxford v Cambridge at Lord's, June 30th, 1892.

A professional cricketer and a gentleman.

Surrey v Kent, August 23 1887.

To Dr Grace on his thirty-ninth birthday, July 18th, 1887.

To Mr Mason, the illustrious Kentish cricketer. Against Warwickshire in the Canterbury Week, 1895, Mr Mason, by sterling cricket, secured a well-earned century.

To worthy Captain Mason and his noble band.

Welcome back again His Highness, the Jam Sahib of Nawanagar (Prince Ranjitsinhji). [1908].

3227 † [**Duncombe, John**]
Surry triumphant or the Kentish-mens defeat: a new ballad being a parody on Chevy-Chace. Bourne (Kent), Bourne End Paddock Cricket Club, 1937. 16p. incl. covers.
reprint of the parody contained in 'Padwick I' 6450, excluding the score.

3228 † **Green, A. H.**
Conflicting conflicts: a selection of poems. Ilfracombe, Arthur H. Stockwell, 1955. 16p.
includes 'Cricket through the candlelight' and 'To cricket'.

3229 **Grosberg, Imogen**
A few quick singles: cricket verse. [Crewe, the Author, 1984]. 17p. incl. inside cover. *typescript.*

3230 Run chase. The Author, [1987]. [17]p. incl. inside cover.

3231 **Harmer, David**
The spinner's final over. Darfield, the Author, 1983. 36p.

3232 † **Hurdis,** *Rev* **James**
The village curate. 1788.
the poem contains an 18 line reference to cricket.

3233 **Manwaring, Randle Gilbert**
The collected poems of Randle Manwaring. 1986.
contains 'The cricket season'.

3234 † **Miller, G. M.**
South African harvest and other poems. Oxford, Blackwell, 1939. 87p.
contains two cricket poems.

3235 **Murrell, Irene**
A tour in the game: being a comment on the West Indies tour by the M. C. C. Lewes, Book Guild, 1986. 31, viiip. illus.

3236 † **Renshaw, Constance Ada**
Freeman of the hills. Oxford, Shakespeare Head Press, 1939. vii, 83p.
contains two cricket poems.

3237 **Shakespeare, Colin**
The five seasons. Bradford, Oak Press, 1988. 30p.
limited ed. of 500 copies.

3238 Seamers. Bradford, Oak Press, 1983. 30p.
limited ed. of 500 copies.

3239 Spinning. Bradford, Oak Press, 1985. 23p.
limited ed. of 500 copies.

3240 **Sheldon, Caroline** *and* **Heller, Richard,** *compilers*
We are the champions: a collection of sporting verse; illustrated by Virginia Salter. Hutchinson, 1986. 124p. illus. index.
some cricketing verse.

3241 **Spencer, Thomas Edward**
The day McDougall topped the score; illustrated by John McIntosh. North Ryde (N.S.W), Methuen Australia, 1985. [32]p. col. illus.
first pub. Sydney, N.S.W. Bookstall, 1906.

3242 † **Studd, Charles Thomas**
Quaint rhymes for the battlefield, by a quondam cricketer. Clarke, 1914. 88p.
some cricket references.

3243 † The **torpedo**, a poem to the electrical eel. Addressed to Mr. John Hunter, surgeon, fourth edition, with large additions. 1777. [iv], iv, 19p.
4th ed. of 'Padwick I' 892-1, 6535-1, 8017-1.

SONGS

3244 **Allen, David Rayvern**
A song for cricket. Pelham Books, 1981. 219p. illus. (some col.) facsims, indices.
appendix lists known cricketing music.

3245 † **Boulanger, E.**
The cricket match schottische. 1857. [5]p. lithograph on cover.
celebrating first intercolonial match between New South Wales and Victoria.

3246 † **Bowyer, Frederick** *and* **Eaton, W. G.**
The Josser's Cricket Club. Hopwood & Crew, c.1880. 5p. col. illus. on cover.
words by Frederick Bowyer; music by W.G.Eaton.

3247 † **Clark, Samuel E.** *and* **Flockton, William**
Cricketers' song (the royal game). Trotter & Co., 1895.
music by Clark; words by Flockton; listed in Mullins.

3248 † Clendon, Hugh
■ I Zingari polka. Metzler & Co., n.d. 7p.

3249 † Giamona, Antonio
■ All England eleven galop. Melbourne, Allan & Co., [1877]. [5]p. illus. on cover.

3250 † Harrow School song book: complete edition 1862-1904. Harrow School Musical Society, [1904]. 166p.
consolidated ed. of 'Padwick I' 6574.

3251 † Henderson, Harry G. M.
■ The Midland Cricket Club: a Derby cricket ditty. Elvaston (Derbys.), the Author, 1899. [4]p.
song dedicated to Hadyn A. Morley and the members of the Derby Midland C.C.

3252 Hinz, Frank *and* **Keogh, Jan**
Leather on the willow. (Singing together; Australia songs: 4). Frankston (Vic.), Sound Austral, [1988]. [3]p.

3253 † Köhler, R. W.
■ The cricketer's polka: introducing airs from *Masaniello* most respectfully dedicated to the cricketers of England. Ewer & Co., 1850s? 8p. incl. covers. col. illus. on cover.
adapted from the opera by Daniel Auber; R.W.Köhler was a member of the Scarborough Cricket Club.

3254 † Lumsdaine, Jack *and* **Bradman,** *Sir* **Donald George**
■ Every day is a rainbow for me. Sydney, D. Davis & Co., [1930]. [3]p. col. illus. on cover.
words by Jack Lumsdaine, music by Don Bradman.

3255 † McBeath, Neil
□ Keep your tail up kangaroo: the big Australian cricket chorus song. Melbourne, Harold Neal, 1932. [4]p. illus.
——reprinted ed. 1937, 'to be broadcast and sung ... during the vital Test match' [26 Feb. - 3 Mar. 1937].

3256 † Marriott, C. H. R.
■ The boys of merry England. B. Williams, 1870s? 9p. col. illus. on cover.

3257 † Parry, John
■ The cricket club polka. Chappell, [1852]. 6p.
'composed for and performed at the Surbiton Cricket Club ball held on Friday October 29th 1852 ...'

3258 † Reade, H. St. John
■ Abbot's Hill v Gentlemen of Herts, August 1st and 2nd 1877. 1912. 6p.
in English with Latin translation by G.A.R. Fitzgerald.

3259 † Sheridan, Mark
■ The josser cricketer: the true story of a Test match; written and sung by Mark Sheridan. Francis, Day & Hunter, n.d. 3p.
——first pub. in the U.S.A. by T.B.Harms and Francis, Day & Hunter. 1904.

3260 † Shorley, E. T. *and* **Benvenuti, V. G.**
■ Cricket is the game. Rockhampton (Qld.), printed by Record Printing Company, c.1924. [4]p. illus. on cover.
words by E.T.Shorley; music by V.G.Benvenuti.

3261 † Sutton, Ken
The cricketers: a national song. Orpheus Music Publishing Co., 1896.
listed in Mullins.

3262 Tocker, James McCallum
Songs of a cricketer. Christchurch (N.Z.), the Author, 1983. xxiv, 89p.
verses set to familiar tunes featured at the annual winter party of the Old Collegians Cricket Club since the early 1970s.

ESSAYS

3263 Arlott, [Leslie Thomas] John
■ Arlott on cricket: his writings on the game; edited by David Rayvern Allen. Willow Books, 1984. xii, 308p. index
——pbk. ed. Fontana, 1985.

3264 The essential John Arlott: forty years of classic cricket
■ writing; edited by David Rayvern Allen. Willow Books, 1989. x, 320p.

3265 Barnes, Simon
■ Sports writer's eye: an anthology. Queen Anne Press, 1989. v, 218p.
some cricket.

3266 A sportswriter's year. Heinemann, 1989. xi, 196p. illus.
■ *includes 'Strange rumblings in Trinidad: how cricket correspondents live on the far edge of sanity' pp. 90-100.*

3267 Blunden, Edmund Charles
■ Cricket country. Pavilion Books, 1985. xii, 224p.
reprinted ed. of 'Padwick I' 6657 with a new introduction by Benny Green.

3268 Cardus, *Sir* **[John Frederick] Neville**
■ A Cardus for all seasons; edited by Margaret Hughes. Souvenir Press, 1985. 237p.
——limited specially bound ed. of 100 numbered copies, 1985.

3269 A fourth innings with Cardus. Souvenir Press, 1981.
■ 254p. scores.
——limited specially bound ed. of 100 numbered copies, 1981.

3270 Carroll, Ray
■ In sun and shadow. [Kilmore (Vic.), the Author], 1986. 112p. illus.
'collection of stories about cricket and cricketers and [Australian Rules] football and footballers'. cricket pp. 7-84.

3271 Engel, Matthew
■ Sports writer's eye: an anthology. Queen Anne Press, 1989. v, 201p.
cricket pp. 5-130.

3272 † Hughes, Donald
Donald Hughes: headmaster: a selection of his writings. Colwyn Bay, Rydal School Endowment Fund, 1970. xiii, 241p. illus. (one col.)
'contains numerous cricket references, [and] extracts from "The Batsman's bride" and text of a speech ... delivered at a Lancashire C.C.C. dinner'.

3273 James, Cyril Lionel Robert
■ Cricket; edited by Anna Grimshaw. Allison & Busby, 1986. xii, 319p. bibliog. index.
includes a complete bibliography of C.L.R.James's writings on cricket.
——pbk. ed. W.H.Allen, 1989.

3274 Joyce, E. Valentine
■ A season for all men. Lewes, Book Guild, 1985. 155p. with 8p. of ports.
seasons 1902, 1928, 1938, 1947, 1955.

3275 Keating, Francis ('Frank')
■ Bowled over! a year of sport. Deutsch, 1980. 220p.
sporting year of 1979; cricket pp. 15-23, 100-112, 157-176.

3276 Gents and players; illustrated by John Jensen. Robson
■ Books, 1986. viii, 218p. illus.
cricket pp. 135-157, and other references.

3277 Long days. Late nights; illustrated by John Jensen.
■ Robson Books, 1984. 224p. illus.
*sporting articles from 'Punch'; cricket throughout
especially pp. 165-194.*
——*pbk. ed.* Unwin, 1987.

3278 Passing shots; illustrated by John Jensen. Robson
■ Books, 1988. 267p. illus.
*includes articles from 'Punch' and 'The Guardian';
cricket pp. 55-96, 173-205.*

3279 Sports writer's eye: an anthology. Queen Anne Press,
■ 1989. v, 282p.
some cricket, especially pp. 41-65 and 235-254.

3280 **Lucas, Edward Verrall**
■ Cricket all his life: the cricket writings of E. V. Lucas.
Pavilion Books, 1989. [iv], 218p.
*reprinted ed. of 'Padwick I' 6724 with a new introduction
by John Arlott.*

3281 † *Manchester Guardian*
■ The bedside *Guardian*: a selection from the *Manchester
Guardian 9*: 1959-60. Collins, 1960. 256p. illus.
*includes 'Four great players' by Denys Rowbotham, pp.
155-60.
see also 'Padwick I' 6618 and 6622.*

3282 **Manwaring, Randle Gilbert**
■ The run of the downs. 1984.
includes a chapter 'Cricketing poets in Sussex'.

3283 **Martin-Jenkins, Christopher Dennis Alexander** *and*
■ **Seabrook, Mike,** *editors*
Quick singles: memories of summer days & cricket
heroes. Dent, 1986. 136p. illus.
31 contributions especially written for this book.
——*pbk. ed.* Coronet, 1988.

3284 **Peebles, Ian Alexander Ross**
■ Batter's castle: a ramble round the realm of cricket.
Pavilion Books, 1986. ix, 191p. illus.
*reprinted ed. of 'Padwick I' 6744 with a new introduction
by E. W. Swanton.*

3285 Bowler's turn: a further ramble round the realm of
■ cricket. Pavilion Books, 1987. [viii], 195p. illus. scores,
stats.
*reprinted ed. of 'Padwick I' 6745 with a new introduction
by Frank Keating.*

3286 **Robertson-Glasgow, Raymond Charles**
■ Crusoe on cricket: the cricket writings of R. C.
Robertson-Glasgow. Pavilion Books, 1985. 320p.
reprinted ed. of 'Padwick I' 6757.

3287 **Robinson, Raymond John**
■ After stumps were drawn: the best of Ray Robinson's
cricket writing; selected by Jack Pollard. Sydney,
Collins, 1985. 237. illus.

3288 **Roebuck, Peter Michael**
■ Slices of cricket. George Allen & Unwin, 1982. xiii,
140p. illus.
——*pbk. ed.* 1984.

3289 **Swanton, Ernest William**
■ As I said at the time: a lifetime of cricket; edited by
George Plumptre. Willow Books, 1983. xvii, 542p. illus.
scores, index.
——*pbk. ed.* Unwin, 1986.

3290 **Wooldridge, Ian Edmund**
■ Sport in the 80's: a personal view. Centurion, 1989.
176p. illus.
articles from 'The Daily Mail'; some cricket.

SPEECHES AND BROADCASTS

3291 **Allen, David Rayvern,** [*editor*]
■ Cricket on the air: a selection from fifty years of radio
broadcasts. British Broadcasting Corporation, 1985.
207p. illus.

3292 More cricket on the air: a further selection from BBC
■ broadcasts. BBC Books, 1988. 190p. illus. index.

3293 **Arlott, [Leslie Thomas] John**
■ A word from Arlott: a collection of John Arlott's
broadcasts, cricket commentaries and writings; selected
by David Rayvern Allen. Pelham Books, 1983. 240p.
illus. index.

3294 † A.C., cricket rhymster; broadcast 22 August 1961. 5p.
■ *typescript.
transcript of radio talk on Albert Craig.*

3295 Another word from Arlott: a further collection of John
■ Arlott's broadcasts, cricket commentaries and writings;
selected by David Rayvern Allen. Pelham Books, 1985.
viii, 312p. illus. index.

3296 **Arlott, [Leslie Thomas] John** *and* **Brearley, John**
■ **Michael ('Mike')**
Arlott in conversation with Mike Brearley. Hodder and
Stoughton, 1986. 143p. illus.
based on the Channel Four television series.

3297 † **British Broadcasting Corporation**
■ 'Bat and Ball'; TV broadcast, 26 August 1954. v.p.
*typescript.
rehearsal transcripts including directions for re-enactment
of Hambledon v All England.*

3298 † 'The Don'; broadcast on 5 July 1961. 15p. *typescript.*
■ *transcript of radio interview between John Arlott and Sir
Donald Bradman.*

3299 † Portrait of Keith Miller; broadcast 11 September 1956.
■ 21p. *typescript.
transcript of radio broadcast including contributions
from Edrich, Evans, Yardley, Bowes, Langley, Graveney,
Bailey, Compton and Miller himself.*

3300 † Sir Pelham Warner; broadcast 1st and 4th May 1958.
■ 20p. *typescript.
transcript of two part radio broadcast including interview
with Sir Pelham Warner and contributions from Wilfred
Rhodes, Patsy Hendren and Denis Compton.*

3301 † Taking stock: 'problems of county cricket'; broadcast 24
■ April 1952; chairman: John Arlott, speakers:
H.S.Altham, R.W.V.Robins, Bill Bowes, H.L.V.Day.
15p. *typescript.
transcript of radio broadcast.*

3302 **Phillips, Caryl**
■ Playing away. Faber, 1987. xii, 79p illus.
text of Channel 4 film.

PLAYS

3303 † **Harkness,** *Mrs* **A. Lawson**
The cricket match: a comedy of school life, in two acts,
for eight females. Manchester, Abel Heywood, c. 1900.
16p.

3304 **Harris, Richard**
Outside edge: a play. French, 1980. [iii], 80p.

3305 † **John, Errol**
Moon on a rainbow shawl. Faber, 1958. 71p.
——2nd. ed. 1963.
play based on the life of a professional Trinidad cricketer;
Errol John is the son of George John.

ANECDOTES, HUMOUR
AND SATIRE

3306 **Allen, David Rayvern,** *editor*
The Punch book of cricket. Granada, 1985. xviii, 174p.
illus.
——*pbk. ed.* Grafton, 1986.

3307 **Andrew, George**
Further tales from the tin tabernacle. Darf, 1989. 96p.
illus.

3308 Tales from the tin tabernacle. Darf, 1989. vii, 74p. illus.

3309 **Badger, Anna,** *pseud* [*i.e.* **Scott, Rosalind S.**]
How to play clicket, as told to Rosalind S. Scott.
Whitehaven, [the Author], 1985. 56p. illus.
feminist tract in children's booklet format.

3310 **Ball, Johnny**
Plays for laughs. Puffin, 1983. 128p. illus.
sketches for children. includes 'Just not cricket' pp. 31-33.

3311 **Barnes, Simon**
A la recherche du cricket perdu. Macmillan, 1989. v,
138p. illus.
cricket parodies of 25 famous writers.

3312 **Bentine, Michael**
The best of Bentine. Granada, 1983. 208p. illus.
includes 'Cricket on the continent', pp. 57-60.

3313 † **Bentine, Michael** *and* **Ennis, John**
Michael Bentine's book of square games. Wolfe
Publishing, 1966. 96p.
cricket pp. 55-60.

3314 **Blofeld, Henry Calthorpe**
Wine, women & wickets; illustrated by Bill Mitchell.
Surry Hills (N.S.W.), James Fraser, 1984. 111p. illus.
——*U.K. ed. published as* 'Caught short of the
boundary', Stanley Paul, 1984.
——*pbk. ed.* Star, 1986.

3315 **Botham, Ian Terence** *and* **Gregory, Kenneth**
Botham's choice; with drawings by Haro. Collins, 1982.
124p. illus.
——*pbk. ed. with title* 'Botham's bedside cricket book',
Fontana, 1983.

3316 **Brayshaw, Ian John**
Funny cricket: a collection of cricket stories; illustrated
by Richard Gregory. North Ryde (N.S.W.), Methuen
Australia, 1983. 255p. illus.

3317 Over the wicket: another selection of cricket stories;
illustrated by Richard Gregory. Sydney etc., Methuen
Australia, 1980. 127p. illus.

3318 The wit of cricket; cartoons by Bill Mitchell. Milsons
Point (N.S.W.), Currawong Press, 1981. 111p. illus.
——*UK ed.* Deutsch, 1982.

3319 **Brooke-Taylor, Tim**
Tim Brooke-Taylor's cricket box; illustrated by Borin
Van Loon. Stanley Paul, 1986. 133p. illus.
——*pbk. ed.* Arrow, 1988.

3320 † **'C.J.'**
'The Ashes of remembrance': the Test match-itis Club: a
cricketer's dream. Melbourne, Barker & Co., [1924].
[8]p.
satirical story cantaining puns on the names of Ashes
protagonists.

3321 **Chappell, Ian Michael** & **Rigby, Paul**
Long hops & larrikins. Sydney, Lansdowne, 1983. 59p.
illus.

3322 **Chappell, Ian Michael, Robertson, Austin** *and* **Rigby,
Paul**
The best of Chappelli. Sydney, Lansdowne Press, 1982.
160p. illus.
incorporating items 3323 and 3324.

3323 Chappelli has the last laugh. Sydney, Lansdowne Press,
1980. 79p. illus.

3324 Chappelli laughs again. Sydney, Lansdowne Press,
1980. 80p. illus.

3325 **Coleman, Vernon**
Thomas Winsden's cricketing almanack, 136th edition.
Severn House, 1983. 126p. illus.

3326 † **Coles, Albert John**
In Chimley corner. Herbert Jenkins, 1927. 256p.
'Ian's cricket match', pp. 156-164.

3327 **Cooper, Leo** *and* **Cooper, Jilly**
Leo and Jilly Cooper on cricket; pictures by Ross. Bell &
Hyman, 1985. 63p. incl. endpapers. illus. (some col.)

3328 **Dunstan, Keith**
A cricketing dictionary; illustrated by Jeff Hook.
Newton Abbot, David & Charles, 1984. iv, 84p. illus.
——*first pub.* Melbourne, Sun Books, 1983.
humorous definitions.

3329 **Dyson, W. F.**
'Cricketdotes': a collection of whimsical anecdotes,
oddities & similes about cricket. Dundee, R. Miller,
1985? 16p.

3330 **East, Raymond Eric** *in association with* **Dellor, Ralph**
A funny turn: confessions of a cricketing clown;
illustrated by Bill Tidy. George Allen & Unwin, 1983.
125p. illus.
——*pbk. ed.* Unwin, 1984.

3331 **Forbes, Ernest**
The world's best cricket jokes; illustrated by Tony
Blundell. North Ryde; London, Angus & Robertson,
1988. 95p. illus.

3332 **Ford, Noel**
Cricket widows: pitch battles between the sexes. Angus
& Robertson, 1989. 96p. illus.

3333 **Gordon, Richard,** *pseud.* [*i.e.* **Ostlere, Gordon**]
Fifty years a cricketer; illustrated by Geoffrey Dickinson.
Harrap, 1986. 101p. illus.

3334 **Grant, John**
The depths of cricket: a random 22-yard stroll. Grafton,
1986. 247p. bibliog. index.

3335 **Gren,** *pseud.*
The duffer's guide to cricket. Columbus Books, 1985.
80p. illus.
Gren of 'South Wales Echo'.

3336 **Hadlee, Sir Richard John**
Hadlee's humour; illustrations by K. S. Clark. Auckland,
Lansdowne Press, 1982. 80p. illus.

3337 Haining, Peter Alexander, *editor*
■ LBW: laughter before wicket! 100 years of humorous cricket short stories. George Allen & Unwin, 1986. xv, 315p.

3338 Heath, Ian
■ The golden rules of cricket. Corgi Books, 1984. 48p. illus.

3339 Holles, Robert
■ The guide to real village cricket; illustrated by Roy Raymonde. Harrap, 1983. 96p. illus.
——*pbk. ed.* Unwin, 1984.

3340 Hughes, Patrick Cairns ('Spike')
■ The art of coarse cricket. Dent, 1986. 123p. illus.
pbk. ed. of 'Padwick I' 6873.

3341 Johnston, Brian Alexander
■ It's a funny game. Star, 1983. 231p. illus.
pbk. ed. of 'Padwick I' 6876-1.

3342 Rain stops play; with cartoons by Bill Tidy; edited by
■ Lynn Hughes. Unwin Paperbacks, 1981. xi, 83p. illus.
pbk. ed. of 'Padwick I' 6876-2.

3343 † Jones, W. M.
Our village parliament. Frome, Ellenbray Press, n.d. xii, 121p.
ch. XII: 'The cricket match'.

3344 The **laugh's** on us: cricket's finest tell their funniest;
■ cartoons by Jeff Hook. Byron Bay (N.S.W.), Swan Publishing, 1989. 208p. illus.

3345 Macey, Kevin *and* **Benyon, Tony**
■ Howzat? Sevenoaks, New English Library, 1985. 120p. illus.

3346 McGrath, Rory, Fincham, Peter *and* **Moore, Ian**
■ Cricket made silly; illustrated by Nigel Page. Century, 1986. 96p. illus.

3347 McKendrick, Fergus
■ Pulpit cricket and other stories; with illustrations by Val Biro. Willow Collins, 1983. 144p. illus.

3348 † Mailey, Arthur Alfred
■ Cricket stories and sketches. [Sydney, Market Printery, 1958]. 20p. incl. covers, illus.

3349 Martin-Jenkins, Christopher Dennis Alexander
■ Bedside cricket; illustrated by McMurtry. Dent, 1981. 88p. illus.
——*pbk. ed.* Coronet Books, 1983.

3350 Martin-Jenkins, Christopher Dennis Alexander, *editor*
■ Cricket's lighter side: a *Cricketer* collection. Simon & Schuster, 1988. 144p. illus.

3351 The *Cricketer* book of cricket disasters and bizarre
■ records; illustrated by S. McMurtry. Century, 1983. 121p. illus.
——*pbk. ed.* 1984.

3352 The *Cricketer* book of cricket eccentrics and eccentric
■ behaviour; compiled by Chris Rhys, illustrations by David Hughes. Century, 1985. 123p. illus.

3353 May, Norman
Sporting laughs. Cammeray (N.S.W.), Horwitz Grahame, 1985. 153p. illus. index.
much cricket.

3354 Mell, George
■ This curious game of cricket; illustrated by Bill Tidy. George Allen & Unwin, 1982. xii, 127p. illus.
——*pbk. ed.* Unwin, 1983.

3355 † Mervis, Joel
Passing show again. Cape Town, Howard Timmins, 1967. 165p. illus.
extracts from The Passing Show column of 'The Sunday Times'; cricket pp. 1-104.

3356 † Milne, Alan Alexander
Once a week. Methuen, 1914. [x], 323p.
includes 'On the bat's back', pp. 253-257.

3357 Moffitt, Ian (Moffinch) *and* **Gore, Philip (Claw)**
■ Great budgie batsmen and bowlers; illustrations by Bill (Beak) Leak. Sydney, Collins, 1983. 96p. illus. (mostly col.)
humorous accounts of the careers of famous cricketers depicted as birds.

3358 Morley, Steve
■ Tales from the tap room. Methuen, 1986. 128p. illus.

3359 † Murali, K. V.
■ Cricket jokes and odds! [The Author, 1976]. 24p. illus.

3360 Naik, Vasant K.
Cricket vasant. Pune, Chandrakala, 1986. 135p.
in Marathi: 'Cricket's summer'.

3361 † Owen, Will
Mr Peppercorn. John Miles, 1940. 279p. illus.
cricket in ch. IX.

3362 Pandit, Bal J.
Trifala. Pune, Metha Publishing, 1981.
in Marathi: 'Clean bowled'.

3363 Parkinson, Michael
■ Parkinsons lore; with drawings by Michael Lewis. Pavilion Books, 1981. 156p. illus.
cricket pp. 19-94.
——*pbk. ed.* Arrow, 1982.

3364 Poddar, Jyotsna, *compiler*
■ Cricketing memories. [Calcutta], Shradhanjali Trust, 1987. 111p. col. illus.
50 cricketing personalities recount amusing anecdotes.

3365 † Reedy, William Curran
■ Cricketers calendar [for 1928]; with a foreword by J.B.Hobbs. Delgado, [1927]. [54] leaves.
anecdotes and humorous sketches for each week of the year;on box 'The "Hobbs" cricketers calendar'.
—— *also pub. for 1929?*

3366 Rice, Jonathan
■ The compleat cricketer; illustrated by William Rushton. Poole, Blandford Press, 1985. 159p. illus.
——*pbk. ed.* Javelin Books, 1986.

3367 Rushton, William George
■ Marylebone versus the world!! Pavilion Books, 1987. 136p. illus.

3368 † Pigsticking: a joy for life: a gentleman's guide to sporting pastimes. Macdonald and Jane's, 1977. 176p. illus. facsims.
cricket pp. 130-139.

3369 † Secombe, *Sir* **Harry Donald**
Goon for lunch. Michael Joseph, 1975. 175p. illus.
chapter 3: 'Needle match'.

3370 Sherwood, Peter *and* **Alderdice, Gary**
■ The world's best cricket book ever; with contributions from Annie Rice and Ted Thomas. Wakefield, E.P. Publishing, 1981. 96p. illus.

3371 Sicka, *Mrs* **Asha**
■ The funny game of cricket!!! Bombay, K. Subramanian for Business Book Publishing House, 1988. 99p. illus.

3372 Tales from around the wicket told by the Lord's
■ Taverners. Newton Abbot, David & Charles, 1989. 126p. illus.
   'A Graham Tarrant book'.

3373 Thompson, Graham
■ Middle stump: an alphabet of cricketing terms. Queen Anne Press, 1987. [95]p. illus.

3374 Tinniswood, Peter
■ The brigadier down under. Macmillan, 1983. [vi], 146p.
   ——*pbk. ed.* Pan, 1984.

3375 The brigadier in season. Macmillan, 1984. 173p.
■ ——*pbk. ed.* Pan, 1984.

3376 The brigadier's brief lives. Pan Books, 1984. 125p. illus.
■

3377 The brigadier's tour. Pan, 1985. 187p.
■

3378 Collected tales from a long room. Hutchinson, 1982.
■ 262p.
   incorporating items 3379 and 3380.

3379 More tales from a long room. Arrow Books, 1982.
■ 140p. illus.

3380 Tales from a long room. Arrow Books, 1981. 128p.
■ illus.

3381 Tales from Witney Scrotum; illustrated by John
■ Lawrence. Pavilion Books, 1987. 125p. illus.
   ——*pbk. ed.* Arrow Books, 1988.

3382 Trueman, Frederick Sewards *and* **Hardy, Frank**
   You nearly had him that time - and other cricket stories; illustrated by David Langdon. Arrow, 1981. 128p. illus.
   pbk. ed. of 'Padwick I' 6915-2.

3383 Tyson, Frank Holmes
■ The cricketer who laughed; illustrated by Vane Lindesay. Hutchinson of Australia, 1981. 147p. illus.
   ——*U.K. ed.* Stanley Paul, 1982.
   ——*reprinted in* 'The sportsmen who laughed omnibus', Hutchinson of Australia, 1982.

3384 Walker, Maxwell Henry Norman
■ How to hypnotise chooks and other great yarns. Glen Waverley (Vic.), Garry Sparke & Associates, 1987. 160p. illus.

3385 How to tame lions and other great tales. Glen Waverley
■ (Vic.), Garry Sparke & Associates, 1988. 160p. illus.

3386 Walker, Maxwell Henry Norman *with* **Coward, Mike**
■ The wit of Walker. Glen Waverley (Vic.), Garry Sparke & Associates, 1983. 160p. illus. stats.

3387 Walters, Kevin Douglas ('Doug')
■ One for the road; cartoons by Jeff Hook. Milsons Point (N.S.W.), Swan Publishing, 1988. 136p. illus.

3388 [Ward, Martin *and* **Oldman, Paul]**
■ The British Academy of Cricket manual for Gentlemen and Players. A mentor and guide on all matters relating to Cricket with notes on PROPER SPORTING BEHAVIOUR, the whole being an AUTHORISED DIGEST of Legislation expressed in simple lessons and Strict REGULATIONS. Pavilion Books, 1988. 240p. illus.

3389 Winkworth, Stephen
■ Famous sporting fiascos; illustrated by Jaques. Bodley Head, 1982. 200p. illus. index
   some cricket anecdotes.

3390 Wooldridge, Ian Edmund
■ Travelling reserve. Collins, 1982. 88p. illus.
   frequent references to cricket.

3391 † Wright, Alan *and* **Stokes, E. Vernon**
■ Comic sport & pastime. Frederick Warne & Co., 1904? 47p. illus. (some col.)
   cricket illus. and poem, pp. 22-23.

3392 Yapp, Nick
■ Bluff your way in cricket. (Bluffer's guide series). Horsham, Ravette, 1988. 62p.

3393 Young, Ken
   A tricky ball and other cricket stories. Chinchilla Newspapers, 1982. 32p. incl. adverts.

DIARIES AND LETTERS

3394 Gregory, Kenneth, [*editor*]
■ The second cuckoo: a further collection of witty, amusing and memorable letters to *The Times*. George Allen & Unwin, 1983. vii, 322p. index.
   cricket pp. 157, 255 and 283-284.
   sequel to 'Padwick I' 6938-1.

3395 † Lucas, Edward Verrall
■ Post-bag diversions. Harper & Brothers, 1934. xi, 259p. illus. index.
   letters elicited by E. V. Lucas; cricket pp. 217-220.

3396 Pearlman, Phil, *editor*
   Dear Australian: an anthology based on a selection of memorable letters to *The Australian* 1964-1981. Sydney, Lansdowne Press, 1982.
   cricket pp. 45-48.

3397 Turner, Thomas
   The diary of Thomas Turner 1754-1765; edited by David George Vaisey. Oxford University Press, 1984. xxxix, 386p. illus. facsims. map.
   ——*pbk. ed.* 1985.
   another ed. of 'Padwick I' 6939.

3398 Williams, Marcus, *editor*
■ The way to Lord's: cricketing letters to *The Times*. Willow Books, 1983. [x], 293p. index.
   ——*pbk. ed.* Fontana, 1984.

RELIGIOUS TRACTS

3399 † Couchman, Mary
■ The noes have it: a temperance tale. S. P. C. K., [1902]. 74p. frontis.
   cricket in ch. 1 and depicted on front cover.

3400 † Hoare, [Maurice] Patrick Blizard
   The beginning of term and other stories. Ilfracombe, A. H. Stockwell, [1944]. 159p. illus.
   includes two cricketing fables.

3401 † **Kelly, Minnie Harding**
Tom Kenyon, schoolboy. Religious Tract Society, [1913]. 320p.
cricket in ch. xix.

3402 † **Manwell, M. B.**
Kit and Co. Religious Tract Society, [1901]. 48p.

3403 **Wingfield-Digby, Andrew Richard**
■ A loud appeal. Hodder and Stoughton, 1988. xiii, 128p.
cover sub-title: 'playing by God's rules'.
also describes the founding of 'Christians in Sport'.

3404 † **Wynne, May,** *pseud.* **[i.e. Knowles, Mabel Winifred]**
The girls of Beechcroft School. Religious Tract Society, [1920]. 255p. illus.
ch. xii: 'The cricket match'.

PICTORIAL RECORDS

PRINTS AND ILLUSTRATIONS
(See also under Cricketana)

3405 **Brodribb, [Arthur] Gerald Norcott**
The art of Nicholas Felix. Ewell, J. W. McKenzie, 1985.
90p. illus.
limited ed. of 220 signed and numbered copies.

3406 **Cardus,** *Sir* **[John Frederick] Neville** *and* **Arlott, [Leslie**
■ **Thomas] John**
The noblest game: a book of fine cricket prints. Harrap,
1986. 30 + [129]p. illus. (some col.)
*reissued ed. of 'Padwick I' 6967 with a new introduction
to cricket prints by John Arlott.*

3407 † The **cricketers** portrait gallery: 34 portraits of noted
players. 1896. 16p. illus.

3408 **Frindall, William Howard ('Bill')**
■ The Carphone gallery of cricketers. Queen Anne Press,
1988. 222p. illus.
autograph album.

3409 **Frith, David Edward John**
■ Pageant of cricket. Macmillan, 1987. 640p. illus. (some
col.) index.
——*limited ed. of 200 leather-bound numbered copies
signed by Sir Donald Bradman and the author, 1987.*

3410 **Goldman, Paul**
■ Sporting life: an anthology of British sporting prints.
British Museum Publications, 1983. 126p. + 10p. of col.
plates, illus. bibliog. index.
cricket pp. 49-59.

3411 **Graddon, Corridan**
■ Cricket: a set of etchings. St. Albans, Graddio Press,
1983. 24 leaves, illus.
limited ed. of 100 signed copies.

3412 **Kamath, Ashok,** *editor*
Sports photography: Wills book of excellence. Calcutta,
Orient Longman, 1989. 204p. col. illus. index.
cricket pp. 108-153.

3413 **Kelly, Ken** *[and]* **Lemmon, David Hector**
■ Cricket reflections: five decades of cricket photographs.
Newton Abbot, David & Charles, 1985. 192p. illus.
(some col.)
——*reissued* Peerage Books, 1989.

3414 **Murrell, Adrian**
■ Cricket impressions. Kingswood Press, 1987. 144p.
illus. (some col.)
——*pbk. ed.* Heinemann Kingswood, 1989.

3415 † **Nottingham Castle Museum & Art Gallery**
■ An exhibition of cricket pictures from the collection of
Sir Jeremiah Colman Bt. March 9 to April 14 1935?
see also 'Padwick I 6968, 6981-3, 6986 and 6996.

3416 † **Photographic** album with portraits of famous cricketers;
■ athletes etc. Slade Brothers, [1880]. 48p. illus.

3417 **Russell, Robert Charles ('Jack')**
■ A cricketer's art: sketches by Jack Russell. Nuneaton
(Warwicks.), Goodyer Associates, 1988. x, 54p. illus.

3418 † **Shepheard, George**
A sketch book. [c.1790].
at Lord's according to 'Allen EBC'.

3419 **Simon, Robin** *and* **Smart, Alastair**
■ John Player art of cricket. Secker & Warburg, 1983. xii,
250p. illus. (some col.) index.
includes catalogue and narrative account of cricket art.

3420 † **Surrey County Cricket Club**
■ Schedule of pictures at pavilion, Surrey County Cricket
Club, Kennington Oval, as at May 1936. The Club, 1936.
40p. typescript.

3421 **Visions** of sport: celebrating twenty years of Allsport,
■ the international sports picture agency. Pelham Books,
1988. 158p. col. illus.
some cricket.

3422 **Wingfield, Mary Ann**
■ Sport and the artist. volume 1: ball games. Woodbridge
(Suffolk), Antique Collectors' Club, 1988. 358p. illus.
(some col.) bibliog. index.
cricket pp. 80-127.

3423 **Wright, Gerry** *and* **Frith, David Edward John**
■ Cricket's golden summer: paintings in a garden; with a
commentary by David Frith. Pavilion Books, 1985. 64p.
col. illus.

CARTOONS AND CARICATURES

3424 **Alexyz,** *pseud.* *[i.e.* **Fernandez, Alex Raphael]**
■ Howzzat! a century of cricket cartoons. Bombay,
Marine Sports, 1987. [110]p. illus.
a collection of 100 cartoons.

3425 **Bechaz, Graeme**
'How's that': cricket through the eyes of an innocent.
Elwood (Vic.), Bridgewater Books, 1988. [52]p. illus.

3426 **Bond, Simon**
■ Stroked through the covers. Methuen, 1987. [94]p. illus.

3427 **Conyers, Paul**
■ The proverbial cricket book. [Bondi (N.S.W.), the
Author], 1984. [64]p. illus.

3428 **Dubbleyoo, L. B.,** *pseud*
■ The lighter side of ... cricket. Auckland, SeTo
Publishing, 1989. [33]p. illus.
cover sub-title: 'what the umpire heard'.

3429 **Emery, Llewellyn** *and* **Horton, Walt**
Cricket: the off side. Hamilton (Bermuda), Emerton
Productions, 1987. 56p. illus.

3430 **Garner, Steven**
■ The golden age of village cricket. Luton, Lennard
Publishing, 1988. [127]p. chiefly illus.

3431 **Hewison, William,** *editor*
Sporting gestures: *Punch* plays the game. Grafton, 1988.
[128]p. chiefly illus.
some cricket.

3432 **Ireland, John** *and* **Martin-Jenkins, Christopher Dennis Alexander**
Cricket characters: *The Cricketer* caricatures of John Ireland; text by Christopher Martin-Jenkins. Stanley Paul, 1987. 96p. col. illus.

3433 **Jawed Iqbal**
How is that? cricket in cartoons. Lahore, the Author, 1980. 254p. incl. adverts. illus.
predominantly caricatures of well known cricket personalities.

3434 **Knight, Mark**
The crowd roars: Australian cricket crowd banners. Narrabeen (N.S.W.), Impress Publishers, 1984. [62]p. illus.

3435 **Larry,** *pseud*
Owzat! Larry looks at cricket umpires. Robson Books, 1987. [96]p. illus.

3436 **Leigh, Paul**
100 puns not out! Adelaide, Rigby, 1984. 100p. illus.

3437 **March, Russell**
The cricketers of *Vanity Fair*. Exeter, Webb & Bower, 1982. 112p. col. illus.

3438 **Piesse, Ken,** *editor*
Cartoonists at the cricket. South Yarra (Vic.), Currey O'Neil Ross, 1983. 128p. illus.

3439 Match drawn: a cavalcade of cricket cartoons. Melbourne etc., Ross Publishing for Lothian Publishing Company, 1988. 94p. illus.

3440 **Plumptre, George**
Cricket cartoons and caricatures. (The MCC Cricket Library). Willow Books, 1989. 159p. illus. (some col.) index.

3441 **Pyne, Ken**
Silly mid-off: how to survive the cricket season. Century Publishing, 1985. [112]p. illus.

3442 **Savur, Bharat** *and* **Savur, Shalan**
Sunny the supersleuth. Bombay, India Book House, [1984]. 28p. incl. covers and adverts. illus.
children's comic book featuring S. M. Gavaskar as the super hero.

3443 **Schofield, Philip**
Sticky wicket: almost 101 uses for a dead cricket bat. Lane Cove (N.S.W.), Hodder & Stoughton Australia, 1982. [64]p. illus.

SPORTS AND GAMES

FOR ADULTS

3444 † **Dimmock, Peter,** *editor*
■ Sportsview grandstand: the TV book of all sports.
Vernon Holding & Partners, [1960]. 192p. illus.
articles on cricket pp. 58-67, 121-128, 135-144, 151-155.

3445 † **George, W. G.**
Training: being section II of the author's work , entitled:
'Athletics and kindred sports'. Southwood Smith, 1903.
134p. illus.
cricket pp. 90-96.

3446 **Gladstone, Francis**
■ Baseball: a cricketer's guide. Kingswood, 1987. viii,
152p. illus. plans.
*similarities and differences of the two games discussed pp.
145-148.*

3447 **Grayson, Edward**
■ Sport and the law. Butterworths, 1988. xviii, 376p.
index.
rev. and expanded ed. of 'Padwick I' 7080-2.

3448 † **In-door** and out-door games for all seasons: being
'parlour pastimes' and 'games for all seasons', complete
in one volume. Blackwood, 1880? 272p. + 280p. illus.
cricket pp. 9-23 (part 2).
see also 'Padwick I' 7054 and 7126.

3449 † A **key** to in-door and out-door amusements. Cassell,
■ n.d. [1870s].
2 vols.
vol. 1, vi, 384p.
vol. 2, vi, 384p. + index.
issued in weekly parts; contains 'Cricket' by C.W.Alcock.

3450 † **Maxwell, William Hamilton**
The field book: or, sports and pastimes of the British
Islands. 1860. 563p. illus.
rev. ed. of 'Padwick I' 7052.
cricket pp. 129-131.

3451 † **Warville's** games or pam-lu, chess and cricket. Boston
(Mass.), printed by J. Belcher, 1809. 60p.
---- earlier U.K. ed.?

3452 † **Watson, Robert Spence**
Cricket and croquet. Newcastle, printed by A. Reid,
1866. 11p.
*paper read out at fundraising concert at Gateshead on
behalf of North Durham C.C.*

FOR CHILDREN

3453 † The **boy's** prize book of sports, games, exercises and
pursuits. S. O. Beeton, 1866. 228p. col. frontis. illus.
by the writers of 'The boy's own magazine'.
cricket pp. 101-110.

3454 † **Peter** Parley's annual: a Christmas and New Year's
present for young people. 1840. vi, 378p. illus.
cricket pp. 129-134.

3455 † **Sports** of youth; or, the good child's remembrancer.
■ Printed by Hodgson & Co., c. 1830. 36p. incl. covers.
col. illus.
cricket p. 7.

3456 † **Williams, Samuel**
The boy's treasury of sports, pastimes and regulations.
Bogue, 1844. 464p. illus.
cricket pp. 65-76p.

REMINISCENCES AND BIOGRAPHY

COLLECTED BIOGRAPHY

(See also under more specific headings, e.g. Batting and Batsmen)

3457 **[Andrews, Gordon B.]**
■ English cricketer-footballers 1888-1939. [Admington, Shipston on Stour], Datasport, [1983]. [21]p.

3458 **Andrews, Gordon B.**
■ English footballers and cricketers who have played English league football and first class cricket since 1946. Admington, Shipston on Stour, Datasport, [1984]. [21]p.
cover title: Datasport English cricketer-footballers 1946-83.

3459 **Arlott, [Leslie Thomas] John**
■ John Arlott's book of cricketers. Readers Union, 1982. x, 180p. illus.
another ed. of 'Padwick I' 7167-1.
——*pbk. ed.* Sphere, 1982.

3460 **Aziz Rehmatullah, A.,** *editor*
■ Masters of cricket. Karachi, the Author, 1982? 112p. incl. adverts. illus.

3461 **Bailey, Philip Jonathan, Thorn, Philip R.** *and*
■ **Wynne-Thomas, Peter,** *compilers*
Who's who of cricketers: a complete who's who of all cricketers who have played first-class cricket in England, with full career records. Feltham, Newnes Books in association with the Association of Cricket Statisticians, 1984. 1144p. stats.

3462 **Bailey, Trevor Edward**
■ The greatest since my time: the best cricketers of the last twenty years and the major changes in the game. Hodder and Stoughton, 1989. 272p. illus.

3463 **Barker, Ralph**
■ Purple patches. Collins, 1987. 288p. illus. index.
Bill Ponsford, Arthur Booth, Bill Johnston, Frank Tyson, Jim Laker, Micky Stewart, Bill Athey, Denis Lindsay, Bob Massie, David Steele, David Hookes.

3464 **Bedser, Alec Victor**
■ Cricket choice. Pelham Books, 1981. 204p. illus.
——*another ed.* Readers Union, 1982.

3465 **Brooke, Robert William,** *compiler and editor*
■ The Collins who's who of English first-class cricket 1945-1984; research assistant Brian Hunt. Willow Books, 1985. xiii, 411p. stats. bibliog.

3466 † **[Carr, James Joseph Lloyd]**
■ Carr's dictionary of extra-ordinary English cricketers. Kettering, J. L. Carr, Sep. 1977. [20]p. incl. covers.
rev. ed. of 'Padwick I' 7183-1 including some additional entries.
——*another rev. ed.* Jan. 1978.
——*rev. and expanded ed. with title 'Carr's illustrated dictionary of extra-ordinary cricketers'* Quartet Books/Solo Books, 1983. [95]p.

3467 **Compton, Denis Charles Scott**
■ Compton on cricketers past and present. Cassell, 1980. xii, 204p. illus. index

3468 **Gavaskar, Sunil Manohar**
■ Idols. Calcutta, Rupa, 1983. [xiv], 293p. illus.
——*U.K. ed.* George Allen & Unwin, 1984.

3469 **Giller, Norman,** *editor*
■ Cricket heroes. Thorpe Bay, Norman Giller Publications, 1981. [66]p. incl. covers, illus.
'England's cricketers select their heroes'.

3470 **Gower, David Ivon** *with* **Hodgson, Derek**
■ Heroes and contemporaries. Collins, 1983. 127p. illus.
——*pbk. ed.* Panther Books, 1985.

3471 **Hunt, Brian** *and* **Brooke, Robert William,** *compilers*
■ Births and deaths of cricketers 1945-1984. Solihull, the Authors, 1984. 19p.
includes only information 'not previously published or difficult to obtain'.

3472 **Johnston, Brian Alexander**
■ It's been a piece of cake: a tribute to my favourite cricketers. Methuen, 1989. xiv, 274p. illus. index.
short essays on 77 cricketers.

3473 **Lemmon, David Hector,** *editor*
■ Cricket heroes: essays by members of the Cricket Writers Club. Queen Anne Press, 1984. 160p. illus. index.

3474 The **Lord's** Taverners fifty greatest: the fifty greatest
□ post-war cricketers from around the world; text: Graham Tarrant. Heinemann-Quixote, 1983. 120p. col. illus. stats.
selected by Trevor Bailey, Richie Benaud, Colin Cowdrey, Jim Laker; illustrations: Mike Francis, Ivan Rose, Rodger Towers, Ron Wootton.
——*limited ed. of 500 copies signed by all the contributors, 1983.*

3475 **Meher-Homji, Kersi**
■ Cricket's great families. Ashburton (Vic.), Garry Sparke & Associates, 1980. 160p. illus.

3476 **Murphy, Patrick**
■ Declarations; photography by Graham Morris. Letchworth, Ringpress Books, 1989. 192p. illus.
cover sub-title: 'leading cricketers talk to Patrick Murphy'.

3477 **Pandit, Bal J.**
101 shreshth patu cricket. Pune, Utkarsh, 1988.
in Marathi: '101 great cricketers'.

3478 **Pemain-pemain** kriket terkenal. (Siri kisah nyata, no.
■ 13). Kuala Lumpur, Whereever Distributors, 1982. 31p. illus.
in Malay; 'The most famous cricket players'; for children.

3479 Randall, David
■ Great sporting eccentrics. W.H. Allen, 1985. 192p.
illus. bibliog.
several cricketing entries.

3480 Rhys, Chris, *compiler and editor*
■ The Courage book of sporting heroes, 1884-1984.
Stanley Paul, 1984. 221p. illus.
includes thirteen cricketers.

3481 Sproat, Iain MacDonald, *compiler and editor*
■ The cricketers' who's who. *annual*. illus. stats.
pub 1980. with title Debrett's cricketers' who's who.
Publishers:
1980 Debrett's Peerage Ltd.
1981-84 Cricketers' Who's Who Ltd.
1985-86 Queen Anne Press
1987 to date Willow Books.

3482 Spurrier, Michael C.
■ Gallant and distinguished. [1986]. 13p. *typescript.*
copy in Cricket Society Library.

3483 Thomson, Arthur Alexander
■ Odd men in: a gallery of cricket eccentrics. Pavilion
Books, 1985. [i], 184p. index.
*reprinted ed. of 'Padwick I' 7254 with a new introduction
by Leo Cooper.*

3484 Tyson, Frank Holmes
■ The test within: talent and temperament in 22 cricketers:
a personal selection. Hawthorn (Vic.), Century
Hutchinson Australia, 1987. ix, 220p. illus.

3485 † [Warner, *Sir* Pelham Francis, *editor*]
British sports and sportsmen past and present; compiled
and edited by 'The Sportsman'. British Sports and
Sportsmen, [1908-1936?]. 16 vols. illus.
vol. 5: 'Cricket and football', 1917. viii, 579p.
*limited royal ed. of 250 numbered copies of 'Padwick I'
7261.*

3486 Wellings, Evelyn Maitland
■ Vintage cricketers. George Allen & Unwin, 1983. xii,
177p. illus. index.

3487 West, G. Derek
■ Twelve days of Grace. Darf, 1989. xi, 220p. illus.
bibliog. index
*biographical sketches of 12 cricketers whose careers
overlapped or ran parallel with the Grace family: William
Buttress, James Southerton, Roger Iddison, R.P.
Carpenter, G.F. Tarrant, Edward Pooley, Henry Jupp, J.C.
Shaw, Ephraim Lockwood, R.G. Barlow, William Barnes,
Edmund Peate.*

3488 † Yeomans, Ron
■ Cricket close ups 1949-50; illustrated by 'Thack'. [1950].
64p.
*privately printed and bound volume of series of
'close-ups' of famous players reprinted from 'Yorkshire
Post' and 'Yorkshire Evening Post'; 64 cricketers featured.*

INDIVIDUAL BIOGRAPHY

Abdul Qadir Khan

3489 Mubashshir Alam, S., *editor*
■ Abdul Qadir benefit cricket match: Pakistan XI vs World
XI at Al Arabi Stadium on 2nd & 3rd Oct. '86. Kuwait,
[1986]. [60]p. incl. adverts. illus. stats.
*much of the contents in Arabic; match sponsored and
organised by the Kuwait Bahrain International Exchange
Co.*

Abel, Robert

3490 Kynaston, David
■ Bobby Abel: professional batsman, 1857-1936. Secker &
Warburg, 1982. xi, 164p. illus. stats. bibliog. index.

Abrahams, John

3491 Foster, Robin *and* **Lorimer, Malcolm George,** *compilers*
■ John Abrahams testimonial brochure, 1988.
[Testimonial Committee, 1988]. 72p. incl. adverts. illus.
(some col.)

Acfield, David Laurence

3492 David Acfield benefit year 1981. [1981]. 60p. incl.
■ adverts. illus. stats.

Agnew, Jonathan Philip

3493 Agnew, Jonathan Philip
■ Eight days a week: diary of a professional cricketer; the
inside story of the 1988 season. Letchworth, Ringpress
Books, 1988. [iv], 184p. illus. stats.

Allen, *Sir* George Oswald Browning ('Gubby')

3494 Swanton, Ernest William
■ Gubby Allen: man of cricket. Hutchinson/Stanley Paul,
1985. xiii, 311p. illus. scores, index.

Amiss, Dennis Leslie

3495 Dennis Amiss ... testimonial year 1985 official brochure.
■ [Testimonial Committee, 1985]. 68p. incl. adverts. illus.
stats.

3496 Goodyear, David William
■ Dennis Amiss, Warwickshire and England.
[Birmingham, the Author, 1984]. 100p. illus. stats.
——*another ed. 1988?, with 4 page insert bringing career
details to completion; on cover: 'full complete 1960-87
record'.*

Arlott, Leslie Thomas John

3497 Arlott, [Leslie Thomas] John *and* **Brearley, John**
■ **Michael ('Mike')**
Arlott in conversation with Mike Brearley. Hodder and
Stoughton, 1986. 143p. illus.
based on the Channel Four television series.

Armitage, Robert Lawrence Sugden

3498 Bassano, Brian Stanley, *editor*
■ The best of South African sport. [Port Elizabeth, n.d.].
103p. incl. adverts. col. illus.
pub. for Rob Armitage benefit year.

Arthur, Ben

3499 **Harragan, Robert**
■ Ben Arthur. The Author, 1980. 1p. *typescript.*
offprint from 'Llanelli Star', 7 June 1980; Ben Arthur played for Llanelli in 1870s.

Asif Iqbal Razvi

3500 **Asif** Iqbal benefit 1968-1981. [Benefit Committee],
■ 1981. 94p. incl. adverts. illus.

Athey, Charles William Jeffrey ('Bill')

3501 **Hall, Geoffrey**
■ Bill Athey: a career so far, 1976-1983. Beverley, the
Author, 1984? 16p. incl. covers, stats.

Austin, G. C. ('Chicko')

3502 † **Warwickshire County Cricket Club**
■ Joint testimonial to E. J. ('Tiger') Smith and G. C.
('Chicko') Austin. [1955]. [4]p. incl. covers, illus.
G. C. Austin was clerk and scorer to the Club, 1904 to 1910 and county match scorer from 1911.

Aylett, Allen James ('Mick')

3503 **Aylett, Allen James** *as told to* **Hobbs, Greg**
■ My game: a life in football. South Melbourne, Sun
Books, 1986. x, 261p. illus. index.
his cricket career, pp. 52-4; Aylett played eleven games for Victoria in the late 1950s.

Bailey, Jack Arthur

3504 **Bailey, Jack**
■ Conflicts in cricket. Kingswood Press, 1989. [ix], 193p.
illus.

Bailey, Trevor Edward

3505 **Bailey, Trevor**
■ Wickets, catches and the odd run. Willow Books, 1986.
240p. illus. index.

Bainbridge, Philip

3506 **Phil** Bainbridge benefit year 1989. [Benefit Committee,
■ 1989]. 120p. incl. adverts. illus. (some col.), stats.

Bairstow, David Leslie

3507 **Bairstow, David** *with* **Hodgson, Derek**
■ A Yorkshire diary: year of crisis. Sidgwick & Jackson,
1984. x, 165p. illus.
the 1984 season.

3508 **Gray, Geoff,** *compiler and editor*
■ The David Bairstow benefit year 1982. [1982]. [96]p.
incl. adverts. illus. (some col.) stats.

Balderstone, John Christopher ('Chris')

3509 **Johnson, Martin,** *editor*
■ Ken Higgs/Chris Balderstone benefit year. [Testimonial
Committee], 1984. 48p. incl. adverts. illus. stats.
brochure for testimonial year.

Banerjee, Sarbindu Surendrakumar ('Shute')

3510 **Bhattacharji, A. N.**
■ Reminiscences about Shute Banerjee, one of the best
all-round cricketers in India. 2nd. ed. Calcutta, Shute
Banerjee Memorial Committee, [1988]. 12p. incl.
covers. illus.

Barclay, John Robert Troutbeck

3511 **John** Barclay benefit year 1986: the year of the Trout.
■ [Benefit Committee, 1986]. 46p. incl. adverts. illus.
(some col.)

Barlow, Graham Derek

3512 **Graham** Barlow benefit '84. [Benefit Committee?,
■ 1984]. 47p. incl. adverts. illus. (some col.) stats.

Barnard, Llewellyn Jamieson ('Lee')

3513 *Kookaburra Telegraph* Lee Barnard benefit year 1989-90.
■ [Johannesburg, New Graphis, 1989]. 120p. incl.
adverts. illus. (some col.) stats.
some articles in Afrikaans.

Barrie, *Sir* James Matthew

3514 **Allen, David Rayvern**
■ Peter Pan and cricket. Constable, 1988. 188p. illus.
facsims. bibliog. index.
J. M. Barrie and cricket.

Barrington, Kenneth Frank

3515 **Scovell, Brian**
■ Ken Barrington: a tribute. Harrap, 1982. 176p. illus.
stats. index.

Batty, David A. ('George')

3516 **Twenty** wonderful years at Bingley: David Batty
■ testimonial brochure. 48p. incl. covers and adverts.
illus. stats.
produced for testimonial match, Bingley v Yorkshire XI, 27 May, 1986.

Beaumont, John

3517 † **[Craig, Albert]**
■ John Beaumont. Wright & Co., [1889]. [4]p. folded
card, illus.

Bedser, Alec Victor

3518 **Bedser, Alec** *and* **Bannister, Alexander James**
■ Twin ambitions: an autobiography. Stanley Paul, 1986.
217p. illus. stats. index.

Beldham, William ('Silver Billy')

3519 **Collyer, Graham**
■ Farnham Cricket Club 1782-1982: a bi-centenary history,
also featuring the life of William 'Silver Billy' Beldham
and cricket in the village. Farnham, Farnham Castle
Newspapers, 1982. 96p. illus. scores, stats.

Benaud, Richard ('Richie')

3520 **Benaud, Richie**
■ On reflection. Willow Books, 1984. 255p. illus. index.
——*pbk. ed.* Fontana, 1985.

Bennett, Donald

3521 **Don** Bennett testimonial 1981. [1981]. [48]p. incl.
■ adverts. illus.

Bestall, Darryl

3522 **Darryl** Bestall benefit year 1987-8. Durban, [1987]. 34p.
illus. stats.

Birch, John Dennis

3523 **John** Birch benefit brochure. [1989]. [48]p. incl.
■ adverts. illus.

Bird, Harold Dennis ('Dickie')

3524 **Bird, Dickie**
b From the pavilion end. Arthur Barker, 1988. x, 160p.
illus.

3525 Not out. New English Library, 1981. x, 150p. illus.
pbk. ed. of 'Padwick I' 7333-1.

3526 That's out! Arthur Barker, 1985. 160p. illus.
■ ——*pbk. ed.* 1989.

Boock, Stephen Lewis

3527 **Colbert, Roy,** *editor*
■ Boocky: cricket's a funny game. [Dunedin, Testimonial
Committee, 1989]. 64p. illus. stats.
pub. for S. L. Boock's benefit year 1989-90.

Booth, Brian Charles

3528 **Booth, Brian** *with* **White, Paul**
■ Booth to bat: an autobiography. Homebush West
(N.S.W.), Anzea Publishers, 1983. xii, 202p. illus. stats.

Border, Allan Robert

3529 **Border, Allan**
■ An autobiography. North Ryde (N.S.W.), Methuen
Australia, 1986. 230p. illus. stats.
——*U.K. ed.* Methuen, 1987.

3530 **Border, Allan** *with* **Bills, Peter**
■ A peep at the Poms ... the Australian captain in England.
Arthur Barker, 1987. [vii], 168p. illus. stats.
the 1986 season.

3531 **Mallett, Ashley Alexander**
■ Allan Border (Master Cricketer series). Richmond
(Vic.), Hutchinson of Australia, 1983. 32p. illus.
for children.

Bosanquet, Bernard James Tindal

3532 **Bosanquet, Reginald** *with* **Reyburn, Wallace**
■ Let's get through Wednesday: my 25 years with ITN.
Michael Joseph, 1980. 190p. illus.
*ch. 2: 'My father was an inventor' contains memories of
B.J.T.Bosanquet.*
——*pbk. ed.* New English Library, 1985.

Botham, Ian Terence

3533 **Andresier, Steve,** *editor*
■ The Ian Botham benefit yearbook. Benefit Committee,
1984. [24]p. incl. adverts. illus. (some col.) stats.

3534 **Bannister, John David ('Jack'),** *editor*
■ Ian Botham's leukaemia celebrity walk. Willow Books,
1986. 96p. illus.
26 Oct - 29 Nov 1985.

3535 **Botham, Ian** *and* **Roebuck, Peter Michael**
■ It sort of clicks: Ian Botham talking to Peter Roebuck.
Willow Books, 1986. 153p. illus. index.
——*pbk ed.* Willow Books, 1987, *updated to include the
1986 season and the 1986-87 England tour to Australia.*

3536 **Botham, Kathy**
■ Living with a legend. Grafton, 1987. 219p. illus.
——*pbk. ed.* 1988.

3537 **Doust, Dudley**
■ Ian Botham: the great all-rounder. Cassell, 1980. xiv,
138p. illus. diagr. scores. index.
——*rev. pbk. ed.* Granada, 1981.

3538 **Eagar, Patrick** *and* **Wright, Graeme**
■ Botham. Tadworth (Surrey), Kingswood Press, 1985.
159p. illus. (some col.) stats. index.

3539 **An evening** with Ian Botham; with special guest David
■ English. [1989]. 20p. incl. covers and adverts. illus.
(some col.)
lecture tour souvenir brochure; Oct.-Nov. 1989.

3540 **Hayter, Reginald James,** *editor*
■ Ian Botham '84: benefit brochure. [1984]. 56p. incl.
adverts. illus. (some col.) stats.

3541 **Keating, Francis ('Frank')**
■ High, wide and handsome: the story of a very special
year. Willow Books, 1986. 218p. illus. scores.
Botham in the 1985 season.

3542 **Langley, Andrew**
■ Ian Botham (Profiles series); illustrated by Karen
Heywood. Hamish Hamilton, 1983. 64p. illus.
——*rev. ed.* 1988.
for children.

3543 **Mosey, Don**
■ Botham. Methuen, 1986. 240p. illus. stats.
——*pbk. ed.* Sphere, 1987, *updated to include the 1986
season and the 1986-87 England tour to Australia.*

3544 **Murphy, Patrick**
■ Botham: a biography. Dent, 1988. xii, 236p. illus.
(some col.) stats. index.

3545 **Naik, Vasant K.**
Ian Bothamchi shouryagatha. Salsette (Goa),
Bandodkar, 1983. 159p.
in Marathi: 'A saga of Ian Botham's courageous exploits'.

3546 **Wilson, Lorraine**
Ian Botham; illustrated by Alex Stitt. Melbourne,
Nelson, 1984. 27p. illus.
for children.

Bough, Francis Joseph ('Frank')

3547 **Bough, Frank**
■ Cue Frank! Queen Anne Press, 1980. 191p. illus.
'Cavalier cricket' pp. 118-135.

Bowen, Rowland

3548 † **Joseph, Andrew**
■ Rowland Bowen. [The Author, 1968]. 9p. *typescript.*
Rowland Bowen and 'The cricket quarterly'.

Bowley, Thomas

3549 † [Craig, Albert]
■ Thomas Bowley. Wright & Co., [1889]. [4]p. folded
card, illus.

Boycott, Geoffrey

3550 **Alton, Fred,** *compiler*
■ The statistical Test cricket career of Geoff Boycott
O.B.E. from June 1964 to September 1981. The Author,
[1981]. [16]p. stats.
cover title: 'Boycott OBE'.

3551 **Boycott, Geoff**
■ Boycott: the autobiography. Macmillan, 1987. 296p.
illus. stats. index.
——*luxury ed. of 151 signed and numbered copies in slip
case, each copy corresponding to one of Boycott's
first-class centuries,* 1987.
——*pbk. ed.* Corgi, 1988.

3552 Opening up. Arthur Barker, 1980. 183p. illus. scores.
■ ——*pbk ed.* Sphere, 1982.

3553 **Callaghan, John**
■ Boycott: a cricketing legend. Pelham Books, 1982.
220p. illus. stats.
——*pbk. ed.* Sphere, 1984, *updated to January 1984.*

3554 Geoffrey Boycott. (Profiles series); illustrated by Karen
■ Heywood. Hamish Hamilton, 1982. 63p. illus.
for children.

3555 **Clark, Christopher D.**
■ The Test match career of Geoffrey Boycott. Tunbridge
Wells, Spellmount, 1986. 144p. illus. stats. index.

3556 **Mosey, Don**
■ Boycott. Methuen, 1985. xii, 224p. illus. stats.
——*pbk. ed.* Penguin, 1986, *updated to include 1985
season.*

3557 **Sheen, Steven**
■ The Geoffrey Boycott file. Hamlyn, 1982. 191p. stats.
*cover sub-title: 'complete match-by-match record of
Geoffrey Boycott's career 1962-81'.*

3558 Sir Geoffrey: 21 years of Yorkshire cricket. Arthur
■ Barker, 1984. [196]p. incl. adverts. illus. (some col.)
stats.
produced for testimonial season.

Bradman, *Sir* Donald George

3559 The **Bradman** albums: selections from Sir Donald
■ Bradman's official collection. Chatswood (N.S.W.),
Rigby, 1987. 800p. illus. (some col.) facsims. scores,
index.
*in 2 vols in slip case:
vol. 1 1925-1934;
vol. 2 1935-1949.*
——*UK ed.* Queen Anne Press, 1988.
——*de-luxe ed. of 500 numbered copies signed by Sir
Donald Bradman.*

3560 **Bradman** v Gavaskar. Lucknow, Lucknow Publishing
House, 1988. 82p. stats.
a statistical comparison.

3561 **Bradman, Don**
■ Farewell to cricket. Pavilion Books, 1988. [iii], 320p.
*reprinted ed. of 'Padwick I' 7354 with a new introduction
by David Frith.*

3562 **Bradman:** the Don declares. [Sydney], ABC Sport
(Radio) in association with the Australian Bicentenary
Authority, [1987]. 17p.
booklet to accompany ABC Radio series.

3563 † **British Broadcasting Corporation**
■ 'The Don'; broadcast on 5 July 1961. 15p. *typescript.
transcript of radio interview between John Arlott and Sir
Donald Bradman.*

3564 **Clarke, Mavis Thorpe**
■ Young and brave. Lane Cove (N.S.W.), Hodder and
Stoughton (Australia), 1984. 183p.
*contains 'Donald Bradman: a country lad with his cross
bat', pp. 85-105; for children.*

3565 **Derriman, Philip**
Bradman: the last portrait. [16]p. col. illus.
*special supplement of weekend 'Sydney Morning Herald',
7 Oct 1989.*

3566 **Derriman, Philip,** *editor*
■ Our Don Bradman: sixty years of writings about Sir
Donald Bradman. Willow Books, 1987. x, 222p.

3567 **Docker, Edward Wybergh**
■ Bradman and the bodyline. Angus & Robertson, 1983.
[v]. 165p. illus. bibliog. index.
pbk. ed. of 'Padwick I' 7357-1.

3568 **Egan, Jack** *[and]* **O'Reilly, William Joseph,** *compiler*
□ The Bradman era. Sydney, Australian Broadcasting
Corporation, 1983. 207p. illus. index.
*produced to accompany the television documentary of the
same name.*
——*pbk. ed.* Sydney, Fontana, 1983.
——*U.K. ed.* Willow Books, 1984.

3569 **Fingleton, John Henry Webb ('Jack')**
■ Brightly fades the Don. Pavilion Books, 1985. 261p.
illus. scores, index.
*reprinted ed. of 'Padwick I' 7359 with a new introduction
by Michael Parkinson.*

3570 **Mallett, Ashley Alexander**
■ Don Bradman (Master Cricketer series). Richmond
(Vic.), Hutchinson of Australia, 1983. 32p. illus.
for children.

3571 **Page, Michael Fitzgerald**
■ Bradman: the illustrated biography. Macmillan, 1983.
[viii], 368p. illus. facsims. stats. index.
'using the private possessions of Sir Donald Bradman'.
——*de-luxe ed. of 100 numbered copies signed by Sir
Donald Bradman.*
——*pbk. ed. (text only) entitled 'Bradman: the biography',*
Sun Books, 1988.

3572 **Page, Michael Fitzgerald** *and* **Fregon, Des**
■ The Don: a photographic essay of a legendary life.
Melbourne, Sun Books, 1984. 97p. illus.

3573 **Piesse, Ken**
■ Bradman and the legends of Australian cricket.
Melbourne, Syme Magazines, 1988. 68p. incl. covers &
adverts. illus. (some col.) stats.
*a 'Cricketer' magazine special, commemorating Sir
Donald Bradman's cricketing feats and his 80th birthday,
August 27, 1988.*

3574 Donald Bradman (Famous Australians series);
■ illustrated by Tanya Bamforth. Lane Cove (N.S.W.),
Hodder and Stoughton, 1983. 33p. illus. (some col.)
glossary, stats. index.
for children.

Brain, Brian Maurice

3575 **Brain, Brian**
■ Another day, another match: the diary of a county cricketer's season. George Allen & Unwin, 1981. x, 115p. illus. stats. index.
  the 1980 season.

3576 **Murphy, Patrick,** *editor*
■ Brainy: official testimonial brochure 1981; statistics by Bert Avery and Les Hatton; photographs by Ken Kelly. [1981]. 40p. incl. adverts. illus. stats.

Brassington, Andrew James ('Andy')

3577 **Andy** Brassington benefit 1988 souvenir brochure.
■ [Bristol, Benefit Committee, 1988]. 96p. incl. adverts. illus. (some col.) stats.

Breakwell, Dennis

3578 **Philpott, Ray,** *editor*
■ Trevor Gard, Dennis Breakwell joint benefit brochure 1989. Benefit Committee, 1989. 48p. incl. adverts. illus. (some col.) stats.

Brickett, David John

3579 **Dave** Brickett benefit brochure. Port Elizabeth, [1983].
■ 76p. incl. covers and adverts. illus. (some col.) stats.

Britcher, Samuel

3580 **Allen, David Rayvern**
■ Samuel Britcher: the hidden scorer. [The Author, 1982]. 16p. illus.
  limited ed. of 100 numbered and signed copies.

Broad, Brian Christopher ('Chris')

3581 **Broad, Chris** *with* **Murphy, Patrick**
■ Home truths from abroad. Arthur Barker, 1987. x, 148p. illus.

Broderick, Vincent

3582 † **Vince** Broderick's testimonial season. [1954]. [4]p.
■ folded card. illus.

Bryant, *Sir* Arthur

3583 † **Bryant,** *Sir* **Arthur**
■ The lion & the unicorn: a historian's testament. Collins, 1969. 367p. illus. index.
  cricket pp. 124, 191-199, 219-220.

Butcher, Alan Raymond

3584 **Alan** Butcher benefit year 1985. [1985]. 40p. incl.
■ adverts. illus. stats.

Butcher, Roland Orlando

3585 **Butcher, Roland** *and* **Lawrence, Bridgette**
■ Rising to the challenge. Pelham Books, 1989. viii, 165p. illus. stats. index.

3586 **Roland** Butcher benefit 1989. [1989]. [80]p. incl.
■ adverts. illus. stats.

Caesar, Julius

3587 **Amey, Geoffrey**
■ The ill-fated cricketer: Julius Caesar and the players of his time. Guildford, the Author, 1987. [iv], 102p. illus. scores.

Cairns, Bernard Lance

3588 **Cairns, [Bernard] Lance**
■ Give it a heave! an autobiography. Auckland, MOA Publications, 1984. 224p. illus. (some col.) stats.

Cardus, *Sir* John Frederick Neville

3589 **Brookes, Christopher**
■ His own man: the life of Neville Cardus. Methuen, 1985. [viii], 280p. illus. bibliog. index.
  ——*pbk ed.* Unwin, 1986.

3590 **Cardus,** *Sir* **Neville**
  Autobiography. Hamish Hamilton, 1984. 288p. illus.
  reprinted ed. of 'Padwick I' 7402.

Carrick, Philip

3591 **Phil** Carrick benefit 1985. [Benefit Committee, 1985].
■ [104]p. incl. adverts. illus. stats.

Chadwick, John Peter Granvillle

3592 The **Peter** Chadwick benefit for 1984. Harrogate,
■ Harrogate Cricket Club, 1984. [10]p. incl. inside covers and adverts. illus.

Chapman, Arthur Percy Frank

3593 **Lemmon, David Hector**
■ Percy Chapman: a biography. Queen Anne Press, 1985. 162p. illus. stats. bibliog. index.

Chappell Family

3594 **Brayshaw, Ian John**
■ The Chappell era. Sydney, Australian Broadcasting Corporation, 1984. 160p. illus. stats.

3595 **Mallett, Ashley Alexander**
■ The Chappell brothers (Master Cricketer series). Richmond (Vic.), Hutchinson of Australia, 1982. 32p. illus.
  for children.

Chappell, Gregory Stephen

3596 **Chappell:** the master batsman. Pymble (N.S.W.),
■ Playbill, [1982]. [25]p. illus. (some col.)

3597 **Chappell, Greg**
■ Unders and overs. Sydney, Lansdowne Press, 1981. 128p. illus. (some col.)
  cover sub-title: 'the controversies of cricket'.
  principally the 1980-81 season.

3598 **McGregor, Adrian**
■ Greg Chappell. Sydney, Collins, 1985. [vi], 286p. illus. stats. index.
  ——*pbk. ed.* Fontana, 1986.

3599　**Murray, Peter Allan,** [*editor*]
■　A pictorial and statistical record of Chappell, Lillee, Marsh: Test cricket. Waterloo (N.S.W.), Waterloo Press, 1984. 168p. illus. (some col.) stats.
with contributions from Max Walker, Sunil Gavaskar, Richard Hadlee, Sarfraz Nawaz, Alvin Kallicharran, David Frith and Henry Blofeld.

3600　**Pollard, Jack**
■　A tribute to Lillee and Chappell [Sydney], Angus & Robertson, 1984. 52p. col. illus.

Chatfield, Ewen John

3601　**Chatfield, Ewen** *with* **McConnell, Lynn**
■　Chats: Ewen Chatfield's life in cricket. Auckland, MOA Publications, 1988. 216p. illus. (some col.) stats.

3602　**Hannah, D. V.** *and* **Alexander, R. S.,** *editors*
Ewen Chatfield 1985-86 benefit programme. Wellington, Wellington Cricket Association, 1985. 55p. illus. stats.

Clarke, Sylvester Theophilus

3603　**Sylvester** Clarke benefit 1987. Wimbledon, Clifford
■　Frost, [1987]. 40p. incl. adverts. illus. stats.

Clift, Patrick Bernard ('Paddy')

3604　**Paddy** Clift benefit year 1986. [1986]. 52p. incl. adverts.
■　illus. stats.

Clift, Phil Brittain

3605　**Phil** Clift testimonial match: Glamorgan C. C. C. v
■　Llanarth C. C. ... Sunday, June 13th. [1982]. [8]p. incl. covers. illus.

Clinton, Grahame Selvey

3606　**Grahame** Clinton: benefit year 1989. [Benefit
■　Committee, 1989]. 52p. incl. adverts. illus. (some col.) stats.

Compton, Denis Charles Scott

3607　**Compton, Denis**
■　End of an innings. Pavilion Books, 1988. xx, 207p. illus.
reprinted ed. of 'Padwick I' 7439 with a new introduction by Benny Green.

3608　**Vivian, Gordon,** *editor*
■　'Fifty years on': 1934-1984; golden anniversary celebration dinner ... Thursday 18th October, 1984. Denis Compton/Bill Edrich Dinner Committee, 1984. [32]p. incl. adverts. illus. stats.

3609　**West, Peter**
■　Denis Compton: cricketing genius. Stanley Paul, 1989. viii, 184p. illus. stats. index.

Coney, Jeremy Vernon

3610　**Coney, Jeremy**
■　The playing mantis: an autobiography. Auckland, MOA Publications, 1986. 279p. illus. (some col.) stats.
——de luxe vellum-backed limited ed. of 110 numbered copies in slip case produced for Wellington Cricket Association, 1986. Nos. 1-10 signed as presentation copies.

Cook, Geoffrey

3611　**Geoff** Cook benefit year 1985. [Benefit Committee,
■　1985]. [48]p. incl. adverts. illus. stats.

Cooper, Kevin Edwin

3612　**Double** act: Kevin Cooper and Franklyn Stephenson.
■　Nottingham, Nottinghamshire C. C. C. Marketing Department, [1988]. 28p. illus. stats.
both took more than 100 first class wickets in 1988 season.

Cope, Geoffrey Alan

3613　**Barrie** Leadbeater, Geoff Cope benefit 1980 souvenir.
■　[1980]. [48]p. incl. adverts. illus. (some col.) stats.

Copland-Crawford, Robert Erskine Wade

3614　**Brock, Richard E.**
■　The Copland-Crawfords of Wembley. Ware, the Author, 1989. 120p. illus. map.
his cricket career pp 41-42.

Cowdrey, Christopher Stuart

3615　**Chris** Cowdrey, Kent and England, benefit year 1989.
■　[Canterbury, Benefit Committee, 1989]. [104]p. incl. adverts. illus. (some col.) stats.

3616　**Cowdrey, Chris** *and* **Smith, Jonathan B.**
■　Good enough? Pelham Books, 1986. 187p. illus. scores.

Cowley, Gavin Selwyn

3617　**Cowley, Gavin**
■　Having a ball. Port Elizabeth, S. A. Sporting Publications, 1983. [iv], 108p. illus.
an account of the author's cricket and rugby career.

Cowley, Nigel Geoffrey

3618　**Symes, Patrick,** *editor*
■　Dougal: Nigel Cowley benefit year 1988. [1988]. 72p. incl. adverts. illus. (some col.) stats.

Cox, George

3619　**Sussex Cricket Society**
A thanksgiving for the life and work of George Cox, cricketer and man of Sussex. [Brighton, the Society, 1985]. [12]p.

Craig, Albert

3620 †　**Arlott, [Leslie Thomas] John**
■　A.C., cricket rhymster; broadcast 22 August 1961. 5p. *typescript.*
transcript of radio talk on Albert Craig.

3621 †　**Craig, Albert**
■　A few of my personal experiences on our famous cricket centres. Printed by T. Hughes, 1902? [16]p.

Crapp, John Frederick ('Jack')

3622　**George, Michael**
■　Sportsmen of Cornwall. Bodmin, Bossiney Books, 1986. 96p. illus.
Jack Crapp pp. 38-41.

Crawley, Aidan Merivale

3623 **Crawley, Aidan**
■ Leap before you look: a memoir. Collins, 1988. 444p. illus. index.
some cricket, especially pp. 49-73.

Creswell, John

3624 **Harte, Christopher John ('Chris')**
John Creswell: cricket administrator supreme. North Adelaide, Sports Marketing, 1989. 64p.
limited ed. of 50 copies.
Creswell was SACA secretary from 1883-1909.

Crisp, Robert James ('Bob')

3625 † **Crisp, Robert**
Brazen chariots: an account of tank warfare in the Western Desert, November - December 1941. Muller, 1959. 233p.
several cricket references.

3626 † **Duffus, Louis George**
Beyond the laager. Hurst & Blackett, [1947]. 168p. illus.
ch. ii 'Sticklebacks are proud of you', pp. 31-46, contains an account of Bob Crisp's life and war service.

Crowe Family

3627 **Crowe, Martin David** *and* **Crowe, Jeffrey John** *as told to*
■ **Crowe, Dave** *and* **Crowe, Audrey**
The Crowe style: Martin and Jeff's world of cricket. Auckland, MOA Publications, 1987. 181p. illus. (some col.) stats.

Daniel, Wayne Wendall

3628 **Wayne** Daniel ... benefit '85 souvenir brochure. [1985].
■ 43p. incl. adverts. illus. stats.

Davis, Charles Percy

3629 **[Gardner, Les,** *editor]*
■ Percy Davis: 33 years in the sun. King William's Town, Old Dalian Union, 1980. 64p. incl. adverts. illus. stats.
the former Northants player coached at Dale College for 28 years.

Davison, Brian Fettes

3630 **Johnson, Martin,** *editor*
■ Davo's benefit year brochure. [1982]. [32]p. incl. adverts. illus. (some col.) stats.

Denning, Peter William

3631 **Peter** Denning testimonial book: 1981. [1981]. 56p. incl.
■ adverts. illus. stats.

Deodhar, Dinkar Balwant

3632 **Deodhar, D. B.** *and* **Naik, Vasant K.**
Shatakakade - cricket, kal, aaj and udya. Pune, Utkarsh, 1986. 254p.
in Marathi: 'Towards a century - cricket yesterday, today and tomorrow'; autobiography published at the age of 94.

3633 **Patakara, Ravindra**
Kriketa Maharshi Pro. Di. Ba. Devadhara. Thana (Maharashtra), Suyasa Prakasana, 1981. 86p. illus.

Dexter, Edward Ralph ('Ted')

3634 **Lodge, Derek Harry Alan**
■ The Test match career of Ted Dexter. Tunbridge Wells, Nutshell Publishing, 1989. viii, 164p. illus. stats. index.

Dilley, Graham Roy

3635 **Dilley, Graham** *and* **Otway, Graham**
■ Swings and roundabouts. Pelham Books, 1987. 160p. illus. index.

D'Oliveira, Basil Lewis

3636 **D'Oliveira, Basil** *with* **Murphy, Patrick**
■ Time to declare: an autobiography. Dent, 1980. xii, 179p. illus. stats. index.
——*pbk ed.* Star, 1982.

Douglas, John William Henry Tyler

3637 **Lemmon, David Hector**
■ Johnny won't hit today: a cricketing biography of J.W.H.T. Douglas. George Allen & Unwin, 1983. [vii], 152p. illus. stats. index.

Dredge, Colin Herbert

3638 **Philpott, Ray,** *editor*
■ Colin Dredge - the Demon of Frome: souvenir benefit brochure 1987. [Benefit Committee, 1987]. 48p. incl. adverts. illus. stats.

Du Preez, John Harcourt ('Jack')

3639 † **[Byrom, Glen,** *editor]*
Jack Du Preez benefit match '79: souvenir programme. 1979. 8p. illus.

Dudleston, Barry

3640 **Johnson, Martin,** *editor*
■ Barry Dudleston benefit year. [1980]. [40]p. incl. adverts. illus. (some col.) stats.

Ealham, Alan George Ernest

3641 **Alan** Ealham benefit year 1982. [Benefit Committee],
■ 1982. [44]p. incl. adverts. illus. stats.

East, Robert John

3642 **van Rensburg, Rudie,** *editor*
■ Robbie East: benefit year 1988-89. Cape Town, Belmor, [1988]. 64p. incl. adverts. illus. (some col.) stats.
some text in Afrikaans.

Edgar, Bruce Adrian

3643 **Edgar, Bruce** *with* **Roberts, David**
■ An opener's tale. Wellington, Bootsie Books, 1987. 75p. illus. (some col.) stats.

Edmonds, Philippe-Henri

3644 **Barnes, Simon**
■ Phil Edmonds: a singular man. Kingswood Press, 1986. xi, 180p. illus. stats. index.

3645 **Phil** Edmonds benefit year calendar. [1983]. [16]p. incl.
■ covers, illus.
includes Middlesex cricket calendar.

Edrich, Geoffrey Arthur

3646 † G.A.Edrich's benefit: Lancashire v Derbyshire at Old Trafford ... July 2nd, 4th and 5th, 1955. [Manchester, Lancashire County Cricket Club], 1955. [4]p. illus. stats.

Edrich, William John

3647 Vivian, Gordon, editor
'Fifty years on': 1934-1984; golden anniversary celebration dinner ... Thursday 18th October, 1984. Denis Compton/Bill Edrich Dinner Committee, 1984. [32]p. incl. adverts. illus. stats.

Elkington, Gerald B.

3648 † Harragan, Robert
Pembrey man's part in sports history. [The Author], 1978. 1p.
Elkington played for South Wales C.C. v Australians in 1878.

Emburey, John Ernest

3649 Emburey, John with Rogers, Martin
Emburey: autobiography Haywards Heath, Partridge Press, 1987. [iv], 166p. illus. index.

3650 John Emburey ... benefit 1986. [1986]. 65p. incl. adverts. illus. (some col.) stats.

Eriksen, Ronnie

3651 Eriksen, Ronnie
A view from the dressing room: the memoirs of a cricket manager. Knysna (Cape Province), Amorique, 1989. xii, 220p. illus. (some col.)

Evans, Talfryn

3652 Harragan, Robert
Tal Evans. The Author, 1980. 1p. typescript.
offprint from 'Llanelli Star', Sep. 1980.

Fairbrother, Jim

3653 Fairbrother, Jim and Moore, Reginald
Testing the wicket: from Trent Bridge to Lord's. Pelham Books, 1984. 144p. illus. index.

Fender, Percy George Herbert

3654 Streeton, Richard Marsh
P.G.H. Fender: a biography. Faber & Faber, 1981. 194p. illus. stats. bibliog. index.
——reprinted ed. Pavilion Books, 1987, with a new introduction by the author.

Ferreira, Anthonie Michal ('Anton')

3655 Chesterfield, Trevor, editor
Anton Ferreira benefit year 1987-88. [Johannesburg, Benefit Committee, 1987]. 96p. incl. adverts. illus. stats.

Fingleton, John Henry Webb ('Jack')

3656 Fingleton, Jack
Batting from memory. Collins, 1981. 266p. illus. index.

3657 Cricket crisis: bodyline and other lines. Pavilion Books, 1984. xx, 313p. illus. index.
reprinted ed. of 'Padwick I' 7527 with a new introduction by Michael Parkinson.

Fletcher, Keith William Robert

3658 Fletcher, Keith
Captain's innings: an autobiography. Stanley Paul, 1983. 156p. illus.

3659 Keith Fletcher testimonial 1982. [1982]. 60p. incl. adverts. illus. (some col.) stats.

Ford, Christopher Gilbert

3660 † Talbot, Edward Keble
Christopher Gilbert Ford 1910-1944: a memoir. Printed for private circulation, 1957. 59p. illus.
Ford played for Harrow in 1928 and 1929 and toured Denmark in 1939 with M.C.C.

Fotheringham, Henry Richard

3661 Henry Fotheringham benefit year 1988/89. [Johannesburg, 1988]. [92]p. incl. adverts. illus. (some col.) stats.

Fowler, Graeme

3662 Fowler, Graeme and Ball, Peter
Fox on the run. Viking, 1988. xvi, 206p. illus. index.
——pbk. ed. Penguin, 1989.

Freeman, Alfred Percy ('Tich')

3663 Lemmon, David Hector
'Tich' Freeman and the decline of the leg-break bowler. George Allen & Unwin, 1982. xii, 144p. illus. stats. index.

Fry, Charles Burgess

3664 † Craig, Albert
Mr C. B. Fry. Wright & Co., 1906. [4]p. folded card, illus.

3665 Ellis, Clive
C.B.: the life of Charles Burgess Fry. Dent, 1984. x, 294p. illus. stats. bibliog.

3666 Fry, C.B.
Life worth living. Pavilion Books, 1986. viii, 423p. illus. index.
reprinted ed. of 'Padwick I' 7538 with a new introduction by Alan Ross.

3667 Morris, Ronald
The captain's lady. Chatto & Windus / Hogarth Press, 1985. 178p. illus. bibliog. index.
the story of Beatie Fry, the wife of C.B.Fry.

Gabriel, Harold Edward Hammond

3668 Gabriel, H. E. H.
76 not out - my cricketing life. The Author, [1980]. [v], 49p. illus. typescript.
limited ed., each copy signed by the author. Harold Gabriel was a stalwart of the Forty Club.

Gard, Trevor

3669 Philpott, Ray, editor
Trevor Gard, Dennis Breakwell joint benefit brochure 1989. Benefit Committee, 1989. 48p. incl. adverts. illus. (some col.) stats.

Garner, Joel

3670 **Coombes, Eric,** *editor*
■ Big Bird 1986: Joel Garner benefit brochure. [1986].
36p. incl. adverts. illus. stats.

3671 **Garner, Joel**
■ 'Big bird' flying high. Arthur Barker, 1988. [vi], 200p.
illus.

Gatting, Michael William

3672 **Mike** Gatting benefit 1988. [Benefit Committee 1988].
■ [88]p. incl. adverts. illus. (some col.) stats.

3673 **Gatting, Mike** *with* **Patmore, Angela**
■ Leading from the front: the autobiography of Mike
Gatting. Queen Anne Press, 1988. [viii], 216p. illus.
index.
——*pbk. ed.* Futura, 1989, *with appendix on 1988
season written by Angela Patmore and final chapter of
self-analysis written in 1989.*

Gavaskar, Sunil Manohar

3674 **Bradman** v Gavaskar. Lucknow, Lucknow Publishing
House, 1988. 82p. stats.
a statistical comparison.

3675 **Clark, Christopher D.**
■ The record-breaking Sunil Gavaskar. Newton Abbot,
David & Charles, 1980. 191p. illus. stats. index.

3676 **Moraes, Dominic Frank**
■ Sunil Gavaskar: an illustrated biography. Madras,
Macmillan India, 1987. x, 197p. illus. (some col.) stats.
index.

3677 **Naik, Vasant K.**
Shatakneer Gavaskar. Salsette (Goa), Bandodkar,
1987. 160p.
in Marathi: 'Centurion hero Gavaskar'.

3678 **Sinha, M. P.**
Cricket samrat Gavaskar: 30 shatakoon ka
sampooran-sachitra vivran. New Delhi, Madha Muskan
Comics, 1984. 36p. incl. covers. illus. stats.
*in Hindi: 'The emperor of cricket: an illustrated
description of 30 centuries'.*

3679 **Tarafdar, Amiya**
■ The hidden treasure: Gavaskar. Calcutta, Suhas
Talukdar, 1987. 110p. illus. (some col.) stats.
*a photo-journalist's record with text compiled and edited
by Atul Mukherjee et al.*

Gibson, Alan

3680 **Gibson, Alan**
■ Growing up with cricket: some memories of a sporting
education. George Allen & Unwin, 1985. xii, 179p.

Giffen, George

3681 **Giffen, George**
■ The golden age of Australian cricket; introduced and
edited by Ken Piesse. South Yarra (Vic.), Currey
O'Neil, 1982. vi, 137p. illus. facsims. stats.
new ed. of 'Padwick I' 7551.

Gifford, Norman

3682 'Giff': Worcestershire and England; testimonial year
■ 1981. [1981]. [66]p. incl. adverts. illus. stats.

Gimblett, Harold

3683 **Foot, David**
■ Harold Gimblett: tormented genius of cricket.
Heinemann, 1982. xi, 148p. illus. bibliog. index.
——*pbk. ed.* Star, 1984.

Goddard, Trevor Leslie

3684 **Goddard, Trevor**
■ Caught in the deep. East London, Vision Media, 1988.
121p. illus.
*some cricket; principally an account of his religious
convictions.*

Goldman, Joseph Wolfe

3685 **Thirlwell, Angela**
■ A century of practice: Isadore Goldman & Son,
1885-1985. Isadore Goldman & Son, 1985. vi, 42p. illus.
cricket interest of Joe Goldman, pp. 27-29.

Gooch, Graham Alan

3686 **Gooch, Graham** *with* **Lee, Alan**
■ My cricket diary '81: the West Indies, Australia, India.
Stanley Paul, 1982. 177p. illus.

3687 Out of the wilderness. Willow Books, 1985. 153p. illus.
■ stats.
——*pbk. ed.* Grafton, 1986, *updated to include 1985
season.*

3688 **Goochie:** Graham Gooch benefit year 1988. [1985]. 88p.
■ incl. adverts. illus. (some col.) stats.

Gower, David Ivon

3689 **Farrar, John** *and* **Hodgson, Derek,** *editor*
■ David Gower benefit brochure. [Benefit Committee,
1987]. 96p. incl. adverts. illus. (some col.) stats.

3690 **Gower, David** *and* **Lee, Alan**
■ With time to spare. Ward Lock, 1980. 120p. illus. stats.

3691 **Powell, Robert D.**
■ D.I. Gower: a statistical appreciation. Sutton Coldfield,
the Author, 1987. 16 leaves, bibliog. *typescript.*

Grace Family

3692 **Jones, Peris**
■ Gentlemen and players. [Bristol], Downend Local
History Society, 1989. [ii], ii, 72p. illus.

Grace, Edward Mills

3693 **Turner, John R. B.**
A doctor cricketer: the other Grace. [1980]. [8]p. incl.
covers.
reprinted from 'The Practitioner', Nov 1980.

Grace, William Gilbert

3694 † **[Craig, Albert]**
☐ Dr W. G. Grace. Wright & Co., [1887]. [4]p. folded
card, illus.
——*another ed.* 1890.
——*another ed.* 1894.
earlier eds. of 'Padwick I' 7577.

3695 **Darwin, Bernard**
■ W.G. Grace. Duckworth, 1981. 128p. illus. stats.
bibliog. index.
pbk. ed. of 'Padwick I' 7579.

3696 **Furniss, Harry**
■ A century of Grace ... with anecdotes of W. G. Grace. Hambledon Press, [1984]. 64p. illus.
new ed. of 'Padwick I' 7588.

3697 † **Gloucester City Library**
Catalogue of the Grace centenary. 1948.
Graciana exhibition; 91 cricket items.

3698 **Grace, William Gilbert**
■ 'W.G.': cricketing reminiscences and personal recollections. Hambledon Press, 1980. xxiv, 422p. illus. stats. index.
another ed. of 'Padwick I' 7583 with a new introduction by E.W. Swanton.

3699 **Midwinter, Eric Clare**
■ W.G. Grace: his life and times. George Allen & Unwin, 1981. [ix], 175p. illus. bibliog. index.

Grant, George Copeland ('Jack')

3700 **Grant, Jack**
■ Jack Grant's story: educator, cricketer, missionary. Guildford, Lutterworth Press, 1980. x, 198p. illus. index.

Graveney, David Anthony

3701 **David** Graveney souvenir benefit brochure 1986.
■ [Bristol, Benefit Committee, 1986]. 92p. incl. adverts. illus. (some col.) stats.

Graveney, Thomas William

3702 **Graveney, Tom**
■ The heart of cricket. Arthur Barker, 1983. 186p. illus. index.

Greenidge, Cuthbert Gordon

3703 **Greenidge, Gordon** *with* **Symes, Patrick**
■ Gordon Greenidge: the man in the middle. Newton Abbott, David & Charles, 1980. 207p. illus. stats. index.

3704 **Symes, Patrick** *and* **Cave, Paul**
■ Gordon Greenidge benefit year 1983: souvenir brochure. Southampton, Paul Cave Publications, 1983. 44p. incl adverts. illus. stats.

Greensmith, William Thomas ('Bill')

3705 † [**Bill** Greensmith benefit brochure]. [1963]. 20p. illus.

Gregory, William Robert

3706 **Smythe, Colin,** *editor*
■ Robert Gregory: a centenary tribute with a foreword by his children. Gerrards Cross, the Author, 1981. 40p. illus.
photographs of Robert Gregory as cricketer, p. 13.

Greig, Anthony William ('Tony')

3707 **Greig, Tony** *with* **Lee, Alan**
■ My story. Stanley Paul, 1980. 188p. illus. stats. index.

Griffiths, Brian James ('Jim')

3708 **Barron, Brian,** *editor*
■ Jim Griffiths testimonial '87. [1987]. [44]p. incl. adverts. illus. stats.

Gunn Family

3709 **Haynes, Basil** *and* **Lucas, John**
■ The Trent Bridge battery: the story of the sporting Gunns. Willow Books, 1985. 208p. illus. stats. bibliog.

Hadlee, *Sir* Richard John

3710 **Farrar, John,** *compiler and editor*
■ Richard Hadlee testimonial brochure. [Nottingham, 1986]. 96p. incl. adverts. illus. stats.

3711 **Hadlee, Richard**
■ Hadlee hits out. Auckland, Lansdowne Press, 1983. 179p. illus. stats.

3712 **Hadlee, Richard** *and* **Brittenden, Richard Trevor** ('Dick')
■ Hadlee. Wellington, Reed; London, Angus & Robertson, 1981. xii, 195p. illus. index.

3713 **Hadlee, Richard** *with* **Becht, Richard**
■ Rhythm and swing: an autobiography. Auckland, MOA Publications, 1989. 303p. illus. (some col.) scores, stats.
——*U.K. ed.* Souvenir Press, 1990.

3714 **Hadlee, Richard** *with* **Francis, Tony**
■ Richard Hadlee: at the double; the story of cricket's pacemaker. Stanley Paul, 1985. 166p. illus. scores. stats.

3715 The **Richard** Hadlee testimonial year book. Auckland
■ (N.Z.), Richard Hadlee Testimonial Committee, [1989]. 64p. illus. (some col.) stats.

Hammond, Walter Reginald

3716 **Howat, Gerald Malcolm David**
■ Walter Hammond. George Allen & Unwin, 1984. xvi, 160p. illus. stats. bibliog. index.

Hampshire, John Harry

3717 **Hampshire, John** *and* **Mosey, Don**
■ Family argument: my 20 years in Yorkshire cricket. George Allen & Unwin, 1983. x, 142p. illus. index.

Hanif Mohammed

3718 **Hanif** Mohammed benefit: Pakistan XI vs New Zealand
■ XI ... Dec 16 1984: official souvenir. [Karachi, 1984]. 164p. incl. covers and adverts.

Hardie, Brian Ross

3719 **Brian** Hardie benefit year 1983. [Testimonial
■ Committee, 1983]. 56p. incl. covers & adverts. illus. stats.

Harris, George Robert Canning
4th Baron

3720 **Coldham, James Desmond**
■ Lord Harris. George Allen & Unwin, 1983. xii, 171p. illus. bibliog. index.

Hawke, Neil James Napier

3721 **Hawke, Neil**
■ Bowled over. Adelaide, Rigby, 1982. 184p. illus.

Hayes, Frank Charles

3722 **Higgs, Peter,** *editor*
■ Frank Hayes ... official testimonial brochure. [1983]. [64]p. incl. adverts. illus. stats.

Hazare, Vijay Samuel

3723 **Hazare, Vijay** *and* **Naik, Vasant K.**
■ A long innings Calcutta etc., Rupa, 1981. viii, 276p. illus. stats. index.

3724 Maze gajalele sa. Pune, Kreedangan, 1987.
in Marathi: 'My famous matches'.

3725 **Menon, Mohandas K.** *et al, compilers*
■ Vijay Hazare: complete statistics in first-class cricket; with end of season summary and biography by Dr. Vasant Naik. (Profiles in Statistics series: 1). Bombay, The Association of Cricket Statisticians and Scorers of India, 1989. 82p. illus. stats.

Headley, George Alphonso

3726 **Whitham, Robert K.**
■ George A. Headley (Famous Cricketers series: no. 5). West Bridgford (Notts.), Association of Cricket Statisticians, [1989]. 30p. illus. stats.
cover sub-title: 'his record innings-by-innings'.

Hearne, George Gibbons

3727 † **[Craig, Albert]**
■ G.G. Hearne. Wright & Co., [1889]. [4]p. folded card, illus.

Hemmings, Edward Ernest ('Eddie')

3728 **Cooper, Peter B.,** *compiler and editor*
■ Eddie Hemmings benefit year 1987. [Nottingham, 1987]. [100]p. incl. adverts. illus. scores, stats.

Hemsley, Edward John Orton ('Ted')

3729 **Holden, Sue,** *editor*
■ E.J.O.: the official brochure of the Ted Hemsley benefit year 1982. [1982]. 64p. incl. adverts. illus. stats.

Hendrick, Michael

3730 **Mortimer, Gerald,** *editor*
■ Hendo: Mike Hendrick's testimonial brochure 1980. [1980]. 44p. incl. adverts. illus. stats.

Hendry, Hunter Scott Thomas Laurie

3731 **Cardwell, Ronald L.** *and* **Hodgson, Thomas L. P.**
■ A cameo from the past: the life and times of H.S.T.L. Hendry. [Sydney], Cricket Publishing Company for the Australian Cricket Society, 1984. 137p. illus. scores, stats.
limited ed. of 325 numbered and signed copies.

Henry, Omar

3732 Omar Henry benefit 1988-1989. Cape Town?, n.p.
■ [1988]. 52p. incl. adverts. illus. (some col.) stats.

Hide, Arthur Bollard

3733 † **[Craig, Albert]**
■ Arthur Hide. Wright & Co., [1889]. [4]p. folded card, illus.
——*another ed.* n.p., 1889.

Higgs, Kenneth

3734 **Johnson, Martin,** *editor*
■ Ken Higgs/Chris Balderstone benefit year. [Testimonial Committee], 1984. 48p. incl. adverts. illus. stats.
brochure for testimonial year.

Hill, Alan

3735 **Mortimer, Gerald,** *editor*
■ The Alan Hill benefit year 1986. [Derby, Derbyshire County Cricket Club, 1986]. 66p. incl. covers and adverts. illus. (some col.) stats.

Hirst, George Herbert

3736 † George Hirst's benefit at Headingley, August 1904: 'my
■ cricketing career'. [Leeds, *Pudsey Echo*], 1904. 16p. incl. adverts. illus.
cover title.

3737 **Thomson, Arthur Alexander**
■ Hirst and Rhodes. Pavilion Books, 1986. viii, 211p. illus. stats. bibliog. index.
reprinted ed. of 'Padwick I' 7687 with a new introduction by J.M. Kilburn.

Hobbs, *Sir* John Berry ('Jack')

3738 **Arlott, [Leslie Thomas] John**
■ Jack Hobbs: profile of the master. John Murray / Davis Poynter, 1981. 144p. illus. stats. bibliog. index.
——*pbk. ed.* Penguin, 1982.

3739 **Hobbs, Jack**
My life story. Hambledon Press, 1981. xviii, 320p. illus. scores, stats.
reprinted ed. of 'Padwick I' 7697 with a new introduction by Benny Green.
——*limited ed. signed by P.G.H.Fender,* 1981.

3740 **Lodge, Derek Harry Alan**
■ J.B. Hobbs: his record innings-by-innings. [Famous Cricketers series: no 1]. [Haughton Mill (Notts.)], Association of Cricket Statisticians, [1986]. 44p. frontis. stats.

3741 **Mason, Ronald Charles**
■ Jack Hobbs: a biography. Pavilion Books, 1988. xi, 212p. illus.
reprinted ed. of 'Padwick I' 7701 with a new introduction by the author.

3742 **Porter, Clive Willoughby**
■ The Test match career of Sir Jack Hobbs. Tunbridge Wells, Spellmount, 1988. [vi], 177p. illus. stats. bibliog. index.

Hobson, Denys Laurence

3743 **Denys** Hobson benefit year 1984/5. [Cape Town, Creda
■ Press, 1984]. 72p. incl. adverts. illus. (some col.) stats.

Hodgson, Alan

3744 Alan Hodgson ... testimonial 1980. [3]p. illus.
■

Hopkins, John Anthony

3745 **John** Hopkins benefit brochure 1986. [1986]. [40]p.
■ incl. adverts. illus. (some col.) stats.

Howarth, Geoffrey Philip

3746 **Geoff** Howarth benefit brochure 1983. [1983]. 32p. incl.
■ adverts. illus. stats.

Hughes, David Paul

3747 **Hemsley, Bill,** *editor*
■ David Hughes testimonial fund 1981. [1981]. [104]p.
incl. adverts. illus. (some col.) stats.

Hughes, Kimberley John

3748 **Mallett, Ashley Alexander**
■ Kim Hughes (Master Cricketer series). Melbourne,
Hutchinson of Australia, 1984. 32p. illus.
for children.

Humpage, Geoffrey William

3749 **Geoff** Humpage benefit year 1987 official souvenir
■ brochure. [1987]. 48p. incl adverts. illus. stats.

Hutton, *Sir* Leonard

3750 **Alton, Fred,** *compiler*
■ Len: the statistical Test cricket career of Sir Len Hutton
from 1937-to-1981 (sic). The Author, [1981]. 18p. illus.
stats.

3751 **Howat, Gerald Malcolm David**
■ Len Hutton. Heinemann Kingswood, 1988. xii, 227p.
illus. stats. index.

3752 **Hutton, Len** *and* **Bannister, Alexander James**
■ Fifty years in cricket. Stanley Paul, 1984. 202p. illus.
stats. index.
——*pbk. ed.* 1986.

Illingworth, Raymond

3753 **Illingworth, Ray** *in association with* **Mosey, Don**
■ Yorkshire and back: the autobiography of Ray
Illingworth. Queen Anne Press, 1980. 192p. illus. stats.
——*pbk. ed.* Futura, 1981.

3754 **Illingworth, Ray** *with* **Whiting, Steve**
■ The tempestuous years, 1979-83. Sidgwick & Jackson,
1987. 152p. illus. index.

Imran Khan Niazi

3755 **Imran** Khan benefit year 1987. [1987]. 52p. incl
■ unnumbered advert. pages, illus. (one col.)

3756 **Imran Khan**
■ All round view. Chatto & Windus, 1988. xiv, 210p.
illus. (some col.) stats. index.
——*pbk. ed.* Pan Books, 1989.

3757 **Imran Khan** *with* **Murphy, Patrick**
■ Imran: the autobiography of Imran Khan. Pelham
Books, 1983. ix, 163p. illus. index.

3758 **Iqbal Munir**
■ An eye on Imran; commentary by Chishty Mujahid.
Karachi, World of Cricket Pakistan, 1987. [122]p. incl
adverts. col. illus. stats.
a photographic record.
——*another ed.* 1988.

Inchmore, John Darling

3759 **John** Inchmore benefit magazine 1985. [1985]. 83p. incl
■ adverts. illus. (some col.) stats.

Ingelse, D. L.

3760 **Ingelse, D. L.**
■ 'Vyftig plus vyf': een cricket leven. Eindhoven, [the
Author], 1983. 71p. illus. index.
*the author's cricketing life in the Netherlands, 1928-83,
covering 50 years of league cricket and 5 years of friendly
cricket.*
limited ed. of 120 copies.

Jackman, Robin David

3761 **Robin** Jackman benefit year 1981. 1981. [48]p. incl.
■ adverts. illus. (some col.) stats.

Jackson, Archibald Alexander

3762 **Frith, David Edward John**
■ Archie Jackson: the Keats of cricket. Pavilion Books,
1987. xv, 111p. illus. stats. index.
rev. ed. of 'Padwick I' 7753-1.

Jackson, *Sir* Frank Stanley

3763 **Coldham, James P.**
■ F.S. Jackson: a cricketing biography. Marlborough,
Crowood Press, 1989. 208p. illus. stats. bibliog. index.

James, Cyril Lionel Robert

3764 **Cashman, Richard I.** *and* **McKernan, Michael,** *editors*
■ Sport: money, morality and the media. Kensington, New
South Wales University Press, [1982]. illus. bibliog.
index.
*includes 'Cricket, literature and the politics of
de-colonisation - the case of C.L.R.James' by Helen
Tiffin, pp. 177-193.*

3765 **James, C. L. R.**
□ Beyond a boundary. New York, Pantheon Books, 1983.
xviii, 255p.
U.S. ed. of 'Padwick I' 7757.
——*pbk. ed.* London, Stanley Paul, 1986, *with a
foreword by Mike Brearley.*

Jardine, Douglas Robert

3766 **Douglas, Christopher**
■ Douglas Jardine: spartan cricketer. George Allen &
Unwin, 1984. xiv, 206p. illus. stats. bibliog. index.

Jarvis, Kevin Bertram Sidney

3767 **Kevin** Jarvis benefit year '87. [Benefit Committee],
■ 1987. [68]p. incl. adverts. illus. (one col.) stats.

Jeanes, William Henry ('Bill')

3768 **Harte, Christopher John ('Chris')**
■ W.H. Jeanes: the man who made modern South
Australian cricket. North Adelaide, Sports Marketing,
1989. 24p.
limited ed. of 50 copies.
Bill Jeanes was SACA secretary 1926-55.

Jennings, Raymond Vernon

3769 **Caught** behind: Ray Jennings benefit year 1987-88.
Johannesburg?, Wiggins Teape, [1987]. 96p. incl.
adverts. illus. (some col.) stats.

Jephson, Digby Loder Armroid

3770 **Meredith, Anthony**
■ The Demon & the Lobster: Charles Kortright and Digby
Jephson, remarkable bowlers in the golden age.
Kingswood Press, 1987. xvi, 192p. illus. bibliog. index.

Jessop, Gilbert Laird

3771 **Brodribb, [Arthur] Gerald Norcott**
The Croucher: a biography of Gilbert Jessop. Constable,
1985. [viii], 239p. illus. facsims. scores, stats.
new ed. of 'Padwick I' 7762.

Jesty, Trevor Edward

3772 **Hawker, Jim** *and* **Neasom, Mike**
■ 1982 Trevor Jesty benefit year souvenir brochure.
Gosport, Trevor Jesty Benefit Committee, 1982. 36p.
incl. covers & adverts. illus. (some col.) stats.

Johnson, Colin

3773 **Colin** Johnson appreciation year '86. [Appreciation
■ Committee, 1986]. [68]p. incl adverts. illus. (some col.)
stats.

Johnson, Graham William

3774 **Graham** Johnson benefit year 1983. [Benefit
■ Committee], 1983. [72]p. incl. adverts. illus. (some
col.) stats.

Johnston, Brian Alexander

3775 **Johnston, Brian**
■ Chatterboxes: my friends the commentators. Methuen,
1983. 214p.
'voices of cricket' pp. 119-149.
——*pbk. ed.* Star, 1984.

Jones, Alan

3776 **Alan** Jones testimonial brochure. Leslie Morris, 1980.
12p.

3777 **Jones, Alan** *with* **Stevens, Terry**
■ Hooked on opening. Llandysul, Gomer Press, 1984.
xxiii, 188p. illus. stats. bibliog. index.

Jones, Andrew Howard

3778 **Boon, Kevin,** [*editor*]
Andrew Jones: what is it like to be an international
cricketer? Petone (Well.), Nelson Price Milburn, 1989.
32p. illus.
*from transcript of interview with Andrew Jones by Liz
Brook.*

Jordaan, Alan

3779 **[Chesterfield, Trevor,** *editor*]
Alan Jordaan cricket brochure 1984. [Pretoria],
Christian Brothers College Old Boys Cricket Club,
[1984]. 52p. illus.

Kallicharran, Alvin Isaac

3780 **[Holden, Sue,** *editor*]
■ Kalli: the official brochure of the Alvin Kallicharran
benefit year 1983. [1983]. 56p. incl adverts. illus. stats.

Kanhai, Rohan Babulal

3781 **Birbalsingh, Frank** *and* **Shiwcharan, Clem**
■ Indo-Westindian cricket. Hansib, 1988. 135p. illus.
*'The Tiger of Port Mourant - R. B. Kanhai: fact and
fantasy in the making of an Indo-Guyanese legend', pp.
41-88.*

3782 **James, Cyril Lionel Robert**
■ At the rendezvous of victory: selected writings. Allison
& Busby, 1984. xii, 303p. bibliog. index.
includes 'Kanhai: a study in confidence' pp. 166-171.

Kapil Dev, Ramlal Nikhanj

3783 **Irani, L.**
Vishua vijeta Kapil Dev. New Delhi, Super Pocket
Books, 1983. 207p. illus. stats.
in Hindi - 'World champion Kapil Dev'.

3784 **Kapil Dev**
■ Cricket my style. New Delhi, Allied Publishers, 1987.
[vi], 118p. illus. stats.
——*U.K. ed. published as* 'Kapil: the autobiography of
Kapil Dev', Sidgwick & Jackson, 1987.

3785 **Kapil Dev** *with* **Verma, Vinay**
■ By God's decree: the autobiography of Kapil Dev.
Arturmon (N.S.W.), Harper & Row, 1985. [viii], 102p.
illus.

Kardar, Abdul Hafeez

3786 **Kardar, Abdul Hafeez**
■ Memoirs of an all rounder. Lahore, Progressive
Publishers, 1987. vi, 287p. illus.

Kidson, Hayward C.

3787 **Kidson, Hayward C.**
■ Over and time. Cape Town, Howard Timmins, [1983].
[xvi], 449p. illus. scores.
cover sub-title: 'an umpire's autobiography'.

Kirsten, Peter Noel

3788 **Peter** Kirsten benefit year 83/84. [Cape Town, 1983].
■ 68p. incl adverts. illus. (some col.) stats.

Knight, Roger David Verdon

3789 **Roger** Knight benefit year 1984. [Benefit Committee],
■ 1984. 48p. incl. adverts. illus. stats.

Knott, Alan Philip Eric

3790 **Knott, Alan**
■ It's Knott cricket: the autobiography of Alan Knott.
Macmillan, 1985. ix, 165p. illus. stats. index.

Kortright, Charles Jesse

3791 **Meredith, Anthony**
■ The Demon & the Lobster: Charles Kortright and Digby
Jephson, remarkable bowlers in the golden age.
Kingswood Press, 1987. xvi, 192p. illus. bibliog. index.

3792 Sale, Charles
■ Korty: the legend explained. Hornchurch, Ian Henry Publications, 1986. [vi], 162p. illus. stats. bibliog. index.

Kourie, Alan John

3793 Coulson, Michael, *editor*
Sporting stars of South Africa: Alan Kourie benefit year 1986-87. Johannesburg, 1986. 128p. incl. adverts. illus. (some col.) stats.

Kuiper, Adrian Paul

3794 [Stuart, Lynne, *editor*]
Adrian Kuiper benefit year 89-90. Cape Town, Creda press, [1989]. 60p. illus. (some col.) stats.

Laker, James Charles ('Jim')

3795 Laker, Jim *and* Gibson, Pat
■ Cricket contrasts: from crease to commentary box. Stanley Paul, 1985. 160p. illus. index.

3796 Mosey, Don
■ Laker: portrait of a legend. Queen Anne Press, 1989. 189p. illus. stats. index.

Lamb, Allan Joseph

3797 Farrar, John, *compiler and editor*
■ Allan Lamb benefit brochure. Northampton, Harvest Studios, [1988]. 96p. incl. adverts. illus. (some col.)

3798 Lamb, Allan *and* Smith, Peter
■ Lamb's tales. George Allen & Unwin, 1985. x, 180p. illus. index.

Larkins, Wayne

3799 Barron, Brian, *editor*
■ Wayne Larkins benefit '86. [1986]. [68]p. incl adverts. illus. (some col.) stats.

Larwood, Harold

3800 Larwood, Harold *with* Perkins, Kevin
■ The Larwood story. Sydney, Bonapara, 1982. 234p. illus. index.
——*U.K. ed.* Harmondsworth, Penguin Books, 1985.
rev. ed. of 'Padwick I' 7790.

3801 Naik, Vasant K.
Vadali golandaz Larwood. Salsette (Goa), Bandodkar, 1983. 92p.
in Marathi: 'Whirlwind bowler Larwood'.

Laver, Frank

3802 † Laver, Frank
■ [Diary].
account of his life, with detailed day by day entries from 1889 - Oct. 1898; two bound ms. vols. housed in Melbourne Cricket Club Museum along with his photgraph albums and scrapbooks.

Lawson, Geoffrey Francis

3803 Mallett, Ashley Alexander
■ Geoff Lawson (Master Cricketer series). Melbourne, Hutchinson of Australia, 1984. 32p. illus.
for children.

Le Roux, Garth Stirling

3804 Garth Le Roux benefit year 1987. [Cape Town, 1987].
■ 79p. incl. adverts. illus. (some col.) stats.
on cover: 'benefit year 1987-88'.

Leadbeater, Barrie

3805 Barrie Leadbeater, Geoff Cope benefit 1980 souvenir.
■ [1980]. [48]p. incl. adverts. illus. (some col.) stats.

Lees, Warren Kenneth ('Wally')

3806 Edwards, Brent
Wally: the Warren Lees story. Dunedin, Otago Cricket Association, 1987. 106p. illus.

Lever, John Kenneth

3807 JK: John Lever testimonial year 1989. [1989]. 86p. incl.
■ adverts. illus. (some col.) stats.

3808 John Lever benefit year 1980. [Benefit Committee,
■ 1980]. 60p. incl. covers & adverts. illus. stats.

3809 Lever, John K. *and* Gibson, Pat
■ J.K. Lever: a cricketer's cricketer. Unwin Hyman, 1989. [viii], 184p. illus. stats. index.

Lever, Peter

3810 † Lancashire County Cricket Club
■ An appreciation of Peter Lever. Manchester, the Club, 1972. [4]p. illus. stats.

Lewis, Anthony Robert ('Tony')

3811 Lewis, Tony
■ Playing days. Stanley Paul, 1985. 251p. illus. index.

Lewis, Vic

3812 Lewis, Vic *with* Barrow, Tony
■ Music and maiden overs: my showbusiness life. Chatto & Windus, 1987. 192p. illus. index, discography.
cricket pp. 149-167.

Lillee, Dennis Keith

3813 Brayshaw, Ian John
■ Caught Marsh bowled Lillee. Sydney, Australian Broadcasting Corporation, 1983. 128p. illus. stats.
——*rev. ed. pub. as 'End of play: caught Marsh bowled Lillee', Australian Broadcasting Corporation, 1984.*

3814 Lillee, Dennis
■ My life in cricket. North Ryde (N.S.W.), Methuen, 1982. 220p. illus. stats. index.
——*new ed.* 1984.

3815 Over and out! North Ryde (N.S.W.), Methuen, 1984.
■ 194p. illus.

3816 † [Lillee, Dennis Keith] *as told to* Brayshaw, Ian John
■ Lillee. Sydney, Angus & Robertson, 1975. [160]p. illus.
pbk. ed. of 'Padwick' 7806-2 updated to include preface on 1974-75 Ashes series.

3817 Lillee: a testimonial 1981-82. Pymble (N.S.W.), Playbill,
■ [1981]. [20]p. incl. covers, illus. (some col.)

3818 Mallett, Ashley Alexander
■ Dennis Lillee (Master Cricketer series). Richmond (Vic.), Hutchinson of Australia, 1982. 32p. illus.
for children.

3819 Murray, Peter Allan, [editor]
■ A pictorial and statistical record of Chappell, Lillee, Marsh: Test cricket. Waterloo (N.S.W.), Waterloo Press, 1984. 168p. illus. (some col.) stats.
with contributions from Max Walker, Sunil Gavaskar, Richard Hadlee, Sarfraz Nawaz, Alvin Kallicharran, David Frith and Henry Blofeld.

3820 Pollard, Jack
■ A tribute to Lillee and Chappell [Sydney], Angus & Robertson, 1984. 52p. col. illus.

Lloyd, Clive Hubert

3821 Clive Lloyd testimonial brochure, 1986. [Testimonial
■ Committee, 1986]. 71p. incl. covers & adverts. illus. (some col.) stats.

3822 Derlien, Tony
■ Lancashire's Clive Lloyd. Altrincham, John Sherratt & Son, 1987. xi, 109p. illus. stats.
his county career.

3823 Lloyd, Clive *with* **Cozier, Tony**
■ Living for cricket. Stanley Paul, 1980. 144p. illus. stats.
——*pbk ed.* 1983.

3824 McDonald, Trevor
■ Clive Lloyd: the authorised biography. Granada, 1985. xiii, 175p. illus. stats. index.
——*pbk. ed.* Grafton, 1986.

Lloyd, David

3825 † Maddock, John, *editor*
■ David Lloyd testimonial year book 1978. Manchester, [Testimonial Committee], 1978. 92p. incl. covers & adverts. illus. (some col.) stats.

Lloyd, Neil

3826 Woodhouse, Anthony, *editor*
■ Neil Lloyd: an appreciation. Wombwell, Wombwell Cricket Lovers' Society, 1983. 32p. incl. covers, illus. stats.

Lockhart, William Peddie

3827 † W.P. Lockhart: merchant and preacher: a life story;
■ compiled by his wife. Hodder and Stoughton, 1895. xi, 262p. frontis.
'behind the wicket', pp. 27-34.

Lockwood, William Henry

3828 † Craig, Albert
William Henry Lockwood. 1890. [4]p. folded card, illus.
earlier ed. of 'Padwick I' 7817.

Love, James Derek ('Jim')

3829 Love, Lindsey, *compiler and editor*
■ Jim Love benefit year 1989. [1989]. [72]p. incl. covers & adverts. illus. (some col.) stats.

Lucas, Edward Verrall

3830 Prance, Claude Annett
■ E.V. Lucas and his books. West Cornwall (Connecticut), Locust Hill Press, 1988. xxxvi, 243p.
bibliography of the writings of E. V. Lucas with introductory biographical note.

Lumb, Richard Graham

3831 Richard Lumb benefit year 1983. [Benefit Committee], 1983. 80p. incl. covers & adverts. illus. stats.

MacBryan, John Crawford William ('Jack')

3832 Foot, David
■ Cricket's unholy trinity. Stanley Paul, 1985. xix, 188p. illus. bibliog. index.
Jack MacBryan, pp. 131-179.

McCabe, Stanley Joseph

3833 McHarg, Jack
■ Stan McCabe: the man and his cricket. Sydney, Collins Australia, 1987. xii, 187p. illus. index.

McEwan, Kenneth Scott

3834 Ken McEwan benefit year - 1984. [1984]. 88p. incl.
■ covers & adverts. illus. stats.

3835 Lemmon, David Hector
■ Ken McEwan. George Allen & Unwin, 1985. [vi], 141p. illus. stats.

Macfarlane, *Sir* David Neil

3836 Macfarlane, Neil *with* **Herd, Michael**
■ Sport and politics: a world divided. Willow Books, 1986. 271p. bibliog. index.
cricket pp. 215-18 and other scattered references.

McGahey, Charles Percy

3837 Kemp, Jan
■ Cheerful Charlie: a biography of C.P. McGahey; statistics: Robert Brooke. Great Wakering (Essex), the Author, 1989. [viii], 152p. illus. stats. bibliog. index.

McGilvray, Alan David

3838 McGilvray, Alan *as told to* **Tasker, Norman**
■ The game goes on ... Crows Nest (N.S.W.), ABC Enterprises for the Australian Broadcasting Corporation, 1987. 220p. illus.

3839 The game is not the same ... Sydney, ABC Enterprises
■ for the Australian Broadcasting Corporation, 1985. 188p. illus.
——*UK ed.* Newton Abbot, David & Charles, 1986.

McKay, Harry John

3840 Harte, Christopher John ('Chris')
Harry McKay: the cause of the last class clash in South Australian cricket. North Adelaide, Sports Marketing, 1989. 32p.
limited ed. of 50 copies.

McKechnie, Brian John

3841 **McKechnie, Brian** *with* **McConnell, Lynn**
McKechnie: double All Black: an autobiography.
Invercargill (N.Z.), Craigs, 1983. 181p. illus. stats.
index.

McKenzie, Kevin Alexander

3842 **Kevin** McKenzie benefit brochure. [Johannesburg,
1983]. 108p. incl. adverts. illus. (some col.) stats.

MacLaren, Archibald Campbell

3843 **Down, Michael G.**
Archie: a biography of A.C. MacLaren. George Allen &
Unwin, 1981. xii, 193p. illus. stats. bibliog. index.

McLean, Teresa

3844 **McLean, Teresa**
Metal jam: the story of a diabetic. Hodder and
Stoughton, 1985. 224p. index.
cricket memories pp. 13-14, 25-26, 103 and 141-142.

Madray, Ivan Samuel

3845 **Birbalsingh, Frank** *and* **Shiwcharan, Clem**
Indo-Westindian cricket. Hansib, 1988. 135p. illus.
*"Da coolie ga mek abi hunt ledda": Ivan Madray in
conversation with Clem Shiwcharan', pp. 89-135.*

Marks, Victor James

3846 Vic Marks benefit brochure 1988. Benefit Committee,
1988. 56p. incl. adverts. illus. (some col.) stats.

Marsh, Frederick Edward ('Eric')

3847 Eric Marsh, Repton coach 1950-80. [Repton, Repton
School], 1980. 28p. illus.
Eric Marsh's testimonial brochure.

Marsh, Rodney William

3848 **Brayshaw, Ian John**
Caught Marsh bowled Lillee. Sydney, Australian
Broadcasting Corporation, 1983. 128p. illus. stats.
——*rev. ed. pub. as* 'End of play: caught Marsh bowled
Lillee', Australian Broadcasting Corporation, 1984.

3849 **Mallett, Ashley Alexander**
Rodney Marsh. (Master Cricketer series). Richmond
(Vic.), Hutchinson of Australia, 1982. 32p. illus.
for children.

3850 **Marsh, Rod**
The gloves of irony. Sydney, Lansdowne Press, 1982.
128p. illus.
1981-82 season.
——*U.K. ed.* Pelham, 1982.

3851 Gloves, sweat and tears: the final shout. Ringwood
(Vic.), Penguin Books, 1984. 179p. illus.
1983-84 season.

3852 The inside edge. Sydney, Lansdowne, 1983. 128p. illus.
1982-83 season.

3853 **Murray, Peter Allan,** [*editor*]
A pictorial and statistical record of Chappell, Lillee,
Marsh: Test cricket. Waterloo (N.S.W.), Waterloo
Press, 1984. 168p. illus. (some col.) stats.
*with contributions from Max Walker, Sunil Gavaskar,
Richard Hadlee, Sarfraz Nawaz, Alvin Kallicharran,
David Frith and Henry Blofeld.*

3854 Rod Marsh: his story in pictures. Pymble (N.S.W.),
Playbill, 1983. [32]p. incl. covers, illus. (some col.)

Marshall, Charlee

3855 **Marshall, Charlee**
I couldn't bowl for laughin'. Thangool, (Qld.), the
Author, 1988. 144p. illus.
memoirs of a bush cricketer.

Marshall, Malcolm Denzil

3856 **Marshall, Malcolm** *with* **Symes, Patrick**
Marshall arts: the autobiography of Malcolm Marshall.
Queen Anne Press, 1987. 192p. illus. stats. index.

3857 **Symes, Patrick,** *editor*
Macko: Malcolm Marshall benefit year 1987. Mark
Nicholas, 1987. [68]p. incl. adverts. illus. (some col.)
stats.

Marshall, Polly

3858 **Marshall, Polly**
'Our Polly'. [Pickering], the Author, 1986. 66p. illus.
memoirs of Yorkshire and England batswoman.

Matthews, Gregory Richard John

3859 Greg Matthews. Pymble (N.S.W.), Playbill, 1986. 27p.
illus. (some col.)

3860 **Fishman, Roland**
Greg Matthews: the spirit of modern cricket. Ringwood
(Vic.), Penguin Books, 1986. 184p. illus.

May, Peter Barker Howard

3861 **May, Peter** *and* **Melford, Michael Austin**
A game enjoyed: an autobiography. Stanley Paul, 1985.
xv, 224p. illus. stats. index.

Menzies, *Sir* Robert Gordon

3862 **Bunting,** *Sir* **John**
R.G. Menzies: a portrait. Sydney etc., Allen & Unwin
Australia, 1988. xv, 222p. illus. bibliog. index.
'a Susan Haynes book'.
'Cricket' pp. 166-181.

Merchant, Vijaysingh Madhavji

3863 **Bailey, Philip Jonathan**
V.M. Merchant. (Famous Cricketers series: no 3). West
Bridgford (Notts.), Association of Cricket Statisticians,
[1988]. 28p. frontis. stats.
cover sub-title: 'his record innings-by-innings'.

3864 **Couto, Marcus D.,** *editor*
Vijay Merchant: in memoriam. Bombay, the Author,
[1988]. [iv], 122p. incl. adverts. illus. stats.

3865 **Naik, Vasant K.**
Vijay Merchant. Bombay, Bandodkar Publishing
House, [1984]. [vii], 151p. illus. stats.

Miller Geoffrey

3866 **Melloy, Doug,** *editor*
■ The Geoff Miller benefit year 1985. [Derby, Derbyshire County Cricket Club, 1985]. 52p. incl. adverts. illus. (some col.) stats.

Miller, Keith Ross

3867 **Bose, Mihir**
■ Keith Miller: a cricketing biography. George Allen & Unwin, 1980. [xv], 175p. illus. stats. bibliog. index.
another ed. of 'Padwick I' 7874-1.

3868 † **British Broadcasting Corporation**
■ Portrait of Keith Miller; broadcast 11 September 1956. 21p. *typescript.*
transcript of radio broadcast including contributions from Edrich, Evans, Yardley, Bowes, Langley, Graveney, Bailey, Compton and Miller himself.

3869 **Whitington, Richard Smallpiece**
■ Keith Miller: the golden nugget. Adelaide, Rigby, 1981. 312p. illus. stats.

Mortensen, Ole Henrek

3870 **Hargreaves, Peter Sanford**
■ Derbyshire's Dane: a bit more about Mortensen. [The Author, 1984]. 48p. illus.

Mosey, Don

3871 **Mosey, Don**
■ The best job in the world. Pelham Books, 1985. vii, 199p. illus. index.

Mushtaq Ali, Syed

3872 **Kahate, Atul,** *compiler*
■ Complete statistics of Syed Mushtaq Ali in first-class cricket; with biographical sketch and the end of the season summaries by Dr Vasant Naik. (Profiles in Statistics series: 2). Bombay, Association of Cricket Statisticians and Scorers of India, 1989. 52p. illus. stats.

Mynn, Alfred

3873 **Morrah, Patrick**
■ Alfred Mynn and the cricketers of his time. Constable, 1986. 224p. illus. stats. bibliog. index.
reprinted ed. of 'Padwick I' 7898 with a new introduction by the author.

Nayudu, Cottari Kanakaiya

3874 **Raiji, Vasant**
□ C.K. Nayudu: the Shahenshah of Indian cricket. Bombay, Marine Sports, 1989. xiv, 101p. illus. stats. index.
——de luxe ed. of [200] numbered and signed copies, 1989.

Neale, Phillip Anthony

3875 **Phil Neale benefit year 1988. [Benefit Committee,**
■ 1988]. 96p. incl. adverts. illus. (some col.) stats.

3876 **Phil Neale testimonial year 1984/85. Lincoln,**
[Testimonial Year Committee, 1984]. 84p. incl. adverts. illus.
Lincoln City Football Club testimonial; includes many cricket articles.

Newham, William

3877 † **[Craig, Albert]**
■ Mr W. Newham. [1891]. [4]p. folded card. illus.

Nicholls, David

3878 **David Nicholls benefit souvenir 1980. [Benefit**
■ Committee], 1980. 40p. incl. adverts. illus.

O'Brien, *Sir* Timothy Carew

3879 † **[Craig, Albert]**
■ Mr T. C. O'Brien. Wright & Co., [1890]. [4]p. folded card. illus.

Ontong, Rodney Craig

3880 **Rodney Ontong benefit brochure 1989. [Swansea,**
■ Sketty Publications, 1989]. 76p. incl. covers and adverts. illus. (some col.) stats

O'Reilly, William Joseph ('Bill')

3881 **O'Reilly, Bill**
■ 'Tiger': 60 years of cricket. Sydney, Collins, 1985. [v], 213p. illus.
——pbk. ed. Sydney, Fontana, 1986.

Parker, Charles Warrington Leonard

3882 **Foot, David**
■ Cricket's unholy trinity. Stanley Paul, 1985. xix, 188p. illus. bibliog. index.
Charlie Parker, pp. 3-75.

Parker, Paul William Giles

3883 **Paul Parker benefit year 1988. [Benefit Committee,**
■ 1988]. 76p. incl. covers and adverts. illus. (some col.) stats.

Parkhouse, William Gilbert Anthony

3884 **Gilbert Parkhouse testimonial brochure. Edinburgh,**
Barr, 1987. 24p. incl. adverts. illus.
published for match between a Scottish XI and Glamorgan at Edinburgh, 13 July 1987.

Parkin, Cecil Harry

3885 **Foot, David**
■ Cricket's unholy trinity. Stanley Paul, 1985. xix, 188p. illus. bibliog. index.
Cecil Parkin, pp. 77-129.

Parsons, John Henry ('Jack')

3886 **Howat, Gerald Malcolm David**
■ Cricketer militant: the life of Jack Parsons. Didcot, North Moreton Press, 1980. 125p. illus. maps, stats. bibliog. index.

Patil, Sandeep Madhusudan

3887 **Patil, Sandeep**
■ Sandy storm. Calcutta etc, Rupa, 1984. 167p. illus.

Patterson, William Henry

3888 † **[Craig, Albert]**
■ W.H. Patterson. Wright & Co., 1893. [4]p. folded card. illus.

Pawson, Henry Anthony ('Tony')

3889 **Pawson, Tony**
■ Runs and catches. Faber, 1980. 155p. illus.

Pearce, Thomas Neill

3890 **Essex County Cricket Club**
■ Dinner to commemorate the eightieth birthday of Tom Pearce ... the County Ground, Chelmsford, Friday 8th November, 1985. [Chelmsford, the Club, 1985]. [14]p. incl. covers. illus.

Peel, Robert

3891 † **[Craig, Albert]**
■ Robert Peel. Wright & Co., [1890]. [4]p. folded card. illus.

Phillipson, Christopher Paul

3892 **Paul** Phillipson benefit 1985. [1985]. 40p. incl. adverts.
■ illus. (some col.) stats.

Place, Winston

3893 † **Winston** Place's benefit: Lancashire v Middlesex at Old
■ Trafford ... July 12th, 14th and 15th, 1952. [Manchester, Lancashire County Cricket Club], 1952. [4]p. illus. stats.

Pocock, Patrick Ian

3894 **Pat** Pocock testimonial 1986. [1986]. 64p. incl. adverts.
■ illus. stats.

3895 **Pocock, Pat** *with* **Collins, Patrick**
■ Percy: the perspicacious memoirs of a cricketing man. Wimbledon, Clifford Frost Publications, 1987. 168p. illus. (some col.) stats. index.

Pollock, Peter Maclean

3896 **Pollock, Peter**
■ Clean bowled: so simple the truth. East London, Vision Media, 1985. ix, 107p. illus.
predominantly an account of his religious conversion.

Pollock, Robert Graeme

3897 † **Hattle, Jimmy,** *editor*
Graeme Pollock: king of the willow. Port Elizabeth, [1977]. 64p. illus. stats.

Ponsford, William Harold

3898 **Fiddian, Marc**
■ Ponsford and Woodfull: a premier partnership. Fitzroy (Vic.), Five Mile Press, 1988. 152p. illus. stats. bibliog. index.

3899 **George, Anthony**
■ W.H. Ponsford. (Famous Cricketers series: no. 2). Haughton Mill (Notts.), Association of Cricket Statisticians, [1987]. 23p. frontis. stats.
cover sub-title: 'his record innings-by-innings'.

3900 W.H. Ponsford: a statistical supplement. [Pyle, the
■ Author, 1986]. [63]p. stats.

Pont, Keith Rupert

3901 **Keith** Pont benefit year 1986. [1986]. 72p. incl. adverts.
■ illus (some col.) stats.

Pridgeon, Alan Paul

3902 **Paul** Pridgeon benefit year. [Worcester, Worcestershire
■ County Cricket Club, 1989]. [76]p. incl. adverts. illus. (some col.)

Procter, Michael John

3903 **Mike** Procter testimonial brochure. [Durban, n.d.] 48p.
■ incl. adverts. illus. (some col.) diagr.

3904 **Procter, Mike** *and* **Murphy, Patrick**
■ Mike Procter and cricket. Pelham Books, 1981. 176p. illus. stats. index.

Quiller-Couch, *Sir* Arthur Thomas

3905 † **Quiller-Couch, A. T.**
From a Cornish window. J. W. Arrowsmith, 1906. viii, 367p.
cricket pp. 159-199.

Radley, Clive Thornton

3906 **Clive** Radley benefit 1987. [1987]. 64p. incl. adverts.
■ illus. stats.

Randall, Derek William

3907 The **Derek** Randall testimonial year souvenir brochure
■ 1983. [1983]. [64]p. incl. adverts. illus. (one col.)

3908 **Randall, Derek** *in conjunction with* **Lee, Alan**
■ The sun has got his hat on. Willow Books, 1984. 144p. illus.

Ranjitsinhji, Kumar Shri, H.H.Maharaja Jam Saheb of Nawanagar

3909 **Ross, Alan**
■ Ranji: prince of cricketers. Collins, 1983. 256p. illus. stats. bibliog. index.
——*reprinted ed.* Pavilion Books, 1988, *with a new introduction by Geoffrey Moorhouse.*

Raven, Simon Arthur Noel

3910 **Raven, Simon**
■ Shadows on the grass. Blond & Briggs, 1982. [viii], 227p.
a cricketing memoir of the author.
——*pbk. ed.* Sphere, 1983.

Read, Walter William

3911 † **[Craig, Albert]**
■ Mr Walter William Read. Wright & Co., [1889]. [4]p. folded card, illus.

Rhodes, Harold James

3912 **Rhodes, Harold**
■ The Harold Rhodes affair. Derby, Breedon Books, 1987. 208p. illus. stats. bibliog.
contains list of all bowlers no-balled for throwing during Rhodes's career.

Rhodes, Wilfred

3913 **Thomson, Arthur Alexander**
Hirst and Rhodes. Pavilion Books, 1986. viii, 211p.
illus. stats. bibliog. index.
*reprinted ed. of 'Padwick I' 7997 with a new introduction
by J.M. Kilburn.*

Rice, Clive Edward Butler

3914 **Clive** Rice benefit brochure. [Johannesburg, 1982]. 80p.
incl. adverts. illus. (one col.) stats.

3915 **Clive** Rice testimonial brochure 1985. [Nottingham,
Testimonial Committee, 1985]. 72p. incl. adverts. illus.
(some col.)

Richards, Barry Anderson

3916 **Barry** Richards benefit brochure. [Durban, n.d.] 52p.
incl. adverts. illus. (some col.) stats.

Richards, Clifton James ('Jack')

3917 **Jack** Richards benefit year 1988. Wimbledon, Clifford
Frost, [1988]. 84p. incl. adverts. illus. (some col.) stats.

Richards, Isaac Vivian Alexander ('Viv')

3918 **Foot, David**
Viv Richards. (Profiles series); illustrated by Susan
Neale. Hamish Hamilton, 1987. 59p. illus.
for children.

3919 **Foot, David,** *editor*
Viv 82. [Purnell Books], 1982. 48p. incl. adverts. illus.
(some col.) stats.
Viv Richards' benefit brochure.

3920 **McDonald, Trevor**
Viv Richards: the authorised biography. Pelham Books,
1984. viii, 200p. illus. index.
——*pbk. ed.* Sphere, 1985.

3921 **Richards, Viv** *with* **Foot, David**
Viv Richards. Star, 1982. 169p. illus.
pbk. ed. of 'Padwick I' 7997-3.

Robertson-Glasgow, Raymond Charles

3922 **Robertson-Glasgow, R. C.**
46 not out. Constable, 1985. x, 206p. illus. index.
*reprinted ed. of 'Padwick I' 8007 with a new introduction
by John Woodcock.*

Roebuck, Peter Michael

3923 **Roebuck, Peter**
It never rains ... a cricketer's lot; illustrated by Mike Tarr.
George Allen & Unwin, 1984. viii, 151p.
the 1983 season
——*pbk. ed.* Unwin, 1985.

Roope, Graham Richard James

3924 **Waddell, V. R.,** *compiler*
Graham Roope benefit year 1980 brochure. [1980]. 44p.
incl. adverts. illus. stats.

Rose, Brian Charles

3925 **Coombes, Eric,** *editor*
Brian Rose testimonial brochure. [Benefit Committee],
1983. 48p. incl. adverts. illus. stats.

Ross, Alan

3926 **Ross, Alan**
Blindfold games. Collins Harvill, 1986. 303p.
scattered cricket references.

Ryle, John Charles

3927 † **Toon, Peter,** *editor*
J.C. Ryle: a self portrait. Swengel (Pa), Reiner
Publication, [1975].
first Bishop of Liverpool; noted Eton cricketer.

Sadiq Mohammed

3928 **Sadiq** Mohammed benefit year 1981-82. [Benefit
Committee, 1981]. 128p. incl. adverts. illus. stats.

Salah-ud-din Mulla ('Sallu')

3929 **Tanvir Ahmad** *et al, compilers*
Tribute to Sallu cricket match 1983. [Karachi], 1983.
[172]p. incl. adverts. illus. scores, stats.
*cover title: 'Tribute to Salu (sic) by West of Scotland
Cricket Club'.*

Sassoon, Siegfried Lorraine

3930 **Siegfried** Sassoon 1886-1967: a centenary celebration.
Lewes, Beacon Press, [1986]. 22p. illus.
*includes article on Siegfried Sassoon and cricket by
J.D.Coldham.*

Scott-Page, George

3931 **Scott-Page, George**
Recollections of a provincial dental surgeon.
Chester-le-Street, Casdec, 1985.
one chapter on his cricketing career.

Selvey, Michael Walter William

3932 **Vivian, Gordon,** *editor*
Mike Selvey benefit year book 1982. [Benefit
Committee, 1982]. [44]p. incl. adverts. illus. stats.

Sharp, George

3933 **George** Sharp benefit year 1982. [1982]. 28p. incl.
adverts. illus.

Shilton, John Edward

3934 **Brooke, Robert William**
John Edward Shilton's book: the triumphs and disasters
of a Warwickshire cricketer. Haughton Mill (Notts.),
Association of Cricket Statisticians, [1984]. 64p. illus.
stats. index.

Shrewsbury, Arthur

3935 **Wynne-Thomas, Peter**
'Give me Arthur': a biography of Arthur Shrewsbury.
Arthur Barker, 1985 xi, 163p. illus. stats.

Siddall, Allan

3936 **[Richardson, Bob]**
Allan Siddall: a Victorian cricketer in East Yorkshire.
The Author, [1988]. 69p. illus. scores. *typescript.*

Sidebottom, Arnold ('Arnie')

3937 **Gray, Geoff,** *compiler and editor*
■ The Arnie Sidebottom benefit year 1988. [1988]. 84p.
incl. covers and adverts. illus.

Simmons, Jack

3938 **Higgs, Peter,** *editor*
■ Jack Simmons testimonial year book 1980. [1980].
[134]p. incl. adverts. illus. stats.

3939 **Simmons, Jack** *with* **Bearshaw, Brian**
■ Flat Jack: the autobiography of Jack Simmons. Queen
Anne Press, 1986. 192p. illus. index.

Slack, Wilfred Norris

3940 **Lawrence, Bridgette**
■ Wilf Slack: an appreciation. Southall, A. & N. Moghul
Printers, 1989. 68p. incl. covers and adverts. illus.
(some col.) stats.

Smith, Anthony John Shaw ('Tich')

3941 Tich Smith benefit brochure. [Durban, Natal Cricket
■ Association, 1983]. 48p. incl. adverts. illus. (some col.)

Smith, *Sir* Charles Aubrey

3942 **Allen, David Rayvern**
■ Sir Aubrey: a biography of C. Aubrey Smith, England
cricketer, West End actor, Hollywood film star. Elm
Tree Books, 1982. xiv, 172p. illus. bibliog. index.

Smith, *Sir* Edwin Thomas

3943 **Harte, Christopher John ('Chris')**
Edwin Smith: the grand old man of early South
Australian football and cricket. North Adelaide, Sports
Marketing, 1989. 28p.
limited ed. of 50 copies.
*Smith founded Norwood District Cricket Club (later East
Torrens C.C.)*

Smith, Ernest James ('Tiger')

3944 **Smith, E. J.** *as told to* **Murphy, Patrick**
■ 'Tiger' Smith of Warwickshire and England: the
autobiography of E.J. Smith. Guildford, Lutterworth
Press, 1981. viii, 132p. illus. stats. index.

3945 † **Warwickshire County Cricket Club**
■ Joint testimonial to E. J. ('Tiger') Smith and G. C.
('Chicko') Austin. [1955]. [4]p. incl. covers, illus.
*E.J.Smith played for the county 1904-1932 and was head
coach from 1946.*

Smith, Gilbert Oswald

3946 **Grayson, Edward**
■ Corinthian - Casuals and cricketers. Havant, Pallant
Press, 1983. 248p. illus. index.
*new ed. of 'Padwick I' 8057 especially revised for the
centenaries of amateur soccer and cricket.*

Snow, Charles Percy

3947 **Snow, Philip Albert**
Stranger and brother: a portrait of Lord (C. P.) Snow.
Macmillan, 1982. xv, 206p. illus. bibliog. index.
includes his cricket memories.

Sobers, *Sir* Garfield St Aubrun ('Gary')

3948 † **Bell, Gordon**
■ Sir Garfield Sobers. Sunbury-on-Thames, Nelson,
1978. 128p. illus. stats.

3949 **Morawalla, Mahiyar**
■ King of kings: the story of Sir Garfield Sobers. Bombay
etc., Jaico, 1982. [viii], 152p. illus. stats.

3950 **Sobers, Gary** *with* **Cozier, Tony**
■ Gary Sobers' most memorable matches. Stanley Paul,
1984. 142p. illus. scores.

3951 **Sobers, Gary** *with* **Scovell, Brian**
■ Sobers: twenty years at the top. Macmillan, 1988. xiii,
205p. illus. stats. index.
——*pbk. ed.* Pan, 1989.

Southerton, James

3952 † **Grand** match at Kennington Oval, on July 17th, 18th and
19th, 1879 ... for J. Southerton's benefit. [1879]. [4]p.
folded sheet. illus.
Eleven of the North v Eleven of the South.

Sparks, Henry Yorke

3953 **Harte, Christopher John ('Chris')**
Yorke Sparks: founder of the Adelaide Oval. North
Adelaide, Sports Marketing, 1989. 24p.
limited ed. of 50 copies.
——*reissued as limited ed. of 100 unnumbered copies for
the Glenelg Council; Sparks was Mayor of Glenelg and
founder of the Glenelg Oval.*

Steele, John Frederick

3954 **John** Steele benefit year 1983. [Leicestershire County
■ Cricket Club], 1983. [28]p. incl. adverts. illus. stats.

Stephenson, Franklyn Dacosta

3955 **Double** act: Kevin Cooper and Franklyn Stephenson.
■ Nottingham, Nottinghamshire C. C. C. Marketing
Department, [1988]. 28p. illus. stats.
*both took more than 100 first class wickets in 1988
season.*

Stollmeyer, Jeffrey Baxter

3956 **Stollmeyer, Jeff**
■ Everything under the sun: my life in West Indies cricket.
Stanley Paul, 1983. 231p. illus. index.

Stovold, Andrew Willis ('Andy')

3957 **Andy** W. Stovold souvenir benefit brochure 1987.
■ [Benefit Committee, 1987]. 56p. incl. adverts. illus.
(some col.) stats.

Studd, Charles Thomas

3958 **Grubb, Norman Percy**
■ C.T. Studd: cricketer & pioneer. Cambridge,
Lutterworth Press, 1982. viii, 231p. illus.
new ed. of 'Padwick I' 8096 with additional postscript.

3959 **Walker, Jean**
■ Fool and fanatic? quotations from the letters of C.T.
Studd. Gerrards Cross, Worldwide Evangelization
Crusade, 1980. 128p.
'The cricketer speaks' pp. 47-51.

Swanton, Ernest William

3960 **Eighty** - not out: an interview, broadcast by the BBC, between Cliff Morgan and E. W. Swanton, OBE recording his eightieth birthday on 12th February 1987. Esher, Penmiel Press, 1987. 16p. frontis.
limited ed. of 110 numbered copies signed by Edward Burrett, designer and printer of the booklet.

3961 **Swanton, E. W.**
Sort of a cricket person. Pavilion Books, 1989. [v], 318p. illus. index.
reprinted ed. of 'Padwick I' 8114, 8114-1 with a new introduction by the author.

Tavaré, Christopher James

3962 **Chris** Tavaré benefit year '88. [Canterbury], Kent County Cricket Club, [1988]. 72p. incl. adverts. illus. (some col.) stats.

Taylor, Leslie Brian

3963 **Les** Taylor benefit year 1989. [1989]. 40p. incl. adverts. illus. stats.

Taylor, Michael Norman Somerset ('Mike')

3964 **Mike** Taylor testimonial year 1989. [1989]. [6]p. folded card. illus. stats.

Taylor, Robert William ('Bob')

3965 **Bob** Taylor testimonial year 1981. [Derby, Benefit Committee, 1981]. 64p. illus. (some col.) stats.

3966 **Taylor, Bob** *with* **Murphy, Patrick**
Standing up, standing back. Willow Books, 1985. 172p. illus. stats.

Thomson, Jeffrey Robert

3967 **Byrell, John**
Thommo declares! Cammeray (N.S.W.), Horwitz Grahame, 1986. 141p. illus.

Townsend, Leslie Fletcher

3968 † **Leslie** Townsend: an appreciation. Northumberland County Cricket Club, 1946. [12]p. incl. covers. illus. stats.

Travers, Benjamin

3969 **Travers, Ben**
94 declared: cricket reminiscences. Elm Tree Books, 1981. xviii, 75p. illus.

Trueman, Frederick Sewards

3970 **Alton, Fred,** [*compiler*]
Fiery: the statistical Test cricket career of Fred Trueman from June 1952 to June 1965. The Author, [1982]. 26p. illus stats.

3971 **Arlott,** [**Leslie Thomas**] **John**
Fred: portrait of a fast bowler. Methuen, 1983. 198p. illus. stats.
new ed. of 'Padwick I' 8151.

3972 **Clark, Christopher D.**
The Test match career of Freddie Trueman. Newton Abbot, David & Charles, 1980. 221p. illus. stats. index.

3973 **Trueman, Fred** *with* **Mosey, Don**
My most memorable matches; cartoons by Roy Ullyett. Stanley Paul, 1982. 141p. illus.
——*pbk. ed.* Arrow, 1985.

Trumper, Victor Thomas

3974 **Mallett, Ashley Alexander**
Trumper: the illustrated biography: the greatest batsman of cricket's golden age. Macmillan, 1985. [viii], 232p. illus. facsims. bibliog. index.

3975 **Sharpham,** [**Edward**] **Peter Leonard**
Trumper: the definitive biography. Lane Cove (N.S.W.), Hodder and Stoughton, 1985. 253p. illus. stats. bibliog. index.

Turner, David Roy

3976 **Mitchener, Tony,** *editor*
David Turner benefit souvenir brochure. North Baddesley, David Turner Benefit Committee, 1981. 32p. incl. covers & adverts. illus.

Turner, Francis Michael ('Mike')

3977 **Leicestershire County Cricket Club**
A collection of cricket memories: the Mike Turner testimonial brochure. [Leicester, the Club, 1985]. 112p. incl. adverts. illus.

Turner, Glenn Maitland

3978 **Cairns, Ray** *and* **Turner, Glenn**
Glenn Turner's century of centuries. Hodder and Stoughton, 1983. 280p. illus. charts, stats. index.

3979 **Turner, Glenn** *and* **Turner, Brian**
Opening up. Auckland etc, Hodder and Stoughton, 1987. 195p. illus.

Underwood, Derek J.

3980 **Underwood, Derek J.**
Uphill into the breeze; illustrations by Martyn Lucas. Autolycus Press, 1984. 152p. illus.
personal memories of London club cricket.

Underwood, Derek Leslie

3981 **Derek** Underwood benefit year '86. [Benefit Committee], 1986. [80]p. incl. adverts. illus. (some col.) stats.

van der Bijl, Vintcent Adriaan Pieter

3982 **van der Bijl, Vintcent** *with* **Bishop, John**
Cricket in the shadows. Pietermaritzburg, Shuter & Shooter, 1984. [xii], 232p. illus. stats.

Verity, Hedley

3983 **Hill, Alan**
Hedley Verity: a portrait of a cricketer. Tadworth (Surrey), Kingswood Press, 1986. xiii, 176p. illus. stats. index.

Vigar, Frank Henry

3984 † **Souvenir** brochure - Frank Vigar's benefit ... 1953. [1953]. [4]p. incl. covers, illus. stats.
brochure to accompany Essex County XI v Hutton C. C. June 14th 1953.

Virgin, Roy Thomas

3985 Roy Virgin testimonial souvenir brochure: Roy Virgin International XI v Walsall C.C. ... 21 August 1983. [1983]. [12]p. illus.

Viswanath, Gundappa Rangnath

3986 **Chopra, Raj Kumar**
Vishwanath: a genius cricketer. Allahabad, Granth Bharti, 1982. 127p. illus. stats.

3987 **Naik, Vasant K.**
Cricket kalavant Vishwanath. Salsette (Goa), Bandodkar, 1981. 164p.
in Marathi: 'Cricket's artist Vishwanath'.

Voce, William ('Bill')

3988 † **Nottinghamshire County Cricket Club**
William Voce's benefit: match, Nottinghamshire v Yorkshire ... June 17th, 19th and 20th, 1939. The Club, 1939. [4]p. illus.

Walker, Maxwell Henry Norman

3989 **Walker, Max**
Back to Bay 13. Ashburton (Vic.), Garry Sparke & Associates, 1980. 160p. illus.

Waller, Christopher Edward

3990 Chris Waller benefit year 1984. [1984]. 51p. incl. adverts. illus. (one col.) stats.

Walters, Kevin Douglas ('Doug')

3991 'About Doug': the Doug Walters benefit year book. [1981]. 64p. incl. adverts. illus.

3992 **Mallett, Ashley Alexander**
Doug Walters (Master Cricketer series). Richmond (Vic.), Hutchinson of Australia, 1982. 32p. illus.
for children

3993 **Walters, Doug** *as told to* **Laws, Ken**
The Doug Walters story. Adelaide, Rigby, 1981. 156p. illus.

Wanostrocht, Nicholas ('Felix')

3994 **Brodribb, [Arthur] Gerald Norcott**
The art of Nicholas Felix. Ewell, J. W. McKenzie, 1985. 90p. illus.
limited ed. of 220 signed and numbered copies.

Wardle, John Henry

3995 **Hill, Alan**
Johnny Wardle: cricket conjuror. Newton Abbot, David & Charles, 1988. 168p. illus. stats. index.

Warner, *Sir* Pelham Francis

3996 † **British Broadcasting Corporation**
Sir Pelham Warner; broadcast 1st and 4th May 1958. 20p. *typescript.*
transcript of two part radio broadcast including interview with Sir Pelham Warner and contributions from Wilfred Rhodes, Patsy Hendren and Denis Compton.

3997 **Howat, Gerald Malcolm David**
Plum Warner. Unwin Hyman, 1987. xv, 240p. illus. stats. bibliog. index.

Watson, William Kenneth ('Kenny')

3998 Kenny Watson benefit 85/86. Port Elizabeth, [1985]. 40p. illus. (some col.) stats.

Webbe, Alexander Josiah

3999 † **[Craig, Albert]**
Mr A. J. Webbe. Wright & Co., 1893. [4]p. folded card, illus.

Wellham, Dirk Macdonald

4000 **Wellham, Dirk** *with* **Rich, Howard**
Solid knocks and second thoughts. Frenchs Forest (N.S.W.), Reed Books, 1988. 160p. illus. stats.

Wells, Bryan Douglas

4001 **Wells, B. D.**
Well, well, wells! an autobiography. Haughton Mill (Notts.), Cabdene, [1981]. 118p.
limited ed. of 500 copies.

Wells, Joseph

4002 † **Eames, Geoffrey Leonard**
Joseph Wells: father of H.G. and of Bromley Cricket Club. 1970. *typescript.*
copy in Bromley Library.

Wessels, Kepler Christoffel

4003 **Wessels, Kepler**
Cricket madness. Port Elizabeth, Aandblom, 1987. x, 158p. illus. stats.

West, Peter

4004 **West, Peter**
Flannelled fool and muddied oaf: the autobiography of Peter West. W.H.Allen, 1986. 215p. illus. index.
——*pbk. ed.* Star, 1987.

Willey, Peter

4005 **Morris, John,** *editor*
Peter Willey benefit year 1981. [1981]. 28p. incl. adverts. illus. stats.

Williams, Richard Grenville

4006 **Blayney, Rob,** *editor*
Richard Williams benefit brochure. 1989. 96p. incl. adverts. illus. (some col.) stats.

Williams, Robert Hugh

4007 † **R.H.Williams.** [1969]. [52]p. incl. covers, illus.
appreciation of northern sports editor of 'Daily Telegraph' who died in 1969; includes some of his cricket writing, pp. 41-48.

Willis, Robert George Dylan ('Bob')

4008 Bob Willis benefit year 1981. [1981]. [56]p. incl. adverts. illus. stats.

4009 **Willis, Bob**
Lasting the pace. Willow Books, 1985. [v], 183p. illus. stats.

Wilmot, Anthony Lorraine ('Lorrie')

4010 † **Summerton, Geoff,** *editor*
■ Lorrie Wilmot benefit brochure 1979-80. [Port Elizabeth, Eastern Province Cricket Union], 1979. 16p. illus.

Wilson, Richard ('Dick')

4011 † **Withington, Neil,** *editor*
■ 50 golden years, 1929-1979: Dick Wilson - fifty years with Wrea Green Cricket Club: official souvenir brochure. 1979. 8p. incl. covers. illus.

Woodfull, William Maldon

4012 **Fiddian, Marc**
■ Ponsford and Woodfull: a premier partnership. Fitzroy (Vic.), Five Mile Press, 1988. 152p. illus. stats. bibliog. index.

Woolley, Frank Edward

4013 **Milton, Howard Roy**
■ F.E. Woolley. (Famous Cricketers series: no. 4). West Bridgford (Notts.), Association of Cricket Statisticians, [1989]. 84p. illus. stats.
cover sub-title: 'his record innings-by-innings'.

Woolmer, Robert Andrew ('Bob')

4014 **Bob** Woolmer benefit year 1984. [Benefit Committee],
■ 1984. 64p. incl. covers & adverts. illus. (some col.) stats.

4015 **Woolmer, Bob**
■ Pirate and rebel? an autobiography. Arthur Barker, 1984. [ix], 160p. illus. stats.

Worrell, *Sir* Frank Mortimer Maglinne

4016 **Tennant, Ivo**
■ Frank Worrell: a biography. Cambridge, Lutterworth Press, 1987. xiii, 121p. illus. stats. index.

Wright, John Geoffrey

4017 **Humphreys, Jeff,** *editor*
■ Wrighty: John Wright testimonial 1987. [1987]. 76p. incl. covers and adverts. illus. (some col.) stats.

Wright, Levi George

4018 **Wright, L. G.**
■ Scraps from a cricketer's memory: being the personal reminiscences of L.G. Wright ... with some additional notes by F.G. Peach. Derby, Derbyshire County Cricket Supporters' Club, 1980. iii, 75p. frontis. stats.

Wyatt, Robert Elliott Storey

4019 **George, Michael**
■ Sportsmen of Cornwall. Bodmin, Bossiney Books, 1986. 96p. illus.
R.E.S. Wyatt pp. 59-64.

4020 **Pawle, Gerald**
■ R.E.S. Wyatt - fighting cricketer. Allen & Unwin, 1985. xviii, 278p. illus. stats. bibliog. index.

Younis Ahmed, Mohammad

4021 **Dubai** international world cricket presents Younis
■ Ahmed benefit match: England vs India & Pakistan (combined). [1981?]. [64]p. incl. adverts. illus.

Zaheer Abbas, Syed

4022 **Zaheer** Abbas benefit year 1983. [1983]. 68p. incl.
■ covers and adverts. illus. stats.

4023 **Zaheer Abbas** *with* **Foot, David**
■ Zed: Zaheer Abbas. Kingswood (Surrey), World's Work, 1983. 159p. illus. stats. bibliog. index.

MISCELLANEOUS

4024 **Davison, Caroline**
■ Cricketers' favourites. Leicester? Printed by Eureka
Press, n.d. 26p. incl. covers, illus. index.
favourite recipes of 20 (mostly Leicestershire) cricketers.

APPENDIX

(Insufficient is known about the following items for them to be
listed in the main sequence.)

4025 † **Becca, Lascell**
Touch of class. Kingston, Hallmark Publishers, 1974.
40p. incl. adverts. illus. stats.

4026 † **Bramshill** Cricket Club. 1810.
*in Taylor ('Padwick I' 39) and Goldman ('Padwick I'
20).*

4027 † **Chaplin, Kenneth**
The happy warrior. Kingston, Dominion Publishing Co.,
1960. 62p. incl. adverts. illus.

4028 † **Gaston, Alfred James**
Cricket 1774-1842.
in Goldman ('Padwick I' 20).

4029 † Cricket talks. 1920.
in Goldman ('Padwick I' 20); 12 copies only.

INDEX

Some titles have been inverted to bring the keyword, usually the name of a club, to the front.